Santa
Monica
Public
Library

4-WEEK LOAN

FOR TELEPHONE RENEWALS CALL:

Main Library 451-1866
Ocean Park Branch 392-3804
Fairview Branch 450-0443
Montana Branch 829-7081

DATE DUE

Harvard Historical Studies · 131

Published under the auspices
of the Department of History
from the income of the
Paul Revere Frothingham Bequest
Robert Louis Stroock Fund
Henry Warren Torrey Fund

From Appomattox to Montmartre

Americans and the Paris Commune

Philip M. Katz

Harvard University Press

Cambridge, Massachusetts, and London, England | 1998

Library of Congress Cataloging-in-Publication Data

Katz, Philip Mark, 1964–
    From Appomattox to Montmartre : Americans and the Paris
Commune / Philip M. Katz.
        p.   cm. — (Harvard historical studies : 131)
    Includes bibliographical references and index.
    ISBN 0-674-32348-3 (hardcover : alk. paper)
    1. Paris (France)—History—Commune, 1871—Foreign public opinion,
American. 2. Public opinion—United States. 3. Cluseret, Gustave Paul,
1823–1900—Views on civil wars. 4. Revolutions and socialism—
France—Influence. I. Title. II. Series: Harvard historical studies : v. 131.
DC317.K37   1998
944.081′2—dc21   98-26867

For my mother,
and to the memory of my father

Contents

Acknowledgments

This book began with a difficult Frenchman, a supportive advisor, and a perplexed graduate student. The Frenchman was named Gustave Paul Cluseret, who was not only difficult (though, conveniently, dead) but also fascinating and fruitful as a starting place for historical research into the transatlantic currents of nineteenth-century political culture. I want to thank my advisor, James M. McPherson, for introducing me to Cluseret, and for all his help and support ever since; much of what I know about the Civil War era and the writing of graceful narrative history can be traced back to his example. As for the perplexed graduate student . . . well, I'm still perplexed about many things, though the people whose names are printed below have helped me solve a few puzzles, both historical and personal, in the years since I began this project. Any perplexities that remain are entirely my own fault.

A number of people read my manuscript in its entirety and offered useful advice, including Daniel Rodgers, Sean Wilentz, Thomas Bender, Patrice Higonnet, and James Rawley. Philip Nord read several chapters and helped keep me straight when it came to French history. Reid Mitchell also read several chapters, and helped keep me straight on American history; his judgment and timely encouragement made this a better piece of scholarship. A number of colleagues, especially Benjamin Alpers and Jonathan Earle, but also Steve Kantrowitz, Jane Dailey, and John Wertheimer, offered valuable advice and fruitful bibliographic leads. I owe a more general debt to the following, who supplied me with various measures of intellectual and personal succor: Steve Aron, Elspeth Carruthers, John Carson, Marcus Daniel, Walter Johnson, John Murrin, Paul Smith, Ben Weiss, and Robert Whitaker. In addition, Gerald L. Geison, William C. Jordan, and especially Kevin T. Downing made contributions that cannot be described in mere words, and I thank them heartily.

This book could not have been written without the Princeton University Library's very competent staff, especially the interlibrary loan office and the reference staff; in particular, I want to thank Mary George for helping me locate dozens of obscure sources. Various scholars around the country also helped me track down hard-to-find material: thanks to Bernard A. Cook, at Loyola College, New Orleans; Lori Davisson, at the Arizona Historical Society; Edward T. LeBlanc, editor of the *Dime Novel Round-Up*; and Jeane T. Newlin, Curator of the Harvard Theatre Collection. The Andrew W. Mellon Foundation gave me the financial support I needed to complete this project. I also want to acknowledge the assistance of Elizabeth Suttell and Donna Bouvier at Harvard University Press, and to thank the editors of *Church History* for allowing me to reprint parts of Chapter 7, which originally appeared (in a rather truncated version) as "'Lessons from Paris': The American Clergy Responds to the Paris Commune," *Church History* 63 (September 1994): 393–406.

My family, and especially my mother, have been patient with me for three decades now, so the least I can do is thank them here. Finally, I want to thank April Grace Shelford, for all the reasons she knows and a few that she does not even suspect.

How much history and what wondrous events are crowded into the [last] two decades. The rebellion of the Sepoys . . . [and the] emancipation of the Russian serf, the allied armies of Balaklava and Magenta, Solferino and the Quadrilateral. Garibaldi and Count Cavour and United Italy. Civil War and emancipation in the United States. Napoleon and Sedan, Paris and the Commune, Von Moltke, Bismarck, William and the German Empire. Political revolution in the Twentieth Congressional District of Ohio, and thunder in the Fifth Ward of Cleveland. The days of the prophecy are fulfilled. The record of twenty-five years is closed.

 —FREDERICK T. WALLACE, *MEN AND EVENTS*
  OF HALF A CENTURY (CLEVELAND, 1882)

Introduction:
An Epoch of Stirring Events

Les deux guerres civiles n'avaient de commun que l'épithète.
—EDMOND LEPELLETIER (1913)

The civil war in France and the Civil War in America had nothing in common except a name. So claimed French historian Edmond Lepelletier in the years before World War I, and, like most sweeping historical judgments, this one compounds truth and falsehood.[1] Who can deny that the War Between the States was distinctly American, or that the Paris Commune stirred to the peculiar rhythms of history in France? Slavery and the Constitution on one side, foreign invasion and a long tradition of urban revolt on the other—these were unique and determining factors. As this book will demonstrate, however, both events were awash in "the broad currents of nineteenth century history." They deserve to be studied in relation to those currents and to each other.[2]

In recent years, American historians have paid more and more attention to the international and transnational settings of American history.[3] This book contributes to that larger research project. The chapters that follow will explain how Americans learned about the Commune in 1871, how they interpreted the events in Paris, how their interpretations were shaped by the recent Civil War at home, and how the Paris Commune in turn shaped American political culture in the 1870s and beyond.

What was the Paris Commune? Many Americans, both in Paris and the United States, were trying to answer that question in 1871. They were flooded with information about the events in Paris and swamped with rumors and speculation, and they wanted to know what it all meant. Indeed, the Commune was a major event on both sides of the Atlantic. Few American media, from small-town newspapers to the New York stage, proved immune to the excitement it generated; their outpourings are the main sources for this study. Gradually, however, the excitement of the Commune faded away, and from today's perspective it is difficult to see what the contemporary fuss was about.

1

This difficulty is compounded by two barriers that stand in the way of any attempt to recapture American conceptions of the Commune from the nineteenth century. First, the Paris uprising no longer has the claim on our national memory that it once possessed. For years the Commune remained a vital issue in American culture because it had the power to mask and illuminate domestic concerns. But when this ceased to be the case (after the 1870s, for reasons that will be discussed later), thinking about the Paris Commune became the exclusive pastime of scholars and activists on the left.

Not that political activists have not tried to retain the Commune as part of the American prospect; they have, but without much success. In 1968, for example, when student radicals occupied the administration building at Columbia University, Mark Rudd referred to their temporary abode as the "Commune" while blithely explaining how they followed in the footsteps of "the Paris Commune and the international socialist revolutionary movement." But Rudd seized upon a hollow image, since few observers really understood or cared about the historical moment that he tried to evoke.[4] Another generation has passed since then, and I have discovered that few Americans (even professional American historians) know very much about the Paris Commune. What they *do* know is filtered through 120 years of ideological contention, the second barrier to understanding what the episode meant to Americans at the time.

The Commune itself was an ideological jumble. French historians have identified at least four major strains of ideology weaving through it: the democratic federalism of Pierre-Joseph Proudhon, the neo-Jacobinism of Auguste Blanqui, the artisanal vision of the utopian socialists, and the nascent Marxism of the First International. Just as important, but less well articulated, were the popular revolutionary traditions dating from 1789 and 1848.[5] While the Commune lived its short span from March 18 to May 28, 1871, most Parisians worried about survival rather than ideology, and did their best to muddle through. But when the Commune died, writes one modern historian, its legacy became that of an "unfinished revolutionary phenomenon . . . [leaving] a door open to all the promises it was unable to keep, and thus to ambiguities."[6] These ambiguities soon generated arguments.

Few events, even in French history, have occasioned such furious post-mortem debate. For more than a decade after 1871 the meaning of the Commune and the fate of its victims remained at the center of French politics. In France and elsewhere, Marxists and their descendants continuously recreated the Commune for their own purposes, generating various models of the state and revolution that had little to do with the actual events in Paris. Conservative opponents reflexively followed suit, with the result that the ideologue's version of the Commune became "increasingly detached from concrete historical circumstances and acquired its own autonomy."[7] By and large, the United States was spared the worst of these European debates; instead we conducted our own ideological debates in the nineteenth century, though largely on borrowed terms, as I will show.

American historiography was not as isolated from Europe, with unfortunate results. Since 1924, a handful of studies have been devoted to American reactions to the Paris Commune, and more than half reflect the subtle distortions of "Stalinist historiography."[8] The rest are simply old; all of them need reexamination.[9] The double challenge, therefore, is to break through the barriers of ideological encrustation and to recover forgotten memories so we can see the Commune through the eyes of contemporary Americans. Only then can we start to explain how they applied the example of the Commune to their own domestic concerns.

One way to begin is with a narrative of the Paris Commune, one as devoid of interpretation as possible, and relying as much as possible on the sources of information available in the United States at the time—in a sense, recreating the experience of watching the Commune from American shores. Indeed, some of that experience is recreated in Chapter 4. But a full narrative of the Commune would require several more chapters, and I think these would prove an unnecessary diversion, since American conceptions of the Commune had less to do with events in France than with events at home. Instead, I have provided a chronology of the major events of the Commune in Appendix A. A good part of the Commune's story is also related piecemeal in Chapters 1–3.

Another, more fruitful place to start is with the story of an individual, whose reaction to the Commune might serve as an "ideal type" against which to measure the reactions of his contemporaries.[10] The individual I have chosen is Gustave Paul Cluseret. A singular Parisian who served in both the French and the American civil wars, Cluseret not only embodied but also articulated the points of comparison between them. He developed an interpretation of the Commune that was strongly shaped by his own experience with American politics, and he presented it in terms that were familiar to Americans in 1871. Whether his understanding and theirs converged, however, will be seen later. For now, let us begin with Cluseret's story.

1

The Two Civil Wars
of General Cluseret

What is good for America is good for France.

—GUSTAVE P. CLUSERET (1887)

In 1868, the French artist Gustave Courbet painted a forceful portrait of his friend and political ally Gustave Paul Cluseret. The somber canvas showed a trim, middle-aged man in a plain blue uniform, sporting a dark beard and mustache in the *impérial* style much favored by soldiers on both sides of the Atlantic. The blue tunic was a clue that Courbet's friend had played a minor role in the American Civil War. But there was no hint that Cluseret would soon play a major part in the Paris Commune, or that he would become a significant link between these two world-shaking events. Indeed, only the penetrating eyes of the subject—at once furtive and melancholy—could suggest the extraordinary life that Cluseret was leading.[1]

Gustave Paul Cluseret was born in Paris in 1823, the youngest in a long line of professional soldiers. Like his father and grandfather, he attended Saint-Cyr (the West Point of France) and became an artillery officer. His first taste of battle came during the Paris uprising of June 1848. There, for probably the last time in his life, Cluseret joined on the side of the bourgeois moderates, earning the Legion of Honor while smashing the workers' barricades.[2] But this sordid, youthful act was not a true harbinger of Cluseret's future political development, for within a year he was relieved from duty for openly criticizing President Louis Napoleon.[3]

After rejoining the French army to fight (with distinction) in Algeria and the Crimea, he left for good in 1858, unwilling to serve under the Second Empire any longer. Temporarily abandoning his military vocation, Cluseret sailed for America and began a quieter life as a New York City bank clerk. But 1860 found him back in Europe, battling for Italian liberation under Giuseppe Garibaldi. There, in September 1861, the Frenchman learned about Secretary of State William Seward's appeal to European military officers, inviting them to join the Union cause. Like dozens of others, Cluseret accepted the invitation.[4]

Thus he returned triumphant to America in 1862, bearing impressive letters of introduction from Garibaldi and the leading French Republicans. With these in hand he gained the attention of Charles Sumner, initiating a correspondence that lasted until the Massachusetts senator's death. With Sumner's political backing, Cluseret became a colonel in the Northern forces, serving for a year as a staff officer and then commanding troops in the Shenandoah Valley; but in March 1863 he resigned his commission, embittered by a feud with superior officers. In 1864 he turned to politics more directly, becoming an ardent supporter of John C. Frémont's ill-advised presidential campaign. The campaign soon fizzled away, but Cluseret continued to hover around the fringes of Radical Republicanism, trying to interest Sumner in various Reconstruction proposals. His direct involvement with American politics, limited as it was, ended in 1866, just months before Radical Reconstruction began.[5]

Cluseret spent the next five years flirting with danger and insurrection in every corner of the Atlantic world. In London, he received a death sentence in absentia for plotting with Irish nationalists. In Paris, he was arrested for attacking the Empire in print, and only managed to escape a long prison term by claiming U.S. citizenship under an obscure wartime statute. In New York, he became the corresponding secretary of the Franco-American section of the First International (in 1869).[6] This was all preparation for a return to France during the Franco-Prussian War of 1870, where he arrived too late to fight the Germans, but not too late to join failed uprisings at Lyons and Marseilles.[7]

In April 1871, Cluseret became Minister of War under the Paris Commune; in May, his colleagues arrested him for supposed collusion with the enemy at Versailles. When the Commune ended, Cluseret escaped the country disguised as a Catholic priest. Soon he was sentenced to death again, this time by a French court. He fled to Geneva; he rejoined the International; he embraced the struggle for Balkan independence during the Russo-Turkish War (1878). In 1884 Cluseret finally returned to his native land, following the general amnesty for Communards. Four years later, he won a seat in the French Assembly, waging a bitter electoral campaign with money from the U.S. government (his payment for an official report on Turkish cotton).[8] The next dozen years passed quietly, while Cluseret served as a Radical Socialist deputy and painted landscapes in his leisure hours. He died in 1900, of natural causes, at the ripe old age of seventy-seven.

So ended a picaresque life, and one that easily lent itself to charges of inconsistency. Cluseret's politics were surely changeable, and contemporaries attributed this to crass ambition. Karl Marx, for one, called the Frenchman a "lousy, importunate, vain and over-ambitious babbler." The *New York Times* added that Cluseret "has no positive principle, being regulated, so far as he is regulated at all, by vanity and self-interest." Historians have not been any kinder.[9] Yet a good deal of their abuse is unwarranted. Cluseret was certainly ambitious; as he himself once wrote, "Who is not?"[10] On occasion, he also lost sight of his principles. But this did not make him merely an adventurer, "adopt[ing whatever principles] . . . his sword upheld."[11]

Indeed, the causes he upheld were consistently progressive (in the broadest sense of promoting liberty, democracy, and equality), and he was shaped by their principles much more than he knew. At no time was this more obvious than during the 1860s. At the start of the American Civil War, Cluseret was a bourgeois soldier with republican leanings and an uncertain record of counterrevolution.[12] His most important literary effort to that point was a pamphlet on military reform addressed to the king of Italy (in fact, a thinly disguised job application). A decade later Cluseret had become a committed social revolutionary; his writings had appeared in a half-dozen journals of the left; his republican friends of the mid-1860s, both French and American, had been abandoned as too conservative.[13] Something had happened: American political culture had radicalized Cluseret.

By most standards, the Frenchman's American career was a flop. In a rare burst of English and candor, he even confessed to Charles Sumner that "I am a loser."[14] Three failures stand out in particular: the failure of Cluseret's military pursuits, the failure of Frémont's presidential campaign, and the failure of Reconstruction under President Andrew Johnson. In each case Cluseret tried to combine his personal ambitions with political ideals, but the combination never worked. The American system always let him down, or so it seemed to Cluseret; worse yet, the system always seemed to renege on its own guiding principles.

For most people, a cycle of failures like this would lead to utter despair. But for Cluseret, like many other committed believers, personal failure only intensified his commitment to external ideals.[15] Through it all he remained convinced that his adopted Yankee ideals were worthy and that the United States was truly a model republic, in theory if not always fact. Later he used these convictions to help make sense of the Paris Commune.

Cluseret arrived in America with an overweening pride in his own martial skills, quickly explaining to Sumner, "I have a military reputation to preserve . . . [and] I am known in France and Italy as an up-and-coming officer."[16] At first, his American prospects looked just as good. He came well recommended and used his letters of recommendation to establish contact with Sumner, Seward, and the Department of War. What he wanted was a commission as brigadier general, a rank he deemed commensurate with his past experience and his ties to French republicanism; what he got was a pile of debts and a colonelcy. With these in hand he joined General George B. McClellan's staff in March 1862.[17]

America's "Little Napoleon" was unimpressed by Cluseret and soon packed him off to General Frémont's command in the Mountain Department of western Virginia. There Cluseret served with distinction, eventually earning his general's star for "skill and gallantry" (in Frémont's words) at the Battle of Cross Keys. Cluseret liked and respected Frémont, and when the latter resigned his command in July 1862, the nation gained but the Frenchman lost—for Cluseret neither liked nor respected his new superiors.[18]

They were timid, he complained to civilian authorities like the Secretary of State, and worse yet they were amateurs. In his professional opinion, men like Benjamin Kelley and Jacob D. Cox were "excellent lawyers no doubt," but they were lousy generals. "It is impossible for me to ignore the radical nullity that surrounds me," he told Sumner finally: "I can do nothing better than to compare [a civilian general] . . . to a professor of rhetoric who comes to the theater to perform *Esther* or *Athalie* under the pretext of having studied Racine, [though] never having seen footlights or audiences, nor ever having trod the boards—he would be the most grotesque character in the world. It is the same with these generals in the field of battle."[19]

For the most part, Cluseret was right about these generals; he also thought he was doing his duty by reporting their faults to his patrons in Washington. Yet in the process he only managed to alienate the military authorities and reinforce his growing reputation as a troublemaker.[20] Cluseret's reputation came to roost when he accused General Robert Milroy of mistreating Southern civilians in the Shenandoah Valley during the 1862 campaign—something "which honor and morality condemn in all countries."[21] Milroy, in turn, complained to his own powerful friends about Cluseret's insubordination. As a result, Cluseret was placed under arrest, and resigned his commission in March 1863 rather than face charges.[22]

It was a hard blow for Cluseret. Yet as he explained to Sumner in a rueful letter some months afterwards, the real tragedy of his short American army career was how it traduced the traditional Franco-American commitment to democracy. "You know," he told the Massachusetts senator, "what motive convinced me to leave Europe and destroy my career in order to come to America . . . [It] was to rebuild democratically what Lafayette had once built in a completely different manner. I believe I can add, without too much vanity, that I was better versed in the ways of my craft than was the young marquis . . . [But the politics of the Union Army] presented me with the sad alternative of sacrificing my dignity, my duty, [and] my conscience . . . to my political ideals." Now Cluseret could never become the new Lafayette.[23]

While Gustave Cluseret came to dislike Union generals (who reminded him too much of European autocrats), he also came to admire the average Union soldier, whose "conduct . . . surpassed all my expectations." Everywhere he served, the men in blue suffered gracefully under adverse conditions without complaining or requiring harsh discipline, "something *unheard of*" in Europe. The reason for this, Cluseret decided, was that Yankee soldiers were citizens first and fighters second.[24] "The soldier," he wrote in 1869, "must never cease to be a citizen; he must, on the contrary, take an active, direct part in the affairs of the country." American soldiers *did* take an active part, and Cluseret was amazed at the effort this sometimes required:

If the American volunteers accomplished prodigies of patience, energy, and devotion at the commencement of the war, it is because they fought with knowledge of the cause. In the midst of the messiest business one could hear the squeaking voice of the *"news boy"* over the sound of the fusillade . . . The soldier . . . [bought his] newspaper, stuffing it under the flap of his pack; and at the first break, he ran his eyes quickly over it. After reading it, one could see his face light up or become somber. But whatever his feelings, there would be a redoubling of his zeal and drive.

The Frenchman thought this a vivid example of the average American's fitness for self-government.[25]

He saw more of this republican capacity at work after February 1864, when he hitched his star to Frémont's presidential ambitions. For reasons that remain unclear, Cluseret was installed in the editor's chair of the *New Nation,* the main newspaper of Frémont's strange campaign.[26] He brought two simple goals to the task: to elect Frémont and and to make his own mark on New York journalism. According to one student of the campaign, he also brought a polemical flair, proceeding to fill the pages of the *New Nation* with equal parts Frémont, vitriol, and "contemporary European ultra-democratic theories."[27]

From Frémont came a platform that anticipated all the major planks of Radical Reconstruction, especially the expansion of congressional authority; it also called for a restructured army, a renewed "national spirit," and a refurbished Monroe Doctrine.[28] The vitriol was aimed mostly at Lincoln. In one inspired swipe, for example, Cluseret noted that "call[ing] one man 'Honest' out of a population of thirty million, is not so much a compliment to him as a sarcasm on all the rest."[29] Finally, Cluseret stressed a number of themes that were as much a part of his old life in French republican politics as his new life in America: an expansion of democratic participation, an end to Napoleon III's adventures in Mexico, and the decentralization of authority.

This last point was the most important. For decades, French opposition parties had focused on centralization as the primary source of all political woes in their country. Cluseret brought this same attitude to American politics in 1864, complaining to Sumner that "there is an America of Virginians, of Georgians, [and so on, but] not of Americans. We must create a spirit of national unity, without falling into the . . . [evils of] centralization." Seven years later, these evils became a major theme in Cluseret's interpretation of the Commune. Some Americans, however, had already begun to realize that (de)centralization was a salient link between the American states' rights debate and the recurrent French struggle against tyranny (see Chapter 5).[30]

On May 31, 1864, a "vast assemblage" of Frémont supporters (four hundred, or perhaps a tenth of the *New Nation*'s readership) gathered in Cleveland to nominate him for president on the "Radical Democratic" ticket.[31] One week later, the Republicans in Baltimore renominated Abraham Lincoln. Frémont immediately began to pursue the regular Democratic party nomination, but Cluseret refused to go along in the abandonment of radical policies that such a pursuit required. Their split precipitated a struggle for control of the *New Nation*. Editor Cluseret wanted to "transform . . . [it] into a purely *independent radical* newspaper"; candidate Frémont wanted to keep attacking Lincoln, in the hopes of extorting political advantage. The struggle ended in a nasty lawsuit, and though the journal limped through the November election and was briefly revived under Cluseret's control a year later, his career in New York journalism was over.[32]

Cluseret's disillusionment with his former commander was acute. The battle for the *New Nation* had cost him $1,148; worse, flirting with Frémont had cost him the trust of European friends and supporters, who had always favored Lincoln's re-election.[33] Worst of all, thought Cluseret, the ambitious Frémont had transformed his presidential campaign into an attack on liberty throughout the world, by "prolonging an uncertainty which can only help [the cause of Democratic candidate] McClellan, which is to say, [the cause of] L[ouis] Napoleon, J[efferson] Davis, and black and white slavery."[34] Fortunately the American Republic retained a basic soundness: *Vox populi vox Dei,* he concluded when Lincoln won a second term.[35] Nonetheless, Cluseret had begun to sense disturbing parallels between America and France.

These parallels became clearer when he turned his attention to the problems of Reconstruction. By his own testimony, Cluseret had always been an abolitionist; in fact, he later boasted that "in 1862, Jefferson Davis placed me outside the law . . . for having freed, on my own authority, the slaves at Madison Court House, [Virginia,] without waiting for Lincoln's proclamation."[36] When the Emancipation Proclamation finally came, he applauded it like "every cultivated man in Europe." Still, it was not until 1864 that he began to correspond with Charles Sumner about the fate of African Americans.[37]

In the early stages of the Frémont campaign, the *New Nation* followed a radical line on Reconstruction, calling for the confiscation of rebel lands, complete civil and political equality for the freedmen, and constitutional guarantees of their rights. When Cluseret parted from Frémont he kept these political views.[38] Nonetheless, he added his own, distinctly Franco-American perspective. The Civil War, he told Sumner in late February 1864, was nothing but a result of the slaveholders' desire to perpetuate a "slave republic." By putting "slavery in the place of liberty," they had "attempted to invert the social pyramid from its natural base[,] attempting as in France to substitute authority for liberty!" Once they were defeated, the pyramid could be rebuilt on the solid foundation of freedmen's liberties. But first the rebel leaders had to be punished, both as a matter of simple justice and an example to "Southern aristocrats." The slave-power could not be allowed to resurrect itself, or America might again succumb to autocracy: this was a lesson that Cluseret drew from the history of his own nation. Bourbonism was Bourbonism, he asserted, and "Lee's head, like that of Louis XVI, must fall, judiciously and in cold blood, in the name of law and morality."[39]

Having dispensed with the rebel leaders, Cluseret went on to prescribe conditions for a durable emancipation of the slaves. Land was the most important condition, and the easiest one to provide: simply confiscate it from the Southern masters and sell it off in small parcels to freedmen and Union veterans. This, he explained to Sumner, was "an analogy with our [French] revolution," whose history suggested that "the best and least expensive army of occupation might be . . . [composed] of small proprietors implanted by a revolution into a newly conquered land."[40] The small proprietor—the yeoman—was also at the heart of the American revolutionary tradition, and Cluseret managed to evoke that tradition in a passage rich with Jeffersonian echoes:

> The soil shall command the vote; therefore let us give the soil to our friends [the freedmen], and let the title of proprietor confer the title of elector without distinction of color and without distinction of origin . . . [I]n the South [the cultivator] will be *ipso facto* a citizen and elector.

"The vote for the blacks," he concluded, "is the revolution accomplished by the small proprietor and safe-guarded by him."[41]

Cluseret thus undertook a synthesis of the first French and second American Revolutions to explain the possibilities of Reconstruction; he combined them again to explain Reconstruction's failure. The early months of 1865 were not an easy time for Cluseret, either personally or politically. Having developed his own plan for the "education, civilization, and definitive emancipation of the black[s] through military organization," he watched the army instead become a tool of counterrevolution. Congress, he admonished the senator from Massachusetts, had ceded all policy initiative to "an executive [who would] weaken the revolution almost as much as if it had taken place in Paris." As a whole, the American political system had succumbed to corruption and vice. In short, "Yet another revolution miscarried."[42]

When Andrew Johnson became president, Cluseret became even less sanguine. "Here we are," he wrote Sumner on May 11, 1865, "in full counterrevolution. Virginia restored as a state by a President who considers himself the [sole] representative . . . of the United States . . . like Louis XIV saying *l'état c'est moi.*" What was worse, Johnson's arbitrary policies had placed him on a par with Napoleon III, still the cynosure of evil in Cluseret's political universe. "Ah! revolutionaries, you spit on your fathers and wish to be conservatives." The second American Revolution was lost.

Lost, perhaps, but not forgotten, as Gustave Cluseret continued to ponder the meaning of the Civil War. He traveled a tangled path through the late 1860s. Then, in the hot summer of 1870, the Emperor of France declared war on Prussia. Cluseret's thoughts hurried homeward, but his body could not follow until September, when the Second Empire expired along with the outstanding warrants for the general's arrest. On September 5, the first full day of the new Republic, Cluseret returned to Paris. Finding that his military skills were not in demand at the capital, he soon departed for the southern city of Lyons.[43]

Like Paris, Lyons had its own share of socialists, neo-Jacobins, and local patriots. Like their Parisian counterparts, they saw the collapse of the imperial regime as a prime opportunity to create a revolutionary Commune (that is, a self-governing municipality organized on democratic principles and rather loosely affiliated with the rest of the nation as part of a federal polity). One of their advisors in this grand project was the Russian anarchist Mikhail Bakunin. He and the Lyonnaise Communards knew Cluseret by reputation, and they invited the general to lead their troops when the revolution came, which he quickly agreed to do. But the fateful day, September 28, 1870, brought fiasco, not triumph.[44]

It began auspiciously enough, when a spontaneous crowd of workers stormed the city hall and peacefully disarmed the guards. Unfortunately, no one on the scene really knew what to do next. They asked Cluseret to guide them, but being a stranger to Lyons and dubious about these eager followers, he declined. As he later explained, "it was evident that this was only a fetus and not a new-born, an impulsive act or, perhaps worse, [the act] of some agitator, the only possible result being . . . a mess. Seeing that nothing had been decided, neither a program nor its personnel, the best thing was to leave well enough alone. Which is what I did." All in all, it turned out to be a wise decision, for within twenty-four hours the local authorities had suppressed any further hint of an uprising.[45]

The story was largely the same a month later at Marseilles, though with two important differences. First, the communal movement at Marseilles was spearheaded by the Ligue du Midi, an affiliate of the First International. This meant a better organization, both in terms of program and personnel.[46] Second, the role of outside agitator, played so well by Bakunin in Lyons, was played in Marseilles by George Francis Train, the only American of that time who might lay claim to a more colorful life than Cluseret's.

During a long career, Train (1829–1904) went from being an innovative capitalist to an outspoken radical to a certified lunatic. In the 1840s and 1850s he made several fortunes in gold, trans-Pacific shipping, British streetcars, and the financing of the transcontinental railroad. The American Civil War then took him to England, where he agitated on behalf of the Union cause (much to the dismay of his wife, close kin to Jefferson Davis). Then he came home to champion the views of Internationalists, Irish Republicans, vegetarians, and especially feminists. Indeed, when Elizabeth Cady Stanton and Susan B. Anthony began to publish the *Revolution* in 1868, Train's money made it possible; he even joined them on the stump to campaign for women's suffrage. Four years later he combined forces with Victoria Woodhull, the outspoken advocate of free love, to battle Anthony Comstock and his bluenose crusade; the result was a stretch in prison, not the first one that Train had suffered. In later years a New York court would find him non compos mentis, and he would spend the rest of his days railing against the system and chatting with toddlers, birds, and squirrels.[47]

In the autumn of 1870, however, Train was engaged in a trip around the world that later became the model for Jules Verne's famous novel. On October 20, Train's ship docked at the port of Marseilles, where he was pleasantly surprised to find a large crowd awaiting his arrival. It seems they had heard about his support of the Fenians and his role in popular uprisings in Italy and Australia, and they greeted him as a "liberator." Train was more than willing to accept the title and the responsibility that came with it, as he explained to a large crowd of workers at the Alhambra club that very evening. Introducing himself as "a citizen of the American Republic," he reminded them of the powerful ties that had always bound the United States and France, embodied in a succession of Franco-American heroes from Lafayette to Train himself. Now he offered them guns and "the moral force . . . [of] a great people," urging them to resist the Prussians and march on Paris. "The Republic in itself is an army," he concluded, "and all Europe fears it . . . If one must fight and die, let it be for liberty and France."[48]

Train later wrote that he was immediately "possessed by the French revolutionary spirit. The fire and enthusiasm of the people swept me from my feet. I was thenceforth a 'Communist,' a member of their 'Red Republic.'" Unfortunately, the revolutionary spirit never manifested itself in the form of the promised rifles. All he could offer the movement at Marseilles was his advice, his belief in Franco-American republicanism, and his aid in getting Cluseret to come fight their battle.[49] On October 21, Train was part of the committee that invited Cluseret to take command of the local units of the National Guard in the name of the Ligue du Midi. Cluseret agreed, though with some reluctance. Yet once he arrived in the city from Geneva, he and Train became inseparable.[50]

Yet not even the combination of their varied and formidable skills was enough to establish the Commune in Marseilles. On October 30, 1870, the fall of Metz to the German troops precipitated a march on the city hall, led by Cluseret and Train; on November 1 a municipal revolution was declared; yet by November 4 the central government had reasserted its complete control over the city.[51] There was barely time for Cluseret to extol "republican austerity" and to rally his guardsmen around the "Universal Republic."[52] There was only one more opportunity for Train to invoke the ties between France and the United States.

On November 3 the American saw troops marching through the streets, which he thought were still under Cluseret's command. "Vive la Commune!" he cried out, but they responded with silence; these were French regulars, sent to quell the uprising. A squad was detached to the front of Train's hotel, where he stood on a balcony behind a red flag. They aimed their guns, and Train decided that if they were going to shoot him, he wanted to "die in the most dramatic manner possible." "There were two other flags on the balcony," he recalled, "the colors of France and America." He wrapped himself in the flags, knelt down at the edge of the balcony, and yelled out in French: "Fire, fire, you miserable cowards! Fire upon the flags of France and America wrapped around the body of an American citizen—if you have the courage!" Impressed with his bravado, or perhaps his insanity, the soldiers slowly rose and marched away. But even Train knew the game was up.[53]

The next day Train and Cluseret departed the city together, though heading in opposite directions. Train was bound for Lyons, and was promptly arrested when he got there. After thirteen days in detention they expelled him from the country, much to the relief of both local officials and the American government.[54] (He will soon reappear in this story, however, on the other side of the Atlantic.) Cluseret spent the next five months evading the French police as they chased him through southern France. Yet all the time he remained in contact with the International in Paris through Eugène Varlin, who like Cluseret would become a part of the Commune's inner circle. He was thus prepared for the uprising that began on March 18, 1871.[55]

Cluseret was not in the capital for the first clash between Parisian forces and the central government. When he arrived in Paris a few days later, the National Guard already had effective control of the city, and the provisional French government had fled to Versailles. Both sides were preparing for civil war, and Cluseret was well placed to command the military operations of the Commune. For one thing, he had strong links to three of the groups that organized the communal revolution: the International, the Central Committee of the Twenty Arrondissements, and the Central Committee of the National Guard.[56] For another, his military reputation, only a bit tarnished by the failures at Lyons and Marseilles, had preceded him, and he was popular with the National Guard's rank and file.

On April 2, 1871, Gustave Cluseret was named "délégué à la Guerre" (War Minister) by the Executive Commission of the municipal Council. (The Council was the newly elected city government; despite the resulting confusion, it is usually called "the Commune" for short.) Their first choice would have been the Italian hero Garibaldi, but Cluseret was both available and competent. Nonetheless, the political leaders of the Commune were never willing to grant him total control over military affairs, a situation that soon made Cluseret's job impossible.[57] From the start, things did not look promising. The day after Cluseret took charge, the Commune's forces suffered a rout at Courbevoie that the new commander compared to Bull Run. He had nothing to do with either the planning or the execution, but the failure was laid at his feet anyway—a portent of things to come.[58]

In general, Cluseret faced the daunting task of organizing defenses for a city with limited supplies, a ragtag army, worthless officers, and a nonexistent chain of command. The ideological confusion of the Commune was more than matched by a tangle of institutional structures. It was never clear, for example, just who commanded the National Guardsmen defending Paris: the municipal Council, the Executive Commission, the special Military Commission created on April 20, the War Minister, or the Guard's own Central Committee. Thus no one fully controlled them, everyone worked at cross-purposes, and Cluseret was caught in the middle.[59]

His own testiness only made things worse; just as he had done in the Civil War, the Frenchman now managed to alienate both the soldiers and politicians of the Commune. He stepped on toes everywhere in his effort to reorganize the municipal forces. The National Guard, for example, was displeased by Cluseret's heavy-handed attempts to fill the ranks with conscripts and to eliminate the traditional privilege of electing officers. The Artillery Committee, perhaps the most efficient defensive force in Paris, hated him for trying to curb its independence. The officer corps both envied and distrusted him, feelings that Cluseret reciprocated.[60]

As in America, the professional soldier found himself surrounded by generals who were really politicians, and he did not hesitate to tell them what he thought about their martial skills.[61] But worse than the incompetence was the corruption, both moral and pecuniary. Wherever he looked, Cluseret saw officers shirking their duties while lining their pockets and strutting about in flashy uniforms. His response was a public reprimand, reminding them of why they fought. "Citizens," he told them,

> I have noted with distress that, forgetful of our modest origins, a ridiculous mania for braid, embroidery, and aigullettes has broken out amongst us.
>
> As workers, we have, for the first time, accomplished a revolution by and for labor . . . We were workers, we are workers, and we shall remain workers.
>
> It is in the name of virtue against vice, duty against abuse, and austerity against corruption that we have triumphed: let us not forget it.
>
> Let us remain virtuous men and above all men of duty, [and] thus shall we create an austere Republic, the only one which can exist, or has the right to.[62]

Here, combined with an emergent socialist vocabulary, was the language of republican virtue that Cluseret had learned in America. The same language had marked his most generous prose during the Frémont campaign, his vision of an African-American yeomanry, and his proclamation to the guardsmen of Marseilles. It shaped his 1869 pamphlet, *Armée et*

Démocratie, where he praised the American citizen-soldier and scathingly contrasted "military virtues" with "virtues [that] are essentially civil and the daughters of liberty."[63] And now it was present visually in the uniform he adopted as War Minister. During the Commune, notes his biographer, "one never saw [Cluseret] except in civilian dress."[64] This misstates the facts, since at least two photographs from the period clearly show Cluseret in uniform; but the uniform is strikingly plain, utterly devoid of "braid, embroidery, and aigullettes," and patterned on the simple tunic of a Union Army officer.[65] (Could it even be the same uniform he wore in the Shenandoah Valley, during "better days when victory was in the service of freedom"?)[66]

Cluseret's self-righteous pronouncements further strained his relations with the political leaders of the Commune. Apparently he failed to learn an important lesson from his American experience: that revolutionary politicians like to play soldier almost as much as revolutionary generals like to play politics. From the start, the neo-Jacobin majority on the Commune Council was displeased with Cluseret's defensive strategy. They wanted a "nation in arms," as it had been in 1792–1794.[67] Meanwhile, the Executive Commission kept the War Minister on a short leash, demanding explanations for every military decision. On April 20 the leash became even shorter with the creation of a Military Commission, composed of five civilians whom Cluseret condemned as "utterly ignorant in all the concerns of the [military] profession."[68]

Although written some months after the Commune, this assessment was typical of the general's brusque treatment of his colleagues. Cluseret was elected to the Commune Council on April 18 but never attended meetings. He joined the Executive Commission on April 20 but only went to its meetings when they forced him to. When called to the chambers of the Military Commission he spoke bluntly, showing open contempt for its members. The Commune was being run by "babblers and busybodies," he later complained—a worthless pack of "engineers without works, doctors without patients, lawyers without briefs, [and] professors without pupils." "If only the Commune had been composed of workers instead of journalists," he lamented in his *Mémoires,* "it would have triumphed."[69]

To many eyes, Cluseret's brisk but brusque attempt to master the armies of the Commune looked like the entering wedge of dictatorship; this, plus his strained relations with the civil and military authorities, led to his arrest on April 30, 1871.[70] The immediate cause was a breach in the defenses at Issy, to the south of the city. Since mid-April the French army had concentrated its attack on this vital fort, whose defenders abandoned it, despite strict orders, on April 29–30. The next morning Cluseret took personal command of a battalion and reoccupied the fort. But the defensive line was permanently weakened, and the entire blame was pinned on the War Minister. Citing the "discouragement that reigned in the National Guard" and hinting at both incompetence and disloyalty, Cluseret's former allies on the Central Committee asked for his removal—and the Jacobin-dominated Executive Commission was more than happy to comply.[71]

In the process, writes Stewart Edwards, Cluseret became "the scapegoat for the failure of the Commune to control the National Guard and of the National Guard to be able to organize itself."[72] But there were four other factors at work: his opposition to the arrest of Monsignor Darboy, the Archbishop of Paris, who was being held hostage by the Commune; his opposition to the new "Committee of Public Safety"; his attempt to parley with the German army and secure its neutrality in the civil war;[73] and, finally, his friendliness towards Americans.[74]

Perhaps the last charge had some merit, though it was hardly the stuff of treason. Conscious of his own debt to the United States, Cluseret did his best to aid the Americans who stayed in Paris during the Commune. As a result, one conservative Yankee who found little else to applaud in that period was forced to confess to "a feeling of security entertained by all Americans in Paris while he remained in power"; another admitted that Cluseret "always displayed an extremely liberal policy towards us." On several occasions Cluseret also offered official assistance to the American minister, Elihu Washburne, who remained in Paris to protect the interests of American and German residents. In particular, he arranged for Washburne to visit the imprisoned archbishop, an act that earned him the hatred of Raoul Rigault, chief prosecutor of the Commune.[75]

All these factors brought Cluseret to a cell in the Mazas prison, just down the hall from Darboy (at least until May 9, when Cluseret was transferred to the Hôtel de Ville). All things considered, he was lucky to be there, for as Paschal Grousset explained to the members of the Commune, "*In a revolution*—the Gospel according to Saint Robespierre—one does not simply recall a War Minister who has lost the confidence of his constituents: one arrests him; and in bygone days one shot him."[76] Behind bars, Cluseret missed the worst excesses of the revolution: the resurrection of the Committee of Public Safety, the destruction of the Vendôme Column, the sack of French premier Adolphe Thiers's home in Paris, and a growing number of arrests and accusations as the Commune began to panic. He also missed the worst of the bombardments by the Versailles government, and a stream of military reverses that began to seal the fate of Paris.

On Sunday, May 21, a gala concert was held in the Tuileries Gardens, in the shadow of the former imperial palace, to benefit those who had been wounded, widowed, or orphaned by the civil war. The audience did not know that just a few miles to the southwest the French army was preparing to storm Paris. Closer to the palace, at the Hôtel de Ville, the Commune Council was holding a frantic meeting in equal ignorance of the invasion. The main order of business was Cluseret's trial. Debate dragged on as Cluseret was grilled about his tenure at the Ministry of War. Suddenly, a messenger arrived with the awful news that the enemy was in their midst. Debate ended, a vote was quickly called, and Cluseret was acquitted, 28 votes to 7. At 8:00 P.M., the final session of the Commune adjourned, *sine die*. "It was the end," said Jules Vallès, the session's chairman: "nothingness!"[77]

Some members of the Commune rushed to join their fellow citizens on the barricades, and most who did so died there. Cluseret was a bit less noble, or perhaps more realistic about the chances for success. While hand-to-hand combat raged through the city's streets, he looked for a place to hide. He went to the apartment of William Huntington, an American acquaintance who was covering the civil war for the *New York Tribune,* but Huntington was reluctant to help him. In desperation, Cluseret sought refuge from a priest, who felt obligated by the man's kindly treatment of Archbishop Darboy. Cluseret spent five months disguised as a pious seminarian while all hell broke loose in Paris.[78]

Just as jail had shielded him from the worst excesses of the revolution, the walls of the seminary shielded Cluseret from the worst excesses of the civil war. The last days of the French civil war, May 22–28, are rightly known as *la semaine sanglante:* Bloody Week. This was the Commune's "heroic last stand on the barricades and self-consummation in the fires of Paris—or, as its enemies saw it, [of] the final convulsive orgy of the fevered city." Twenty-five thousand Parisians were killed on the streets or summarily shot by the troops from Versailles, who sacked the city while German soldiers and the French bourgeoisie cheered them on. On the other side, the Commune executed more than seventy hostages, including the archbishop, while Parisians set the city aflame. Their primary targets were the symbolic structures of the old regime, including the Tuileries Palace, the Hôtel de Ville, and the Palace of the Légion d'Honneur, all of which burned to the ground.[79]

The last pocket of resistance was crushed on May 28 at the Père-

Lachaise cemetery. The Mur des Fédérés, where the last defenders were executed, remains "a place of pilgrimage for French Socialists and Communists" even today.[80] On October 29, 1871, Cluseret slipped out of Paris disguised as a Belgian priest. A squad of French soldiers at the Gare du Nord even asked for a blessing, which Cluseret kindly provided; then he boarded his train and left the city. It was the end of another revolution, the end of another failure.[81]

A few months later in Geneva, Gustave Cluseret sat down to record his analysis of the Paris Commune for *Fraser's Magazine,* the most progressive of the mainstream British monthlies.[82] Just as he once used the memory (and experience) of French revolutions to interpret American politics, he now used his American experience to make sense of the latest revolution in France. Indeed, his interpretation of the Commune struck three themes that were deeply resonant with contemporary Americans: republicanism, centralization, and the emancipation of labor. Of the three, the last was least important.

Despite his active role in the First International, socialism was always a secondary part of Cluseret's ideology.[83] But this did not diminish his understanding of the Commune as a workers' revolution, nor his ability to link it to the recent struggle for emancipation in America. After his own brush with Reconstruction, and after his failed bid to resurrect the *New Nation* as a workingman's paper, Cluseret noted in frustration that the United States "presents that strange anomaly of enslaved labor in a free nation. Politically free, the worker is socially the capitalist's serf." Nonetheless, "it belonged to the great Republic that freed the black slave to liberate the white slave, thereby assuring him a future." Part of that future could be seen in Paris in 1871.[84]

Like many others on both sides of the Atlantic, Cluseret described the Commune as a struggle of the "working-classes (which, after all, constitute the only real people, those who work and fight)" to free themselves from the shackles of the old imperial regime.[85] Unfortunately, the workers were led astray by irresponsible leaders who were less interested in pursuing "justice and freedom" than in recreating the Jacobinism of 1793. Because of them, the workers' struggle ended in violence that was both unsought and unnecessary. Yet all was not failure, for "I have faith," wrote Cluseret, "in the great mass of the working people, which knows what it wants, does not trust in words, and . . . made the revolution of March 18.

They want to work for themselves henceforth, not for others. I hope they will not allow themselves to drop the substance to grasp the shadow."[86]

Part of that faith was grounded in Cluseret's embrace of American political principles. For while the workers of Paris were struggling against the old regime, against the French army, and against their own leaders— while they were waging the "universal and eternal protest of the employed against the employers"—they were also striving "to realise the great truth inscribed on the Constitution of America: 'Every man has a right to human happiness . . .'" During his fight against Southern slavery, while commanding Northern citizen-soldiers, Cluseret had witnessed "the reward[s] of free labour" that Parisians still longed for. "I have seen the difference in America," he wrote in 1872. "I have seen consumption, rendered almost universal by the absence of classes, become co-extensive with the population." Indeed, he added, "To the United States belongs, in virtue of their liberty, the solution to the great problem of the nineteenth century: 'What are the equitable relations between labour and capital?' . . . After having fought victoriously for the emancipation of the Negro race, [they] will fight again and conquer for the emancipation of white labour . . . The social party in America will conquer." By implication, the social party in France would conquer too, for Cluseret construed their cause to be the same.[87]

In one of Cluseret's several summations of events in Paris, he noted that the "Commune . . . comprised two great ideas, namely, the idea of a Socialist Republic and that of a simple Republic." His earnest words echoed the Commune Council's pronouncement that "the flag of the Commune is that of the universal Republic."[88] They also reflected what many Parisians in the street actually believed: they were fighting to create a republic, or at least to save one from Thiers's quasi-monarchical designs. Cluseret's conversion to socialism was fairly recent, but his commitment to republicanism was of long standing. And though born in France, it was profoundly shaped by his American experience.

"Is it not," he asked rhetorically, "the history of the United States which, at a distance and without a blow, republicanises Europe by the sole force of its example?" Cluseret was hardly concerned about future historians' struggles to define "republicanism," or even that Reconstruction had put the contemporary meaning of "the republic" up for grabs.[89] *He* knew what a republic meant—no standing army, plus virtue, democratic suffrage, and the unlimited right of free association—and he knew it first-hand. He knew that "where such liberty exists, no revolutions need be feared. Evolutions only take place."[90] Finally, he knew that "what is good on one side of the ocean is good on the other, [just] as my friend Charles Sumner said one day . . . [to a Frenchman] who was trying to prove that the Republic was good for the Americans, but not for the French."[91]

The final theme in Cluseret's interpretation of the Commune was de-centralization. Readers of Tocqueville know it as an abiding theme in French politics. Through every change of regime, one thing remained constant: the central government tried to enhance its power, and the opposition tried to resist. Opposition was particularly acute in the major cities of Paris, Lyons, and Marseilles, which despite their size were directly governed by the national authorities. This arrangement and the frustration it bred were important precipitating factors in the local uprisings in all three places. Whatever else they wanted, revolutionists in all three cities wanted municipal autonomy, preferably as part of a national federation. As the Parisians put it: "Unity such as was imposed upon us until now is only a despotic, unintelligent, and arbitrary centralization. The political unity that Paris wants is . . . voluntary association."[92]

Cluseret could not have agreed more. As he explained to an Englishman during the French civil war, "I am not fighting for Communism, but for Communalism, which, I need not tell you, is quite a different thing . . . Paris and Lyons should be judged . . . capable of managing their own municipal affairs without the interference of the State."[93] He elaborated on this in his *Mémoires:*

> For me, the Revolution of March 18th never signified and never will signify anything more than a municipal Council invested with full powers by the municipality to administer all its affairs [while] uniting with the central power in a simple federative bond, such as happens in America . . . One does not have to look elsewhere to find the secret of [America's] prosperity, for it is [located] in a freedom and economy based on and maintained by municipal independence. What is good for America is good for France . . . And, just as we have accustomed ourselves to the word "Republic," we will grow accustomed to the word "Commune." For without the Commune, it is impossible to maintain either the Republic or liberty.

He made similar claims to a German army officer as they parleyed in April 1871, and again in his articles for *Fraser's.* Each time he managed to blend the French concern for decentralization with the American example. The comparison was not unique to Cluseret, but it still demonstrates his heightened awareness of the parallels between the French and the American civil wars.[94]

Louis Greenberg notes that the decade ending in 1871 "proved a period of questioning of central power everywhere"—in France and the United States especially, but also in Germany, Italy, and Britain. In France the locus of opposition was the municipality, in America it was the states (though New York City was also fighting for a municipal charter while the Commune raged in Paris). Nonetheless, as Jean T. Joughin explains in her study of the Commune in French politics, there is a "meaningful comparison that can be made between the two civil wars . . . in terms of the conflict between centralization and decentralization in government": "Just as the Confederacy represented an obsolescent concept of the relationship between the state and the federal government, so the Paris Commune had an antique view of the role of the municipality vis-à-vis the national government. Both 'lost causes' were victims of the swing toward centralization of political power at the top which has been characteristic of the late nineteenth and the twentieth centuries."[95]

Southerners may well have had an "obsolescent concept" of states' rights, but it remained a deeply ingrained part of American political culture, widely shared by Northerners and hardly dispelled by the Civil War. Recall that, even before Appomattox, Cluseret had warned Charles Sumner about the persistence of Southern state loyalties, stressing the need to "create a spirit of national unity, without falling into the . . . [evils of] centralization." Unfortunately, a Union victory without centralization was impossible. Cluseret recognized this. Yet he never resolved the irony of fighting *for* central government in Italy and America and *against* it in Paris, while fighting for republics in all three places.

Even in the 1870s, when the North began to back away from Reconstruction, centralization remained a fact in American politics. Thomas Cooley, a moderate Northern jurist who later became a preeminent Constitutional scholar, complained that the Federal government was attempting an "extraordinary, . . . organized and forcible revolution in the State government[s]" through its aggressive policies. "One thing is clear," concluded Cooley in 1875: "to concede to the Federal government [the] authority to take to itself State powers, on an assumption that the people of a State have shown themselves incapable of self-government, and must consequently be ruled by the strong hand of the central power, would be to concede the failure of the American experiment in government." One can easily imagine Cluseret making the same judgment in 1871, as he pondered the same elements in the Paris Commune: the people, the central power, a revolution, and the American experiment in government.[96]

Gustave Cluseret's ultimate comment on the French civil war was that the Communards' program "was the American programme, and not even the whole of that. What the people of Paris demanded is what is practised . . . [wherever] good sense and human dignity have united to give to mankind a human government."[97] For their part, American observers were skeptical that Cluseret was the man to make such a judgment. Some doubted his American credentials, others grumbled that "no Americans in Paris . . . would have had anything to do with him under any circumstances," while others complained that he gave *real* Americans a bad name.[98] *Appleton's Journal* saw Cluseret's prominence as "one of the strongest indications . . . of the folly and desperation of the Communal insurrection." Even *The Spirit of the Times,* a publication broadly sympathetic to the Commune, was forced to admit that "the difference between French republicanism and American republicanism is shown in the difference of Cluseret's reception in New York and in Paris."[99]

They might have had a point. After all, Cluseret's unique life journey seems reason enough to exempt him from the role of exemplar, much less ideal type. Yet in many ways he was a microcosm of the world of his day. To borrow a description from Carl Schorske, Cluseret was like an "ideological collage . . . made of fragments of modernity, glimpses of futurity, and resurrected remnants of a half-forgotten past."[100] An unsettled man in an unsettled time, he perfectly embodied the "epoch of stirring events" bracketed by civil wars in America and France. His amphibious Franco-American career also puts a triple lie to Edmond Lepelletier's blithe assertion about the commensurability of those events.

The Paris Commune and the American Civil War were in fact connected on three levels. On the global scale, both were part of an "age of democratic civil wars" that swept across the Atlantic world in the middle years of the nineteenth century.[101] From central Europe in 1848, to Mexico in the late 1850s, to Spain in 1873–1874, Western societies were bent on resolving "the cardinal problems of the nineteenth century," which one historian conveniently lists as "the crusade to end human bondage, the complexities of the Industrial Revolution, the drive toward nationalism, and the advance of democracy." The list is hardly exhaustive, and was meant to be more suggestive than precise, but even so it could be a list of headings on

Gustave Cluseret's curriculum vitae, describing the causes for which he fought.[102]

On a smaller scale, the two civil wars were linked as common parts of a "co-tradition" shared by America and France. Rooted in the common legacy of eighteenth-century revolution, the co-tradition showed itself in the peculiar interest displayed by both French and American observers in the political development of their counterparts. "Sister republics" was often the shorthand code for this mutual interest, even when France lacked a republican form of government. According to Marvin Trachtenberg, for French liberals (like those whom Cluseret claimed as his patrons in 1862), "notions of liberty and republicanism . . . [were always] associated with the image of the United States." As a result, they closely scrutinized the American Civil War for signs of their own political future. When it came to the Paris Commune, Americans returned the favor, as the rest of these pages will show.[103]

For now, three things can be said about the Franco-American co-tradition. First, it was genuine and heartfelt on both sides of the Atlantic (as the Statue of Liberty, if nothing else, ought to prove). Second, its representatives were both illustrious (like Lafayette and Tocqueville) and quirky (like Cluseret and Train). Third, its existence helped Cluseret create an image of the Commune that should have been persuasive on both sides of the Atlantic, constructed as it was from common pieces of political culture.

The final link between the Paris Commune and the American Civil War was a human link. The two civil wars had participants in common, like Cluseret. And they had observers in common: men and women, French and American, who experienced both events and were ready to compare them. Sometimes the comparisons were similar to Cluseret's, sometimes very different. Sometimes observations were made from across the ocean, and sometimes from the middle of the action. The American community in Paris experienced the Commune up close, and their reactions to the French civil war are the subject of the next two chapters.

2

La Colonie Américaine

> If I was not an American I would certainly be a Frenchman.
> —JOHN SHERMAN (1895)

Years before the Commune, a "wise man of Boston" declared that "Good Americans, when they die, go to Paris."[1] But how do you count shades in the City of Lights? Even counting the live Americans in nineteeenth-century Paris presents a challenge. A rough estimate is that by 1870, on the eve of the Franco-Prussian War, at least 5,000 Americans called the city their home. With tourists and temporary residents included, the number swelled to perhaps 13,000.[2] They lived as strangers in a strange land, always removed from the inner rhythms of the French capital. Both a cause and a symptom of their isolation was the fact that American expatriates liked to stick closely together. Their favorite part of the city was a western stretch of the Right Bank, near the sixteenth arrondissement. In the 1870s, even native Parisians called this area the "American quarter" or the "American colony." Its boundaries described a rough triangle, with the Seine along the hypotenuse, the Bois de Boulogne on the western edge, and the Arc de Triomphe at the northern vertex. The third edge, running towards the east, was formed by the Champs-Elysées, probably the most popular place in Paris for Americans to reside.[3]

The political center of the colony, if not the geometric center, was the American legation, located at no. 75, Avenue de l'Impératrice. Just a short walk away was the American Chapel, at no. 21, Rue de Berri. Nearly as close was the office of the *American Register,* the colony's local newspaper, whose reading room was a clearinghouse for gossip and other forms of information. (Its editor, John J. Ryan, was "a very accomplished and experienced journalist.")[4] Freshly arrived Americans rushed to stay at the Grand Hotel on the Boulevard Italiens. Homesick old-timers strolled off to Charley's on the Rue Godot-de-Mauroy to savor their American specialties (like buckwheat pancakes and pumpkin pie). And tucked all around these landmarks were the local tradespeople who catered to American tastes and overcharged their customers for the privilege: the saloons that mixed "the latest American contrivance in beverages"; the "bazaars" that introduced American women to the latest fashions; the booksellers, boot-makers, cabbies, and clothiers—plus hundreds more—all exclusively engaged by *la colonie américaine.*[5]

These tradespeople did as much as the colony's formal institutions to help maintain cohesion among the Americans in Paris. All the same, "the Colonie has its little gradations of rank," status distinctions that French observers often failed to notice. John Russell Young, an American journalist who covered the Commune for the *New York Tribune,* later described some of the persistent divisions within the American community: "The colony draws lines. There is the old resident and the new resident; the American in trade; the idle American; the American who speaks French; the one who does not . . . the colonist who has family relationships—[and] the colonist who never obtrudes his domestic life upon friends."[6] Behind these obvious lines, Young noted, were even finer distinctions of wealth—though again, French observers often failed to see them.

Thus, according to one French woman, "Money being the sinews of travel, those citizens of the Union who come to Paris, ought to be, and are in general, the rich."[7] Her assumption was flawed, for as the *Nation* pointed out, "quick travel and low fares" had rendered the Atlantic Ocean a surprisingly minor obstacle to mid-nineteenth-century Americans. The result was that many of "our citizens, male and female, manage to beg, borrow, or steal at least one trip to Europe."[8] To their delight, when they arrived in Paris in the late 1860s they discovered that Americans lived "without personal taxation or exactions of any sort in this most magnificent of modern capitals." Compared to cities at home, the cost of living was wonderfully low. A favorable exchange rate meant that the dollar gained as much as 35 percent in buying power when converted into francs.[9] With incentives like these, both the rich and the middle class flocked to Paris.

Of course, the former usually managed to live better once they arrived. It was wealthy Americans who smoked big cigars at the exclusive Washington Club (if they were men), or who bought luxurious gowns at the House of Worth and hunted for husbands among the poorer French nobility (if they were women).[10] These Americans often lacked polish, or kept themselves arrogantly aloof from "the habits, behavior, and feelings of Europeans." Snobs on both sides of the ocean called them boors. Yet for every rich tourist or colonist who deserved the label, there was another who honestly appreciated the social, cultural, and educational opportunities of the French capital.[11]

Both varieties of American wealth received a warm welcome at the gilded court of Napoleon III—and where wealth was lacking, good looks and good connections might easily bridge the deficit. Every month, complained a French critic, the American minister was "obliged, upon a simple request, to present a batch of some hundred of his countrymen" to the Imperial Court, regardless of whether they were "serfs or seigneurs." (The number was really just twenty-eight, and Elihu Washburne retained a large degree of discretion.)[12] Others were brought to the Tuileries by Dr. Thomas W. Evans, the emperor's personal dentist. "Handsome Tom," as they called him, was one of the great success stories of the American colony. He had barely a nickel when he came to Paris from Philadelphia in 1847. Yet here he was in 1870: rich, famous, a member of the Legion of Honor, and the emperor's confidant. On the basis of that confidence, Evans could boast that Napoleon III "appreciate[d] the greatness of our rapidly-growing country, the energy of our men, the beauty and elegance of our women, their sparkling wit and self-dependence." Perhaps it was true. In any case, Evans continued, "Americans were always well received at the Imperial Court, especially if they were men or women of distinction, intelligence, and refinement."[13]

Most colonists never made it to the Tuileries or Fontainebleau, yet they still found Paris an attractive place. Health, repose, a child's education, a dose of "general culture," a dash of the night-life: these were the things they mostly wanted, and they could easily be obtained.[14] That was enough for the Yankee bourgeoisie—but there was also a Yankee bohemia. The great transatlantic pilgrimage to the École des Beaux-Arts had barely begun in 1870, yet Paris was already a mecca for American artists and students. Artists included architect Charles McKim, sculptors Olin Levi Warner and Augustus Saint-Gaudens, illustrator James Wells Champney, and a score of others at work in every medium.[15] "Miss Taggart of Indianapolis" was a typical student, in Paris to "pursue her musical studies"; dozens just like her were learning to dance or speak French. The Faculté de Médicine also attracted many students from the United States, including Mary C. Putnam, daughter of a leading New York publisher, who would soon became the first American woman to receive a French medical degree.[16]

Finally, Paris was home to a motley collection of expatriates that John Russell Young derided as idlers and exiles: "business exiles, driven away in the bankruptcy revolutions; political exiles, suffering from the fall of Tammany and the Southern Confederacy; social exiles, who seek oblivion in absence."[17] Young might easily have added criminals, adventurers, and vagabonds to the list, but it would only increase his unfairness to Southerners. The "Southern contingent" of the American colony, as Evans labeled it, was disproportionately large. Yet its membership was not restricted to bitter old Rebels. Some, like Confederate diplomat Ambrose Dudley Mann, were indeed fleeing from the political collapse of the South; but others were simply fleeing the region's economic collapse, and were happy to find a place where they could maintain a comfortable lifestyle on straitened resources.[18]

In the end, the various lines that divided the colony were never completely rigid. Furthermore, they were always cross-cut by a common national identity. Sometimes the strength of this identity waned, and sometimes it became overbearing. It was always strongest on July Fourth. In the "ancient days" before the Civil War (as Young called them), Independence Day was the highlight of the social season for *toute Paris américaine*—as it would be again in years to come. But in 1870, passions still ran too high for the American minister to attempt an official celebration of the national holiday. Instead, the leading members of the colony, both Southern and Northern, came together for an unofficial *fête* at Bella Rosa, the home of Dr. Evans.[19]

As the name suggests, Bella Rosa was a beautiful, stately mansion, constructed on a sunny lot just down the street from the American legation. On that warm Monday afternoon in July, the large saloon at the center of the house was decorated with flowers and bunting-draped portraits of Washington and Lafayette. Outside, a large tent was festooned with French and American flags. At half-past one, more than a hundred guests sat down in the tent to enjoy a sumptuous meal. Above their heads were the watchful portraits of an emperor, a president, and a Yankee saint (Daniel Webster). Dinner was followed by drinks and cigars, by toasts and speeches; as the host's biographer drily notes, many "patriotic sentiments were expressed." Yet there was also an undercurrent of apprehension to this happy American gathering, for everyone knew the truth behind Evans's whispered warning: "Within a few days this country may be at war."[20]

And the war came. One year later, on July 4, 1871, Paris would still be sifting through the wreckage of war and revolution, and there would be no public celebration of American independence.[21]

Without a Franco-Prussian War, there would never have been a Paris Commune. The war against Prussia, however, was hardly an unforeseeable event. In Berlin, Otto von Bismarck's policy of internal consolidation through external conquest had become transparent even before the Austro-Prussian War of 1866, and it was brilliantly executed in the years that followed. In stark contrast, Napoleon III pursued a foreign policy that was both aggressive and inept. At home, his empire was trapped in a fatal swoon of domestic legitimacy that the successful plebiscite of May 1870 did little to check. Yet war was a popular idea with many segments of the French population, who filled the streets with cries of "À Berlin." These factors, plus an inflated estimate of French military prowess, made it fatefully easy for Napoleon III to back himself into a war against Prussia.[22]

The United States was officially neutral, but this did not prevent its citizens in Paris from picking a side. Many, including minister Washburne, were quick to blame the conflict on Napoleon III, whose imperial regime was fundamentally obnoxious to American political ideals anyway.[23] According to the *American Register,* many others "who were not unfriendly to the French people were nevertheless disposed to grant that the Prussians were right."[24] Yet a third group was convinced that, empire or no, *la belle France* and her capital city deserved to be protected against the German aggressors.

In some cases, it was a conviction for which American men would fight, to the death if necessary. In July 1870, a group of young colonists, many of them Civil War veterans, tried to form a "Paris American Legion," but they were rebuffed by the military authorities. Later, however, Americans could be found serving in the French forces at all levels, ranging from a Mr. Moller in the Amis de la France (a foreign legion specially created to defend Paris) to Charles Carroll, a former lieutenant in the Army of the Potomac, who led a unit of French regulars.[25] Yet another veteran of the Civil War, General Régis de Trobriand, traveled to the seat of war but declined the offer of a French command because he remained on active duty with the U.S. Army.

Like Cluseret, the Count de Trobriand (to give him his ancestral title) was a native son of France who fought for the Union, but there the similarity ended. As a child, Trobriand was a page in the household of King Charles X, and his family followed the Bourbons into exile after the 1830 revolution. For the rest of his life, he continued to support the forces of reaction in France, even after becoming an American citizen. When he took command of the 55th New York Volunteers in 1862 (the "Gardes Lafayette," largely composed of French émigrés), Trobriand wore the spangled full-dress uniform of a French officer—in striking contrast to

Cluseret's plain blue tunic as Minister of War.[26] Still true to character, he later condemned "the 'Reds,' [and] the socialists of the Commune" as "the greatest and most dangerous enemies" of his native land.[27]

In the end, a contemporary newspaper reckoned that "forty or fifty" Americans had given their lives for the love of France. Among them was a Civil War hero from New Jersey, Colonel Burr Porter, who died shouting "I will show you how we fight in America."[28] But few of his fellow citizens in Paris were willing to risk so much on a war that seemed so pointless. "On both sides," complained one Pennsylvanian, "there is a sense of injury sustained which the American, at least, cannot appreciate."[29] With all its internal divisions, the colony never reached a consensus on the cause of the war. The effect of armed conflict on the lives and property of innocent bystanders was, however, universally recognized. As a result, the French declaration of war led to a mass exodus of Americans from Paris.[30]

In the first six weeks of the war, the U.S. legation in Paris issued passports to more than 3,300 Americans. Another thousand still held valid passports issued by the State Department at home, and at least a thousand more obtained credentials from other sources, or left the city without any papers at all.[31] At the start of December 1870, Washburne and Consul-General John Meredith Read estimated that no more than 175 Americans remained in Paris.[32] Hundreds had gone home to the United States. Thousands more had chosen to sit out the war in European havens like Brussels, Torquay, and the Italian Riviera—any place but France.[33]

The Americans who remained behind found themselves more integrated than ever into the life of the city. Foreign residents possessed no special immunity from the hardships of war, or from the burdens of the long Prussian siege, which stretched from September 19 until late January 1871. When Paris froze, so did Americans. When the French were reduced to eating horses, mules, rats, and exotic beasts from the city zoo, so were Americans.[34] When Prussian artillery pounded the city, American homes were also destroyed, and a few Americans were even killed by wayward shells.[35] At the same time, the colony reached out to assist the Parisians whose lot they shared. Under the leadership of Dr. Evans, a Franco-American Ambulance was established on the pattern of the United States Sanitary Commission, and by the consensus of French, American, and British observers it was "decidedly the best managed" field hospital of the war.[36]

Still, there was a special burden to being an American in Paris during the war: the burden of suspicion. At the end of August 1870, Paris was gripped by a spy scare. Innocent Germans were arrested, summarily tried, and then shot. One American tourist, with the unfortunate ability to speak fluent German but absolutely no French, would have shared their fate except for a gendarme who eventually understood his plea of "Ich bin ein Americaner."[37] Other accusations followed, but spy mania did not reach its hysterical peak until the siege, when foreigners were routinely fingered as *espions prussiens.* One Yankee clergyman was seized by police while jotting a note in his diary. Later, Nathan Sheppard and two American friends were arrested while "sauntering along the Champs Elysées" on their way home from a visit to General Read; their "crime" was speaking in a foreign tongue.[38]

Perhaps the most notable victim of the spy mania was John O'Sullivan, the ancient Jacksonian who, decades before, had coined the magic phrase "manifest destiny." Just a few days before the siege began, O'Sullivan anointed himself peacemaker and set off on a mission of mercy across the lines that separated Paris from the German headquarters. The mission was a failure, but he did manage to get himself arrested *twice* by the French authorities, both going and coming back.[39]

War and suspicion walk hand in hand, and this is probably enough to explain the spy mania in Paris that season. But why were Americans particularly distrusted? One reason, certainly, is that the American minister also served as the official protector of any unlucky Germans who remained in France. When war first broke out, the Berlin government asked Washburne to assume the local duties of *chargé d'affaires* for the North German Confederation, at least on a temporary basis. As the representative of a neutral power, Washburne was naturally reluctant to do so, but since Paris and Washington were both willing to accept the unusual German proposal, he agreed. For almost a year, until the two European nations renewed their diplomatic ties, the American minister did what he could to protect his unsought German charges, whether that involved granting visas to 30,000 *personae non gratae,* distributing charity to destitute noncombatants, protecting their property from illegitimate seizure, or springing false arrestees from French prisons.[40]

Washburne later wrote that protecting the Germans had placed him in "a very difficult . . . [and] embarrassing" position. Inevitably, the regular contacts between the leading American in Paris and the enemy outside made French patriots suspicious.[41] To make things worse, Washburne enjoyed the unique privilege, personally granted by Bismarck, of sending mail through the siege lines. Usually this involved official correspondence, but on occasion Washburne also received the back issues of British and

American newspapers. This, he complained to a colleague in London, made him "the only person in a city of two millions of people receiving any outside news. It . . . become[s] a great annoyance." The Germans thought he was passing secrets to the French, and asked Washburne to stop sharing his newspapers with the local press; the Parisians thought he was withholding information from their side. Washburne couldn't win.[42]

Yet even more than what the American minister did, the Parisians were suspicious of what America had failed to do. The land of Lafayette was in dire need, but where was American assistance? As we shall later see, public opinion in the United States was profoundly divided by the Franco-Prussian War, with many people supporting Germany in the early stages of the war and then favoring France once the empire was replaced by a new republic.[43] It was mostly the pro-German sentiment, however, that filtered into Paris before the siege cut it off from the outside world. To many French patriots, especially those who forgot which side Napoleon III had supported in the American Civil War, this seemed like a gross violation of the traditional bonds between their country and the United States.

This misplaced sense of historical injustice was only reinforced by the creation of the Third Republic on September 4, 1870. Even if the United States remained properly neutral in a war between empires, wondered Parisians, shouldn't it throw its full support behind a republic fighting a despot? Robert Sibbet, a Pennsylvania physician, was amazed at how earnestly the Paris press began to discuss the chances of armed intervention: "The example of Lafayette and his brave soldiers, crossing the ocean with arms and ammunition to help the American colonists to establish a republic is prominent before them, and they refuse to believe that assistance will not be sent. Strange hallucination indeed! Nevertheless it seems to be an honest conviction of many intelligent Frenchmen." John Meredith Read had a similar experience. On September 9, 1870, while riding through Paris in his coach, he was hailed by two drunk workers. When he explained that he would not stop for them because he was on official business, "the driver & the two drunken men took up the cry, 'Vive la Republique Americaine!' and then they cheered me, & they wished to know how soon the 300,000 soldiers from America would arrive to help France, [whether] there would be a Universal Republic, etc. etc." The troops, of course, never came, and America remained a neutral power; at about the same time, President Grant began issuing official statements that seemed to favor Germany over France.[44]

Hope denied thus fed suspicion and encouraged the search for American spies, on the theory that neutrality really meant collaboration. Both the hope and the suspicion, however, point to a significant fact: the Parisians were eagerly looking to America for examples and assistance. Perhaps because the United States was so far away, their sights were most tightly focused on the representative colony in Paris, whose physical and ideological movements were watched with a scrutiny that exceeded normal bounds. As the colony shrank in size, it grew in significance, even while it became more integrated with the daily life of the city. And while Paris watched the Americans, the Americans watched back.

Ideologically, the most significant event of the Franco-Prussian War, for French and Americans alike, was the creation of the Third French Republic to replace the defunct Second Empire of Napoleon III. On the French side, the "republican idea" had sustained a long, tangled history, frequently informed by comparison with the transatlantic "Sister Republic." On the American side, as a generation of historians has continuously remarked, "republicanism" was one of the central ideas of nineteenth-century political culture. Just twenty-two years earlier, the creation of the Second French Republic had been the cause for rejoicing among Americans in Paris. This reaction was echoed in 1870 by the decimated American colony.[45]

On September 1, 1870, the main French army under Marshal MacMahon was badly mauled at the battle of Sedan, and both MacMahon and the emperor surrendered to German forces. Paris received the news on September 3. One day later, "at precisely four o'clock and forty-five minutes in the afternoon," Léon Gambetta proclaimed the new republic before a huge crowd gathered outside the Hôtel de Ville in Paris. Many Americans joined the crowd, among them Judge John Erskine of the U.S. District Court in Georgia, who later recalled how he stood "amid thousands and thousands of people . . . in front of the Hôtel de Ville . . . [L]ooking up at an open window, I saw the tricolor and Gambetta; and at the moment I beheld the national flag and the MAN, the régime of the *coup d'état* toppled and crumbled to dust. Then arose the gladdening shout, 'Vive la République.' I thought to myself *La chaîne est brisé[e]*; and came away."[46]

Elihu Washburne came away from the same throng and confided to his diary: "Republic proclaimed. It has been a historical day . . . I have seen all." To this hard-bitten statesman from Illinois, veteran of the long struggle to preserve a republic in his own land, the birth of a new French

Republic "seem[ed] . . . almost like a dream." As he confessed to his sister-in-law a few days later, "I am so tickled at what has taken place that I can hardly contain myself . . . Only think, breakfasting in an Empire and dining in a Republic, all so quick as to make your head swim."[47] Other Americans in the city were quick to share his enthusiasm. Mary Putnam, for example, rhapsodized to her father that "I have heard the Republic proclaimed!" She gushed that "such days, in which a people lives, in which individual lives are absorbed into a Social Being that for a moment has become conscious of itself—such moments realize the old conceptions of ecstasy among the Neo-Platonists." Closer to Earth, the *American Register* spoke for many colonists when it wrote that "we are bound to sympathize with a government modelled after our own . . . [and we] give our hearty support."[48]

Private support for the French Republic was matched by official support on September 7, 1870, when the United States became the first foreign power to recognize the new regime—just as it had been the first to recognize the previous French Republic in 1848.[49] In his official communication to Foreign Minister Jules Favre, Washburne stressed the historical and ideological ties that bound the two countries together:

> [T]he government and the people of the United States . . . have learned with enthusiasm of the proclamation of a *Republic in France* . . . and they will associate themselves in heart and sympathy with that great movement . . . Enjoying the untold and immeasurable blessings of a republican form of government for nearly a century, the people of the United States can but regard with profoundest interest the efforts of the French people, to whom they are bound by the ties of a traditional friendship, to obtain such free institutions as will secure to them and to their posterity the inalienable rights of "life, liberty, and the pursuit of happiness."

In response, M. Favre agreed that "No one can better remind us . . . of the appreciable benefits of a republican form of government than the representative of a people which has given to the world the salutary example of absolute liberty."[50]

Favre's fellow citizens obviously agreed, for a large crowd of them gathered outside the American legation on September 8 to publicly thank Washburne. The United States, proclaimed their spokesman with obvious pride, "have always been in communion with the ideas of France. America and France are sisters, sisters as Republics, that is to say, sisters in Liberty.

The ocean that separates us is less deep than the sentiments which unite us."[51] Victor Hugo gave voice to the same sentiment just two days earlier, on the occasion of the great novelist's return to Paris from exile abroad. As he stepped from the train the first thing he saw was an American flag, and he promptly declared that the United States was a great inspiration to France. One American who witnessed the event strongly disagreed, and he offered a response as far removed from Washburne's as possible: "Fudge," he sneered, "the United States Republic has about as much sympathy with this one, as a well ordered family circle has with a lunatic asylum."[52] Once again, the American colony had failed to achieve a consensus on the events that transpired around them.

Those who supported the new French regime saw a clear reflection of the republic they knew at home. A sense of history also prompted warm feelings towards the Republic, which Dr. Sibbet (among others) prayed would now produce a leader like Washington or Lafayette.[53] Yet the implications of this link between France and the United States were never fully articulated, though the *American Register* came closest to doing so. John Ryan's rallying cry was "Americans, remember France! Frenchmen, remember America!" Behind this simple cry, however, lay a spirited defense of republican solidarity. For decades, Ryan argued, France had "indicated profound Republican tendencies"; this fact alone made it "cruel in the extreme . . . to take any other stand but that distinctly in favour of the French Republic."[54] Yet there was more at stake than just the fate of France, since republicanism anywhere was a blow against despotism everywhere.[55]

The key to this world-historical republicanism was political liberty, as "the brilliant example of the United States" clearly demonstrated. To be sure, France had struck a blow for liberty when it overthrew the Second Empire, but that action merely foretold "the spread of Republicanism throughout Europe, such Republicanism as has led America to . . . her [place] at the head of the nations who love liberty."[56] More than once, the *American Register* stressed that "Republican Institutions" were better than "Divine Right Nonsense"; not just freer, but more likely to foster prosperity and peace.[57] Like Washburne the diplomat, Ryan the editor implicitly understood the benefits of a republic (life, liberty, peace, and the pursuit of happiness). In crude terms, their common argument came to this: the American Republic is good; "republicanism" is good by definition; thus the French Republic is good, and deserved Americans' support. Ryan took this argument a step further, predicting an expansion of the republican phenomenon across the world, yet even for him, optimism was more important than analysis.

As already noted, not every American colonist shared this transcendent optimism; while they may have loved their own republic, they didn't much like the new one being created in France. They had various reasons for this sentiment. Some, roundly denounced by Washburne as "American flunkeys," were committed fans of the Second Empire, who "shed tears for 'poor Eugénie.'"[58] Their undisputed chief was Tom Evans, who owed so much to the old regime. Mindful perhaps of his debt, on September 4 the empress fled from the Tuileries palace (and Marie Antoinette's tender fate) directly to the American dentist's parlor; the very next morning he whisked her away to exile in Great Britain. From Evans's colored perspective, the latest French revolution was a direct result of the emperor's "irreconcilable" and "scurrilous" enemies, who had fomented "a protest of the proletariat against every form of orderly government." Afterwards, with the advantage of hindsight, he tied the events of 1870 back to those of 1848, and thence to the "Red Republic," the First International, and the Paris Commune, creating thereby a seamless web of infamy.[59]

Evans's rejection of the Republic had very little to do with his nationality or even his politics (back home, he was a solid Republican). The same could be said for those Americans who simply disliked the social caliber of French republicanism. Consul-General Read, for example, could find "nothing impressive" about the "gaping, laughing crowds" who applauded the new government. As he confided to his private diary:

> Since the 4[th of] September it has really been unpleasant to drive in a private carriage, to wear a clean shirt, or don new gloves. The worst elements of the people, the scum of society seem floating on the top, & pervading the city at all points. Yesterday a drunken Agrarian in a white blouse stood near me, and looking up at a handsome hotel opposite belonging to one who had earn[ed] his fortune by hard work[,] hiccupped: "What right's that man to own that house[?] I don't even own a hat."

The only thing particularly "American" about this exercise in snobbery was Read's use of the term "Agrarian" to describe the socially rebellious; otherwise, it could have flowed just as easily from the pen of a French elitist trapped in the same upheaval.[60]

Ironically, it was an exiled Confederate who drew most directly upon American republicanism to condemn the French Republic. Mrs. F. J. Willard, an "authoress of Louisiana," peered at the new regime through the misty lens of Southern memory. The fall of the Empire, like the fall of the Confederacy, was proof to her eyes that "all things fair" were destined to "trail in the dust." Like Evans, she and her circle of Southern ladies prayed for Empress Eugénie; like Read, they wept in empathy for "the better class" of French people, to whom "the name Republic . . . was synonymous only with bloodshed and riot." But while the "good" French were haunted by the ghosts of 1793, Willard saw a darker specter. "A Republic," she shuddered, "has for the French people the same signification as liberty has for negro slaves; they interpret it to mean license and all manner of idleness and wantonness, and freedom to insult all that is good and worthy of distinction."[61]

Even when she managed to suppress the Southerner's traditional fear of servile revolt, Willard still could not believe that the French Republic bore any resemblance to its American counterpart. How could it? How could "any Frenchman" be expected to "conceive the true signification of republicanism"? They simply did not understand American institutions, she asserted, and so "a republic for the French is a mere farce!" Consequently, the new Republic was "like an intruder, . . . [to be] saluted, but not welcomed."[62]

That being said, the lady then dipped into a vivid pool of misogynistic imagery to illustrate the difference between the two republics. "In my own country," Willard began, the Republic "stands in . . . flowing garments, her cap of liberty on her brow. She has there room for her majestic stride—she has there voices that answer her call . . . she has there a people of decision and character." "Thus," she concluded, "you will not be surprised to learn that I failed to recognise her on this side of the Atlantic . . . shrunken, haggard, and wild . . . Her garments dripping with blood: her cap of liberty a crimson rag, wound round her head in turban-style, had a most disreputable and unbecoming air. Her gait was wanton, and her language maudlin. Her voice a brazen trumpet, full of blatant sound . . . [T]his imposter . . . was not the Goddess of Liberty as she is known in America."[63]

In the end, Willard's encounter with the French Republic was simply an extension of her life in the old Confederacy, and all her perceptions were shaped by preconceptions of America. She looked at Paris, but she could only see how it differed from the South, her idealized native land. She compared the two constantly, which made Willard a surprising exception among the American colonists who stayed in Paris after the summer of

1870. In most cases, they were so caught up in the revolutionary swirl of the city that it left them little time to dwell on comparisons with the United States. Even when they did have time, the comparisons remained superficial, like those of the *American Register*. This was true during the Franco-Prussian War, and it remained true for the duration of the Commune.

On January 28, 1871, an armistice was signed that put a formal end to the Franco-Prussian War. For Americans who had suffered through the long siege, it was an opportunity to leave the city for a well-deserved rest. For the scattered American colony, it was a time to return to Paris and renew, as best as possible, the familiar lifestyle of prewar days. Unfortunately, they did not reckon on the clashing ambitions of Adolphe Thiers and the people of Paris.[64]

On the morning of March 18, 1871, a line of French troops filed into Montmartre, the working-class district of northern Paris. Their immediate goal was to seize the cannon controlled by the National Guard in that part of the city. The larger goal was to reassert the authority of the central government over the Guard, a predominantly working-class organization whose strength and autonomy had grown immensely while defending the capital. Neither goal was achieved. The regular troops, drawn from the same social ranks as the guardsmen, chose to fraternize with their counterparts rather than fire upon them as ordered. Two of their generals, Thomas and Lecomte, were seized by guardsmen and put to death, to the cheers of a gathering crowd. The cannon remained where they were, but within hours the central government had withdrawn from Paris to Versailles, leaving the city under the effective control of the Central Committee of the National Guard.

In the crowd at Montmartre that day was a young correspondent with the unlikely name of Januarius Aloysius MacGahan. He was the first American to observe the French insurrection up close, and smelling a scoop, he dashed off a dispatch to his editor at the *New York Herald*. Young MacGahan was overwhelmed by what he saw, and soon was writing home to friends and family, "Although you knew I was a French Republican, you did not know, perhaps, that I was also a Communard."[65] Other Americans in Paris were just as overwhelmed by the outbreak of civil war (though rarely so willing to pick sides). On March 19, for example, one of them wrote home to her mother in Massachusetts that "there was a revolution in Paris and *I was here.*" Elihu Washburne was in the city as well, and explained to a colleague in London that "the most fearful state of things [exists] here . . . [I]t is impossible to predict what will take place from hour to hour."[66]

For most American colonists, the first response to the Commune was the same as their first response to the Franco-Prussian War: run for cover. European cities like Brussels once again became the temporary haven for displaced Americans. But, as Washburne recalled, a "large number" braved the tide of history and stayed in Paris until the bitter end, comprising a rump colony of at least dozens and probably hundreds of people.[67]

Once again, those who remained found themselves caught in the turmoil of a city under siege, sharing hardships with the native population. Physically, they remained at the very heart of the French civil war, yet they often failed to see beneath the surface of events around them. This despite the fact that some Americans came to play an active role in the Paris Commune; others were victims, though most were simply observers. Just as their countrymen had fought for France in the German war, a handful of Americans now fought for Paris in the Commune—contrary to claims by Washburne and the *American Register* that "no . . . single native-born or adopted American citizen [was] to be found in its ranks."[68] Certainly the most prominent "American" was General Cluseret, whose checkered career as military commander of the Commune has already been discussed. But there was also a whole battalion of Franco-Americans, veterans of the Civil War who had returned to their native land. Other soldiers had even better claims to an American identity: a man named Witton (or Wetton), who served as a surgeon in the National Guard; another, called "Colonel" Block, who knew Cluseret in America and was tapped by him to command a volunteer corps; and another, William DuGas Trammell, who was later described as "the only native-born American known to have fought at the barricades."[69] Two years after the fighting, *Harper's Weekly* even reported that France was about to pardon "three Americans—Alfred Watson, Nathaniel Berry, and Consider Tinkler—who had been sent to [prison] . . . for participating in the Communist insurrection," which suggests that the list of American Communards could easily be extended.[70]

Other Americans participated in the Commune in less direct ways. The American field hospital, for example, remained in operation for at least the opening fortnight of the revolution.[71] On April 29, a visiting Freemason from Lima, Ohio, named Beer joined the local Freemasons at a demonstration in support of the Commune.[72] In the early days of May, the

Herald's MacGahan sometimes overstepped his role as a neutral journalist and joined General Jaroslav Dombrowski in midnight raids against the French army.[73] Indeed, all these actions must have contributed to the "universal pass with the officers and soldiers of the Commune" that one American observer claimed he and his countrymen enjoyed.[74]

At the same time, notes one historian, many Americans became "involved" with the Commune "simply because of their presence in Paris." They were the victims, and the worst hazard they faced was the bombardment of Paris, begun by Versailles on April 7. In ferocity, this new attack easily exceeded the Prussian shelling of a few months before, and a large number of bombs landed with devastating effect in the American colony. Washburne's own house was hit twice, and the apartment of his assistant, Wickham Hoffman, on the Rue de Presbourg, was struck no fewer than eight times; Hoffman's neighbor, a Mr. Pell from New York, had an entire flat destroyed from under him.[75]

Even if bystanders were lucky enough to avoid being hit by a shell, they might still be arrested by suspicious officials of the Commune as they busily searched for Prussian spies and other enemies of their government.[76] Worse was yet to come during the *semaine sanglante* (Bloody Week) of late May, when Versailles began to suppress the Commune. Caught in the crossfire, Americans suffered. On one side, the Commune's defenders pressed Americans into service to help construct barricades; refusal to do so was deemed a crime against Paris.[77] On the other, Versailles and its sympathizers within the walls of the city harbored strong "suspicions of American complicity with Communism." Thus, according to a British eyewitness, more than one American was tossed into prison by advancing French troops on the "frivolous and unfounded charges . . . of not being a Frenchman, and not being where he ought to have been." (Minister Washburne spent weeks afterward getting them released.)[78] And they were fortunate, compared to the Americans accosted by anti-Commune crowds on the mere suspicion of being sympathizers, or worse yet *pétroleuses* (the dreaded female arsonists).[79] Remarkably, though, no American seems to have been killed in the fierce final days of fighting and recrimination.

Instead, most Americans in Paris were observers and nothing more. At every important turn of events in the short life of the Paris Commune, an American was present, and sometimes many Americans. Yet because they could never agree on just what they had seen, conflicting observations gave way to disparate conclusions.

Consider two events that took place in the Place Vendôme (the seat of the revolutionary government), one near the start and the other near the end of the Commune. The first, on March 22, was a peaceful demonstration against the new municipal government, staged by the so-called "friends of order." There were perhaps 2,000 protesters, brought suddenly face to face with a small detachment of National Guardsmen. Someone fired a shot, and a ten-minute fusillade followed. What began in peace ended in bloodshed, and among the dead was the first American victim of the Commune, a man from St. Louis named George S. Hanna.[80]

In the midst of all this confusion, two U.S. diplomats chanced to meet at the edge of the crowd: Frank Moore, an assistant secretary to the Paris legation, and General Augustus Chetlain, visiting from the American consulate in Brussels. Neither man considered the mêlée a very serious matter. Yet one of their fellow citizens who also witnessed the event described it as a massacre—a "frightful" consequence, moreover, of the "rampant spirit of red republicanism."[81] Still another eyewitness, with another point of view, was General Philip Sheridan, the great Union hero of the Civil War. Sheridan had been in Europe for several months as an official observer of the Franco-Prussian War. He and his staff reached Paris in early March, and on March 22 they found themselves at the window of the Hôtel Westminster, directly above the fighting in the Place Vendôme. To Sheridan's expert eye, it looked as though the first shot came from the crowd of civilian demonstrators, and not from the soldiers themselves. But either way, he offered his blunt opinion that the crowd merely got what it deserved. "Served them right," said Sheridan. "No civic body has a right to attack men who hold military positions with military equipments. This is a law of common sense. If they do, they must expect to receive, as they deserve, summary treatment." (Neither side, it must be said, was pleased by the Yankee general's attitude, and the Versailles government was relieved when Sheridan finally left the country at the end of March.)[82]

Two months later, another crowd of Parisians returned to the Place Vendôme. This time they came to watch the fall of the Vendôme Column, an ugly shaft commemorating the military victories of the First Empire. It was clad in the bronze of 1,200 captured cannon and topped with a statue of Napoleon I. On April 12, the leaders of the Commune (largely inspired by Gustave Courbet) declared the monument a "perpetual affront" to Republican France and ordered its destruction; on May 16 the sentence was finally carried out. A few days earlier, a "well-known American banker" had offered to buy the column and transport it, piece by piece, to Central Park in New York; failing that, one of his compatriots was said to have offered either £80 (about $400) or 2 million francs (about $400,000) "for the privilege of being the last to climb to the top of the Column."[83]

The destruction of the column, when it finally came, called forth two very different reactions from American observers. On one side of the Place Vendôme, reporter John Russell Young joined a group of Americans on a hotel balcony overlooking the square. They watched in disgust while the Communards wrecked the column. One of the observers sidled up to Young, and in "a choking voice" he sputtered: "I am trembling with rage! The scoundrels! I could kill every one of them!" Simultaneously, on another balcony directly across the square, an Englishman witnessed the reaction of another group of Americans. This reaction could only be described as jubilant:

> Right quickly [after the Column fell] did one of the [National] Guard's bands strike up the "Marseillaise," but amidst and above it I suddenly heard the strains of "Hail Columbia!" played violently on a piano by some Yankee girl belonging to a party of Americans who had installed themselves on the first floor of the Hôtel Mirabeau. They came out on to the balcony and were loud in their plaudits.

These balconies, facing across the Place Vendôme, were a graphic demonstration of how divided American opinion in Paris could be.[84]

3

First Impressions

Of course every American who happened to be shut up in the French capital . . . must tell his story in print. Thus there will be accumulated a vast store of material to perplex the future historian.

—*EVERY SATURDAY,* OCTOBER 7, 1871

According to one historian of Americans in the Paris Commune, eye-witness observers had just two ways of explaining what they saw: either the Commune was a revisitation of the Terror of 1793, or it was an or-derly experiment in popular government.[1] In fact, things were rather more complicated, with reactions on the scene that ranged from condemnation through disappointment to cheerful acceptance. Taken together, these initial impressions defined a roomy set of possible (or even likely) Ameri-can reactions to the Paris Commune. Yet only some of these possibilities were echoed back home in the United States, where new reactions also surfaced. Whether home or abroad, Americans had been reared in the same political culture. As a result, they brought the same general concerns to their encounters with the Commune. But their responses were also shaped by specific and immediate concerns, and these were very different on the two sides of the ocean.

Within the American colony, the most negative reactions were also the most common. They were also the least interesting, as they mostly echoed the opinions of the French bourgeoisie. This type of response was epito-mized for Americans by W. Pembroke Fetridge, a longtime resident of Paris who made his living writing guidebooks for the Harper brothers in New York. Fetridge described the Commune for his readers across the Atlantic as the "most criminal [act] the world had ever seen," and the "saddest which has ever appeared on the page of history."[2] The Com-mune, he continued, was "a revolution of blood and violence" (72) and "a melancholy example of *universal republicism* [sic], *cosmopolitan revolu-tions, and misdirected intellect*" (his emphasis, 104). Its leaders, he added, were "ruthless desperadoes" (15), "the refuse of France" (16), "malcon-

44

tents" (61), "bandits" (354), "atheists and free-thinkers" (364), and "madmen, drunk with wine and blood" (426). Worse yet, they acted under the orders of the dread "*International* society, recognized as prime mover in this insurrection" (478).[3]

These sentiments were repeated in the intensely negative description of the Commune that Emmeline Raymond sent off to *Harper's Weekly*. For Raymond, who witnessed both sieges of Paris, the Commune came as a terrifying lesson in social anarchy—terrifying *and* unexpected. By her own testimony, prior to March 18 she "did not [even] know the meaning of Socialism, the Commune, and the International Society; and, moreover, I did not believe in the possibility of crimes such as we have witnessed." But the next nine weeks made for quick study, and by the end of the Commune she felt herself "sufficiently well taught" in the ways of anarchy that "should I be so unfortunate as to live long enough ever to witness the reappearance of the red flag, which is the symbol of blood, fire, pillage, and assassination, I will flee to the ends of the earth, were it among the cannibals, who, at least, if they robbed and killed me, would not pretend to do it for the sake of progress."

"Cannibal" was just one of the dehumanizing labels that Raymond affixed to the leaders of the Commune; others included "dwarf" and "brute." In her account, the Commune was neither a human event nor a natural part of the political order, but some perverse deviation. Even to describe the perversion required a convoluted sexual metaphor: "Bedlam," she wrote, "fraternized with the galleys, and this monstrous union produced [the Commune]." Strange offspring indeed, and hardly capable of being born without assistance. Thus Raymond implied the presence of an evil midwife in the shape of the International, whose non-French members used the illusion of rights to injure and deceive the good people of Paris.[4]

As with the French Republic a few months earlier, various Southern observers brought the memory of historical misfortunes at home to their analysis of the Paris Commune. Although they offered a strained comparison between the Lost Cause and the Commune, it was the most intriguing Franco-American comparison generated by the colony. Typically, former Confederate diplomat A. Dudley Mann read the events around him as a gloss on the fate of Southern nationhood. As he explained to Jefferson Davis, the "wars of the Yankees against the South and the Prussians against the French" had furnished him with "a verification, (that which I doubted until the prosecution of the former) of the old Latin adage:—*Homo homini lupus.* In the ferociousness of the inhabitants of Paris, one against another,

I see an ample corroboration of the brutalness of men's nature; and almost despair of its Christianization." At the same time, the evils of the Commune had set Mann to thinking that the "astonishing scientific discoveries of this century . . . [are] employed as to produce a thousand devils instead of a solitary saint. In such a consummation Yankeedom has contributed more than its fair share . . . [with] its hypocritical engenderings and diabolical deeds." Out of these musings he forged his own causal links between Yankee crimes (like the hanging of Mrs. Surratt for her role in the Lincoln assassination) and the general declension of the age, culminating in the Paris Commune.[5]

Six months later, Mann offered a yet more insidious comparison between the two civil wars. In a sullen letter to the Confederate president, he alluded to the Commune as a dark inspiration for a new uprising against the North: "I scarcely need be more explicit; but . . . if the 'Union' in its reckless career, shall in its already rickety condition upset itself I will, with the utmost alacrity, endeavor to make the most of the event in Western Europe in behalf of the Confederate States." Davis did not respond, and it is hard to imagine a Paris-based conspiracy of Southerners bent on revenge. Still, the fact that *any* Southern partisan was dreaming along these lines says something about the unsettled state of affairs on both sides of the Atlantic in 1871.[6]

Mann's fellow Confederate, Mrs. Willard of Louisiana, never went to such interpretive extremes. To be sure, she was even less enamored of the Commune than she was of the French Republic. To her eyes one was simply a continuation of the other, and both were products of political rabble-rousing.[7] Like Fetridge and Raymond, she considered the Commune and especially its leaders to be "an unholy conspiracy" of "cannibals" (265) and "villains" (281). Yet she also managed to relate the Commune to race relations in America, in the same way that she had compared the French Republic to a servile rebellion.

The racial comparison emerged during a supposed conversation with a French nobleman:

> "I assure you [he said] these people [in the Commune] are worse than the 'niggers.'"
>
> "A great deal worse." I replied, "I think it quite a disgrace to the negroes that such a comparison should be made, for negroes were faithful to their masters." (281)

Whether real or reconstructed, this dialogue spoke to the need for an idealized past and an idealized future, as the Southern master-slave relationship was giving way to a new relationship between bosses and wage-earners. The fact that *French* workers (rather than Americans) are part of the comparison is merely incidental; the fact that black slaves are being invoked as model laborers is highly significant. Whether she knew it or not, Willard was introducing a powerful analogy that Southerners at home would also use to interpret the Commune (see Chapter 5).

To distrust the Republic in September 1870 and then reject the Commune six months later was a consistent, even plausible, response to events in France. John Meredith Read, for example, who openly despised the hoi polloi of republican Paris, later saw the Commune as one giant act of vandalism.[8] Just as consistent was the growing sense of disappointment exhibited by early supporters of the Republic when confronted with the violence and excesses of urban revolution. Elihu Washburne was probably the most striking example of this.

As we have seen, Washburne was an early and ardent supporter of the French Republic. When the Commune began, the first thing he did was notify the State Department and offer his opinion that "the insurrectionary movements in Paris . . . would not amount to much, and that no great degree of violence was probable."[9] But less than two weeks later the American minister was describing "the horror of the situation in Paris" to an old constituent in Illinois. "I told him," Washburne recalled, "that anarchy, robbery, murder, assassination reigned supreme . . . [and] that I had come to Paris hoping for repose and quiet, but instead of that I had found myself plunged into the most terrible events of the century."[10]

Seven years later, when Washburne sat down to write his memoirs, his opinion of the Commune had hardened to the same reactionary contours displayed by Fetridge and friends in 1871. At the time, however, Washburne managed to preserve a degree of flexibility toward the temporary government of Paris. For example, though neither he nor the American government was willing to recognize the Commune, they were nonetheless willing to postpone normalization of relations with the Versailles government. In part, says one historian, this was because Washburne had no "great confidence in either of France's rival governments."[11]

When the rest of the foreign diplomatic corps fled to Versailles, Washburne decided that the United States should preserve an official presence in Paris. As he explained to Washington, "We still have here a large number of Americans, and while I hope that they may not be molested or have their property injured, yet no one knows what may happen from hour to hour. Under such circumstances I deem it my duty to remain in Paris as much as possible."[12] While carrying out his duties, which still included the protection of German nationals, Washburne necessarily remained in constant contact with the leaders of the Commune. He was also in constant contact with the government at Versailles *and* the German government in Berlin, with the net result that no one wholly trusted him. Indeed, even after the Commune was suppressed, each of the two sides continued to accuse him of aiding the other.[13]

To his surprise, Washburne discovered that many of the leaders of the Commune, including Cluseret and Paschal Grousset, were quite agreeable; Charles Delescluze, however, struck him as the "most perfect type of the Jacobin and revolutionist of 1793."[14] But all of them, he was glad to report home, retained sufficient respect for the United States that proper "consideration . . . was always given to American passports as well as what were called 'protection papers.'" (These, he explained, "were simply certificates put up on the door of an apartment wherein it was certified that the owner of the apartment . . . was an American . . . [whose] property was to be respected.") Because of this respect, and despite various threats of perquisition by the revolutionary government, "no material damage . . . [was] done to the property of Americans." Likewise, most Americans and even Germans were well treated by the Commune, even when its own citizens were threatened by a return of the Terror.[15]

Washburne was much less successful in his diplomatic attempts to save the life of Archbishop Darboy. Recall that early in April, Darboy and other clergymen were arrested by the Commune and held as hostages, with hopes of swapping them for political prisoners held by Versailles (notably Auguste Blanqui, whose disciples were prominent among the Commune's leaders). But Thiers stubbornly refused to consider any exchange, despite appeals from prominent intermediaries like Washburne. The Commune was no more tractable, and the most that Washburne could secure from them was permission to visit the archbishop in his dank cell at the Mazas prison, where he was being held incommunicado. Even that required a personal favor from Cluseret.[16]

On May 24, in one of the last desperate acts of the Commune, the archbishop and his fellow hostages were lined against a wall and executed by firing squad. Like many Americans on both sides of the Atlantic, Washburne was shocked and disgusted by the act. More important, it confirmed his developing belief that the revolution in Paris was nothing more than a "fight for power and plunder on the part of . . . desperate and wicked men, unlimited, unchecked, and unrestrained by any human power"—in all, a "poor imitation" of 1789, perpetrated by the International.[17] In a final note of disappointment, he explained to Secretary of State Hamilton Fish that the "frightful excesses of the Commune have brought reproach upon the sacred name of the Republic, and the good name of Republicanism suffers."[18]

Despite its abundant hopes for French republicanism, the *American Register,* like the American minister, grew progressively more disappointed with the course of the Paris Commune. The seeds of disillusion were sown early, but did not immediately germinate. In November 1870, news reached Paris of the stillborn insurrection at Marseilles. This outbreak was an opportunity for the *Register* to reaffirm old beliefs while expressing new doubts about the possibilities of French politics: "We, with the majority of Americans, hailed the advent of the Republic with satisfaction, but we had not bargained [on] the sacred name of the glorious free institution [being] profaned by fanatics, who, however sincere may be their intentions, are misguided by unprincipled leaders, who would bring the people's government to ruin and contempt." Unfortunately, "unprincipled leaders" were to be found not just among the Marseilles conspirators but also among the founders of the new national regime, who seemed to be gambling with the unpreparedness of the French people for a lasting Republic.[19]

Until March 18, 1871, these budding doubts still lay dormant beneath the early layers of optimism. That Saturday the *Register* ran a small item on page two noting that the National Guard at Montmartre still refused to surrender its cannon, but adding that the "revolt . . . will soon quietly terminate." A week passed and it became clear that "a Revolution . . . is being accomplished, and not the temporary triumph of the small faction denominated 'the Reds.'" Yet the paper insisted that Paris was still "thoroughly Republican," that the temporary government under Thiers was "a miserable sham," and that even civil war would be preferable to the old Empire.[20]

Another week passed, and the realities of civil war began to rub away at the outer layers of optimism. Was the Republic really a suitable government for France? The *American Register* was no longer sure, and said so in a lengthy editorial on April 1, 1871. John Ryan, the editor, began by repeating his belief that American republicans were bound to "sympathise with . . . political changes that appear likely to bring other countries within the sphere of the institutions . . . best adapted to secure popular liberty." But in the case of France, "we do not know that a Republican form of government is the best adapted to the idiosyncrasies of . . . that mercurial people . . . [and] we might well be excused for doubting their capacity for it." Echoing Tocqueville, Cluseret, and Pierre-Joseph Proudhon, Ryan argued that the problem with France was that it repeatedly succumbed to the evils of centralization. This, combined with the mind-numbing effects of ignorance and Catholicism, left the people unprepared to live in a republic.

Ryan's paradoxical solution to the French dilemma was a "compulsory system of [public] education" administered by the central authority. Unfortunately, he found it hard to believe that "Republican Government by the Commune . . . [could] accomplish this great object." Yet he still hoped France might achieve a viable republic by adopting American-style federalism, with semiautonomous states rather than autonomous cities as the representative units. "Under this system, an analogous one to that of the United States, we shall hear no more of socialism . . . [while] surprises by ambitious generals, dynastic pretenders, or fractions of the populations of the large cities would become impossible."[21]

In America, the argument between states' rights and centralization was perdurable. Like Cluseret, Ryan now attempted to apply the lessons of that debate to the Paris Commune. The French were interested—especially Emile de Girardin, a liberal reformer who supported the Union cause in 1861 and who was now in the midst of drafting his own plan for a federal French Republic modeled on the United States.[22] Most Americans in Paris, however, actively resisted the comparison. Washburne flatly denied that Parisians were "fighting for their liberty and their municipal rights." Fetridge went even further, denouncing the Commune as a retreat from national unity to "the federation of medieval times," a "retrogression of eight centuries" that had nothing in common with the municipal institutions of Switzerland or the United States.[23]

Unfortunately, Ryan and the *Register* never mooted a fuller discussion of federalism in the United States and France. Instead, the newspaper fixated on the tragic particularities of the French civil war. The remnants of early expectation melted away. By the end of April the *Register* declared a plague on both houses; in mid-May it called for compromise again, but expected "disastrous" outcomes for France "as well as all true friends of liberty"; in June it cursed the "dreadful scenes" of the Commune as a blow to republicanism around the world. Ryan also condemned the International, fearing that it might spread to America.[24]

To his credit, Ryan never let the *Register* sink to the rhetorical depths of Fetridge or Raymond. When Bloody Week ended his publication denounced the Commune as "a terrible page in the history of our times," but more in sadness than rancor.[25] The *Register* had always allowed that Parisian workers were airing legitimate complaints, however inappropriate their methods. It even condoned the fall of the Vendôme Column as a proper response to Louis Napoleon's "vanity" and "inordinate personal ambition." Finally, turning to Versailles, the *American Register* noted, "We have but one sentiment in common with the members of the Central Committee [of the Commune], and that is distrust of the sincerity of M. Thiers."[26]

For the *Register*, distrust of Thiers and distaste for the leaders of the Commune were only partial factors in the process of disillusionment; its main concern was always the fate of republicanism in France.[27] For Lillie Moulton, in contrast, personal considerations always came first. Hers was a happy life: a family of Boston Brahmins, a well-known banker for a husband, and enough talent and charm to make her a celebrated chanteuse and the star of the American colony. When the Prussian siege began, she chose to remain in Paris, and the Moulton home became the Sunday-night meeting place for the American elite. When the Commune started, she again chose to remain in the city.[28]

The outbreak of the Commune filled her with anticipation. She expected good things from this revolution. One reason may be that despite her impeccable social background, Lillie Moulton had married into a family with several close ties to the French revolutionary tradition: her father-in-law, for example, had been an eyewitness to the Paris uprisings of 1848, while her husband was friendly with leading French republicans and Communards alike. One of the Communards was artist Gustave Courbet, whom she met in the first days of the civil war.

Lillie was impressed by the man's sincerity. As she explained to her mother, "Courbet belongs more to the fraternity part of the [revolutionary] motto than he does to the equality part of the Commune! He is not bloodthirsty, nor does he go about shooting people in the back. He is not that kind! He really believes (so he says) in a Commune based on the principles of equality and liberty of the masses."[29] Barely a week passed, however, before she wrote that her enthusiasm for the movement had been tempered by a meeting with Raoul Rigault, chief Prosecuter of the Commune and head of its police. No one connected with the revolution was ever more feared or more hated, and not just by Moulton. When she called on Rigault at the end of March, she went in hopes of obtaining a passport to leave Paris. But despite a personal letter of introduction from the American minister, she was rudely received and "diabolical[ly]" cross-examined, and she walked away convinced the man had "a wicked expression . . . [in] his cunning eyes," a vivid mark of "all the horrors which belong to revolutions."[30]

Although she obtained her passport, Moulton remained in the city. Early in May she noted that gay Paris had become a somber place, where "soldiers slink about, looking ashamed of their shabby uniforms." A week later she despaired at the "mob . . . [of] madmen" who pillaged Thiers's home in Paris. Then, in the final days of the civil war, she contrasted the early ambitions of the Commune with the harsher tactics employed by Rigault and his sympathizers on the Committee of Public Safety: "[Rigault] wants the Commune to finish in fire and flame as a funeral pile. I hope he will be on the top of it, like Sardanapalus [the ancient Assyrian tyrant], and suffer the most. Horrible man!" (May 18). And again on May 23, "they have all lost their heads . . . Everything is in a muddle; you can imagine in what a fearful state of anxiety we live." Her own anticipation had turned to disappointment.[31]

While Moulton wavered in her support of the Commune because of the strong personalities she encountered, Mary Putnam remained firm in her support for much the same reason. She had been boarding with the Reclus brothers and their families since 1869, and had developed a very close friendship with them. Their friendship reinforced her support of the Republic and the Commune, for the Reclus brothers were both republicans and Communards. The older brother, Élisée, was a prominent geographer who spent most of the Commune as a prisoner at Versailles. Élie, the younger sibling, served as interim director of the Bibliothèque Nationale, where he did his best to protect the collection from the fighting; when the Commune ended, he barely managed to avoid a cell like his brother's.[32]

Her biographer writes that Mary Putnam "suffered the same overwhelming disappointment at the turn of events, after the first enthusiasm for the Republic, as did her French friends." Yet the Commune's own actions were never the source of their disappointment. Instead it was Thiers's bloody reprisals, which soon forced the Reclus brothers into exile.[33] In defense of the Commune, Putnam explained to her brother that "the origin of the whole trouble was the attempt on the part of that arch mischief-maker Thiers, to deprive Paris . . . of its municipal rights, and to reduce it to as great a state of nullity as under the Empire." In her opinion, the Commune was therefore a worthy struggle for municipal rights and the Republic, and as such it was simply "a mild edition of '93, minus, decidedly minus, the guillotine."[34]

Putnam was just one of several American observers to comment on the apparent orderliness of the Commune—in striking contrast to the visions of disorder eventually conjured up by Americans at home. The American astronomer Simon Newcomb, for example, made it quite clear that *his* experience with the Commune did not involve violence or barbarism. In 1871, he wrote to a friend from Paris that "they are all very well behaved": "There is nothing like a mob anywhere, so far as I can find . . . The stores are all open . . . [and] in all the cafés I have seen, the habitués seem to be drinking their wine just as coolly as if they had nothing unusual on their minds." Thirty years later, Newcomb still insisted that he saw "nothing suggestive of violence within the limited range of my daily walks, which were mostly within the region [near] . . . the Arc de Triomphe." He also maintained that, although the leaders of the Commune engaged in certain desperate acts (e.g., killing Darboy), these acts "constitute[d] but a small part of the history of Paris during that critical period."[35]

The Commune left a similar impression on a rather different observer, a wealthy, conservative Californian named Frank M. Pixley. In his time Pixley had been a lawyer, a politician, a real-estate magnate, and finally a newspaper editor; he witnessed the Parisian events in that last capacity.[36] In January 1871, a San Franciso newspaper began to print a series of Pixley's letters from abroad, which one Franco-Californian reader described as "very sympathetic towards the French." Like Judge Erskine in the previous chapter, Pixley was impressed by Léon Gambetta and excited about the French Republic.[37] Like Professor Newcomb, he was subsequently impressed by the orderliness of the Commune; indeed, a decade later Pixley was still defending this aspect of revolutionary Paris:

> The Commune is held up as the personification of misrule and destruction . . . and Paris of 1871 is described as a scene of frightful disorder, submitting to anarchy, pillage and murder.
>
> I was present in the city of Paris during the entire period that the Commune held sway . . . And yet during the five weeks—weeks of menace from without and suffering within—I saw and heard of no single *act of pillage and murder.*

The Communards, he added, "*may* have been wrong and misguided, but that they were thieves, murderers and incendiaries, I most indignantly deny."[38]

Yet Pixley was not content merely to answer the Commune's critics. He also offered a positive vision of the French civil war as an extension of the glorious American struggle for freedom. "The war of the Commune," he wrote, "was to the Great Revolution what the mad raid of John Brown was to our civil war . . . It will ultimate in the adoption of all the great principles for which the Commune contended. The Commune was . . . a band of patriots."[39] This was a bold statement. One can almost see Dudley Mann and Mrs. Willard nod their heads in sad and fearful assent; one can almost hear them say, "Yes, the Communards *were* just like John Brown."

As a positive vision of either civil war, however, the comparison found few takers. A notable exception was John Russell Young, correspondent of the *New York Tribune*. From the start, Young admitted that "this revolution, like any movement of the human mind which means an innovation upon its established customs, had its follies and crimes." Yet he was broadly sympathetic towards the Commune and its goals—even sympathetic towards its leaders, including those "who went into the Commune with a sombre fanaticism which our good old conservatives saw in John Brown—suspicious, distrusting, hoping against hope, afraid of betrayal, their minds worn and subdued by years of disappointment and betrayal."[40] Young saw the Commune as a struggle between desperate insurgents and the "cowardice and bigotry of France" (that is, Thiers and his government). In the end, he also saw the Commune as a tragedy, born of old and admirable aspirations, yet ending in fire, "sadness and . . . pathos."[41]

Young dispatched a long description of the Commune to his editors at the *Tribune*, with a soaring peroration of a kind rarely encountered in newspaper journalism, even in the nineteenth century. "My friends," it began, "let us be just, and see what is truly true and false in these tragic scenes. The Commune is dead."

> [But] out of it all I believe France will rise again, strengthened, purified, chastened—to be in the future what she has been for so many years, the champion of liberty and humanity and progress. And whatever the passionate impulse of the hour may be—we may mourn the crimes and follies of the day—I am confident the time will come when Frenchmen will look back with pride and emotion at the men of Paris who fought Prussia for four months . . . and who for two months longer held at bay the combined armies of Bonapartism, legitimacy and reaction—dreaming a dream of liberty, equality and fraternity and giving their lives in a desperate endeavor to make it true.[42]

This was certainly a far cry from Fetridge's interpretation, or even Washburne's, yet some went even further toward accepting the Commune.

The Paris Commune left its best impression on an unlikely pair of American observers. One was an obscure young Georgian who fought on the barricades, William DuGas Trammell.[43] The other was George Wilkes, a prominent New Yorker, famous Civil War correspondent, and editor of *The Spirit of the Times* (a pioneering effort in sports journalism); Wilkes was also an old acquaintance of Gustave Cluseret's.[44] Though their backgrounds could not have been more different, when it came to the Commune they reached the same conclusion: it deserved the support of workingmen everywhere, especially in the United States.

Trammell did not get around to saying so until 1874, when he published a fictionalized account of his adventures under the Commune entitled *Ça Ira,* after the famous revolutionary anthem of 1792. By no definition, aesthetic or otherwise, could this be considered a well-written novel; it was a "silly book," wrote one Northern reviewer, and "[if Trammell] pretends to be anxious for the emancipation of labor, he can help the critic to this by laying aside his pen."[45] But Trammell *was* anxious for the emancipation of labor, as well as the emancipation of the South from the yoke of "New England civilisation." In fact, he believed that the forces of labor and republicanism, set loose in the South as they had been set loose in France during the Commune, might "some day [make] our country . . . *la belle France* of America."[46]

More than that, Trammell believed that his eight weeks of fighting for the Commune in Paris were of a piece with the four years of Southern fighting in the War Between the States—with this crucial difference: "Here our heroes were killed and our chief imprisoned; there, chiefs and heroes died behind the barricade, or were brutally murdered by monster assassins . . . Long live the Universal Republic!"[47] The other Confederate observers in Paris, Mann and Willard, could not have been much happier with this comparison than the one between the Commune and old John Brown (though Trammell, like Mann, did hint at an international conspiracy to continue the struggle for the Lost Cause).[48] The main burden of *Ça Ira,* however, was to combine New South advocacy with praise for the Communards. The two were combined in the personal odyssey of Trammell's protagonist, Mirabeau Holmes, from the backwoods of Georgia to the back alleys of the Faubourg St. Antoine, and finally back home to Atlanta. This was the author's odyssey, too.

In many ways, *Ça Ira* is less about the Paris Commune than about Trammell's own politics in the mid-1870s. By 1874, Trammell had rethought his Parisian experience and reworked it in light of his developing career as a New South reformer and member of the First International. Yet even if he left no immediate account of the Commune, it is clear that his support for labor dated from that event.[49] Trammell declares as much on the dedication page of *Ça Ira,* which is offered to "the WORKINGMEN, and to the memory of all who have ever suffered in their Cause, . . . [and to] the Great Revolution to which all Humanitarians must look with the greatest concern, The Emancipation of Labor." On the pages that follow, Trammell emphasizes the links between the Commune, the International, and the Universal Republic, praising them all as expressions of workers' desire for a better civilization. (Fetridge, of course, condemned the same trio as expressions of anarchy.) The Commune's government, Trammell insisted, was "the most perfect that ever existed, the prototype of the ideal government of the future."[50] In the end, the Commune's leaders were the "best hopes of Humanity," while their opponents from Versailles were "bloodthirsty butchers," conspirators, and assassins.[51]

George Wilkes could not have agreed more. In a series of letters to the *New York Herald* and his own *Spirit of the Times* (later reprinted as two pamphlets, one on the Commune and one on the International), Wilkes defended the Paris uprising as a labor movement.[52] It was a defense based on surpisingly little firsthand observation. In fact, Wilkes spent most of the Commune in Brussels, only arriving in Paris on May 13, when he came "to witness the fall of the Vendôme Column."

Wilkes's initial impression, based on "diligent personal observation and inquiry (assisted by the advantage of being [t]here on the ground)," was completely in favor of the Commune. His first weekend in Paris convinced him of several things. To begin with, there had "been no plunder, no disorder, no violence"; and if there *had* been any violence (for example, in the deaths of the generals at Montmartre), it was either the work of "unauthorized" mobs or justified by the laws of war. More important, Wilkes perceived the Communards to be "rugged democrats," motivated by that "sentimental fraternity, which overflows geographical boundaries, and excels ordinary patriotism"—very different from the crypto-monarchists who ran the government at Versailles. Unfortunately, he wrote, the motives of the Commune had been "greatly misrepresented" at every turn. As a result, and much to his dismay, Wilkes discovered that there were even Americans in Paris who wished the Commune ill.[53]

In the weeks that followed, Wilkes became more and more set in his convictions about the French civil war. On one side, he saw the Commune acting "upon th[e] highest warrant that men can have," fighting the good fight for democracy and municipal self-government. On the other, he saw Versailles as "a degenerate vagabond," fronting a movement for monarchy and Catholic reaction while pursuing an "orthodox assassination" of Communards that made the Reign of Terror pale in comparison.[54] On both sides of the Atlantic, moreover, he saw the interested parties of Capital, Church, and State willfully distorting the record:

> Thus we see the Commune, who were guilty solely of making a struggle for municipal independence against a rural conspiracy to subvert the cities in the interest of a monarchy on the plan of Church and State, howled down throughout the world as godless miscreants . . . whose very names should not be mentioned without a shudder or a malediction! But I have looked behind this noise, and have seen the Commune at their task—brave, patient, merciful, and long-forbearing—cheerfully accepting all their sacrifices and quietly enduring the malignant storm of calumny, in the stout reliance that the future would do them justice.

For his part, George Wilkes would do them justice now, excusing every crime charged against them, including the archbishop's murder and the burning of Paris. "The Communists," he concluded, "on all occasions, exhibited integrity, morality, moderation, and respect for human life, while the track of their opponents was red with ruthless slaughter and characterized at every step by perfidy."[55]

As for the future, that belonged to the labor movement and the International—and not just in France or Europe, but in this country, too. The United States, Wilkes feared, was suffering from the same ills as Europe, plus a few that were all our own. These included a re-electable president, a national land policy that favored monopolization, and a corrupt system of patronage. "Thus far," he noted with relief, "there is nothing the matter with the great bulk of our people." "The real trouble is, that American society is wrongly organized, and the wrong classes are in power. It is organized, in short, on the European aristocratic plan, and is more in need of the purification of a thorough revolution than even the society of Europe." The source of this revolution, according to Wilkes, must be an "unpolluted source which has never held power before[:] . . . the banded workmen of the New World—the Internationale." In concrete terms, that meant the National Labor Union, the American counterpart of the International Workingmen's Association to which Wilkes dedicated his pamphlet.[56]

In a final burst of rhetoric, Wilkes offered the Paris Commune as a rebuke to American politics and as a model for American reform:

> Will it be pretended that the miserable slaves of politics in the United States—[by which] I mean the hundreds of thousands of poor party dogs who sniff about the public offices for crumbs, who daily crawl on their bellies for some place-giver's smile, and who dare not utter an independent thought, or, indeed, to speak at all, except at their patron's nod; I say, will it be pretended that the shoulders of such creatures as these are a safer foundation for the support of a republican State than the honest artisans who fought for the Commune in Paris, and who died for their principles at the barricades?

No American observer would ever read a more positive, indeed radical, lesson for his own country in the tragic annals of the French civil war.[57]

At this point, readers might be asking themselves: Why spend so much time on this tiny group of Americans, caught in a place where they did not belong, so very far from home? What light could their experience and opinions possibly shed on the byways of American political culture in the Gilded Age?

The answer, I think, lies in this crucial fact: in 1871, the Americans in Paris represented a cross-section of the American middle class—if not a microcosm, then at least a broad sliver of the bourgeoisie in the United States. They were part of the same political culture as their counterparts at home, and they brought with them to France all the same ideological preconceptions—all the same lenses and frameworks for converting raw reality into meaningful visions of the world. We might expect both sets of Americans to use their conceptual apparatus in roughly the same way, producing images of the Commune that were also roughly similar. But this was not the case. Though each group of Americans generated an impressive set of reactions to the Commune, the sets were *different* (though overlapping) on the two sides of the ocean. Because Americans at home and Americans in Paris were faced with different needs, both personal and political, they responded to the Commune differently. For us, these differences provide an opportunity to explore the links between American culture, foreign revolution, and domestic social transformation in the immediate postbellum era.

For all its diversity, two things united on-site reactions to the Paris

Commune: the excitement of living through a revolution, and a general reluctance to compare that experience with life in the United States. When Paris defended itself against Germany and Versailles, the American colony was caught up in the turmoil. Americans who remained in Paris found themselves enfolded by the city in unexpected ways, and the story of shared danger bulked large in their eyewitness accounts. They also drew comparisons between France and the United States, some more fanciful than others, and some more explicit than others. But the comparisons remained superficial, for when it came to extending the analogies between the two nations, most local observers balked (with the notable exception of the *American Register*).

Why, in the end, were they so reluctant to identify the Commune with American conditions when objective parallels clearly existed? George Wilkes had one answer. In the days that followed the Commune's suppression, he wrote with undisguised contempt about Americans who applauded the Versailles government's harsh measures. He described them as "denationalized Americans":

> By denationalized Americans, I mean those persons of American birth who have abandoned their country to become residents abroad. These persons, in nine cases out of ten, adhere to their nationality only that they may retain the protection of the American Legations; and they are always ready to acknowledge the inferiority of republican institutions, [in order] to be tolerated in circles by which they are despised. These worthless, degenerate, and denationalized Americans are the worst enemies which our country has abroad; and I have . . . often been mortified at their being quoted against republicanism.

Wilkes was not alone in condemning the American colony on this score. And he was right: some Americans in Paris did turn their backs on the republican tradition while courting French society, to the point of adopting an elite French perspective on the French civil war.[58]

The worst offender of all was probably Pembroke Fetridge (though a case could also be made against Dr. Evans, Mrs. Willard, and Consul-General Read, among others). John Russell Young indicted Fetridge by name as the type of American who despised the Commune because it "deprived [him] . . . of his Paris," the shining city of "Heaven-appointed Bonaparte" and orderly streets.[59] The account of the Commune that Fetridge left us corroborates Young's opinion. As we have seen, its pages contain not a single kind word for the Commune, while the emperor and Thiers are lauded. Moreover, Fetridge has little to say to Americans, as such, about the events he is describing. Although the book was written for an American audience, it could just as well have been written by a Frenchman. One would never know that the author was secretary of the exclusive Washington Club in Paris, a pillar of the American colony, or a personal friend of the U.S. minister; indeed, he waits until the very last pages of a very long book even to mention that Washburne played a role in the Commune. Fetridge did not seem to have America in mind.[60]

Yet to be fair to Fetridge and the other American colonists, snobbery was only one reason why they failed to engage more fully in comparisons between the United States and France. Lillie Moulton suggests a more sympathetic reason in a letter she wrote home to her mother in the final weeks of the Paris Commune. "I cannot write history," she said, "because I am living in it."[61]

Revolutions are all-consuming events, even to mere observers. When the Commune ended, Elihu Washburne admitted that he felt "a good deal used up and run down." Washburne was hardly a typical bystander, but this was a typical feeling after the months of war and weeks of civil strife.[62] During that period, he and the other Americans in Paris were preoccupied with simple things: avoiding arrest, avoiding shells, finding enough to eat. Rightly enough, ideology took a back seat to personal security, and we should be surprised that they found any time at all to think about the transatlantic implications of a revolution in progress. When they did find time, their thoughts and interpretations were constrained by immediate experience. To some extent, they were also constrained by the memory of recent events leading up to the French civil war. As a result, the Franco-Prussian War and the birth of the Third Republic cast disproportionate shadows over eyewitness views of the Commune.

At home across the sea, Americans were no less constrained in their vision, yet by a different set of circumstances and ideological needs. The same Parisian events, even when viewed through the same preconceptions, yielded a different set of images. Of course, the American colonists were an important pipeline for information about the Commune and a plentiful source of raw interpretations, which their fellow citizens drew upon freely. The visible presence of Americans in Paris also drew extra attention to the events there. But the images of the Paris Commune that had the most impact on American political culture were shaped by mediated experience and domestic anxiety, not by firsthand observations. These domestic images are the subject of the next four chapters.

4

Ripples across the Atlantic

The telegraphy operators and correspondents . . . are permitted to
make history for us in our day.

    —JAMES R. BAYLEY, BISHOP OF NEWARK (1870)

The Commune is one end of the telegraph wire of Liberty; the
United States are the other.

    —WENDELL PHILLIPS, *NATIONAL STANDARD*, AUGUST 26, 1871

All the Americans in Paris, both before and during the Commune, were
living testimony to a shrinking world. New ways of travel and communication were quickly drawing the United States closer to other nations and
Americans closer to each other. In fact, when he looked back on the 1870s
a generation later, magazine writer Joel Benton was still amazed at the
growing sense of "solidarity . . . [in] the country, brought about by the
general continuity and pulse-beat of the telegraph and railroad, the ubiquity of the daily newspaper, the vast multiplication of periodicals, magazines, and books."[1]

The process Benton described was well under way when France declared
war on Prussia in the fateful summer of 1870 but was still far from complete. Americans had access to an unprecedented flow of news about the
European war and the Commune, yet the news arrived in fragments that
were rarely coherent or consistent. A new technology was in place by 1870
that could turn distant events into everyday parts of American life; an
expanding commercial network was able to broadcast multiple versions of
the same events; but neither was sufficiently developed to offer a complete
account of what was happening in France. As a result, stay-at-home Americans were forced to construct their own versions of the Franco-Prussian
War and the Commune, by somehow fitting the ragged foreign scraps into
familiar domestic patterns.

It was nearly impossible for contemporary Americans to ignore the war
and the Commune. One reason was the ideological affinity between the
European events and the recent war in the United States—the common
factors that made them all part of the "age of democratic civil wars." Some
of these common factors have already been discussed, and I will return to

them in the next chapter. However, in this chapter I focus on another reason why the French war and Commune were so compelling to observers in this country: the development of a commercial culture that could turn foreign tidings into news and then transform the news into a national event.

What Joel Benton remembered about the 1860s and 1870s was a national culture being formed. Nowhere was the truth behind his recollection more apparent than in the rapid evolution of the American newspaper press. In 1850, a total of 2,526 periodicals (newspapers and magazines combined) were being published in the United States, with a gross circulation of 426 million copies per annum. By 1870 the number of periodicals exceeded 5,800, with a total yearly circulation of more than 1.5 billion. This new total included 574 daily newspapers (versus 254 in 1850) with an aggregate circulation of 2.6 million copies a day—or about one paper for every fifteen Americans. Most of these gains had come during the Civil War.[2] European observers were amazed at what they saw: in 1870 the United States was producing 43 percent of the world's periodicals and three times as many newspapers as the entire United Kingdom. As one Englishman concluded, "America is the classic soil of newspapers; everybody is reading . . . [and] there is a universality of print."[3]

These impressive quantitative changes were matched by qualitative changes in the way that news was gathered and distributed. Improvements in printing and paper technology made it cheaper and faster than ever to print the news. One contemporary properly called the improvements "a revolution in journalism."[4] He also noted how "the extension of railroads" and "the improved mail service conducted by the government in connection with them, . . . [had] made it possible for the morning journals of a great city to be delivered at the breakfast-tables of people living hundreds of miles away," turning great metropolitan newspapers like the *New York Tribune* into national organs.[5]

The most significant change, however, was the expanding use of the telegraph, which allowed news to be gathered and spread across great distances. Newspaper publishers in the 1850s used the new tool sparingly, to report only the most important events or the most timely shipping and market news. Telegraph tolls were exceedingly expensive, and for most ordinary purposes the cheap mails were fast enough.[6] But with the outbreak of the Civil War telegraphic news suddenly went from being a luxury to being both a necessity and a challenge.

Understandably, Americans on the home front became desperate for the latest tidings of war (as did soldiers in the field: recall how Cluseret's troops in the Shenandoah Valley paused in their fighting to buy newspapers). To meet this new demand the Northern press mounted an unprecedented news-gathering campaign. The big New York papers, led by the *Herald* and the *Tribune,* each spent between $60,000 and $100,000 a year to cover the war, while their smaller competitors in Boston, Philadelphia, and Chicago spent between $10,000 and $30,000.[7] Most of this went to pay for the telegraphic dispatches that dozens of reporters (called "special correspondents," or "specials" for short) were filing from the front. The *New York Herald* alone had as many as forty specials tagging along with the Union troops at any given time. According to the standard history of American journalism, "Probably no great war has ever been so thoroughly covered by eye-witness correspondents as the American Civil War."[8]

As they covered the war, these men were also inventing a new way to report the news, what dubious European observers would soon be calling "the American way."[9] The emphasis was on speed, and any journalist with "energy, talent, devotion, persistence, and . . . good luck" had an advantage in the race to scoop his colleagues. Meanwhile, the high cost of telegraphy forced reporters in the field to create a writing style that was concise yet compelling, a combination that we still call "telegraphic." Accuracy was less important than speed and concision.[10] Editors at home also went through a learning process, discovering how to coordinate the coverage of far-flung events and fill a day's columns with more news—plus maps, illustrations, cartoons, and other embellishments—than Americans had ever seen.

The Civil War permanently altered the relationship between American journals and their readers. Not only did newspaper readership soar during the war years, but readers grew accustomed to an expanded supply of telegraphic news. To their chagrin, publishers found out that the journalistic precedents of the war were "awkward to disregard thereafter."[11] Readers now demanded the freshest wire news they could get. A publisher from Wisconsin complained that subscribers threatened to stop buying his paper altogether unless he fed them a steady stream of "conflagrations [and] calamities, . . . commotions, revolutions, wars, fallings of dynasties, . . . conflicts, strifes and rivalries, . . . and an unceasing round of exciting, thrilling and astounding events."[12] His readers in La Crosse, like those across the nation, were both anxious and curious about the world that the telegraph now brought to their fingertips, though curiosity was plainly the dominant emotion. Americans craved their "little pellets" of telegraphic news (as *Scribner's* derisively called them), even when they knew the pellets were likely to be inaccurate.[13]

Consequently, by the end of the 1860s more than 2.25 *million* news dispatches a year were being whisked along the 50,000 miles of Western Union telegraph wire.[14] A growing number of these dispatches were coming from across the sea in Europe, arriving in the United States by way of the most impressive addition to the domestic news network: Cyrus Field's Atlantic cable, completed in 1866.[15] Journalist Edward S. King, who covered the Franco-Prussian War and the Commune for New York and Boston newspapers, noted in his memoirs that the laying of the cable resulted in a "consequent increase of interest in European affairs . . . by the whole American people." The increase in interest was naturally reinforced by the postbellum flood of Americans into Europe, and vice versa. According to King, Americans in the years just before the transatlantic link "had been . . . [too] passionately absorbed in the strengthening and asserting of . . . [their] own national life" to spend much time looking eastward. "But after the cable was laid . . . the panorama of Europe's events passed under the daily notice of the most omnivorous readers in the world . . . [E]vents which had been but vaguely heard of . . . [now] were at once recited for the benefit of Americans with a minuteness and . . . detail which were not accorded them even in the countries where they took place."[16]

American editors quickly realized that telegraphic news from Europe sold papers and that bad news from Europe sold even more papers.[17] If they needed additional proof they got it from the Franco-Prussian War. The European conflict was the perfect opportunity for American newsmen to capitalize on all the recent developments in their trade: the public's sharpened appetite for news, the Atlantic cable, their own hard-won expertise at reporting combat. It was also a welcome break from a summer of torpid domestic affairs.[18]

Thanks to the foresight and skill of George W. Smalley, the paper's "foreign commissioner" in London, the *New York Tribune* took the lead in reporting the Franco-Prussian War. Whitelaw Reid, the *Tribune's* editor, explained to Smalley that he was willing to spend whatever it took to keep "first class correspondents with both armies"[19]—and spend he did, mostly on cable tolls. On some days these mounted to more than $4,000 in gold; the telegraph bill for covering the six months of war totaled $125,506.97. But Smalley and the correspondents in the field got results. A *Tribune* man, for example, became the first reporter ever to describe a European battle completely by wire, allowing Americans back home to read about the German victory at Gravelotte (August 18, 1870) just two days after it happened. Two weeks later, the *Tribune* scooped the competition again at the decisive Battle of Sedan on September 2.[20]

Still, the other big New York papers were never far behind the *Tribune* in their coverage of the European conflict; collectively the New York press led the nation, as it had during the Civil War.[21] James Gordon Bennett's *Herald,* for example, fielded twenty-four of its own reporters, among them Januarius MacGahan.[22] In an effort to augment its coverage the *Herald* also struck an agreement with the London *Times* to pool their news-gathering resources, which brought to American readers the astute reportage of William H. Russell, a veteran correspondent of bloody wars in the Crimea and the United States. The *Tribune* formed a similar alliance with the London *Daily News* and its star reporter, Archibald Forbes, yet another veteran of Civil War journalism.[23]

Some of the best reporting of the war, however, was done by men representing less affluent papers than the *Herald* or *Tribune*—such reporters as Moncure D. Conway of the *New York World,* Murat Halstead of the *Cincinnati Commercial,* and Edward King of the *Boston Journal.* What they wrote was literally correspondence: long, thoughtful descriptions of events in Europe that were sent home through the mails. Outside of New York and a few other large cities, that was all most newspapers could afford in the way of exclusive coverage of the Franco-Prussian War or later the Commune.[24]

Smaller journals had to rely on the Associated Press for their primary coverage of the war. The Associated Press (AP) was a consortium of New York publishers that held a virtual monopoly on telegraphic news from abroad. Its agents in London made digests of the European news, generally by clipping the London and Paris journals, and then sent the digests to New York via the transatlantic cable. From there the digests were distributed to over 200 daily papers that subscribed to the AP's service.[25] Meanwhile, editors who did not subscribe to the wire service (and many who did) simply reprinted the news as it appeared on their colleagues' and competitors' pages. Most editors also exchanged subscriptions with out-of-town newspapers as an easy way to assemble more material for their own columns. This meant that exclusive dispatches to the *Tribune, Herald,* or *Times* in fact became widely distributed, though at varying rates of speed (sometimes by telegraph, sometimes by domestic mail). This pattern of dispersion assured that while a large volume of foreign news circulated in America, most of it derived from a small set of original sources passing through New York City.

The extensive newspaper coverage of the Franco-Prussian War continued during the Paris Commune. The news-gathering apparatus put in place for the European war remained intact, as did the domestic appetite for foreign news. Once again, the large New York papers took the lead, and others followed as best they could through the telegraph and mails.[26]

Yet there were new constraints on the coverage. For one thing, the Communards seized control of the Paris telegraph lines almost immediately, maintaining sporadic control for the next two months, while the Versailles government likewise strived to cut the Parisians' links to the outside world.[27] Both sides also tried to prevent even noncombatants from leaving or entering the city. As a result, the best eyewitness reporting on the Commune came from the first and last days of the civil war, when the siege lines were relatively porous. Although some American correspondents stayed in Paris until the bitter end,[28] most covered the Commune from the safe distance of Versailles. Too often, an anti-Commune bias was the result. In many cases, writes a modern critic, seemingly objective dispatches were simply cribbed from the "official . . . French press or the information given out by Versailles and its foreign envoys." Even when they tried to be conscientious, American newsmen at Versailles were more likely to see things from the local perspective.[29]

Still, the greatest restraint on American coverage of the Commune was the fact that events in Paris were downright confusing—certainly more confusing than the events of the Franco-Prussian War. There was a tangle of ideology and, then as now, journalists thought that ideological struggles made for boring copy. In any case, they were too difficult to compress into brief reports. By comparison, the mayhem and fighting in Paris were easy to convey in telegraphic dispatches and were certainly exciting, even if they were peripheral to the real meaning of the Commune. As the *New York World* observed in an editorial, the coverage of the Commune was "a very striking illustration of the evils which the electric telegraph has brought upon us, commingled with its good":

[It is] not yet possible to know with accuracy what ha[s] actually happened in Paris . . . [T]he story of this tremendous conflict comes [to us] in the short, sharp, fragmentary, and unqualified accents of the telegraph, reflecting from day to day and from hour to hour the excited and necessarily incomplete impressions of observers who are near enough to the terrific drama to be shaken by its terrors without being near enough to analyze its action.

A telegraphic dispatch, the *World* continued, was by necessity brief, un-reflective, and too often misleading. The "inevitable result" was that read-ers no longer looked for analysis or worried about accuracy, all to the detriment of informed opinion-making.[30]

Despite this troubling observation, and despite the various constraints, news from Europe flowed unabated into the United States. The *New York Times,* which by the spring of the Commune had already established itself as a staid, gray journal, sometimes ran as many as nine decks of front-page headlines announcing the latest news from Paris. The headlines were often sensational, such as "Red Flag Floating over the Louvre and Tuileries" on April 2, 1871. On April 8, a random but typical day of coverage, the *Times* ran six headlines under the general rubric "The Civil War in France," followed by a set of dispatches relayed from Versailles via London—in all, two columns of copy, dealing mostly with the battle at Neuilly, northwest of Paris. There was also a prominent editorial, in which the editors "mar-vel[ed] . . . that the well-disposed majority inside Paris did not manage to give the socialists occupation enough to render the entrance of the Ver-sailles troops a matter of comparative ease."

The *New York World*, a more flamboyant paper than the *Times,* also ran six headlines about the Commune on April 8—plus another that simply read "&c., &c., &c." In all, it devoted seven columns of type to the French civil war. That same day, the *New York Herald* offered eleven headlines (including "The Rouge Revolt" and "A Reign of Terror in Paris"), four columns of reporting, and a pious editorial note that fighting on the eve of Easter would make the world "indignant." The *Tribune* had a similar amount of coverage, while the smaller New York journals carried propor-tionately lesser amounts. But every paper, and probably every paper across the country, had *some* sort of coverage. For example, even in the tiny mining town of Corinne, Utah, the local paper managed to publish what it called a humorous "clipping"—"It is said that Paris capitalists are continu-ally wishing they 'nary Red'"—along with a few brief wire-service items (under five sentences each), dated a day or two before.[31]

Urbane New Yorker George Templeton Strong was certainly not your average newspaper reader in 1871, but he did read several papers each day. As a result, his diary entries give an idea of how closely events in Paris might have been followed from the vantage point of New York: "News (more or less veracious) from *Gallia Infelix* . . . Latest news [from France] . . . Fighting around Paris continues . . . Paris is much the same . . . Reports from Paris are cloudy but lurid . . . [More] news from Paris . . . Reports from Paris . . ." Similar entries appeared for months.[32] Yet for all his perusal of the daily press, Strong was chagrined to discover that he still didn't know what was happening in France. As he complained to his diary at the end of May, the "telegrams from Versailles and St. Denis are many, muddled, and contradictory."

> Whether the Versailles men are giving no quarter and the streets of Paris are running with blood, the Rouges are pumping petroleum out of fire engines into burning buildings, and the Palais de Justice is destroyed; or, whether the converse of all this be true, no man can tell at present . . . "Fifty thousand dead and wounded lie unburied in the cellars and the streets of Paris," say the telegraphists. Possibly it may prove that there are only forty-nine thousand.

Here Strong simply repeated the *New York World*'s complaint that American journalism had failed to capture the intricacies of the Paris Commune, even with the help of the transatlantic cable—and not just the ideological intricacies, but even the simpler complexities of fact.[33]

Other observers expanded on this basic complaint. French sculptor Frédéric-Auguste Bartholdi, who was in the United States promoting an embryonic version of the Statue of Liberty, wrote to his mother that he could not even keep *"au courant* with what is happening at home, [because] all I can find in the papers are the large events." Part of the problem was the chaotic state of the French press accounts cribbed by American journalists. According to Pembroke Fetridge in Paris, "there was much discrepancy in the various accounts given [in the French press] . . . Each succeeding day corrections were made in the original reports, of which readers in the United States could never be thoroughly informed through the newspapers." Fetridge's grubstreet colleague, Dr. Linus P. Brockett, reached a similar conclusion in Brooklyn, adding only that "the confused and contradictory reports and letters in the daily papers concerning the insurrection in Paris . . . have rendered the whole affair a hopeless muddle."[34] The final result was that despite the heap of American newsprint devoted to the Commune, when it came to making sense of what happened, Americans were largely on their own.

According to one Marxist historian of America and the Commune, the "guardians of 'culture'" in the United States actively curtailed any "public discussion of subjects as vulgar as the Commune." He was wrong, even if his argument is confined to the most elite cultural outlets.[35] Unlike the Franco-Prussian War, the Paris Commune touched every corner of American culture. Depictions of the Commune appeared in all popular media, with the possible exceptions of opera and sheet music. In part, this was simply more evidence of the growing interconnectedness of American commercial culture after the Civil War.

But it was also a sign of how large an impact the Paris Commune had on American culture, when culture is broadly defined. Part of being human is the constant striving to make sense of the world around us. Better yet, as anthropologist Clifford Geertz writes, "man is an animal suspended in webs of significance he himself has spun." Like Geertz, "I take culture to be those webs."[36] Culture is also dynamic, since new events constantly get caught up in the web and have to be assimilated, consciously or unconsciously, into the pre-existing patterns. As another social theorist writes, "[new] forces cause people to change their notions of what kind of situation they are in, and to sustain these new notions sufficiently long to build them into institutions."[37] Of course, big events disturb the cultural web more than small ones do, and big forces shake a settled notion more than a small force ever can. Beginning in 1871, the Paris Commune became such an unsettling force for many Americans, a big event that demanded assimilation into their view of the world. For some, this was only because they were beset by media reminders of the French civil war. Nonetheless, the flood of cultural artifacts inspired by the Commune was both a cause and a sign of just how momentous an event it was.

The Paris Commune was like a flat pebble that skipped across the surface of American culture. With every skip it propagated ripples, which interacted with subsequent ripples across the entire surface; and even later, when the pebble sank from view, it continued to alter the flow of things around it, however subtly. It was no surprise that the very first splash hit New York City, which not only had the closest ties to Europe (both commercial and intellectual), but also sat at the terminus of transatlantic communication. The initial ripples were carried along by the nation's press, which spread the news from Paris almost as swiftly as it arrived in New York. Yet neither the newspapers nor even the Eastern cities would be large enough to contain the entire American response to the Commune.

The geographic ripples across the land are the easiest to trace, especially when frozen in columns of black and white: in AP dispatches to the *New Orleans Picayune;* in editorials from the *New York Herald* reprinted in Utah's *Daily Corinne Reporter;* in headlines that stretched down the pages of the *Cleveland Leader,* the *San Francisco Chronicle,* and hundreds of other regional papers; in popular weekly magazines that were published in New York, Boston, and Philadelphia, but circulated everywhere; and so on through all the pathways of national culture mentioned by Joel Benton at the start of this chapter. This meant that not just elite New Yorkers like George Templeton Strong, but average Americans from every part of the country could—and did—pay close attention to events in Paris. For example, just two days after the Commune began, a farmwife in rural Massachusetts confided to her diary that "the papers are full of accts. of violence and bloodshed among the French people in Paris. I should think they were in the midst of a bloody revolution, but we wait [for] further confirmation of news. Have they not had enough of *war, devastation & carnage*[?]" Another diary, by a local editor in Virginia City, Nevada, sadly noted, "Our telegrams give the fearful . . . scenes of the Paris rebellion—Paris on fire & nearly or quite destroyed."[38] From a small town in Minnesota came an anxious letter to Senator Charles Sumner, written mid-Commune: "I fear [that] Thiers & Co are murdering the best people in France. When we first read of the Communists in Paris, a few weeks ago, a frenchman near here said: Ils ne sont [pas] les communists de Pére [*sic*] Cabet, but I begin to think they are. I wish I could go there. What can be done?"[39] Meanwhile, far south in New Orleans, a creative dry-goods firm tried to profit from the French unrest by running a provocative advertisement: "The Paris revolutionists have raised the black flag. Guéblé & Nippert have lowered all their standards of prices."[40]

Americans everywhere noticed the impact of the Commune. For all that it was a national event, however, the easiest place to spot the cultural ripples of the Commune was still at their point of origin: the big cities of the East. Like transatlantic news, commercial culture in the Gilded Age typically flowed outward from New York City, though also from Boston, Philadelphia, and increasingly Chicago. Yet it would be wrong to invert the pattern and insist that New York was somehow typical of the entire nation. On the contrary, New York always managed to sustain a wider variety of cultural forms than any other spot in America. For that very reason, it becomes useful to catalogue the various ways that an "ordinary" New Yorker might have encountered the Paris Commune in the 1870s, as the fullest cultural reckoning of the event's impact.

Imagine a New Yorker who could read English, who became mildly curious about the Commune, and who had the means to participate in the commercial culture of the day.[41] In the spring of 1871, he or she could begin to satisfy that curiosity by browsing through half a dozen newspapers every day—and, like George Templeton Strong, probably finish in despair at the different accounts of the Commune they offered. On Saturdays our Gothamite could wade through another pile of *weekly* papers and magazines. This pile might have included Wilkes's *Spirit of the Times,* the *Christian Union,* the *Nation,* or *Harper's Weekly*—though probably not all four, since they scrupulously cultivated different audiences (race fans, churchgoers, liberal reformers, and the public at large). Nonetheless, they were all published in New York, and each had a national circulation. More important, each of them carried extensive coverage of the Commune, with a mixture of weekly summaries, rehashed newspaper accounts, original correspondence, editorial comment, and even illustrations.

The illustrated weeklies deserve special mention. Like other types of newspapers, illustrated weeklies reached new heights of popularity and influence during the Civil War, when Americans were eager to read *and* see what was happening on the battlefront. After the war, the picture papers struggled to maintain their new circulation levels, often relying on sensationalism (especially in the case of *Frank Leslie's Illustrated Newspaper*) and exposé (like the attack on "Boss" Tweed in *Harper's Weekly*), but always relying on the appeal of their illustrations. Pictures sold papers, and in 1871 the three major American illustrated weeklies—*Frank Leslie's* and *Harper's* in New York, and *Every Saturday* in Boston—competed fiercely to offer the most recent pictures of the French civil war. Every week, engravings of the Commune were spread across three or four pages of each publication, with such descriptive captions as "Paris,—The Red Flag on the Column of July"; "The Revolution in Paris,—Meeting of a Red Republican Club"; "Outside of Paris,—Waiting for the End"; "The End of the Commune,—Execution of a Pétroleuse"; and "The Communist Prisoners in the Orangerie, Versailles."[42] Especially common were crude portraits of Commune "celebrities" and bird's-eye views of Paris in flames.[43]

In many cases, illustrations in the American weeklies were simply copied from their counterparts in England and France, with or without consent.

Every Saturday was the exception: it struck a formal arrangement with the London *Graphic* to reprint electrotypes of the *Graphic*'s original wood-cuts—a potentially valuable scoop in the days of the Franco-Prussian War and the Commune, when the *Graphic* had several talented artists at work in Paris. Unfortunately, *Harper's Weekly* went right ahead and copied the same pictures from the London *Graphic* without permission, "and thus robbed *Every Saturday* of most of what it had paid for." As a result, it was common for the same illustrations and even the same captions to appear in both places.[44] Whatever the original source, one thing is obvious about the pictures of the Commune that appeared in American weeklies: they were not chosen for their truth-value, but instead for their visual, sensational, and ideological appeal. Consequently, these illustrations were eye-catching but not particularly accurate renditions of the Commune.

After reading the various dailies and weeklies—not to mention the monthlies and quarterlies[45]—our ordinary New Yorker could then turn attention to a trio of "instant histories" that were rushed into print soon after the Paris uprising. Before the end of the summer, the prestigious New York firm of Harper and Brothers published Pembroke Fetridge's *The Rise and Fall of the Paris Commune in 1871.*[46] Two less reputable publishers had beaten them to print, however: H. S. Goodspeed and Company (also of New York), with Dr. Linus P. Brockett's *Paris Under the Commune; or, The Red Rebellion of 1871: A Second Reign of Terror, Murder, and Madness,* and the National Publishing Company of Philadelphia, with James D. McCabe's *History of the War between Germany and France . . . To Which is Added a Complete Account of the Revolt of the Commune, and the Second Siege of Paris.* Both volumes were marketed through the subscription trade, where books were sold on prospectus by agents who plied the backroads of America, through regions where few bookstores were handy. (In larger cities, the books were also sometimes distributed via normal retail channels.) This was another field of commercial culture that prospered thanks to the Civil War; in the postbellum decade, veterans usually became the most aggressive salesmen, and Civil War topics usually sold the most books. At best, offerings in the subscription trade sold hundreds of thousands of copies and made books available to eager readers who had no other access to current literature. Even so, subscription books were often hastily and cheaply produced, then grossly overpriced.[47] The two books on the Commune were no exceptions.

The first thing a subscription book needed was a ready-made audience to canvass, for publishers in the trade would not proceed unless they could easily identify their market. Fortunately, James Dabney McCabe understood both audiences and publishers, learning the hard way while churning out "several hundred short stories, essays, poems, and translations" in the 1860s and 1870s.[48] McCabe was living in New York when the Franco-Prussian War erupted, and he immediately recognized that "everybody will now be looking to Paris and Berlin." Quickly convincing his Philadelphia publisher that "the excitement ought to help to sell . . . book[s]," McCabe started gathering material for a history of the war: newspaper clippings, cable dispatches, and illustrations from *Harper's Weekly* and *Frank Leslie's Illustrated Newspaper*.[49] With these in hand, McCabe was soon "writing up the history fast," as he liked to put it. By the middle of May 1871, a scant three months after the surrender of Paris to the Germans, his 700-page chronicle of the Franco-Prussian War was rolling off the presses.[50]

By then McCabe was already thinking about incorporating the Paris Commune into a second edition. Originally, he was not keen on the idea. On April 10, he even begged his publisher to "think *twice* about asking me to include the Paris riots in the War History . . . I had better not touch on the subject, for no man living can say where these things will end." But McCabe knew there was a book-buying audience for the Commune, and seven weeks later he capitulated: "If you wish it I will, of course, make the addition to the War History, and as soon as possible. I fear it will not be as complete and full as the rest, as the events of this insurrection are but imperfectly known here as yet."[51] Like his competitors Brockett and Fetridge, McCabe was reluctant to rely on "scanty" and confusing newspaper accounts to reconstruct a narrative of the Commune—but like them, he did it anyway. Casting reluctance aside, he wielded scissors and paste with alacrity, and by mid-July the second edition of McCabe's "War History" was ready for distribution.[52] This edition shared a number of things with the Fetridge and (especially) Brockett volumes, starting with the same sensational illustrations and recycled newspaper accounts. More important, in all three cases the emphasis was squarely on the narrative, with little effort to explain what the Paris Commune *meant*, except to note that it was largely an undesirable event.

Contemporary Americans who avoided nonfiction writing in either newspapers or books could still read a good deal about the Commune. At least twelve novels were published in the United States between 1872 and 1904 that used the swirl of the Paris uprising as a backdrop for fiction. One was written by Edward King, the same reporter who covered the Paris Commune for the Boston and New York press. Another was written by Robert W. Chambers, the most popular author of historical romances at the time. Both books were published in 1895.[53] Several of the novelists, including Chambers and King, managed to introduce fictional Americans into the Commune, or even to use Gustave Cluseret and Elihu Washburne as minor characters. But as far as I can tell, the only American novel that tried to use the Paris Commune to talk about domestic affairs directly was William DuGas Trammell's *Ça Ira* (1874), discussed in Chapter 3. For the rest, the Commune was nothing more than another exotic setting for tales of danger, romance, and family intrigue. In some cases, the authors did strive to describe the historical setting accurately; as one of them proudly noted in the 1890s, that meant consulting "the most effective records" of the time, especially the old newspaper files![54]

The Paris Commune served the same atmospheric function in various short stories[55] and dime novels[56] that it did in the longer works of American fiction. A good example can be seen in "Cacique: A Story of the Commune," a short but complex tale published in early 1877.[57] The story begins on a sunny day at the Bois de Boulogne, just at the end of the German siege. The narrator, a young American, is ice-skating when he first beholds the title character. She is "bright-eyed, lovely, laughing" (217)— but alas, she has a tragic past. Of course the narrator falls in love with Cacique. Only later does he learn the secret of her tragedy: she is the daughter of a Creole nobleman, with a hateful half-sister who has sworn to destroy her. In his youth, the nobleman had married a French peasant girl and had a daughter. A few months later mother and daughter disappeared, and the husband returned to Martinique to claim his inheritance. There he marries again and has another, unloved daughter, the evil Irene, who grows up "wild, uncultivated, selfish and willful" (219). The second wife dies, the first wife and daughter suddenly reappear on the island, and Cacique replaces Irene as the father's heiress. "Selfish and cruel by nature," the younger Irene vows retribution (220). She tries to kill Cacique, so Cacique and her fiancé flee to Paris—and into the arms of the Commune.

"Day by day," recalls the narrator, "the horrors of the insurrection deepened around us," as the fate of Cacique and the fate of the city began to converge. A half-page later "the insurrection was crushed" (222). The troops from Versailles pour into the city, and Cacique runs to find her new husband in the "wild excitement." Suddenly, she is confronted by the "maniac" Irene, who finally gets her revenge by denouncing Cacique as a *pétroleuse*. "I could not stifle the mad woman's cries," says the rueful narrator: "I could not resist the frenzy of a furious mob thirsting for blood" (222). And so Cacique—his "noble, glorious Cacique!"—is wrongly shot for being a Communarde.

As this brief summary suggests, "Cacique" was neither great literature nor an accurate (much less sufficient) depiction of the Commune—but it wasn't meant to be. It was meant to be entertaining, and on that score it succeeded. More to the point, it appeared in a magazine with almost 100,000 subscribers, any of whom might be set to thinking about the Paris Commune by this one short story.[58]

Even poetry, the most esoteric of the lively arts, rippled with the impact of the Paris Commune. Like the novelists and story writers, American poets produced their versions of the Commune for widespread consumption. First among them was the leading poet of American democracy, Walt Whitman. "O star of France!" he apostrophized when news of the Commune began to reach these shores,

> The brightness of thy fame, and strength, and joy, . . .
> Beseems to-day a wreck, driven by the gale . . .
> Dim, smitten star!
> Orb not of France alone—pale symbol of my soul,
>   its dearest hopes,
> The struggle and the daring—rage divine for liberty,
> Of aspirations toward the far ideal—
>   enthusiast's dreams of brotherhood,
> Of terror to the tyrant and the priest.
>
> Again thy star, O France—fair, lustrous star,
> In heavenly peace, clearer, more bright than ever,
> Shall rise immortal.[59]

Whitman composed these stirring lines for the popular *Galaxy* magazine, and no other American poet, writing for a general audience, ever came so close to applauding the Commune. The *Saturday Review* in England complained shrilly about poets who "prostituted [their] . . . genius to apologize for the worst excesses of the Commune," but it was difficult to find that sort of poetic work in mainstream American culture.[60] Walt Whitman, for example, was engaged in neither prostitution nor apologetics. Rather, he was trying to connect the Commune with the Franco-American tradition of republicanism. That was nothing new for him. As a Free Soil Democrat in the 1850s, the young Whitman had loudly praised the 1848 revolution in France as an exercise in popular sovereignty; in 1871, the older Whitman simply remained optimistic about French uprisings and the democratic possibilities they contained.[61]

At the other end of the poetic spectrum—in temperament, not talent—was Herman Melville, who transformed the Commune into one long, apocalyptic allusion. He did this in *Clarel,* a powerful but obscure epic that has perplexed its readers ever since it appeared in 1876. On the surface, *Clarel* is the story of a pilgrimage to the Holy Land by four world-weary Americans. But as always in Melville's work, there are deeper levels of meaning. At the very least, notes Melville scholar John P. McWilliams, the poem is both a meditation on "America's complex fate" and a sullen reflection of the poet's own disillusionment with America after the Civil War. Like the characters in *Clarel,* the postbellum Melville increasingly felt like a man "without a country, without a social creed, . . . without religious faith." By 1866, when he published *Battle-Pieces,* a collection of bitter poems, Melville was already convinced that the Civil War "brought the nation to flawed maturity."[62]

For Melville, the Commune was another instance of what material-ism and license could bring to a postlapsarian nation. Unlike Whitman, Melville never applauded a French uprising in his life. Quite the opposite: in the novel *Mardi* (1849), he used a political fable to denounce the "violent eruption" of 1848 and to ridicule its American admirers.[63] For Melville, the Paris Commune was a new outbreak of the same violence. Artistically, however, it could not have happened at a better time, for he was in the midst of composing *Clarel* when the Commune began. Accord-ing to his modern editor, Melville closely followed the events in Paris on the pages of the daily New York papers, and what he read in them was quickly translated to the pages of his own manuscript. As a result, *Clarel* bristles with negative references to Communists, Atheists, Red Caps, and the Red Republic. Some allusions to the contemporary Commune are relatively straightforward, like this terse jeremiad by one of the American pilgrims:

> Repent! repent in every land
> Or hell's hot kingdom is at hand! . . .
> While now the armed world holds its own,
> The comet peers, the stars dip down; . . .

> While Anti-Christ and Atheist set
> On Anarch the red coronet!
>
> (II.xxxiv.30–38)

Yet in other passages, Melville's editor notes, "it is not entirely clear which of 3 major revolutions is being referred to, the sense often being collective—1789, 1848, or 1871."[64] What *is* clear is that Herman Melville perceived a strong link between the unsettled state of America and these foreign upheavals, however much he obscured the link with his art.

Whitman and Melville were not the only American poets to engage with the Commune, just the most talented. Americans in the 1870s were much less wary of poetry as a public art than they have become since. No important civic event was complete without a special ode or anthem specifically written for the occasion. Ordinary Americans gathered in the parlor to read poetry aloud. Almost every magazine or newspaper carried verse as a regular feature. And because the poets of the day were just as likely to versify current affairs as they were to write about love and death, there was always an abundance of mediocre poetry inspired by the headlines.[65] The headlines from Paris were a case in point.[66]

The average poetaster's view of the Commune usually fell somewhere between Melville's and Whitman's, though they all worked from the same raw material: what they read in the papers. One poet, however, not only read the accounts from Paris but even wrote some of them: Edward King, the Boston journalist and future novelist of the Commune. In September 1871, his poetic sketch entitled "A Woman's Execution, Paris, May, '71" was printed in *Scribner's Monthly*.[67] A few months later, the *Atlantic* published a similar poem by another aspiring journalist, future Secretary of State John Hay. While both poems focus on the bloody suppression of the Commune—what Hay called "the joy of killing . . . / In the glut of those awful days"—the poets managed to condemn Versailles without condoning the Commune.[68] Avoiding politics altogether, Charles Sibley adopted a purely threnodic tone for his contribution to the *Galaxy*, "The Burden of Paris": "No longer the Beautiful City, / Paris, shalt thou be called, / But the City of Sadness, / The City of Sorrow, / For many years!"[69] The extremely popular "Howard Glyndon" (real name Laura Searing) adopted the same tone for *Harper's Weekly*. She concluded, however, that the Commune was "the hand of God" sent down to strike France.[70] Another female poet, Margaret Junkin Preston of Virginia, was neither as popular as Howard Glyndon nor as dubious about the Commune. As a result, her lines on the uprising include both heroic Parisians and "short-sighted zealots of Order!"[71]

All these poems appeared in mainstream American periodicals in either 1871 or 1872, amidst the early ripples of the Commune. None was particularly distinguished as poetry, nor could any of them be called apologies for the Commune. Soon, however, poetic defenses of the Commune began to flow from the pens of labor advocates in praise of the working-class heroes of Paris. By the late 1870s, two writers with middle-class followings had also produced pro-Commune poetry: the ex-Fenian John Boyle O'Reilly and the ex-Chartist William J. Linton.[72] Despite their solidarity with the workers, however, neither poet was actively engaged in the labor movement, nor could they claim to speak in the authentic voice of workingmen. Unfortunately, when worker-poets wrote about the Commune themselves, as happened increasingly in the 1880s and 1890s, their output was consigned to obscure publications like the *Denver Labor Enquirer,* where few of their fellow-workers (and fewer members of the bourgeoisie) could ever read them.[73] In contrast, Whitman's *Leaves of Grass,* which included "O Star of France" after 1871, was almost continuously in print. Margaret Preston's "The Hero of the Commune" also reappeared in three standard anthologies of American verse, the last published in 1927.[74]

After fifty-six years, the final anthologizing of Preston's poem was a feeble, late ripple of the Commune's first impact on American culture. Its initial publication, however, reminds us again how thoroughly interlinked American commercial culture had become by the early 1870s. Preston's poem (see Appendix B for the text) is framed around the following anecdote from Bloody Week at the end of the Commune: A young boy is rounded up with the other Communards and is about to be executed. At the last minute, he begs a favor from the French officer in charge: Can he go return a watch that he borrowed from a friend, and then come back to be shot? The officer, who wants to spare the boy's life anyway, quickly agrees—and then, to his great surprise, the boy actually returns after the errand. Impressed at this display of honor, the officer lets the *garçon* go free.

This story, which is probably apocryphal, first appeared in a French journal, *Le Figaro,* on June 3, 1871. An American correspondent then copied it directly from *Le Figaro,* or perhaps indirectly from a British newspaper, and cabled it home. From New York it spread to newspapers across the country, and then reappeared (and was recirculated) in magazines like *Harper's Weekly* and *Appleton's Journal.* Preston and Hay then built poems around the anecdote, and these in turn were variously re-printed. Pembroke Fetridge clipped the story from an American paper and used it for his history of the Commune. William DuGas Trammell in-cluded it in *Ça Ira* three years later. It even resurfaced in Francis Gribble's 1895 novel of the Commune, *The Red Spell;* who knows where he clipped it from.[75] No doubt this minor anecdote of a French boy and his pocket-watch could be tracked through hundreds of such repetitions, with all the variations to the story catalogued and queried. But such an investigation would only reinforce my main point: that the Commune made ripples across the entire surface of American commercial culture.

Let us return to the "ordinary" New Yorker in 1871. If all the poems, books, magazines, and newspapers did not fully satisfy his or her curiosity about the Commune—or if our subject preferred listening to reading—there were also public lectures on the subject. (Another option was to go to church; sermons on the Commune are discussed separately, in Chapter 7.) In the summer of 1871, the leading impresario of the American lecture circuit, James Redpath, wrote to Elihu Washburne and invited him to come home and give a series of lectures about his exciting ordeal. Red-path's Boston Lyceum Bureau was only three years old and still finding its feet, but Redpath was so certain the American public wanted to hear about the recent upheavals in Paris that he offered Washburne $500 a lecture for an exclusive engagement—$100 more than the highest prevailing rate.[76] The diplomat politely refused.

If Washburne was reticent, other eyewitnesses were eager to mount the podium in his stead. The first, in October 1871, was a Protestant clergy-man from France named Athanase Coquerel, who spoke on the "Two Sieges of Paris" to appreciative (and paying) audiences in New York and Boston.[77] The next was New York merchant Elliott C. Cowdin. Although he spent most of the 1870s as part of the American colony in Paris, Cowdin still managed to return home and entertain New Yorkers with a pair of well-received talks about the Commune: one at the Cooper Union in 1872, another at the American Institute in 1877.[78] Another Yankee eyewitness, Nathan Sheppard, thrilled New Yorkers in 1876 with his lec-ture "Shut Up in Paris."[79] One year later, Elihu Washburne finally deliv-ered his own lecture on "the terrible events of the Commune" to a gather-ing of German Americans in his hometown of Galena, Illinois. Most of the lecture was a personal narrative of the events of six years earlier. In retrospect, the former diplomat admitted to his audience that he now considered the Paris Commune simply an exercise in "force and terror."[80]

Back in New York City in 1871, an important group of public speakers strongly disagreed with Washburne's later assessment. These were the Commune's middle-class sympathizers, who either endorsed the Commune's revolutionary program or insisted that Americans keep an open mind about the experiment in Paris. The most prominent member of this group was Wendell Phillips, the old-line abolitionist, who never shrank from endorsing a radical cause. Indeed, Phillips was one of the few abolitionist ideologues to make the transition from antislavery to prolabor agitation, and he was always willing to link those reforms with the world-historical drive towards freedom. On December 6, 1871, at Steinway Hall in New York, Phillips made the connection again in a speech on the labor problem. "The French Commune," he declared, "has always seemed to me to deserve the cordial respect of every lover of the progress of the masses throughout the world . . . I have no doubt that in due time its good name will be vindicated, and its leaders lifted to the unqualified respect of the civilized world . . . There was never . . . more highminded and disinterested effort made in the long history of Freedom's struggle, than in Paris." According to the *New York Times,* his words were received with polite applause.[81]

No doubt the applause was mingled with nervous laughter from those who felt less warmly toward the masses than Phillips. But there was no reason for the audience to be surprised by what Phillips said about the Commune. After all, the speech in New York was just a milder version of one he gave at Steinway Hall in Boston seven months earlier, which had been widely reported in the press. It was also consistent with Phillips's other public pronouncements on the Commune, including his statement at the beginning of this chapter. The occasion for the Boston speech was the first anniversary meeting of the New England Labor Reform League on May 10, 1871. Before a mixed crowd of working people, reformers, and veteran abolitionists like Julia Ward Howe and Lucretia Mott, Phillips argued that the class struggle in America was really no different from the class struggle in France, and might well lead to "such scenes as devastate the city of Paris today." If that happened, the greedy capitalists would only be getting what they deserved. Phillips concluded with a striking (some said ominous) turn of phrase: "Scratch a Russian, and you will find a Tartar underneath; scratch New York, and you will find Paris just below the surface . . . [I]mpressing the laboring classes with the belief that there is no such thing as justice, and that law is not sacred, will yet develop into revolution in the country."[82]

Because Wendell Phillips was famous and because he made such good newspaper copy, his provocative remarks in support of the Commune were widely reprinted. Similar, though usually less tendentious, declarations were uttered by middle-class reformers on New York stages throughout 1871, but they received less attention.[83] Nonetheless, their speeches were another way for New Yorkers to encounter the Paris Commune—very different from commercial lectures, and with the intended goal of persuading rather than amusing, but a significant ripple all the same.

Even if New Yorkers strongly disagreed with the reformers' pro-Commune stance, they still might go hear them speak for the fun of it, as a kind of lurid spectacle. Henry James captured this attitude perfectly in *The Bostonians* (1886), his caustic portrait of Boston in the early 1870s. James described a city enervated by the Civil War, where the fires of antebellum reform were reduced to a few glaring embers like Wendell Phillips. Somewhere, perhaps, serious crusaders still commanded the public rostrum, but not in Boston. "Enterprise and puffery" were the new order of the day, and James's narrator complains that "momentary fad[s]" and the "unprecedented success of curiosity" were all that really attracted a Boston audience. In the novel's final, sardonic episode, James has "all Boston . . . packed into" the magnificent Music Hall on Hamilton Place to hear Miss Verena Tarrant lecture on the women's question—"several thousand people stamping with their feet and rapping with their umbrellas and sticks." Most had come "to gape and grin and babble," not to hear about feminism. They were there for the entertainment, supporting the novelist's contention that "prima donnas," "natural curiosities," and women reformers had all become equivalent spectacles on the American stage. Clearly he overstated the case. But to the extent that Henry James was correct and not just rehearsing his own misogyny, the conclusion applied to pro-Commune lecturers as well pro-feminist ones.[84]

Though pro-Commune lectures attracted their share of mirth and wonder, New York in 1871 was also home to deliberate spectacles inspired by the events in Paris. Late that spring, for example, San Francisco Hall exhibited a large "view in relief" of the city of Paris. A few months later, and a few blocks further north on Broadway, Apollo Hall offered a "double stereoscopicon" show entitled "Paris en Feu—Ruines de Paris et ses Environs—

La Commune de Paris à New York." According to the advertising puff, it promised to be a "GREAT NOVELTY" and an "EXTRAORDINARY ATTRACTION." The reviewer at the *New York Herald* was more specific, explaining that the "main features presented were the ruins of Paris and its environs, from photographs taken immediately after the terrible and disastrous fires, after which followed a presentation of portraits of the leaders of the Commune." In the end, he pronounced the "whole exhibition well worth attending."[85]

The autumn of 1871 brought a new theater season to New York City, and with it two original plays about the Paris Commune. Dedicated first-nighters could have seen Ada Gray starring in *Paris, or Days of the Commune* at the Grand Opera House, or traveled across the East River to Brooklyn's Park Theatre to watch Kate Ranoe in *The Revolt of the Commune; or, Paris in 1871.*[86] But they probably would not have enjoyed either production. Reviewers thought they were terrible. "From beginning to end," sniffed the critic from the *New York Times,* Thomas C. De Leon's *Paris, or Days of the Commune* was "unmitigated trash of the dreariest and most common-place sort." (Indeed, he thought it was so bad that he refused even to describe the plot.) More important for us was the fact that the play had very little to do with the Commune at all; revolutionary Paris simply became the backdrop for a conventional melodrama. As the *Times* critic explained, "A number of people come upon the stage, declare themselves to be Frenchmen, Zouaves, Communists or Americans, as the case may be, utter sentiments of various degrees of insipidity, interspaced with various eccentric mispronunciations . . . to give local coloring, and go off without apparent purpose or aim. The rest is blue fire and calcium lights . . ."[87] Another reviewer, more kindly disposed toward the Commune, felt that De Leon had badly mishandled "a subject so full of possibilities." In the hands of a better playwright, the public might have learned something about the Paris Commune "without knowing it, under the delicate disguise of an entertaining play." But he sadly concluded that a "dramatist of the Commune" who could combine both entertainment and explanation was "yet in the unknown future."[88]

Unfortunately, that dramatist of the Commune never did appear, at least not in the United States. There were other plays about the Paris Commune: by the end of the century, at least three had been staged in Boston alone, another in nearby Falmouth, and probably two more in Memphis and San Francisco. During the same thirty-year period, reenactments of the Paris Commune in the form of plays and tableaux vivants also became part of the radical subculture of the labor movement, especially among German Americans.[89] But none of these performances attracted much attention outside of the immediate circle of spectators.

The largest theatrical audience was reserved for yet another spectacle inspired by the Commune: a lifelike panorama of the two sieges of Paris. Panoramas (also known as cycloramas) are huge, cylindrical paintings of famous events or places, designed to provide viewers with the illusion of actually being there. Although they were in vogue for most of the nineteenth century, there was a "golden age of the panorama . . . in the 1870s," when the field was dominated by French and German artists. Most were veterans of the Franco-Prussian War, which became a favorite subject.[90] For Americans, the most important cyclorama of this era was a vivid rendering of the Battle of Gettysburg by French painter Paul Philippoteaux, which can still be seen at Gettysburg today.

Another product of the golden age, no longer in existence, was Fortuné Liénard's panorama *The Great Siege of Paris, 1870–71,* which opened for business at the New York Colosseum in the winter of 1875. Joining Liénard's canvas of the Prussian siege was *The Shooting of the Archbishop of Paris by the Commune of 1871* by Monsieur Desbrosses—a "splendid picture," claimed the program, that "becomes, by the aid of well-devised mechanical accessories, a surprisingly realistic scene."[91] In 1876, the entire operation moved from the Colosseum in Manhattan to the Centennial Exposition in Philadelphia, where it drew thousands of visitors from around the nation. For a mere fifty cents, spectators could file into a "huge circular building of corrugated iron" and once again be thrilled by "the saddest memories . . . [of] the terrible SEVENTY-THREE DAYS, during which the [Paris] Commune controlled the city." The printed program never failed to emphasize the thrill and the terror captured by the panorama. Even when it set out to narrate the "circumstances of this painful historical event" (that is, the executions), it wound up extolling the verisimilitude of the "horribly mangled" bodies in the painting.[92]

This was typical, as we have seen. Excitement preceded explanation as the Commune rippled across American life; at first, telling stories was more urgent than understanding them. Singly, the stories were trivial and tragic by turns. But there were so many stories (and images) from Paris that it became impossible to ignore the Commune in Gilded Age America. Thanks to a growing commercial culture, with its own dynamics and demands, the French civil war became a cultural event of national scope in the United States. It was everywhere: a catchpenny version of the Commune even stood just outside the gates of the Centennial Exposition in Philadelphia, the official jubilee of American exceptionalism.

There was something ironic about the juxtaposition, for the panorama of the Commune, like all the other accounts of Parisian unrest, implicitly called into question the truth of American distinctiveness. Was the Great Republic really special? Was it immune from European varieties of unrest? Though the spread of the Commune can easily be mistaken as a surface phenomenom, just below the surface lay a deep pool of American apprehension. Unresolved doubts about the long sectional crisis and new fears about structural changes in American society roiled together, and both were revealed in domestic interpretations of the Paris Commune. The Commune was a problem for American culture, in the broad sense of culture defined earlier. It demanded explanation. But unlike Americans in Paris, Americans at home could not fall back on the rich raw material of immediate experience to construct an explanation; all they had was the thin, scattered stuff of telegraphic dispatches, partly reworked and extended by other cultural media. What both groups of Americans shared, however, was a vague but powerful sense that the civil wars in France and the United States were comparable. That vague sense was the next step toward turning the Commune into something usable at home.

5

Civil Wars by Analogy: Party, Section, and the Paris Commune

Hardly any two nations afford wider contrasts or more of them than the United States during our war against secession, and France during her struggle against the Commune. Yet . . .

—*NEW YORK EVENING POST,* JUNE 29, 1871

Barely a year after the Commune, *Harper's Weekly* noted how "difficult [it was] to realize the remarkable story of the rise and fall of the Communists of France. History has been too swift for us to take proper note of events. We have a general idea concerning the second siege of Paris, but what do we [really] know? . . ." Images and descriptions were one thing, but what was the Commune's real meaning? What were its deeper consequences? More important, did it have a special meaning and consequence for Americans?[1] These were all good questions, and they were frequently asked. Thoughtful Americans were deeply confused about the Paris Commune and the significance it held for their own nation. If nothing else, its ubiquity cried out for explanation: what sort of event could produce so many ripples?

At a more profound level, the French civil war cried out for explanation because Americans were still struggling to make sense of their own fraternal conflict. According to historian Edward Gargan, contemporary Americans brought nothing but anticipation to their encounter with the Paris Commune. In his view, "the events of the Commune were fed into a kind of simulator . . . that permitted important groups in America to experimentally choose the options they would employ if a similar crisis occurred in their country."[2] Gargan was correct, but only in part. Americans in the 1870s were certainly looking to the future, and they did use the Commune to speculate about future events at home (a subject of later chapters). But they also looked back to the past or glanced sideways at the current political scene. And when they looked in those directions they could see that a crisis similar to the Commune had already occurred in the United States: the Civil War.

Americans were thus quick to match the Commune against the patterns of their own recent past. Indeed, a common and compelling way to explain what happened in France was to offer analogies between the Commune and the American Civil War, including Reconstruction. As a collective mental pattern, the Civil War was simply inescapable. From the start, the painful memory of combat between states and brothers was the obvious model for understanding warfare, even when the fighting took place in France. Just as painfully, the recent war continued to be the touchstone for domestic politics. For most Americans in the 1870s, to think about politics was to think about the unresolved issues of the Civil War; quickly enough, to think about the Paris Commune also became a way to think about those issues. Indeed, like all analogies, the Franco-American comparison was two-sided and reciprocal: even when the Civil War was being used to make sense of the Commune, the Commune itself was being incorporated into the ongoing debate about the meaning of the Civil War.[3]

In time, Americans from all parts of the country and all circles of political life discovered that the Commune was "good to think with." At best the Paris Commune could broaden their understanding of the Civil War while offering new perspectives on sectionalism, party politics, and class conflict. At worst it provided an excuse for demolishing Reconstruction. Too often, Americans discovered that the Commune made a useful ideological weapon—although, to their dismay, they also frequently discovered that the weapon had two edges. But always the comparisons came first.

Comparisons between events in France and events in the United States began early in the Franco-Prussian War. Leaving aside the tangled dynastic dispute that became a casus belli, the war between France and Germany was a straightforward fight, perfectly suited to the news-gathering skills of the recent Civil War. The movement of large armies and the clash of arms were all too familiar. Men who had been at Bull Run or Shiloh had little trouble describing Woerth and Sedan; from the outside, the German siege of Paris looked just like the siege of Richmond six years earlier. In many cases the same correspondents covered both wars. As a result, except for the datelines and place-names, dispatches filed from the European battle-front were often indistinguishable from Civil War dispatches filed a decade before.[4]

General Adam Badeau, a once and future aide to Ulysses S. Grant, was an eager eyewitness to the European war. His professional view was that "it need[ed] no peculiarly close or skillful observation to detect the points in which the two greatest wars of the last half-century bear a marked resemblance."[5] George Templeton Strong, the patrician New York lawyer, demurred, writing in his diary that "no such question" divided the Europeans "as that which stirred up the New Yorker against the Charlestonian ten years ago."[6] But clearly it was Badeau's opinion of military equivalence that prevailed, and on this level the war was simple for Americans to write about and easy for them to understand.

If describing the Franco-Prussian War was easy, so was picking sides: it simply depended on how you remembered the Civil War.[7] President Grant, for example, remembered that bigger armies tend to win battles. Thus, despite the inflated military reputation of France, he was on the side of the heavier (Prussian) battalions; although the United States was officially a neutral power, the public and private statements flowing from his administration displayed a clear preference for German arms. In Congress, too, the news of war was met by scattered applause in favor of Germany.[8] Outside Washington, however, both sides had their champions.

The best survey of American reactions to the Franco-Prussian War is contained in John Gazley's dated but valuable study, *American Opinion of German Unification, 1848–1871* (New York, 1926). After consulting hundreds of newspapers and other sources, Gazley outlined the following generalizations:[9]

First, as President Grant noted at the time, "every unreconstructed rebel sympathize[d] with France, without exception." Grant was largely correct: most ex-Confederates were on the French side, because they recalled that Napoleon III's France had been on their side during the Civil War while most German-Americans fought for the North. At the same time, Southrons drew an explicit analogy between Prussian hegemony over the Germans and Northern hegemony over Americans. "By force or fraud," proclaimed the *Richmond Whig,* the government of Prussia (read: "the North") "has deprived other states of their liberties. Hanover, Sleswick [*sic*], Nassau, [etc.] . . . have been completely absorbed while Baden, Bavaria, and the rest of the Southern states [read: "the Southern states"] are threatened with speedy extinction." There was also a peculiar romantic tradition in which the white men of the South imagined themselves to be the racial descendants of ancient Celts; this only served to reinforce their sympathies in a war that pitted good Gallic patriots against invading Teutonic hordes, in a sadly familiar pattern.[10]

Second, Irish Americans, the nation's largest ethnic group, also sided with France. In August, the New York Fenians (whose former allies included both Gustave Cluseret and George Francis Train) formed a "liberal committee" to support the French cause, which sponsored a rally on September 3. At this rally they loudly declared that France was the last, best hope for European republicanism, despite the current Empire; furthermore, France was a longtime friend of the Irish and America's first ally, while Germans (and "above all, the Hessians") had ever been enemies of America, fair Ireland, and republicanism itself.[11] Yet the most important factor in their support of France was that the French, like the Irish, hated England. Also, Irish Catholics were not about to support Protestant Prussia over Catholic France, especially when they were having problems with their own Protestant enemies here in the United States.[12]

Third, as Senator Carl Schurz, the leading German American in the Republican party, indignantly noted, most Democrats had also "taken the side in the present war for France." The main reason was simple: in 1870, Irishmen and Southerners were more important Democratic constituencies than were German Americans. At the same time, Democratic party leaders thought they saw a disturbing similarity between German militarism and the Republican policy of military Reconstruction. In any case, they were happy to adopt a position contrary to Grant's.[13]

Finally, the vast majority of Republicans and Northern independents took the side of Prussia. Parke Godwin, the New York editor, was only voicing a sectional bias when he wrote in the middle of the war that "with few and inconsiderable exceptions, the American people have sympathized entirely with the Germans."[14] The broad sympathy for Germany was the flip side of the deep antipathy many Americans felt for Napoleon III. As Mary C. Putnam had learned for herself in Paris, an empire built on a coup d'état was fundamentally obnoxious to American sentiments. Parke Godwin expressed the same sentiment when he wrote that "every sincere lover of liberty sees in the Emperor of the French the most deadly enemy that genuine freedom has."[15] On a less abstract level, there was also the fact that Napoleon III had supported the Confederate States and had tried to establish a puppet regime in the neighboring republic of Mexico. These adventures were hardly calculated to gain the Empire any friends in the North. At best, said one Republican orator, they demonstrated how completely the French emperor "has forgotten the traditions of his [own] nation."[16] Under different circumstances, the Franco-American co-tradition would have led more Americans to support the French cause. But the fresh memory of Napoleon's role in the Civil War removed potential support for France while smoothing over the uncomfortable fact that Prussia, too, was a despotic imperial regime.

During the Franco-Prussian War, Republicans and especially their German American supporters routinely portrayed the Second Empire as an aggressor. Apart from this negative view of France they also maintained a positive conception of Germany as a nation struggling to achieve political unity, in much the same way that the United States had struggled through the Civil War to restore its own national unity. Starting with the Austro-Prussian War in 1866, American observers began to note a certain similarity between the internal consolidations of Germany and America. The *New York Times*, still flushed with postbellum success in 1866, had opined that "national unity is intrinsically a noble idea, and, wherever you find it, it appeals to all generous sympathies—unity in America; unity in Italy; unity in Germany." Four years later, America's chief diplomat in Berlin was still convinced that "our victory [in the Civil War had] . . . sowed the seeds of the regeneration of Europe" by establishing a model for Germans to follow. While many Northern Republicans seemed to agree, Democrats and Southerners were justifiably skeptical of a German unity that came at the price of Prussian invasions and an autocratic central government.[17]

Finally, an important caveat: significant as they were, none of these generalizations about America and the Franco-Prussian War can be taken as absolutes. Individual opinions depended on many factors, and no single factor was sufficient to predict a given American's viewpoint. As one historian of the subject has warned, "the great majority of Americans were not governed purely by party affiliations in this case, but exercised their judgment independently, on the basis of available information."[18] If anything, this warning carries more weight in the case of the Commune, where events were more complex and the available information less clear. Still, the American response to the Franco-Prussian War well shows how foreign events could be drawn into the web of domestic politics and even reinforce prevailing sectional and party alignments in the process. At the same time, the ease with which Americans assimilated the Franco-Prussian War into postbellum politics made it easier—and perhaps more imperative—to assimilate the Commune as well.

The Civil War, the Franco-Prussian War, and the Paris Commune each posed the question of republicanism in its starkest form: Shall "the people" be sovereign? The global expansion of popular government, or at least an attempt to expand its blessings, was central to the age of democratic civil wars.[19] In their own separate ways, Abraham Lincoln and Gustave Cluseret both knew this; they both understood that a second American Revolution was being fought to secure the blessings of republican government for all people everywhere. Ordinary Americans understood this too. Like Cluseret, some even saw the disparate events in America and France as part of the same world-historical trend toward popular government.[20] But defining what "popular" (much less "republican") government required proved elusive, as the bitter politics of Reconstruction showed. Reconstruction was a struggle to define what it meant to be a republic, and to decide who was fit to participate in such a polity; in short, it was a struggle to define Lincoln's "new birth of freedom."[21] Reconstruction both shaped and was shaped by American views of the new republic in France.

Compared to the military cheerleading that greeted the Franco-Prussian War, the declaration of a new French republic evoked a more nuanced reaction in the United States. Americans in Paris welcomed the new regime with noisy enthusiasm, with only a few skeptics and nay-sayers to sour the chorus of approving voices. At home there was also enthusiasm, but it was much more qualified. In New York the mayor ordered City Hall to be decked with tricolored bunting in France's honor, and joyful Franco-Americans in St. Louis and New Orleans held public rallies to support the new regime. Another New Yorker crowed, "The young Republic was born without an American enemy, and she will die (may God forbid!) with an American benediction . . . [The press] all joined voices in one warm VIVE LA RÉPUBLIQUE!"[22] Elsewhere, however, the public acclaim that had marked the coming of the Second French Republic in 1848 (or even the first Republic in 1792) was notably absent.[23]

In fact, there was a general wariness toward the new republic that often had little to do with the French regime itself, but that nonetheless tempered the traditional American passion for popular government abroad. Some, like Radical Republican Charles Sumner, were still fired by that old passion; he quickly announced that "a great hour for Humanity sounded when the Republic was proclaimed."[24] President Grant, who did not often agree with Sumner on matters of foreign policy, did in this case and was soon ordering his friend Washburne to recognize the new government in Paris. Three months later, in his annual message to Congress, Grant expanded on the theme of world-historical republicanism: "The reestablishment in France of a system of government disconnected with the dynastic traditions of Europe, appeared to be a proper subject for the felicitations of Americans. Should the present struggle result in attaching the hearts of the French to our simpler forms of representative government, it will be a subject of still further satisfaction to our people." Yet Elihu Washburne's own brother, a Republican congressman from Wisconsin, declared in response to Grant's message that "We hardly know here [in Washington] what to think about the great conflict."[25]

Representative Washburn (as he preferred to spell the family name) had a right to be confused. To begin with, the French Republic was fast becoming a political football between the two American parties. Most Republicans, Radical or otherwise, followed Grant and Sumner in their early embrace of the new government. After all, the target of their animosity in the current European war was the French Empire, not the French people. They also remembered, though sometimes dimly, that their party had been founded on the proposition that democracy is better than despotism. And while there was still sympathy for the German project of national unification, it was matched by a growing suspicion that Prussia was "pursuing a criminal career of conquest, seeking, as far as possible, to obliterate France." In John Gazley's nice phrase, many Republicans now saw the "positions of the 'Hohenzollern lamb' and the 'French wolf' . . . [as] almost completely reversed."[26] This reversal was clearly reflected in a letter that Elihu Washburne received from a close Republican ally, the Appraiser of the Port of New York: "When this French Prussian war [*sic*] first commenced public sentiment was strong on the side of the Prussians. Napoleon you know has not been in favour since our rebellion, and the success of the Prussians at first was hailed with delight and very few regretted the fall of the Emperor, but King William must not crowd Republican France too far and expect that feeling to continue."[27]

Unfortunately, loyal party men like the appraiser found it difficult to maintain such broad sympathy for the French Republic because of the inconvenient fact that Democrats and Republicans now inadvertently shared the same opinion of France. The Democratic press was openly applauding Grant's decision to recognize the French Republic. Even the Irish Catholics, most steadfast of Democrats and usually Grant's most implacable foes, had begun to praise him warmly. Support from such unlikely places made Republicans nervous, but it made German Americans, who were already upset at the President's mild display of sympathy for France, positively furious. According to one pro-French observer, the German American response was to "shamelessly lay down conditions" to the leaders of the Republican party: either back away from an active endorsement of the French Republic, or risk losing an important bloc of ethnic voters. Caught thus between principles and politics, most party members quickly withdrew from their hasty embrace of the French Republic; as the same observer put it, "in order to preserve . . . [German American] support, the radical Yankees abandoned poor France to her fate."[28]

Electioneering was one thing, but some "radical Yankees" had also begun to attack the legitimacy of the French regime as a republic. This repudiation can be traced not to some narrow calculation of political advantage, but to growing doubts about the inherent desirability of popular government. During the sectional crisis and Civil War, most of these doubts had remained submerged, because "theories and methods of government were lost sight of in the slavery conflict." But Reconstruction brought them to the surface, as weary Northerners found themselves "face to face with a pure democracy from one end of the country to another"; they were not heartened by what they saw.[29] As Jonathan Baxter Harrison ruefully noted in 1879, "Thirty or forty years ago it was considered the rankest heresy to doubt that a government based on universal suffrage was the wisest and best that could be devised . . . Such is not now the case . . . To express the case in a few words, there is a considerable body of intelligent and patriotic men in the United States who fear and distrust their sovereign [the people]."[30]

In fact, a mistrust of popular government in all its forms had been spreading for years among the genteel elite of the late nineteenth century—the so-called "Best Men," many of whom had once been active antislavery Republicans.[31] Evidence of their mistrust is easy to find in the 1870s, starting with the ruins of the Fourteenth and Fifteenth Amendments, but also including the rejection of women's suffrage, the Northern acquiescence to Southern "home rule," urban reforms designed to limit local autonomy, voting reforms designed to limit the franchise, and the entire Liberal Republican movement. The same mistrust tempered enthusiasm for the French Republic. Conversely, in the midst of Reconstruction the French Republic and later the Commune became useful ways to focus and excuse the ideological shift away from popular government.

This dynamic began with a curt denial that France could even be called a "republic," regardless of what the French thought about it. Thus, according to the venerable abolitionist (and prominent Grant supporter) Lydia Maria Child, "Wendell Phillips, and others [like him], are blinded by the name of a Republic; and it is a mere *name*."[32] E. L. Godkin of the *Nation*, whose influential journal stood at the forefront of "liberal reform," argued much the same thing: "The wild exultation which followed the proclamation of the Republic at Paris was really due to the secret belief that there was some magic in the name . . . The mania, too, as might have been expected, crossed the Atlantic, and found plenty of victims here."[33] In a series of editorials that stretched into 1871, *Harper's Weekly* also denounced the charisma that seemed to adhere to the word "republic." But editor George William Curtis went a step further, declaring that France could not be considered a legitimate republic because "it [was] not yet evident that . . . [the Republic was] really the choice of the French people." Paris alone had declared the new regime, while "the preference of rural France, and of the middle class in the cities, is monarchical. To them the Republic is not *démocratique* [i.e., political] only, it is *sociale;* and that, in their judgment, is sheer anarchy."[34]

Curtis's argument gained new force with the advent of the Paris Commune, which was clearly not the preferred government of most French citizens. His argument also had serious implications for domestic politics. The Radical wing of the Republican party had dominated Congress since 1867, arrogating to itself the power to decide when Southern states became "republics," often without regard to local preferences or conditions. Yet now Curtis and others from the moderate wing of the party were using the French example to highlight an uncomfortable fact: calling a regime a "republic" did not make it so. Radical Republicans already knew this; indeed, they had recently used this fact to invalidate Redeemer governments in the South.[35] Following their lead, then, moderates could have used the supposedly mislabeled French Republic to argue that the post-Confederate South still needed fundamental alterations before it became truly "republican." Instead, their treatment of French republicanism indicated a withdrawal from the revolutionary possibilities of the postbellum order and a widening split within the party. Consider Child's attack on her old ally Phillips for supporting a foreign revolution, or Curtis's tacit agreement with reactionaries in France that social change meant "sheer anarchy"; neither was a promising sign for Radical Reconstruction, whose end would be hastened by association with the Paris Commune.[36]

In 1873, one newspaper recalled that the "atrocities of the Commune made . . . popular government . . . for a while distasteful to conservative men."[37] But if Jonathan Baxter Harrison was right, popular government had become distasteful to them before the Commune. Nonetheless, the Commune provided Americans across the political spectrum with a timely opportunity to reconsider the most important element of popular government: the people. Contra the trend that Harrison reported, most Americans remained instinctive democrats. Yet, despite their better instincts, many accepted the assertion that French people were incapable of popular government as a sufficient explanation for the Commune. This explanation was not shaped by events in Paris but rather by growing doubts about the innate capacity of certain domestic groups to participate in the American republic—women and former slaves in particular. Not surprisingly, doubts about the Parisians helped to reinforce these domestic doubts in turn.

Conservative Americans had always harbored a certain distrust of the French capacity for self-rule, which they usually combined with a self-righteous disdain. Indeed, they had been using the "three national traits" of France (i.e., fickleness, sexual license, and military pride) to explain and condemn Parisian unrest since at least the 1790s.[38] This traditional sense of Gallic unfitness was an important component of the general wariness that greeted the new French Republic in 1870. As *Scribner's Monthly* scornfully explained, "there is not enough of intelligence, principle, and virtue in France to sustain a republic." *Harper's Weekly* agreed: "Nothing so shows the fitness of a nation for self-government so distinctly as its will and capacity to restrain itself"; unfortunately, it noted, the people of France just did not seem to possess "the character and heroism which are essential in the establishment of a republic."[39]

Supporters of the Third Republic tried to repulse these assaults, but attacks on the French capacity for self-government continued to mount, especially during the Commune. Cluseret, of course, thought that the Paris Commune was a natural extension of American republicanism, as exemplified in the Civil War. Some of his Yankee peers, such as Wendell Phillips, Benjamin Butler, and Theodore Tilton, agreed. According to the controversial Butler, "the Commune of Paris were [*sic*] fighting for the right of local self-government, and that . . . principle embodies all republican institutions . . . I might [even] have said that the Commune had the example of our fathers as a precedent."[40] For Tilton, prominent editor of the New York *Golden Age,* the Commune *was* "republicanism, and Americans ought everywhere to honor it. The Commune offered to France what the Republic [under Thiers] refused it—namely, local self-government . . . It was the Commune, not the Republic, that should have triumphed."[41] One of Tilton's admirers even claimed that "the mass of the French people (especially of the cities and more especially the Communists) are *more* capable of self-government, more economical, more industrious, and more honest and conscientious, and more chaste than the mass of the American people."[42] But this view of the Commune was not accepted by most Americans.

Instead, the same moderate Republicans who were then parting with

Phillips et al. on the wisdom of Radical Reconstruction launched a broad attack against the political capacity of the Communards. Its main thrusts were a denial of the French Republic's legitimacy, as described above, plus a mounting wariness of popular government everywhere. Significantly, political elites from the Democratic party and the South also joined the assault. In a typical foray, the *San Francisco Morning Bulletin* announced that the Commune "was destroying genuine republicanism and individual liberty."[43] Worse yet, Paris was turning its back on the salutary example of the United States. Deploying a homey metaphor, the *New Orleans Picayune,* a leading Democratic paper, complained that "the seed corn of American republican ideas" was being blighted by the Commune. Its bitter Republican rival, the *New York Times,* agreed: "For many years to come the crimes of the Parisian socialistic Democracy will be charged upon liberty, and the first demands of . . . [the people] will be confused with the wild ideas and savage crimes of the French Communists."[44] Still another Republican journal, the *New York Evening Post,* reinforced the entire line of attack against the Commune: "The condition of affairs in Paris . . . is well calculated to inspire the well-wishers of a French republic and the lovers of law and order with the liveliest apprehensions . . . [In] looking for the cause of this political and social demoralization of the French we are driven to the old rationale of the decay of private virtue."[45]

In the face of this onslaught the Commune also acquired allies, notably *Frank Leslie's Illustrated Newspaper.* In a strongly worded counterattack, the popular weekly denounced the vigorous criticism of Paris as a city unprepared for democracy as "part of the tactics of the enemies of popular rights, self-government, and Republican institutions throughout the world." These enemies did not care about the actual events in Paris; instead, the Commune was being "made a scarecrow for the timid, and a pretext for persecutions and violent and irresponsible repression of liberal sentiments everywhere in Europe . . . [and even] here, in the United States."[46] Although *Leslie's Illustrated* should have swept the field with this perceptive observation, the "enemies of popular rights" were more powerful. In part, this was because they had the loudest voices in the dominant political culture (the most money, the best political connections, the largest audiences). But their strength also lay in the ability to ask and answer a compelling question—What was wrong with Paris?—while confronting authentic fears about the changing shape of the American polity. The result was another series of analogies between the United States and the Commune.

What was wrong with Paris? According to this view, the same thing that was "wrong" with the foreign-born masses in American cities, with female voters, and especially with former slaves when they tried to become active members of the polity. Parisians, this argument began, were "poorly prepared to govern themselves."[47] "It has taken all of a thousand years to educate England and America to the point of self-government," while poor France (and especially Paris) was still ignorant, priest-ridden, and immoral—not just unschooled in the ways of popular government, but perhaps unteachable.[48] Not surprisingly, the foreign element in American cities (especially the Irish) was just as "brutalized" and ignorant as the Communards, "transplanting their bigotry and incapacity for self-government from the Old World."[49] Native-born women, though neither brutalized nor ignorant, also lacked "the austere education of facts" that turned their sons and husbands into virtuous electors. As a result, distaff dabbling in politics was likely to make America more unruly, more licentious, and more fickle—in short, more like the Paris Commune.[50] Yet the most Commune-like threat to the nation, in this elitist view, came from the former slaves.

From the start, Radical Republicans had hoped that freedmen were capable of democratic citizenship, and many agreed with Cluseret that experience in the militia and tenure on the land would turn them into virtuous yeomen. In the extended debate on Negro suffrage in 1866–1867, even moderate Republicans like Senator Frederick T. Frelinghuysen of New Jersey argued that "the ballot itself is a great education" and would serve to encourage and inspire the black race; at the very least, they thought that Negro suffrage was necessary to secure the fruits of Northern victory.[51] Democrats responded that it was "utterly impossible [to maintain] a free government, or free institutions, . . . [with] ignorant and degraded races like the negro." According to one midwestern Democrat, the white race was the only one "in the history of the world . . . [to] have shown any capacity for self-government," and Southern whites were not about to disagree.[52]

As the disappointing results of Reconstruction became clearer, "the doctrine of the immediate fitness of the Negro for all the rights of citizenship came more and more to be questioned, and the way was rapidly being prepared for *laissez faire* in the South." By 1871 many moderates, including Republicans, had started to agree with the Democrats that African Americans were innately incapable of democracy.[53] Montgomery Blair, a border-state Democrat who served as Lincoln's Postmaster General, spoke for moderates in both parties and sections when he called for the disfranchisement of the enslaved people whom Lincoln had freed. "The negro," claimed Blair in the late 1870s, "is not [of] a self-governing nature"; nor could he be taught a self-governing nature. "Hence to incorporate him in our system is to subvert it. His nominal enfranchisement is but a mode of disfranchising the white man."[54] The *Nation*'s editor agreed, and taking the argument one step further, Godkin railed against the "Socialism in South Carolina" that came from allowing incompetent black men to govern and vote. Finally, at the end of one of his sharp polemics against Radical Reconstruction, he offered what must have seemed like a clincher: when it came to political incapacity, South Carolina was just as bad as "Boss" Tweed's New York with its ignorant foreign-born masses—or even, he hinted, as bad as the Paris Commune.[55]

Godkin's comparison of the Commune and Reconstruction was neither isolated nor random. If the main theme for Godkin and his like was "the people's" incapacity for republican government, then attacks on Communards, on domestic women's suffrage, on immigrants and freedmen, were simply variations on the same theme. The domestic theme and the foreign theme weaved in counterpoint, and both were amplified in the process. Yet in this debate on republican capacity, comparisons of Communards and immigrants, or of the Commune and the American woman's movement, were usually implicit, or else absorbed into a larger explanatory pattern: the dual identification of the Commune as something both foreign to and imminent in America. Not so with the comparison of the Commune and freedmen. Indeed, this last comparison, which Godkin merely implied, only becomes clearer in the light of explicit analogies between the Commune and the American Civil War.

One of the first, and still one of the best, analyses of the Paris Commune was produced by Karl Marx in 1871. He called his work *The Civil War in France*. As he sat down to write, his thoughts may well have turned back to the recent Civil War in America. After all, he and Friedrich Engels had closely followed the American struggle, and both had written about it extensively. In 1865, Marx even drafted a letter to Abraham Lincoln on behalf of the First International in which he praised Lincoln as "a single-minded son of the working class," struggling for the cause of workers everywhere.[56] In ways very different from Lincoln or even Cluseret, Marx perceived the Civil War in a world-historical context. Marx was also quick to recognize a parallel between the French and American civil wars. In one early draft of *The Civil War in France* he noted that "Southerners fought for the slavery of labour and the territorial secession from the United States. Paris fought for the emancipation of labour and the secession from power of Thiers state parasites, of the would-be slaveholders of France!"[57] Cluseret had recognized the same parallel from the start. But Americans were slower—or perhaps just reluctant—to offer the same comparison.

Not that Americans were slow to use the language of the Civil War to describe the Commune. Consider what they did with Marx's study of the events in France. Although it first appeared in the United States in pamphlet form as *Defence of the Paris Commune* (Washington, 1871), it was soon reprinted in various places under Marx's original title. Long before then, however, the title had become commonplace. Americans didn't need to wait for a German socialist to tell them what to call a fraternal conflict, because they had their own hard-earned vocabulary. Indeed, from the start American headline-writers had been calling the Commune the "Civil War in France" and the "Civil War in Paris," or less often the "French Insurrection" or the "European Rebellion"—all labels that harked back to the bloody days of 1861–1865.

Sometimes the War Between the States was evoked subtly. One midwesterner, for example, wrote in a letter to the *Cleveland Leader,* "We cannot sympathize with the communists," yet he had to admit that civil war in France was the inevitable result of the "hate that comes in a house divided against itself." In the South, the Paris rebellion was sometimes referred to as "the existing 'unpleasantness,'" in just the same way that genteel Southerners were beginning to call their own rebellion "the late unpleasantness." The *New York Herald,* however, was hardly being genteel when it reverted to antebellum malediction to denounce the leading Communards as "Fire-Eater[s]."[58]

Broad comparisons between the Commune and the Confederate South should have been doubly attractive to partisan Northerners. Even on a superficial level, like the *Herald*'s swipe at Fire-Eaters, the analogy was a way to explain the Commune while waving the bloody shirt. Yet not every Yankee was keen on it; indeed, Northerners were reluctant to explore the analogy's domestic implications, even when they acknowledged that such a comparison was plausible. In the words of one leading Republican organ, "no two nations afford wider contrasts or more of them than the United States during our war against secession, and France during her struggle against the Commune."[59] Less dismissive, but just as cautious, was William

Seward's version of the Civil War analogy. Lincoln's former secretary of state happened to be traveling through Europe just after the Commune. Reporters were naturally eager to know what he thought about French affairs. As one of them noted, the old Republican was "amply able to judge and discuss civil war"; indeed, he probably knew more about the political aspects of the recent American conflict than any man alive. Perhaps feeling chastened by that knowledge, Seward offered the Northern press only a modest commentary on the French civil war, quietly suggesting that "if the [American] parties had been more equally divided, and if sagacity and moderation had not been at the helm, who knows but that we, too, might have had our Commune?" Beyond that, he refused to speculate on other Franco-American comparisons.[60]

The *New York Times,* lacking either Seward's modesty or the *Post*'s complacency, refused to dismiss the Civil War analogy out of hand. Instead, in a tortured twist of logic, the *Times* introduced the comparison only to deny its salience. The occasion was an English journalist's assertion that the Commune was simply an act of secession, with "Paris separating from France, [just] as the Southern States wished to separate from the Northern in America." The *Times* strongly disagreed. Secession, it argued, "scarcely explains the matter," because the "[Parisian] Reds want not to separate from France, but to govern France."[61] For years, the paper had been denouncing the South on the very same terms that it now used to denounce the "Reds," as rebels who wanted to control the nation rather than leave it. Thus, even in the process of overtly rejecting the Civil War analogy, the *Times* seemed covertly to embrace it.

Perhaps unwittingly, the *Times* had stumbled upon some of the tensions inherent in this sort of political analogy. Once it mentioned a possible parallel between the two civil wars, it became impossible to un-mention or even to ignore it. As long as the Commune remained a current event, it evoked comparisons with the Civil War and Reconstruction. In a larger sense, to offer any comparison between the Paris Commune and conditions in America made it difficult to forestall any other comparison, no matter how unintended or undesirable. To say that the Commune was somehow like America made it difficult to deny that America was also like the Commune. This was a problem in 1871, and became even more of a problem as the 1870s wore on.

Most Republicans who used the Civil War analogy to explain the Commune while scoring points against Southern and Democratic opponents were not concerned about the tensions within the analogy. For Henry C.

Bowen, editor of the *Independent,* it was enough to say that the "proper and fit synonym" for the self-styled *fédérés* of the Commune was "Confederates," as if that explained everything; in each case, a militant minority had tried to "subjugate" the proper majority.[62] Yet Bowen was keen to elaborate, to compare the Commune to the Civil War and its painful aftermath. In his very first editorial on the Paris Commune, Bowen described it as a "French Ku-Klux." The choice of terms was significant, for like many other Northerners, Bowen saw the Ku Klux Klan as the ultimate symbol of anarchy and arrogance in the unrepentant Confederacy—especially in 1870 and early 1871, when Congress passed a series of enforcement acts to curb Klan violence in the South. In Bowen's editorial the contemporaneous Commune became an easy way to emphasize the Klan's horrors.

He began, like Godkin and others, with the elitist observation that France was "incapable of settled government." He noted, moreover, that any observer's "first impulse [was] to draw a parallel" between the Commune and the French Revolution. Yet he insisted that "we can find a nearer parallel":

> The Reign of Terror has come back to Paris; but have we had no reign of terror in our own South? Three or four generals [*sic*] have been brutally murdered there. Have we had no civil and military officers, no mayors, no president murdered since the Rebellion? The only excuse offered for France pleads her exasperation because a better nation [i.e., Germany] has conquered her. Is not the spirit of the Lost Cause nursing the same exasperation in our own Southern States[?]

For his own part, Bowen was convinced that the parallels between France and America were significant, "if not the most obvious." With the timely return of terrorism to Paris, he urged his Northern readers to "see an American reflection in a French glass" (though he was using an American mirror himself to look at France). Both France and the South, he explained, had recently shed their "barbaric institutions" (that is, the Empire and slavery); both were still saddled with "dense ignorance"; both were trying to deny the obvious benefits of conquest by a "superior civilization"; and both displayed a "local pride and contemptuous disregard for others." In short, neither Paris nor the South was ready for self-government. The parallel had a moral, too: the armed strength of the national government was necessary to "put down the Ku-Klux principle in Mississippi and Paris."[63]

Still other Republicans, secure in the dubious assumption that blame for the Civil War should rest squarely on Southern shoulders, tried to use the civil war in France to remind the South of its culpability. This was a tactic that party members in both sections could use. Julia Ward Howe, whose "Battle Hymn of the Republic" was still a Republican rallying cry, offered a typical Northern assessment. "No matter what advantage of reason the *Commune* may have had over the Versailles Government," she noted in 1871, "the *Commune* committed a civil crime in attempting military enforcement of its political opinions. Such was the crime which our South committed and which we resisted as one defends one's own life." The South, she continued, "differed from us and [was] determined to coerce us forcibly," and in the end received the same deserved punishment as Paris after the Commune: reduction to a "weltering mass of ruin and corruption."[64] In Mississippi, meanwhile, the Radical Republican governor bluntly converted Howe's description of just retribution into a threat. In the midst of the 1871 election campaign, which was marked by intense Klan violence, an exasperated James L. Alcorn declared that Southerners had "surrendered all rights of citizenship" as soon as they began the Civil War. Thus, he reminded his opponents, the proper punishment afterwards should have been death by the sword or at "guillotine[s] . . . moved by steam." He added that "no voice in all the world would have been raised in your behalf," and for proof he told them to "look at the treatment of the commune by the French government. The world endorses that, and would have endorsed similar treatment . . . [by] ourselves." In 1865, of course, the victorious Northern Republicans had shown forbearance; in 1871, in the wake of the Ku Klux Klan, Governor Alcorn was suggesting that mercy might yet have its limits.[65]

Party propagandists continued to wave this bloody-shirt version of the Commune for a surprisingly long time. As late as the 1876 presidential campaign, one Republican organ contained an article comparing "The Slaveholders' War and the Paris Commune." Like Julia Ward Howe's early commentary, the article began with an almost sympathetic view of the French civil war, recalling that "however mistaken the means, the leaders' object [in Paris] was not a blind striking at order, but rather, an effort to remove the causes of chronic disorder by restoring self-government and breaking down an autocratic centralization." But this was scarcely an attempt to praise the Commune, or even to understand it. Sympathetic aspects of the Commune were only introduced to make Southern Democrats seem worse by comparison, and to undermine the Southerners' own claim of "restoring self-government." The writer explained that even to compare the "Commune rebellion" with the "civil war started by our slaveholders" would be "an insult to the Paris Communists." For unlike the Paris Commune, the "Democratic rebellion . . . was inaugurated to make slavery permanent, to insure the continuance of poverty as a social system and political fact; to prepare the way for the perpetuation of an oligarchy by the destruction of free government and the Union based thereon." The worst thing about it, he concluded, was that guilty Confederates went unpunished for their part in the rebellion. A decade later, Americans even "allow[ed] statues in honor of rebel generals to be erected . . . [and let] Southern rebels rule the House of Representatives"; by comparison, France had punished the guilty *and* the innocent in Paris, at the very least removing the latter's political rights. The article ended with a veiled threat, à la Alcorn, that something similar could still happen in America.[66]

But few Republicans, North or South, were quite so vehement in pursuing the Civil War analogy, either in 1871 or later. In fact, the most penetrating attempt to compare the Commune with the Confederacy did not even flow from a Republican pen; it appeared in a leading Democratic newspaper, the *New York World*. Although the *World* was a loyal party organ, its view of the Commune was framed by the ambivalent yet high-minded aspirations of its publisher and editor, Manton Marble. In the words of his best biographer, Marble was a "genteel partisan," trying to balance the dictates of party against those of his conscience. For example, even though the *World* was financed by the national Democratic party and generally cleaved to its pro-Southern politics, Marble refused to forgive individual Southerners for starting the Civil War.[67] Even though the *World* represented the pro-business, hard-money Democrats of New York City, Marble adopted a sympathetic stance towards workingmen.[68] And even though the *World,* like most Democratic papers, supported the French Republic in the Franco-Prussian War, Marble went much further, displaying an unfashionable measure of sympathy for the Paris Commune.[69]

With events in Paris barely a week old, the *World* began to explicate the Commune in terms of domestic politics. Like Bowen at the *Independent,* Marble first used the Commune as a metaphor for illegitimate force— though for Democrats this meant Reconstruction, not the Confederacy or the Klan. Thus, when President Grant used Federal troops to prop up the "bastard [Republican] state government" in South Carolina in March 1871, the *World* denounced it as an unwarranted use of centralized power for partisan gain. The Republicans, Marble complained, only wanted "to create a state of things in the South favorable to the success of the[ir] . . . party in the Presidential election." And such a "design [was] worthy of . . . the Paris 'Reds,'" who likewise seemed eager to force their intentions on an unwilling nation.[70]

By the end of the Commune, however, Marble had turned the Franco-American parallel around. No longer was it a case of the Republican administration being as bad as Paris revolutionaries; instead, the Communards began to look *better* than the homegrown Republicans. Marble even offered a twist on the argument that French people were incapable of republican government. "Americans," he conceded, "have been educated in the principles and invited to the practice of liberal thought and of political freedom for many generations," while Parisians had to suffer "under a persistent system of bureaucracy." Nonetheless, "the stupid outrages just perpetrated upon [the Vendôme Column] . . . were more than paralleled during the dark days of our civil war, and are doubtless more than paralleled still in certain regions of our country, by the 'ultra loyal' of our own race."[71] In other words, Communards might be ignorant vandals, but American Republicans were positively vicious, because as Americans they ought to know better.

On June 1, 1871, Marble's evolving comparison between the Commune and Reconstruction was captured in a *World* editorial entitled "Communists and Secessionists." His theme was the abiding American one of states' rights. The main similarity between the French and American civil wars was their common emphasis on issues of local autonomy, as historian Jean T. Joughin noted in a passage cited in Chapter 1. As she put it, "the Confederacy represented an obsolescent concept of the relationship between the state and the federal government, . . . [while] the Paris Commune had an antique view of the role of the municipality vis-à-vis the national government."[72] Yet many American observers in Paris, like Washburne and Fetridge, tried to deny the similarity. Back at home, and thus closer to the daily politics of Reconstruction, Manton Marble faced the subject more squarely.[73]

"There is," he began, a "similarity in one point between the secessionists of this country under Jefferson Davis and the communists of Paris under their hydra-headed leadership. Both misused, disgraced, and finally desecrated a good idea." The good idea was that states had rights. But rights also implied duties, and when they conveniently forgot that fact the "Southern nullifiers perverted beyond recognition . . . [the noble ideas] of

Jefferson, Madison, and Sam Adams." Secessionists "ignored all the obligations of duty to the nation and unconstitutionally exaggerated the rights of the States." Similarly, "the Paris communists had hold of one end of a good idea, which was enlarged communal self-government; but, like the Southern secessionists, they so mistook and misapplied it that ruin came on them and whatever of good underlay their movement." Marble conceded that, like the people of the prewar South, the people of Paris had legitimate complaints against the central government—so many, indeed, that an "irrepressible conflict" had arisen between Paris and the rest of France. It was thus "very easy to see that the municipal idea of the Paris communists had much of justice in it." In both America and France, then, the "problem to be worked out, patiently and thoughtfully, was how to secure sufficient . . . aggregate strength for national purposes and [still] preserve communal self-government." Unfortunately, the impatient Parisians had opted for a revolution instead, probably destroying their chances for self-government in the process.

Despite the horrors of the Civil War, Marble still thought that Americans were luckier when it came to states' rights. Southern secessionists might have strayed, even been foolish, but at least "our forefathers frame[d] a Federal government which . . . justly reconciled national power with community independence." By contrast, there was nothing *but* national power in France. Before 1870 the Empire had dominated the entire political life of the nation, and now the new government was attempting to do the same. Marble thought this contrast helped explain the Commune, while providing a timely lesson for Americans. "The spectacle of the awful struggle around . . . Paris," he warned, "should nerve us to more vigorous efforts to avoid the vicious state of things which the empire [and now Thiers] had created in France, and to that end prevent completion of the chain of centralization which the Grant Republicans are forging." For Manton Marble, a strong-willed Democrat, the Commune was not nearly as bad as the type of centralizing regime that made civil wars necessary—or reconstructions so painful and repressive. By contrast, President Grant's loyal supporter, Henry Bowen, drew an entirely different lesson from the Commune: that a strong central government was the only way to *prevent* pain and repression in the South. From different domestic politics came different meanings for the Commune.

Within the space of a few months, Manton Marble managed to turn full circle from his first description of the Paris Commune as an example of brute, misguided force. In the process, he forged a version of the Civil War analogy that differed quite markedly from the Republicans'. Yet there was still another aspect to Marble's comparison of the civil wars. As a Democrat, he attempted to fit the pieces of the Commune into a coherent restatement of party ideology while rendering the foreign event in familiar American terms. As a Northerner, he also tried to make the Commune fit with his guiding ideas about section. Of course, party and sectional ideologies were closely intertwined in the era of Reconstruction, yet it is important to disentangle them as much as possible—especially in a case like Marble's, when sectional loyalties chafed against party orthodoxy.

The friction was apparent in the final lesson that Marble derived from the Paris Commune: that Jefferson Davis (and other ex-Confederates) should abstain from re-entering American politics. According to Marble's analysis, Napoleon III had precipitated the Commune by declaring war on Prussia in precisely the same way that "Jefferson Davis and his abettors [had] promoted a condition of things among the ruling politicians of the South which precipitated the rebellion." It was a flawed analogy between two imperfect causal explanations. Yet however muddled Marble's history and logic might have been, his argument was crystal clear: if you start a civil war and you don't win, you are out of the game. He offered this opinion bluntly:

> The truth is that Jefferson Davis is not only a badly beaten general, a failure as an executive head of a resisting people, a thoroughly whipped rebel, but a politician who stupidly, criminally (to use the mildest phrase) *blundered*. As the representative of all this, those can honor him who see fit . . . [But] Jefferson Davis must take a back seat in the new order of things, if for no other reason than because his judgment cannot and will not be trusted, South or North.

The *New York World* might be a Democratic paper, and the national party might be welcoming former rebels back into the ranks, but as a Northerner, Manton was indignant. The Commune gave him a convenient opportunity to vent his anger.[74]

Marble's bitter words may have cheered Republican foes in the North (who generally shared his views about Davis), but his Democratic allies in the South were deeply offended. The *New Orleans Picayune,* which in most things political agreed with the *World,* was quick to note this Yankee attempt to "liken the communists of Paris to the secessionists of America," and quickly rose to the challenge. It would not permit such an unfortunate comparison between the Lost Cause and the Paris Commune to go unanswered.[75]

"Comparisons," it began, "are always odious, but this [one] is especially odious and unjust." Secession and the Civil War were "among the bygones" of American history, so why compare them to the current disorder in Paris? It was time for a fresh start and a fresh attitude, what Democrats had taken to calling the "New Departure" (though the *Picayune* did not use the expression here). Inevitably, the leading roles in this new departure would be played by "our neighbors, our readers, our patrons and our friends"—who happened to be the same ex-Confederates maligned in the columns of the *World*. According to many white Southerners, these were the best men their section had to offer. Inspired by their worthy eminence, the *Picayune*'s editor submitted a list of "immense differences" between the Confederacy and the Commune.

The first difference was that the Commune represented only "a meagre minority of adults in a single city," while the "secessionists were the whole of the people of several large States." Secondly, the "aim of the Communists was innovation and conquest; [while] the aim of secessionists was conservatism of the strictest kind as to their home governments." A corollary was that the "Communists tried to make a revolution and to introduce radical changes into the system of government . . . [while the] secessionists honestly professed to resist a revolution." A third difference was that the "madmen of the Parisian Commune were never more than a gang of usurpers and desperadoes," while the Confederacy was governed by the most respected (and respectable) Southern leaders. The final difference, which seemed to incorporate all the others (while strangely echoing Northern views), was that the "insurgents of Paris promulgated and sought to enforce a Government exactly the opposite to all sound republican theory," while the Confederacy tried to cleave to the purest model of republicanism ever: the American Constitution.

For all these reasons, the *Picayune* announced that there was "no way in which . . . [the two civil wars] can be compared except by absolute contrast, and any attempt to class them together in any respect is to slander the whole of the people of the once seceded States." Yet the *Picayune*'s rejection of the Civil War analogy still managed to express some of the same political viewpoints as the *World*'s embrace of the analogy: praise for states' rights, the idea that the Civil War was fought to defend local autonomy, the postbellum resistance to centralized authority, and so on. And while both the *Picayune* and the *New York Times* overtly denied the Civil War analogy, they used their strenuous denials to advance very different arguments about the meaning of the War Between the States.

There were still other ways to insinuate the Commune into domestic arguments about the Civil War, and Southerners found most of them. Not even the hot-tempered *Picayune* was consistent. Although it generally condemned the Commune, the New Orleans paper also used the revolution in Paris as a retroactive justification of the Confederacy. Looking to Paris in mid-April, when it seemed like the Communards might succeed, the *Picayune* offered a pungent essay on political legitimacy:

> A revolt by one person against the laws sanctioned by all the rest is a crime. A revolt by a few [as it later described the Commune] . . . is still a crime, and the revolters are to be held and treated as criminals; but when an insurrection assumes vast proportions [as the Confederacy had done], is sustained for a long time with ample military power, and takes the shape of an orderly, independent government, its adherents, coadjutors and sympathizers can no longer be held as amenable to criminal laws . . . Insurgent sway . . . [then takes on] the insignia of legitimate power.[76]

Other Southerners felt the same way. So long as they could describe the Commune as a wholesome revolt against an oppressive centralized power, ex-Confederates were ready to applaud. They were even ready to applaud the Commune as a parallel to the Klan; after all, explained one Democratic congressman, both began as secret conspiracies, and "conspiracy [is] ever the result of bad government . . . [and] repression the father of revolution."[77]

To be sure, no one in the South ever applauded the Commune as loudly as William DuGas Trammell did in *Ça Ira*. Ben E. Green of Georgia, a kinsman of John C. Calhoun's and a prominent Greenback reformer, probably came closest. Within a few months of the Commune, Green completed a timely translation of Adolph Granier de Cassagnac's *History of the Working and Burgher Classes,* a labor-reform pamphlet of 1838. Green appended a long essay to the English text in which he promised to explain the "much calumniated French Commune," though he devoted most of its pages to attacking the Republican party and its autocratic tendencies instead.[78] Ultimately, like Trammell, Green was an eccentric case. Yet even completely respectable papers like the *Atlanta Constitution* and the *Charleston Republican* were willing to express "profound sympathy" for the Communards and to endorse their goal of local autonomy, if not their methods.[79]

Almost a decade later, one leading Southerner was still applauding the Paris Commune for its position on states' rights. The year was 1880; the place, a small, damp office near the Capitol building in Washington, D.C. Two notorious Southerners were meeting for the first time. One was a slight, withered man, burdened by age and illness and history: Alexander Stephens, the former Vice-President of the Confederate States of America, and now a member of Congress from the same Georgia district that he had represented before the war. The other man, both younger and decidedly more robust, was Albert Parsons. Texas-born and a proud veteran of the Confederate army, Parsons was already one of the country's most radical working-class spokesmen. He was in Washington as a representative of Chicago's Eight-Hour League, attending a conference on land reform, which Stephens also endorsed.

According to a reporter who described their encounter for the *Chicago Daily Telegraph,* a third man introduced young Parsons, noting that he was "a Communist." Parsons stepped forward and offered his hand; Stephens took it, quickly "announc[ing] that he himself was . . . a Communist." The elderly statesman then explained that "as Communism has developed in France, Spain, and other countries the past few years, and as it relates to the sovereignty of local Government, and the nature and functions of State rule, it develops a marvelous bearing on the future of America." Despite this clarification, the reporter was shocked.[80]

What the reporter failed to recognize was that the two men had very different things in mind when they called themselves communists. For Stephens, communism and the Commune were understandable only in relation to the past. In 1880 he was still guided by the beacons of sectionalism and states' rights that had defined the Civil War era. His young admirer was on a different path. Although he despised slavery, Parsons had spent four years in the Confederate army. Yet his view of the Paris Commune had nothing to do with the Civil War. Instead, it was shaped by his postbellum life in the Chicago labor movement.

Chicago in the 1870s was home to the most outspoken critics of the capitalist system in America, and after 1873 Albert Parsons was one of them. He began with a mainstream critique of "wage slavery," but then continued drifting to the left. Finally, as editor of the *Alarm* in the 1880s, he became the leading native-born exponent of the violent form of European anarchism preached by Johann Most.[81] Along the way Parsons played leading roles in two events that anxious Americans tried to compare to the Paris Commune: the Great Strike of 1877 and the Haymarket bombing of 1886. In 1877, the *Chicago Tribune* even singled him out as "the leader of the Commune" in Chicago.[82] Though it was hardly accurate, Parsons must have been pleased with the title, having claimed during the strike that the Commune was a glorious "attempt by force of arms to secure labor's economic emancipation." Indeed, his final act, as he trudged with his comrades to the gallows at Cook County Prison in 1887, was to invoke the working-class martyrs of Paris.[83]

In a sense, the curious exchange between Stephens and Parsons was also a collision between two different meanings that Americans gave to the Paris Commune, one political, the other social. Stephens saw it as a struggle for home rule. Parsons saw it as an attempt to change capitalist society. Either view could find some support in the actual events of the Commune; Cluseret maintained both views at once. But which meaning Americans adopted had more to do with domestic conditions than with the Commune itself, and the Commune could be made to reinforce any number of domestic ideologies. By 1880, few Americans were choosing to interpret the Commune as Stephens still did, or as other Southerners and Democrats had done in 1871, when they described the Paris Commune as a sectional conflict. Domestic conditions had changed, and Parsons's view of the Commune as a working-class uprising had become more common (though unlike Parsons, most Americans saw it as an *undesirable* model of social change). I will come back to this later, especially in Chapter 8. Here I want to repeat a point made before: that earlier uses of the Commune, like Stephens's, made it more difficult to ward off later uses, like Parsons's. Analogy fostered more analogy, with unexpected (often unwelcome) results.

At least one Southerner recognized this danger in Stephens's interview with Parsons. The Reverend Charles Hubner was shocked that a fellow Georgian, much less a Confederate leader, was still willing in 1880 to conjure with a positive image of the Commune. Hubner was convinced that Vice-President Stephens must have been misquoted by the Yankee newspapers, so he wrote the old man directly for an explanation, and received a prompt reply. Once again, Stephens admitted to being a "Communist," but only "in the sense in which the term was used . . . [to denote] the revival of representative government" in France and Spain. ("To be a

Communist in that sense," noted Hubner, "is to be an advocate and defender of home-rule and State rights, and Mr. Stephens has, in heart and soul, always been the advocate and defender of such a Commune.") He also admitted to a certain "sympathy for [American] Socialists and Communists in such of their grievances as are just, [though] he is grieved at, and utterly condemns, their methods." But in the end Stephens categorically rejected Parsons's definition of Communism, which aimed to "overturn" private property.

This is what Hubner was waiting to hear. Heaving a sigh of relief, he could now rest assured that "call[ing] Mr. Stephens a Communist . . . was a perversion of the language used by Mr. Stephens, and a misstatement of fact." Still he felt it would have been better if Stephens had never invoked the Commune in the first place, with all its unfortunate implications of social upheaval.[84] Hubner knew that the line between sectional conflict and social upheaval was never very distinct in the South. When Confederate partisans favorably compared the Commune to their own struggle for independence, whether in 1871 or 1880, they risked another comparison between the Commune and the worst form of social upheaval that white Southerners could imagine, namely racial unrest. Indeed, Southerners always had this problem when they tried to borrow images of national revolution from abroad—especially in 1860–1861, when some of them offered the French Revolution as a model for secession.

In the final weeks of 1860, South Carolina was the hotbed of secession, and everyone in Charleston seemed to be talking about revolution. Often their speeches were embellished with the image of French patriots overthrowing tyranny in 1789. As secession fever spread, fire-eaters across the South repeated the Charlestonians' allusions to revolutionary France. In the same heady spirit of appropriation, notes historian James Ford Rhodes, they borrowed the French national anthem as "the music of this nascent revolution." (Even later, the "Marseillaise" remained one of the most popular anthems of the Confederacy.)[85] Other Southerners were more prudent about invoking foreign revolutions—among them, ironically, Alexander Stephens. As Stephens admonished one rash young colleague, "Revolutions are much easier started than controlled," especially in societies with a rigid hierarchy.[86] The French Revolution of 1789 was a case in point, for what began as a patriotic uprising soon devolved into social anarchy; the first Republic even emancipated the French slaves. With that example in mind, thought Stephens, Southerners were better off avoiding the topic of foreign revolutions altogether, much less having a revolution of their own, or "just the sort of thing as was seen in France in 1792" (that is, the Terror) could be seen in the South.[87]

Stephens lost the secession argument in 1860, and soon forgot his own good advice about playing with the image of revolution. Despite a reputation for obtuseness, other Southern Bourbons actually learned something from their foolish, headlong embrace of revolutionary rhetoric. As a result, they were wary of praising the Paris Commune in 1871, even when it looked like a noble civil war. Again, the "Marseillaise" was an index of their attitudes toward revolution. As one Alabama writer explained for the benefit of Northerners who wanted to compare the Commune to the War Between the States, proper Southerners had changed their tune on that beloved Confederate melody as soon as they learned about the Commune. Before 1871, no one could fail to "observe the delight with which the multitude ever listen[ed] to the 'Marseillaise.'" The song was a perennial of the Southern stage; whenever its familiar strains "came up from the stage or the chorus-echoing pit, the pit, dress-circle and galleries were . . . wild with delight, [and] the theatre rent with acclamations." But the Commune, with its fearful arson and destruction, "made the name of France hideous." Now, "when the 'Marseillaise' was sung in the Mobile theatre there was no voice to take up the swelling chorus and no sign of applause in pit or gallery. The 'Marseillaise' will become a vague memory divested of all its charms and heard no more in southern theatres."[88]

When they discussed the Commune, most Southerners thus steered clear of positive interpretations, even of the provisional kind sometimes advanced by the *New Orleans Picayune* and other ex-Confederates. Praising the Commune seemed too much like praising anarchy. Instead they tended to echo the negative interpretations advanced by Mrs. Willard and by Ambrose Dudley Mann in Paris. Remember Willard's nasty comparison between the Communards and African Americans: the horrid Parisians were much "worse than the 'niggers,'" who at least displayed a degree of loyalty to their former masters.[89] In making that comparison, Willard breached the conceptual boundary between two very different laboring classes—and into the breach rushed Southern racial fears.

Seen as an act of social upheaval, the Commune was a convenient amplifier for Southern fears of social (that is, racial) transformation at home. For many decades, Southerners had complained that the real revolutionaries in America were Northerners who wanted to transform race relations below the Mason-Dixon line. The old complaints grew even louder during Reconstruction. And they were often embellished with imagery drawn from the French Revolution and the Terror. Jonathan Worth of North Carolina, for example, bluntly referred to the Radicals in Congress as "those red Republicans." Stonewall Jackson's former chief of staff, the Reverend Robert L. Dabney of Virginia, condemned every Republican who hailed from New England as a French-style "Jacobin," hell-bent on galvanizing the freedmen.[90] (What would he have thought about General Cluseret's 1865 plan to turn the freedmen into a revolutionary army of occupation?)

The Commune was easily transplanted into this ideological climate, as both a symbol of unwelcome social change and a souvenir of the French Revolution. The *Charlottesville Weekly Chronicle,* speaking for the Conservative party in Virginia, compressed both aspects of the Commune into a succinct passage: "The French Reds, like their brethren, the black Radicals of this country, are appealing to a higher law to justify their crimes. They threaten the guillotine in Paris. [Wendell] Phillips and company would send halters to the leading men of the South. One set is as bad as the other. There is little choice between them." It seemed almost obvious for white Southerners to equate the Commune with "social equality," and social equality with racial equality. In a sense, they had been programmed for the equation by a lifetime's input of racial ideology.[91] When Robert Nelson, a Texas-based agent for the Colored National Labor Union, issued a call for a labor conference to be held in Houston in the summer of 1871, a Galveston newspaper was ready to respond with a typical, dire warning: "The beginning is here—the little rippling stream, so weak as to be insignificant—the end is like that of Paris. It is the Commune with its sea of blood and its ocean of fire."[92] And when a regiment of armed black militia marched through Edgefield County, South Carolina, in 1874, local Democrats were convinced that "no orgie [*sic*] of the Paris Commune surpassed this in the subversion of God's law and order."[93]

Finally, if white Southerners were prepared to denigrate the Commune as a way to express some of their own fears about racial discord, they were also prepared to offer the Paris Commune as a warning against making black men into citizens. Here, political conditions in the postbellum South converged with elitist Northern arguments about republican incapacity. It is hardly surprising that one of the first and most anxious warnings about black citizenship and the Commune was delivered by a Northern observer with Southern sympathies. It was bad enough, he wrote, that Georgia had six thousand illiterate *white* men on its voting rolls, who were obviously unfit for self-government. But add to that "the whole bulk of the Negro population," and "so vast a mass of ignorance would be found that, if combined for any political purpose it would sweep away all opposition the intelligent class might make." In the end, "the ignorant voters . . . [might even] form a party by themselves as dangerous to the interests of society as the communists of France."[94]

Robert A. Toombs, the Confederacy's first secretary of state, had a similar reaction to the Commune. When a reporter from the *New York Tribune* asked him about Negro suffrage, Toombs declared that it was "an unmixed evil" by which a "great lump of ignorance and vice had been made part of the governing class." Nor did he "think an intelligence qualification for suffrage would remedy the evil"; intelligence without property or political education just was not enough. After all, the "Paris mob were intelligent, but they were the most dangerous class in the world to be trusted with any of the powers of government."[95]

At first glance, Toombs's reference to the Commune looks gratuitous. What did freedmen and Parisians really have in common? Yet he must have thought that a reference to the Commune would bolster his main argument that a "property qualification was . . . necessary for a stable government," else poor whites and blacks would combine together and "attack the interests of the landed proprietor." Toombs was correct in his assumption, for the Commune was already becoming a shorthand tag for political incapacity in the North. By alluding to the Commune, Toombs reinforced the idea that African Americans were likewise incompetent to take part in a democratic polity. At the same time, by describing the Paris Commune in the same terms that some Northern elites (including Republicans) were using, Toombs might have been asking them to support his view of Negro suffrage. In the process, Southern Democrats like Toombs conveniently forgot how they had cheered French armies and supported the French Republic just a few months earlier.

Perhaps Toombs was being generous when he claimed that the "Paris mob were intelligent," or perhaps he was just attempting to make black Southerners look worse by comparison. Reverend Dabney, however, felt little generosity toward either group. To his way of thinking, both "lower classes," the Parisian and the African-American, were irredeemably ignorant. Unlike a white Southerner, a black man could never be made fit for republican government, and the common school system that radical Yankees were trying to foist on the South was only "prepar[ing] the way for . . . the horrors of the Paris *Commune*." Governor Hugh S. Thompson of South Carolina agreed with him: "If the dreaded Commune shall ever be established [in the South], its success will be owing in considerable measure to the public school systems . . . which are now accustoming the people to be cared-for and controlled by a central government."[96] Fortunately, not everyone in the South felt that way about education or its effects on citizenship.[97] For years to come, however, leading white Southerners would continue to describe their black fellow citizens as a "foreign and incongruous element" (Lucius Q. C. Lamar, 1875), akin to "the Anarchist, the Communist, the Nihilist, and all the other scum of European cities" (Wade Hampton, 1890).[98] Increasingly, white Northerners agreed with those descriptions.

For those who doubted that black people were fit for the rigors of self-government there was no better proof than the "black and tan" legislatures that governed several Southern states during Reconstruction. These legislatures were dominated by freedmen, lower-class whites, and Northern newcomers (the infamous "carpetbaggers" of Lost Cause legend), while indigenous antebellum elites were disqualified from serving because of their part in the Rebellion. Given their composition, these bodies were usually short on political experience, and the undeniable result was blunder and peculation—together with a surprising amount of wise and progressive legislation. Southern opponents ignored the positive results and only focused on the ignorance of the black lawmakers. In 1873, for example, "one of the most distinguished gentlemen of the South" complained that the Louisiana legislature, with its large percentage of black men and carpetbaggers, was nothing better than "an exhibition of baboons . . . a profane caricature of the human race," and "a parody of republican institutions." He even referred to the black legislators as "African communists."[99] Similar statements flowed unabated from the pens and platforms of Southern Redeemers. It took a Republican, however, to raise the attacks on African-American political capacity to their highest level. His name was James Shepherd Pike, and he was from Maine.

Pike began his career in the 1850s as an ardent antislavery man, though he eventually became a disgruntled independent. During the Civil War he served as the American minister to the Netherlands. Yet even then he had his doubts about black men as citizens, and his doubts about democratic government in general (doubts that Jonathan Baxter Harrison would surely have recognized and Abraham Lincoln abhorred). As Pike explained to Salmon P. Chase in 1865, the African American was "ignorant, debased, & totally unfit to exercise the duties of citizenship"—just as unfit, perhaps, as the ignorant Irishman, whether at home in "Donnybrook" or away in the United States.[100] Nonetheless, he accepted Negro suffrage out of party loyalty—until 1872, when he abandoned the party to become a Liberal Republican. Horace Greeley, the Liberals' candidate, ran that year on a platform of sectional reconciliation, and Pike worked hard but in vain to get him elected. Afterward, Greeley's old paper, the *New York Tribune,* sent Pike to South Carolina to report on Reconstruction and its supposed failures.

The result was a series of articles that soon became a best-selling book, *The Prostrate State* (New York, 1874).[101] In its pages Pike described an appalling state of affairs, a woeful tale of corruption and ruin that he explicitly blamed on Republican policy. He explained how the "old aristocratic society" of South Carolina was replaced by "the most ignorant democracy that mankind ever saw, invested with the functions of government" (11). He told how a mass of "rude and unlettered" black men now filled the ivory legislative halls (47), munching loudly on bags of peanuts, propping their muddy boots on the desks, making grandiose speeches, and stealing the white people's money. He noted the "immense proportion of ignorance and vice that permeates the mass" (48) and voiced his opinion that such men as these could never be turned into worthy citizens, much less worthy lawmakers.

It was as if Pike had resurrected all the old labels used to announce the supposed incapacity of Frenchmen for self-government. In the same spirit, he sadly proposed that the South had witnessed "a descent into barbarism" of the sort that could only be produced by a "foreign tyranny" (11). "Is this the self-government for which a war of seven years [*sic*] was waged, that justice and liberty might forever be maintained in the States of the model American Republic?" he asked bitterly. "Tell us what government of any civilized state of the Old World, if imported into South Carolina, would be as oppressive upon, and as unfitted for, the 300,000 white people of that State, as that which now curses it under the name of republican!" (70).

Pike's black despair was confirmed by another unlikely Northern observer of conditions in the South: Edward King, the journalist, poet, and novelist of the Paris Commune. After the Commune ended, King returned to the United States with a reputation as "one of the ablest of the younger American journalists."[102] The editor at *Scribner's Monthly* thought especially well of King, and in 1873 the magazine sent him South, like Pike, to report on the effects of Reconstruction. During the next two years, King covered some 25,000 miles of the old Confederacy, and the result of his travels was an exhaustive series of articles for *Scribner's*. Like Pike's, these pieces soon reappeared as a best-selling book, *The Great South* (New York, 1875).[103]

Unfortunately, King's personal observations were compromised by his constant exposure to Southern white elites while researching *The Great South*, and their views often crept into his writing.[104] This was especially obvious in his descriptions of African Americans as citizens and politicians, which owed more to racist ideology than to reality. He wrote, for example, that North Carolina had a "great mass of densely ignorant and ambitious blacks" to whose "villainy and robbery . . . the white population of the State was compelled to submit" (468). Likewise, he described black members of the Louisiana state legislature who were "so completely ignorant that they cannot follow the course of debate" (95) and who were "evidently unfit for any public duty" (295). Worse yet, in South Carolina black Republicans perpetrated "mighty theft[s and] . . . colossal impudence" (457). "Never," King cried, "was a revolution, originally intended as humane, turned to such base uses" (457). "Ignorance must not be allowed to run riot. If we saw it consummating, as a Commune assembled in Paris, one thousandth part of the infamy which it effects as a Legislature in South Carolina, we should cry out angrily for interference" (461).

Edward King knew better than to make this comparison between the Commune and the postbellum South. He was no cross Southern Redeemer, railing against "African communists" to gain white support, nor even a disillusioned elitist like Pike. Instead, he was a Northern Republican in good standing, who still believed that, given the right chances and the right education, African Americans would make perfectly capable citizens.[105] More important, he had seen the revolutionary assemblies of the Commune, and he knew that Parisians were far less ignorant and more capable of self-government than most Americans gave them credit for. Yet in the end, he echoed a description of the Commune that had been shaped by the demands of domestic politics, both party and sectional, rather than by the actual events in Paris.

A dozen years later, in a striking demonstration of metaphorical tension, King inverted the comparison between the freedmen and Communards originally offered in *The Great South*.[106] Now, in 1887, he suggested that popular politics under the Commune resembled the biracial politics of the South during Reconstruction. Looking back at the Commune, he explained that there was "scarcely an absurdity in politics, religion, finance, or economy, the adoption of which . . . [the radical Parisian] clubs did not counsel. That American readers may understand them, they may be compared to the early reconstruction conventions in the Southern States after the Civil War, when the negro was beginning to try his 'prentice hand at parliamentary form. The vaporings of the club orators in France are as ridiculous as those of the liberated slave, and often have less practical importance."[107] The analogy still rang false, but it showed how strongly domestic conditions and mental patterns shaped American interpretations of the Commune. In search of a way to explain the Commune to Americans, King fell back on a familiar (hence meaningful) image that Democrats, and some Republicans, had been spreading for years: the freedman who was woefully unsuited for republican government. Yet this was ultimately a circular description, for the idea of a politically incapable black population had been powerfully augmented by descriptions of incapable French republicans in 1870 and incapable Communards in 1871.

In the beginning, there seemed to be many ways to compare the Paris Commune to the American Civil War—as wars, as rebellions, as experiments in popular government, and so on. At best, Americans were able to use their own experience with sectional conflict to make sense of what was happening in France. Thinking about the events in France also allowed them to sharpen their understanding of domestic politics, and especially to examine the impact of new voters on the American republic. But not every comparison between the civil wars was useful, intentional, or even pleasing. In the hands of shrewd politicians, the Commune became just another blunt weapon of partisanship. Or it became an excuse to assert a bolder elitism, or even to retreat from Reconstruction. Some comparisons, like the states' rights analogy between the Commune and the Confederacy, backfired, leading their proponents to political adversity and ideological confusion. Others, like Pike's and King's analogy between Communards and the black politicians of the South, only succeeded by distorting reality on both sides. But in the end, every comparison asked the same question, however implicitly: What did Paris and America *really* have in common?

6

The View from the 1870s

> [France's] troubles are not hers alone: they are but symptomatic of
> the evils that exist everywhere in modern society.
>
> —CHARLES ELIOT NORTON (1872)

Thomas Nast was the perfect embodiment of many of the cultural trends described in the last two chapters. On the eve of the Paris Commune, Nast was easily the most famous political cartoonist in the nation, employed by the "most important weekly journal of the time," *Harper's Weekly*.[1] Both the artist and the journal were prominent links in the expanding web of American commercial culture, and both had achieved their leading place in the days of the Civil War. Nast became an even greater force in politics after the war. As the vigorous partisan of a section (the North) and a party (the Republican), his cartoons were engaged in all the fierce battles that raged over Reconstruction and the other issues of the day. These drawings both reflected and shaped Northern public opinion in the 1860s and 1870s. As one biographer argues, Nast "sense[d] intuitively the public mood. More important, his convictions during his great days coincided with the public's."[2] Thomas Nast was indeed a powerful champion, and a good part of his power came from the fact that he was dealing in images, not just words.

William Marcy Tweed, the "Boss" of Tammany Hall, was painfully aware of that fact. When Nast sketched his scathing attacks on municipal corruption in New York City, Tweed is said to have cussed, "I don't care so much what the papers say about me—my constituents can't read; but damn it, they can see pictures!"[3] That was in 1871, and the Boss had good reason to be worried. After almost four years of flagrant corruption, during which the "Tweed Ring" skimmed some $30 million from the public coffers, the city's political elite had finally begun to fight the machine. The attack was led by George Jones at the *New York Times* and by Thomas Nast at *Harper's Weekly:* while Jones printed damning extracts from Tammany's secret ledger books, Nast produced even more damning caricatures of Tweed and his cronies, illustrating their public and personal vices. The cartoonist used a varied set of images to convey this double sense of corruption. At different times he portrayed Tweed et al. as small-time crooks and would-be Caesars, as corpulent gluttons and Falstaff's buck-ram army, and often as skulking, rapacious vultures.[4] In a potent conflation of the two leading stories of the day, he even attacked the corrupt Tweed Ring by comparing it to the Paris Commune.

Nast was not alone in making the comparison. "No issue of 1871, save political corruption," notes historian Samuel Bernstein, "was given more headlines in the American press than the Paris Commune."[5] What Bernstein fails to indicate is how the two sets of headlines interacted. The apparent expansion of political corruption through every level of American government was one of the great public anxieties of the Gilded Age, and this anxiety was clearly reflected in American responses to the Commune. Charles Eliot Norton, the reform-minded Brahmin, was so appalled by the spoilsmen at home that he (briefly) condoned the Commune's attempt to remove by force the "deepseated evils" of corruption in France.[6] In New York, however, where the battle against the Tweed Ring gave the issue particular salience, most local elites presumed that the Paris Commune was a case of corruption, and not the cure for it.

According to one New York editor, corruption and demagoguery had spawned the Commune in Paris, and now the same forces were at work in New York: "If the United States were made up of the same materials, in the same proportions, that now constitute the city of New York, they would be in the present condition of France. There is no overwhelming public opinion in New York city that controls its governing politicians."[7] The *Nation* complained that, like the leaders of the Paris Commune, the "Boss" and his associates only pretended to rule in the name of "the people," and this was sufficient proof that neither New York nor Paris was prepared for self-government.[8] Tammany Hall was corrupting public opinion and, even worse, it was corrupting public morals. Thanks to the Tweed Ring, said *Harper's Weekly,* "the rising generation is largely infected with the fallacy that money must be made by short-cuts to fortune." Tweed flaunted his ill-gotten wealth with an arriviste vulgarity that also reminded reformers of the Paris Commune.[9]

Placed side by side, the parallel examples of Tweed and the Commune reassured the local elite that New York City's government had to be protected from the misguided will of the "people."[10] As we have seen before, the Paris Commune provided Americans with a handy critique of democracy at home, which they might have been reluctant to offer without a foreign catalyst. Not surprisingly, Tweed's critics were often the same "intelligent and patriotic men" that Jonathan Baxter Harrison noticed assaulting popular sovereignty during Reconstruction; indeed, the attack on urban politics and the disowning of Reconstruction were part of the same transformation in American political culture.[11]

The *New York World,* which was friendly toward both the Commune and Tammany Hall, tried to convince antidemocratic reformers that "'The Commune,' pure and simple, is not a bad sort of thing, nor, to Americans at least, is it a new thing. You in New York have your commune in your own way. That is, you have local self-government. New York governs herself by officers elected by her own people."[12] But the Republican *New York Times* quickly rejoined, "We should certainly not like to see [ex-] Mayor Wood's idea carried out in this country, and New-York become a 'commune,' free and independent. Nor does Paris seem any more fit for such a liberty."[13] Here again, New York and Paris were linked by doubts about republican capacity.

In July 1871, Thomas Nast gave visual expression to the verbal link in a large, multipanel cartoon that not only attacked the Ring and the Commune, but also lampooned Irish Americans and Southern Democrats.[14] In the upper-right panel, the four main members of the Tweed Ring cower before the ghost of Benjamin Franklin, who warns them that "all good Americans when they die go to Paris." At the same time, two placards behind the figures present another set of warnings: the one behind the specter says "Paris . . . Reign of Terror," while the one behind the Ring says "New York City. The Rule of Four. We Will Make New York the Paris of America." To drive the point home, another panel at the bottom of the page illustrates the destruction of the Vendôme Column in Paris, a visual portent of New York's potential fate.

Nast recycled the same image a year later, in a full-page cartoon for *Harper's Weekly* (see facing page).[15] A thin, dark line stretches diagonally across the drawing, connecting the two main elements of the composition. The line is a rope, and the rope is attached on the left to a large Roman column labeled "The Republican Column." On the top of the column stands a statue of Liberty (or perhaps Columbia), flanked by an eagle and the national flag; the words "U. S. Grant" and "Union" are written in large letters on the capital just below her feet. The same words reappear on the pedestal, while the honored name of Lincoln is emblazoned along the column's base. Meanwhile, the shaft of the mighty Republican Column is inscribed with the glorious record of President Grant and his party: the names of the great Union generals and victories; the names of the great

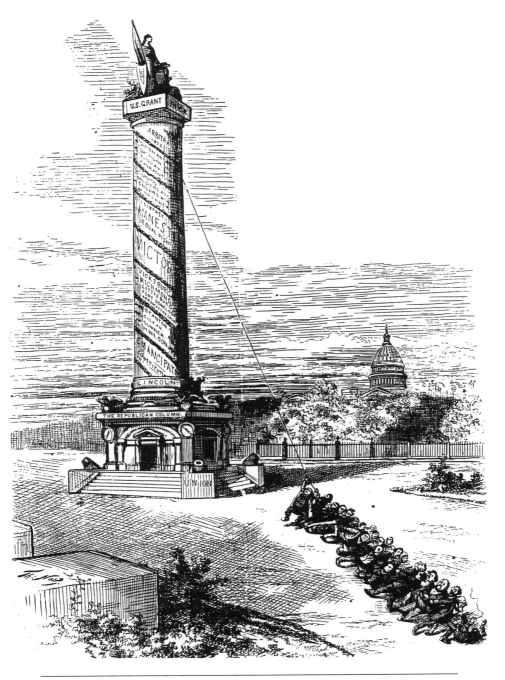

Thomas Nast, "'ANY THING FOR REVENGE!'—À LA COMMUNE,"
Harper's Weekly, July 27, 1872. (Courtesy of HarpWeek, Inc.)

party leaders; the words "Liberty," "Equal Rights," and "Constitution"; and in the biggest letters of all, "Victory" and "Emancipation."

At the other end of the tightly strung rope, in the lower right-hand corner of Nast's cartoon, a mob of small figures is striving to topple the edifice of republican (and Republican) government. Many figures in the mob are recognizable caricatures, starting with Tweed and his three main cronies. Along with the Ring, however, Nast also managed to include all the major political foes and bogeymen of Northern Republicanism. Jefferson Davis and a masked Klansman represent the intransigence of the South and the section's incapacity for self-rule. A stereotyped Irishman represents the immigrant threat to American institutions. Carl Schurz, another foreigner, represents the Liberal Republican faction that threatened to unseat Grant. And there at the very front of the rope, tugging with all his might, is Horace Greeley, Grant's opponent in the 1872 presidential election.[16]

The title of the cartoon is "'ANY THING FOR REVENGE!'—À LA COMMUNE." But even without the caption, it should have been clear to his viewers that Nast was borrowing a well-known episode from the Paris Commune to make his point about American politics. Disorderly vandals on one side, a column representing order and government on the other: the cartoon was meant to recall the destruction of the Vendôme Column. Yet as Nast drew it, the Republican Column looked nothing at all like the structure that American eyewitnesses saw tumble to the ground in Paris.[17] Though inspired by the Commune, his own column was purely a figment of the American imagination, just as the cartoon around it was purely a figment of American politics. But the reference to the Paris Commune still had an ominous implication for Americans: the column of order had fallen in France, and it still might fall in America, however stalwart and steady the column appeared in Nast's 1872 depiction.

At the end of the Paris Commune, the United States was poised—like the thin, taut rope in Thomas Nast's cartoon—between the forces of order and the forces of disorder. To many worried observers, the forces of disorder appeared to be gaining. As Nell Painter reminds us, Americans in the late nineteenth century continuously thought that the nation was "standing at Armageddon," and not without good cause.[18] Yet perhaps the 1870s deserve a special place in the annals of American apocalypse. As one scholar has it, the Civil War and its lingering "after-results" profoundly "disturbed the settled status of classes and raised questions concerning settled opinions"; as a result, the "thinking minds" of the 1870s were "re-examining some of our fundamental notions."[19] The decade was marked by an ongoing struggle to make some sense of the Civil War and Reconstruction. It was also marked by Indian wars in the West and racial violence in the South; by ethnic discord and devastating fires; by the fight against corruption, which threatened the status quo in politics; and by the fight for women's rights, which threatened the status quo in society at large. The decade was also marked by economic dislocation and violent labor unrest. At some point every one of these American developments, and more, were compared to the same foreign event: the Paris Commune. In the process, the Commune became Americanized.

What did it mean to "Americanize" the Commune? To my mind, it involved two different but closely related processes. One was a *descriptive* process, in which various aspects of the Commune were compared to roughly similar aspects of American life (or simply recast in American terms) in order to make the events in Paris seem familiar, hence understandable. The comparisons might be concrete and simple; for example, one *New York Times* correspondent tried to describe the bombardment of Paris by asking his readers to "fancy batteries in the Central Park firing down Fifth-avenue." Or they might be complex and abstract, like many of the comparisons between the Commune and the American Civil War.[20]

The second type of Americanization was *predictive*. It turned around a disturbing question: Could what happened in France also happen here? The question itself was fraught with uncertainties; as often as not, answers came in the form of fearful, complacent, even fierce denials: it can't happen here. Even so, "what happened in France" became a convenient reflection of what some people feared *might* happen in America (instead of what actually occurred in Paris). In this way, the Commune became both a signifier and a context for the unprecedented social transformations in postwar America, a way to discuss domestic woes that might otherwise be difficult to discuss.

Description inspired prediction, since any comparison made later comparisons easier to assert. Whenever the Commune was likened to America, it became more plausible that soon the United States would be like Paris—a frightening thought, if the Commune signified disorder. Ironically, the expansion of order, as seen in the transatlantic cable and the web of commercial culture, had opened the way for a new variety of American disorder. And all of these elements—order and disorder, description and prediction, America and the Commune—came together in a rather unlikely event: the Great Chicago Fire.

On Sunday night, October 8, 1871, somewhere near Mrs. O'Leary's barn, a fire broke out that quickly destroyed a third of the Windy City. Property damages mounted to nearly $200 million as the walls of fire swept along a four-mile path. By Monday night, 100,000 Chicagoans found themselves homeless. Meanwhile, the telegraph allowed horrified Americans across the country simultaneously to follow the holocaust's progress. In the process, claims one scholar, the Great Chicago Fire became the first great "national" event, in the sense of "a symbolic drama . . . of [national] unity staged in mass communication media"; it "demonstrated that news could create for Americans a commonly available simulation of national life. Nationally disseminated telegraphic news reports could bind all Americans instantaneously to a common experience." Yet by this definition the Paris Commune was also a national event, so perhaps it was not strange for the two events to be compared by contemporary Americans.[21]

The connection began with simple descriptions. Just after the fire, for example, one survivor wrote that a ride through "the burnt district . . . was more dismal than a walk through Pompeii, or an excursion among the wrecks of Paris, wrought by the Communists from within, and [the] Prussians from without." A poet for the *New York Evening Post* expanded on this comparison in his elegiac tribute, "Paris and Chicago":

> O bird with a crimson wing
> > And a brand in thy glowing beak,
> Why did'st thou flutter o'er seas to bring
> > A woe that we dare not speak?
>
> Fly hence on thy wing of flame,
> O bird! for thy work is done;
> And the queens of a different clime and name
> > In their ruin and grief are one.

With nearly as much poetic license, *Appleton's Journal* wrote that a "fire-fiend" had jumped from Paris to "a cow-shed to consume the busiest of our Western emporiums."[22] Americans across the nation saw the burning rubble of Paris as a twin to the burning rubble of Chicago.[23]

But the comparisons soon grew invidious. From reports in the popular media, Americans knew that the recent Paris inferno had had a cause as well as a smoldering aftermath. That cause—incendiarism—was quickly imputed to the blaze in Illinois. Even before the fires went out, panicky Chicagoans began to pass rumors of petroleum-wielding arsonists. General Philip Sheridan, who had recently witnessed part of the Commune, knew better. Now in command of the Federal troops in Chicago, he personally assured the city's mayor that "no authenticated attempt at incendiarism" could be discovered.[24] Regardless, the press continued to brim with ominous accounts.

Perhaps the most ominous came on October 23 when the *Chicago Times* published the "confession" of a "Communist incendiary."[25] The man claimed to be an agent for the "Société Internationale," deputized by Communards in Paris to establish a branch of the International in Chicago. "The avowed purpose . . . of the society," he explained, was "to elevate the workingman to the level of the rich." He and his co-conspirators had worked toward this goal for months, trying to "stir up strife between the mechanics of the city and their employers." When their attempts at agitation failed, the society turned its hand to arson. The weapon of choice was a "petroleum mine": on October 8 they set half a dozen and watched Chicago burn. But this was just the start, for as the "confessor" warned in conclusion, "Other cities, both in this country and Europe, have been threatened with [similar] fire."[26]

Not even the *Times* was willing to take the story it printed quite seriously (indeed, it openly disclaimed "any opinion as to its authenticity"). Across town, the *Chicago Tribune* scoffed at the very concept of *pétroleurs* or *pétroleuses* in Chicago, noting that the "crowning evil of all times of tumult and disaster is suspicion. We cannot burn witches now . . . [b]ut we can shoot old women for pumping petroleum if we are Parisians, and we can resurrect them in back alleys if we live in Chicago." The *Tribune* returned to this editorial line a few months later, writing about the International. "The great bugbear of modern times," it began, "is the International Society. Timid men have traced to its influence almost every calamity of the past year . . . There are plenty of people to-day who believe that the Internationale fired Chicago; that they committed the Communist atrocities in Paris; . . . and that they are a secret power, working behind every throne for its overthrow, and undermining society to reduce the rich to the level of the poor and make property common,—all of which is pure stuff." Instead, the International Workingmen's Association (IWA) was a "purely reformatory organization," with little in the way of devious political intent; its influence in America, never great to begin with, was already on the wane. Firebombs or no, the *Tribune* concluded, this foreign creation had nothing to do with America.[27]

Unfortunately, the *Tribune*'s denial had little effect on the diffuse fears of other Americans. Their fears were conveniently focused by the unguarded pronouncements of George Francis Train, Gustave Cluseret, and Wendell Phillips—especially Train's. Returning to America after the excitement in Marseilles, he embarked on a political fantasy tour that became a quixotic run for the White House. It began when he stepped off the boat in April 1871. Almost immediately, Train told a New York audience that revolutionary methods were needed to solve the city's municipal corruption. "To the lamp-post!" he exhorted them: "All those in favor of hanging [Boss] Tweed to a lamp-post, say aye!"—and the crowd shouted "aye!"[28] This was followed by a lecture series at Wood's Museum that left worried critics calling him "an Irishman, a Fenian, [and] a French Red . . . sworn to set up the French Republic."[29] After this great success, Train went stumping across the nation, mixing tales of the Paris insurrection (which he never witnessed himself) with reckless comments on domestic affairs.

In October, Train's speeches began to include a gleeful account of the fall of Chicago. According to one report, "Two hundred American audiences have seen . . . [Train] map out on a blackboard the destruction of the doomed city of sin (Chicago)." Rumors, fears, and Train's unconventional past all came together, and many newspapers, recalling the man's role in various uprisings and international intrigues, concluded that he had something to do with the Great Chicago Fire. The papers even reported that "a strange man, the description of whom answers for the prophet from Omaha," had been seen in the vicinity of Mrs. O'Leary's barn on the night of the conflagration. Again, however, the main culprit was the International, "and [since] Mr. Train is supposed to be a leading member of that society," his having a hand in the blaze helped make some sense of a senseless event.[30]

Train scoffed at the idea, denied the charges, and tried to sue the offending journals, all to no avail. He continued to be linked to the Chicago Fire, as did Cluseret and Phillips. One Catholic writer was truly convinced, for example, that Cluseret had called for the torching of *Chicago* when he threatened "to burn Paris rather than surrender it" (a threat, by the way, that Cluseret never uttered). As for Wendell Phillips, the same writer com-

plained that he was a staunch friend of the Commune and a labor reformer. Thus, it was no surprise when Phillips appeared "to threaten incendiarism as a means of accomplishing his purpose":

> What means this, the closing sentence of his lecture [on the Great
> Fire]: "The lesson taught by Chicago is that wealth cannot afford to
> neglect poverty"? Does this mean that the Internationals burnt Chi-
> cago? or does it simply mean that other cities may be burnt as well as
> Chicago, and will be, if wealth continues to neglect poverty or refuses
> to yield to the demands of the International Association of Working-
> men? This gives the question a startling aspect.

Here was the writer's "question": Could foreign unrest, epitomized by the
IWA and especially the Commune, be coming to America? Much as he
tried to deny it, he was afraid of the possibility. And the Chicago Fire, as a
lurid reflection of the fires in Paris, gave him and others like him a chance
to express their fears.[31]

At the very core of predictive Americanization was a dipole of fear and
denial. Both forces came into play as Americans contemplated a bizarre
attempt to *truly* Americanize the Commune by importing Communards
to the United States. In fact there were two simultaneous attempts,
launched by two competing groups of American entrepreneurs, each of
whom thought they had an answer to the question "What do you do with
40,000 political prisoners?" The question was hardly moot for the French
government in 1871, because in the bloody wake of the Commune they
had arrested nearly that many Parisians. Alas, they soon discovered this
mass of humanity was too large to execute, court-martial, or even transport to faraway penal colonies.[32] This is where the Americans stepped in,
with grandiose schemes to expatriate Communards to empty tracts in the
desert Southwest, all at nominal cost to the French taxpayers.

One group of entrepreneurs was represented in Paris by George Wilkes,
who was there not only as a correspondent for the *Spirit of the Times* and
the *New York Herald*, but also as a trustee of the Lower California Company. Already this corporation had led a short but corrupt and colorful life.
The board of directors, notes one historian, "comprised a *Who's Who* of
eastern Democratic wealth," including Samuel Barlow, August Belmont
(soon to be chairman of the Democratic National Committee), and even
"Boss" Tweed, along with Generals John Logan and Ben Butler (two

converts from the Democratic party to Radicalism).[33] On paper its assets included $35 million in stock and 30 million acres of land near Magdelena Bay in Baja California. In truth, its only real asset was a conditional charter to the territory, extorted from the Mexican government in 1862 by a predecessor corporation.[34]

The main condition of the charter was for the Americans to establish a viable colony on the peninsula within a reasonable period of time. Unfortunately, the land was arid, inconveniently situated, and utterly devoid of exploitable resources. Only through shameless huckstering was the company able to persuade a tiny group of ill-prepared San Franciscans to settle on the land. At the end of 1870, that colony failed, leaving nothing behind but bad publicity. A colony of Communards looked like the only way of keeping the land in the speculators' grasp.[35]

In June 1871 Wilkes offered the French government a colonization plan that combined genuine sympathy for the victims of the Commune with sheer entrepreneurial gall. The terms were simple: in exchange for a million francs (about $200,000) up front, plus transportation and sixty days of food for every *déporté,* his company would accept "several thousand political prisoners" as colonists in Baja, where they never again would disturb the domestic tranquility of France.[36] Amazingly, Versailles gave the scheme some serious thought. Wilkes gave his plan to the Minister of the Interior, who approvingly passed it on to Thiers, who soon (August 12) offered to present it to the National Assembly.[37] On September 23 the *American Register* recorded that Wilkes's proposal had been "regularly noticed in the *Journal Officiel,* as pending before the [Assembly] Committee to which it was referred." The plan was also referred to the Ministry of Justice, on the important question of whether it was legal for the French government to export its prisoners under the guise of foreign colonization. The answer must have been no, for shortly thereafter the government dropped the plan; and though Wilkes tried one last time in December to get the scheme adopted (in the form of a personal petition to the Assembly), no Communard would ever be sent south of the border.[38]

Versailles was offered a second colonization plan by Charles Debrille Poston, a former territorial delegate from Arizona with a checkered career in government service and land speculation.[39] Like George Wilkes, Poston was a part-time journalist for a leading New York paper, in this case the *Tribune;* he also enjoyed close ties with the Lower California Company. (Nonetheless, Poston's scheme to bring Communards to Colorado and Arizona seems to have possessed independent backing.) Though many details remain unclear, the gist of the final plan was to resettle the least dangerous class of French political prisoners in mining colonies on the Great Plains, on lands adjacent to the Apache Indian territory. In earlier forms, however, the plan envisioned a veritable "French State in America," with 40,000 industrious Parisians toiling away at mines, at farms, and on the Southern Pacific Railroad.[40]

Unlike Wilkes's scheme, Poston's drew little attention from the French authorities, except from the Minister of Commerce, whose say in the disposition of Communards was practically nil.[41] What it did draw, together with the Lower California plan, was a great deal of fire from newspapers on both sides of the Atlantic. The Parisian press was incensed. One local paper, noted the *American Register,* was "dreadfully outraged by the propositions," while another sputtered, "The dignity of the nation would not permit of such a transaction."[42] This view was echoed by *Le Soir* and *Le Figaro,* two of France's leading journals.[43] Meanwhile, the ultraconservative *La Patrie* was shocked that "one would [even] dream of assimilating French citizens, however guilty . . . If France once again has had the misfortune of numbering in her midst men whom she is forced to banish, she is by no means reduced thereby to selling them off like raw material to foreign speculators."[44]

However, it was the centrist journal *La Verité* that managed to phrase French skepticism in terms that skeptical Americans might understand. "The Americans," they wrote, "come and say, we will take these men whom you reject, we ask for them, we will make free, quiet and happy citizens of them. Such language is without an answer. Who seeks out the radical vice that turns men into dangerous disruptions when other countries see [in them] only elements of strength and prosperity[?]"[45] Why, asked *La Verité,* should Americans be so eager to accept into their midst a mass of foreign rebels? The answer was that most Americans really were *not* that eager, especially not out West, where the Communards seemed to be headed. For example, some editors in northern California thought that banishment to Baja was "just punishment for the wicked Paris 'Reds,'" yet only because the Baja region was so clearly inhospitable—and so far away from San Francisco.[46] In Denver, the popular *Colorado Monthly* claimed to be "more directly interested in . . . American citizens" coming West than any foreign communists doing so.[47] Meanwhile, a leading Tucson paper concluded that Poston's scheme was simply part of the "alliance of the Eastern press and the Apaches against the struggling pioneers of Arizona."[48]

The Eastern press was little more pleased than the Westerners, however. *Every Saturday* aired a common view when it wrote that "a great colony of . . . [Communards] who immigrate to escape prison is a thing for which the [Western] State[s] cannot be eager." "Five thousand French communists may possibly make good American citizens," it concluded, "but as yet we fail to see any cause for going into rapture or rhapsody about the matter."[49] The American government seemed to agree, judging from one insider's comment "that under pretext of sending us political offenders only, prisoners of a very different class may be shipped."[50] At best, worried observers were inclined to treat the colonization schemes as a bad joke. The *New York Herald,* for example, saw them as a way to lampoon the presidential ambitions of its crosstown rival, Horace Greeley: "We say to the Communists, 'Come' . . . If half the things that are told of the members of the Commune are true they could not fail to be pleased with the Great West. Those of them who . . . like debating societies might go to Greeley, Colorado, where there is a colony of very mild Communistic ideas . . . [I]n many ways they are exactly suited to the country; so we hope that they will not wait till Greeley is President, but go west and buy land at once." This sneer was launched despite the *Herald*'s close connection with Wilkes and the prominent space it gave to his colonization venture.[51]

Yet if some were afraid of the impact that real, live Communists might have upon the peaceful United States, there were other middle-class Americans whose faith in the redeeming features of the American landscape and polity led them to welcome the rebel Europeans. Colonel Poston himself proclaimed that "happy will be the Frenchmen [*sic*] who exchanges the uncertainties of European governments for the certain rewards of labor under a Government whose onward progress no earthly power can impede . . . My plan of colonization offers advantages which neither Emperor, King, nor Kaiser in Europe can give, . . . [in particular] the *reality,* not the *phantom,* of LIBERTÉ, EGALITÉ, FRATERNITÉ."[52] Perhaps he was being disingenuous. But Ryan of the *American Register,* who like Poston had seen the prisoners up close, agreed that "thousands of intelligent and labourious artizans [*sic*] who have engaged in the communistic insurrection . . . will make good citizens of [the United States]."[53]

The view from New York was even more optimistic. According to the *Christian Union,* "the assimilating qualities of American climate and character" would soon turn Communards into good Americans. Even the *Herald,* in a surprisingly generous mood, said: "Let them come and work out their own regeneration on the Pacific Slope."[54] Even those who strongly distrusted the American entrepreneurs sometimes felt that "[French]men who come over of their own accord may make good citizens in a few years."[55]

The last few citations, and dozens more like them, offered a clear argument: vaguely defined "Communism" might be bad, but it was really a European syndrome. Once they were brought to America, undesirable Communards would cease to be communists because communism cannot flourish under American conditions; thus they would cease to be bad. It was an optimistic argument, and one that was strongly undercut by comparisons between Communards, Indians, and the domestic working class.

One of the most interesting patterns to emerge from the New World's encounter with Old World unrest was a conflation of Communards with Native Americans. Comparing "Reds" to "Red Indians," and vice versa, was more than just a colorful play on words. For one thing, the comparison was too widespread. It echoed, naturally enough, in the murmurs that greeted the scheme to make next-door neighbors of Apaches and Communards. As one New Mexican editor complained, "We of this western country, accustomed as we are to the frequent murders and plundering excursions of our Indian element, stand appalled before the horrible details of the French barbarities . . . [Their] acts of vandalism . . . would put to shame a horde of Apache Indians." His colleague at the *Colorado Monthly* agreed; hinting at moral equivalence between the two groups, he went on to predict that "fierce Apaches will . . . welcome" French colonists "with bloody hands to hospitable graves."[56]

But it was not just Westerners faced with the possible influx of Communards (and the very real presence of hostile Indians) who saw a resemblance between these two disorderly forces. According to one American in Paris, the French government had started to "fear the Red Indians" of the French working class long before the Commune threatened.[57] Others were quick to echo this comparison once the Commune began. Far off in Italy, the famous patriot Joseph Mazzini was moved to describe the "doings . . . in France . . . [as] marked by an 'Irokese [*sic*] ferocity,' by an 'insane blood-thirstiness more characteristic of wild beasts than of men.'"[58] Closer to home, influential spokesmen like George W. Curtis and E. L. Godkin took turns railing against the "red Indians" and "bloodthirsty Indian squaws" of the Commune, while the *Chicago Tribune* unfavorably compared the Parisian workers to Comanche hordes.[59] Indeed, even at the level of popular culture represented by the dime novel, publicists managed to equate French radicalism with Indian hostility.[60]

The equation persisted for years in American culture. In 1874, for example, a Catholic journal argued that "Western savages . . . [and] Parisian revolutionists" were wholly similar threats to Jesuit missionaries. A dozen years later, a Nebraska lawyer still thought that our native "untutored savages" (the Indians) were comparable to "the Communist[s] of France, the Socialist[s] of Germany, the Nihilist[s] of Russia, and the cut-throat murderers of Ireland." Each, to his eyes, was a parallel threat to America's republican institutions.[61]

As suggested already, comparisons between the two "red" groups could flow in both directions.[62] The *New York World* demonstrated this in the summer of 1871. For Manton Marble, the Commune was proof that "the wrappage of civilization" was painfully thin, when "scenes can be enacted [in Paris] which are not outdone in atrocity by any story of . . . Wyoming which history has rescued from the annals of savage tribes."[63] Yet his paper would also use the image of the Commune to describe America's own "savage tribes." Thus, the Darien Indians of Panama became "The Reds of America" by virtue of "their communal chiefs and system of government"; Western Apaches on the warpath, like rebels in Paris, became "savages" and "the red enemy," plunging Arizona (like Paris) deep into "Red Ruin"; the chief of the Arapahoes, who disdained private property, became a "Red Republican."[64] The elision between the two groups became complete on June 20, 1871, when the *World* published an article on Indian fighting in Texas headlined "The Red Spectre," only to reuse the phrase a few columns later to describe the International's supposed role in the French civil war.

Why this twinning, at a glance so incongruous, between the Indian and the Communard—the one so innately American, the other so apparently foreign? There are, I think, three answers. The first is that many Indians were really on the warpath in 1871. Despite the Grant administration's vaunted "Peace Policy," the years that followed the Civil War were punctuated by continuous skirmishing between the Army and Plains Indian tribes like the Kiowa, Arapahoe, Apache, and Comanche. Sadly, war between Indians and whites was nothing new. It had persisted for centuries, leaving in its wake a corrosive discourse of hatred and dehumanization. By 1871, even the most sympathetic Christian reformers were apt to call Native Americans "savages" and "heathens," while frontiersmen were as likely to label them "barbarian monster[s]" or even "red devils."[65]

This language was quickly applied to descriptions of the Commune. According to one historian of the war on the Plains, the Western Indians "were more active than ever in the spring of 1871"—just as violence was wracking Paris.[66] Bitter violence also broke out *against* the Indians on April 29, 1871, when a mob of Mexicans, Indians, and white settlers massacred 144 Apache women and children at Camp Grant, Arizona.[67] Western violence, in all its forms, was a cruel but timely parallel to the shaved-down version of the Commune that sped across the wires. As a result, the familiar, indigenous modes of violence became the obvious pattern for the foreign "savagery" in France—especially when a bad pun to link them was so readily available to clever headline writers.

A second explanation for the link between Indians and Communards can be found in Richard Slotkin's persuasive description of the "reconstruction of class and racial symbolism" that took place in the decade after the Civil War. According to Slotkin, the "traditional American symbolism of class" represented class as "an aspect of race." Within that symbolic world, "the spectrum of class relations [was projected] on a scale determined by the degree of likeness to the Indian at the lower end of the spectrum, and the Anglo-Saxon natural aristocrat at the other. The Indian [was] characterized by his savagery, his closeness to nature and to animalism, his lack of a sense of private property . . . [and] his politics [took] the form of violence . . . directed to cruel and destructive ends." Before the Civil War, the spot on the scale nearest the Indian was shared by Southern slaves and Northern paupers. But later, as the dislocations of rapid industrial growth began to propagate a native class of the dispossessed, "the increasing tendency [was] to invoke the Indians as analogues for the proletariat of the city."[68]

The Commune catalyzed this trend, which Slotkin locates in the mid-1870s. As we have seen (and will see again), the Commune gave focus to scattered fears that the United States was becoming a class-based society like Europe. With the right set of optics, a link could be seen between *their* uprising and *our* native workers; similar links were visible between *their* uprising and *our* savage Indians, and again between *our* savages and *our* workers. As Slotkin puts it, the new Yankee proletariat was "'interpreted' by the Indian analogy, [while] Indians [were being] . . . interpreted by a pauper analogy."[69] Taken together, it was a vicious circle of analogies, with the Commune as the third, inextricable component.

At its most vicious, this circular equation of Worker = Communard = Indian was used to describe and decry the Great Strike of 1877. But

Charles Loring Brace was the first to set up the triple equation, in his book *The Dangerous Classes of New York* (1872). (Others had developed the separate comparisons, but not with all three terms at once.) Brace was part of the clerical establishment that, even by 1872, had developed grave misgivings about the Commune. He was also a leading urban reformer. Deeply disturbed by the social effects of urbanization, in 1853 Brace founded the Children's Aid Society in New York to combat what he thought was the worst of those effects: the growing number of homeless working-class children.[70]

When he wrote *The Dangerous Classes* twenty years later, Brace was still dismayed by the unsettling presence of the deskilled masses in America's cities, still typified by Gotham's street urchins. According to Brace, "There seemed to be a very considerable class of lads in New York who bore to the busy, wealthy world around them something of the same relation which Indians bear to the civilized Western settlers. They had no settled home, and lived on the outskirts of society, their hand against every man's pocket, and every man looking on them as natural enemies." While they reminded him of American Indians, the urban masses also reminded Brace of the recent upheaval in Paris. "It has been common," he noted, "since the recent terrible Communistic outbreak in Paris, to assume that France alone is exposed to such horrors." But this reformer, with his two long decades of street experience, thought he knew better. He warned his readers that "the same explosive social elements [are] beneath the surface of New York as of Paris . . . [L]et the civilizing influences of American life fail to reach them, and . . . we should see an explosion."[71]

Yet the somber prediction of a Commune-like catastrophe in the United States came with a disclaimer. America is not Paris, Brace wrote, and with "Christian reform . . . and education," the danger could be averted.[72] These were the common anodynes of the optimistic bourgeoisie: with Christian reform and education, both Communards and workingmen might be saved; with Christian reform and education, Southern freedmen and Native Americans might both become good citizens. At every point, this optimism eroded as the 1870s wore on.

Finally, the Communard and the Indian were linked as part of a larger pattern of distancing and dehumanization. Although it was never the exclusive American response, a fear of the Paris Commune's domestic reprise certainly fixed the attention of many bourgeois minds. One way to deflect that fear was to represent the Commune as something foreign—not just geographically distant, as every dateline from Versailles or Paris confirmed, but essentially alien to the American way of life and even to human nature itself. Because the white man's image of the Indian already combined this sense of the foreign with an ominous presence, it became a convenient model and reinforcement for similar images of the Commune.

From the start, Indians were unavoidably present in the New World. Yet for the white settlers, the native inhabitants gradually came to represent something alien, something exotic to normal experience, something "other." This duality, which James Fenimore Cooper and his colleagues parlayed into a national romance, was reflected in the ambiguous status of Indians under American law. The Constitution acknowledged their physical presence but denied them any political rights, while the government's awkward treaty system categorized the Indians as semisovereign nation-tribes, *in* but not *of* the United States.[73] But there was more. The Indian was simply out of place in the dominant vision of an ideal America: a savage in a civilized land, a heathen in a Christian nation, and a communal property holder in a capitalist society. "The idea of the separate possession of property by individuals," complained one Pennsylvania congressman in 1880, "is as foreign to the Indian mind as communism is to us." It was hardly a new complaint, and during the 1870s two solutions were generally offered to the Indian's troubling dual presence: extermination or assimilation (through education, Christianity, and republican citizenship).[74] In 1871 the same solutions were offered to the hypothetical problem of Communards in the West, who likewise threatened to become a troubling dual presence, in but not of the United States.

Indeed, the Indian's negative attributes were widely ascribed to the Commune even when no direct comparison was being offered. Like the supposed wild Indians, Communards were brutes and barbarians, committing "sins against civilization" with "means such as savages would shrink from using." War paint and feathers were optional; instead of Indians, Communards could also be "desperadoes," "Mohammedan fanatic[s]," "Greek brigands," "Feejee Islanders," or "Goths and Huns"—to give just a partial list of the epithets. In any case, they were clearly uncivilized, and thankfully absent from the American scene, despite one editor's ardent warning that "the barbarians who threaten modern civilization are within its boundaries, not outside."[75]

For some Americans, even "barbarian" was too good a label for the Communards, as it implied a vestige of humanity. Similar thinking made the Communards a frequent target for bestial adjectives. According to the *New York Post*, the Commune showed the "frenzy of a people, when the restraints of culture are thrown off, and the ape and the tiger in them work their wild will, unrestrained." It "savored," said the *Atlanta Constitution,* "more of the hyena than of the human being."[76] Was the Commune atavistic? asked one New York editor: "Gallic blood . . . [must] possess a savage taint, of which our healthier Anglo-Saxon is happily free. Is Darwin then correct? and have the French in but half their nature developed into men[?]" In the same vein, a religious journal marveled at "the freaks of the Communists," and a short-story writer five years later would happily dismiss the Commune as "fierce, maddened, [and] wild." In sum, said Linus P. Brockett, "the Communists . . . acted like wild beasts . . . and it was natural, though possibly not politic, to treat them like wild beasts, whose extermination was necessary for the safety of society."[77]

Thomas Nast was a master of dehumanization. His numerous cartoons of brutish "Paddies" and crude, debased Negroes are proof that Nast knew how to wield a dehumanizing pen. In the 1870s he brought his special talent to bear on depictions of the unnatural, un-American Commune.[78] As drawn by Nast, "Communists" usually came from France and took the form of leering skeletons. In one cartoon from 1874, for example, the wife and the son of a stolid Yankee worker can barely restrain him from shaking the hand of a grinning, bony wraith. A sash across the skeleton's chest identifies him as a "Communist"—though he also wears the symbols of American gentility: a top hat, greatcoat, and gloves. Clear signs of disorder are everywhere, from the skull and crossbones on the skeleton's chest to a riotous mob in the far background. Just as clear is the skeleton's foreignness, signified by a French mustache, a distant building marked "Foreign," and a placard announcing the "Committee of [Public] Safety."[79] When he got bored with skeletons, Nast lampooned the Commune as a toadstool with French features (a pointy beard and mustache); a redundant caption called it "A Foreign and Poisonous Weed." Sometimes he even drew Communists as frogs, repulsive creatures that signified Frenchness and thus confirmed the Commune's double foreignness.[80] But why did Nast have to prove that the Paris Commune was foreign? And why did he work so hard to prove it?

Again and again, attempts to remove the Commune from the normal bounds of human or American experience led back to a fear that the Commune was coming to the United States. Consider a typical argument,

that the Commune was "insane." Despite the best efforts of leading physi-
cians, most Americans in 1871 still linked insanity with moral failure.
Nonetheless, both experts and laymen agreed that madness was a form of
deviance.[81] As Edward Gargan notes, this view of madness was also applied
to the Paris Commune; by calling the Commune "insane" Americans were
able to dismiss it "as fundamentally antihistorical, as antihuman as the
actors in the drama of madmen."[82]

"Insane" was an unfair label, claimed Henry Ward Beecher from his
Brooklyn pulpit, but few cared to listen.[83] Instead, they described the
Commune as "lunacy" and "wicked madness"; as an asylum of "half-
crazy" leaders and "madmen" followers; as a mob that had "run amok"
when prodded by "men of insane ambition and recklessness."[84] This dismal view of the Commune was even confirmed by an "illustrious" French
physician, who called the upheaval a "contagious mental alienation" exac-
erbated by absinthe and tobacco—a diagnosis often reprinted in the
United States.[85]

The Frenchman used "alienation" as a technical word to describe a
specific mental pathology. In the American context, however, the word
became a résumé of the entire effort to distance the Commune, to represent it as something *alien* to the United States. Was the French insanity
really contagious? Lydia Maria Child, the veteran reformer, perused the
French doctor's analysis and wrote that it was "truly frightful. If the state
of things prevailed every where that prevailed in their *cities,* they must
become a nation of outright maniacs" (original emphasis). Could the same
"state of things" prevail in the United States? Were French cities all that
different from American cities? Child was afraid that the answer might be
no.[86] For now, at least, the *New York Times* disagreed. Studying the same
French doctor's report, its editors concluded that a "sirocco of madness
had swept over Paris," a freak wind not likely to be found on these shores.
With mock generosity, the *New York Tribune* allowed that "dishevelled
fanatics dancing amid the blazing ruins . . . and shrieking for blood . . .
[was] too gross a burlesque upon human nature—even for Paris." It went
without saying that healthy American minds were immune to "the crazy
doings of the Paris Communists."[87]

Or were they? What about "addle-brained" Yankees like George Francis
Train who sympathized with the Commune? Were they infected with its
madness?[88] Even without direct contact, American cities were beginning to
display the early symptoms of a Commune-like disorder. Calling the Paris

Commune "insane" would not make those symptoms disappear—as the editor of *Harper's Magazine* noted. "The madness, the folly, the cruelty of mobs and revolutions are not all of them," he wrote:

> A frantic Commune is not merely an illustration of the moral depravity of man, as it is called. No; it is as significant as the cloud that portends the the tornado. If a man can not walk through the new city of New York, looking into its worst slums, its dreadful dens, and reflecting upon its fifty thousand human beings unhappier than brutes and as ignorant, . . . without feeling that society is justly reproached, what must be his reflections in crammed and suffocating Europe?

In the end, talking about the Commune became just another way of talking about America, and descriptions of foreign madness became portents of future upheavals at home.[89]

According to some observers, the burning of Paris proved that the Commune was madness itself. By definition, the incendiary was insane. Or so claimed Eugene Benson, a popular magazine writer, in a prophetic short story called "The Fire-Fiend" (published in 1869). Combining amateur psychology with commonplace antifeminism, Benson portrayed a "fiendish" woman who was driven "by terrible and fatal impulses" to light deadly fires. Two years later, she became a type for the demented "fire-fiend" that *Appleton's Journal* saw at work in Paris and Chicago, and that many Americans identified with the Parisian *pétroleuses*.[90]

Of course, many *Parisiennes* were active in the Commune; like all wars and revolutions, this one provided women with unusual opportunities to engage in direct political action. But their influence was never as pervasive or demonic as contemporary Americans liked to suggest.[91] The *pétroleuses* sent shivers of actual fear through the French middle class, and shivers of anticipatory fear through their U.S. counterparts. According to American accounts, the female "petroleum-thrower" was a double threat. First, she threatened to wreck Americans' belongings, as the harbinger of a "great Pandemonium, of which the burning Paris of May . . . [was just] an epitome and a warning."[92] Worse, she threatened to wreck their society by upsetting the bourgeois gender order. A string of ungracious adjectives said that female Communards were different from the idealized women at home. From her window in Paris, Mrs. Willard wrote that the women of the Commune were "wanton," "brazen," "shrunken, haggard, and wild."[93] A New York editor opined that the *pétroleuses* were "coarse, brawny, unwomanly"; a female poet added "pale, frenzied, . . . [and] fierce"; they all agreed that the *pétroleuses* were unnatural and un-feminine.[94]

By their own admission, just thinking about the female revolutionists in France made some American men feel distinctly "unmanned."[95] Still worse, they feared that the desexed (or hypersexed) *Parisienne* had counterparts in America. The Reverend Charles Boynton, for example, saw ominous links between the foreign Commune and the indigenous women's movement. Just blocks from the nation's Capitol, he preached that the "woman movement" was just another "form" of the International, that "world wide association in sympathy with the French Communist[,] which proposes the destruction of all government, all social order and all religion." Its goal, he added, was to "place *man* on the road to Atheism."[96]

Victoria Woodhull, the controversial feminist, probably embodied all of his fears. She defended the Paris Commune, befriended Ben Butler and George Francis Train, and petitioned the Senate for women's suffrage. She believed in "free love." She joined the International. And not surprisingly, she and her followers reaped the same gendered epithets as the original *pétroleuses:* "half-crazed females . . . and lean, irrepressible women."[97] Susan B. Anthony was another of Train's occasional allies.[98] Just as the Paris Commune ended, she began a speaking tour on behalf of women's rights. In the Pacific Northwest, editors delighted in linking her to both Woodhull and Train, and even wrote that she represented the "immoral views and sentiments of the French Commune," which was "rapidly developing and attempting to organize under the Women's Rights standard" in America.[99]

For years to come, explains Meredith Tax, a feminist reformer could expect to be denounced as "a 'Commune-ist'—advocating something like the Paris Commune." Henry James was a case in point, equating a feminist reformer in *The Bostonians* (1886) with "some feminine firebrand of Paris revolutions, erect on a barricade."[100] Here was a way for middle- and upper-class men like James to avoid their fears about a shift in gender relations. All you had to say was "Feminists are foreign, just like the women of the Commune." But unlike the *pétroleuses*—and more than Native Americans—American women were undeniably present in the

United States. Comparing them to the Paris Commune only made it harder to deny that a "Commune-ist" upheaval of any sort was possible in America.

American reactions to the Paris Commune reflected pre-existing social and cultural divisions in the United States. Some contemporaries interpreted these divisions as a breach between order and disorder, and in this chapter I have focused on their perspective (without endorsing it). On one side of the breach stood a middle-class establishment epitomized by the Protestant clergy, which enjoyed privileged access to the new commercial culture that was integrating the nation. Generally speaking, this establishment was white, male, Protestant, and self-consciously devoted to policing the status quo. On the other side of the breach stood "the other" in all its different avatars: the Indian and the incendiary, the heathen and the beast, the immigrant and the criminal, the madman and the feminist, "Boss" Tweed and the democratic masses—every embodiment a threat to domestic tranquility. Images of the Commune were plastered across the breach in the process of predictive Americanization, as worried members of the bourgeoisie used the Paris uprising to express their fears of similar unrest at home and simultaneously to deny that similar unrest was even possible at home.

Although Americans generally understood that the Commune was a foreign event with distinctive causes, they readily compared it to domestic phenomena, starting with the Civil War. This helped them make sense of the Commune. It also helped them make sense of domestic disorder, by providing a handy foreign reference. Both those who feared disorder and those who were relatively confident about social stability could point to the French uprising as an example. If the result was a paradox, then at least it was consistent with other American reactions: The Commune was like America, but the United States wasn't like Paris. Americans tried to have it both ways, and for a while they succeeded.

On Independence Day in 1871, for example, the *New York Times* calmly suggested, "If we have the material of a bloody Commune among us, we can regard its development as capable of control. It has no necessity of scaling the Capitol . . . and there will be no need of a siege of New-York by the authorities at Washington to drive it out." But the *Times* was less complacent two years later when it grumbled at the "spread of communistic ideas on the Continent" and the spread of "Communistic claims in

New-York."[101] In the summer of 1877, the grumbling finally turned to grief: "The days are over in which this country could rejoice in its freedom from the elements of social strife which have long abounded in old countries."[102]

Foremost among those elements was the growing strife between capital and labor, which had come to overshadow the other divisions in American society. In the process, the role of the Paris Commune in American culture changed until it finally became what Karl Marx and Friedrich A. Sorge prematurely described in 1871: a vicarious battleground for workers and bosses.

7

Apocalypse Where?
Apocalypse When?

Paris is preaching mankind a most instructive sermon, . . . to which
New York may listen with advantage.

—GEORGE TEMPLETON STRONG (1871)

In 1871 many Americans complained that the version of the Commune
offered by their newspapers was muddled, incomplete, and often grossly
inaccurate. Some complained ruefully, some complained bitterly, and some
complained from the perspective of class conflict. In particular, Americans
on the left complained that the press and the privileged class that controlled it were intentionally distorting the news from France. As Friedrich
Sorge, the German-born labor radical, explained to his mentor, Karl Marx,
"the Commune in Paris gave to the American Press a fresh opportunity to
renew their venomous attacks, calumniations & execrations of the Parisian
Workingmen, our [International] Association . . . and its members."[1] One
indignant reader of *Woodhull & Claflin's Weekly* likewise complained that
"persistent misrepresentations of the position and objects of the Paris
Communists . . . [are] evidence of the 'Holy Alliance' between the American press and European despotisms, civil and ecclesiastical." The *Weekly's*
editors were quick to add their own attack on the *New York Times, Herald,*
and *Tribune* for supporting "the money power of France" in their bloody
repression of the Commune. "Why not squelch every other workingman's
organization," they asked sarcastically, "and therein give full scope to the
money powers, who now only tolerate suffrage while they can manipulate
it and get sanction and endorsement through the honey-fugling [*sic*] and
wire-pulling of *plébiscites* and primaries[?]"[2] Wendell Phillips was more
temperate but no less direct when he protested that American reporters in
Europe were all "lying about the Commune" in order to feed the middle-
class loathing of working-class movements.[3]

These protests, paired with blatant attacks from American conservatives
on both the Commune and domestic reform, have led historians to con-
clude that "'communism' . . . quickly became an all-purpose epithet applied by conservatives to anyone or anything found distasteful."[4] This

142

analysis nicely conforms to the orthodox theory of class conflict, but it suffers from two basic shortcomings. The first is that conservatives, even when defined as a small segment of the bourgeoisie, were not monolithic; while their reaction to the Commune was generally negative, it was also genuinely nuanced.

Second, there is a tendency in the works of these historians to examine early responses to the Commune through the lens of subsequent conflict, thus distorting the lines of cause and effect. Edward Gargan, for example, asserts that in 1871 the "social program represented by the Communards provoked in America an unlimited will to violence in the defense of conventional beliefs," and then immediately concludes that the "violence of the 1870's and during the labor strikes of 1877 . . . illustrate[d] the consequences for a society that willed to be free of inhibiting mechanisms against official violence." Art historian Albert Boime makes a similar elision from the "chorus of abuse in the American press" in 1871 to the "obsession of the American press with the Commune . . . during the early 1870s" to the "dire example of the Commune" offered by various popular novelists at the end of the century—all in the space of just over three paragraphs.[5]

Although I have singled them out, Gargan and Boime are far from the worst offenders. Moreover, as they and many other scholars properly note, "communism" and "the Commune" did serve as antilabor epithets during and after the Great Strike of 1877 (see below). But Americans reached that point only after struggling through the problem of Americanization described earlier: that is, after considering the vital question of whether the Paris Commune, and all that it represented, was alien or applicable to American society. In this chapter, I look at some of the ways that conservatives wrestled with the problem of Americanization in both 1871 and 1877. In the next chapter, I examine the cultural threat that "Commune-like" labor represented to non–working-class Americans both before and during the Great Strike.

There was no consistent conservative response to the Paris Commune in 1871. To be sure, trying to find a hostile response to the Commune that year was like trying to find hay in a haystack. Almost every editorial, magazine article, and book on the subject at some point compared the Commune to the dark days of Terror under the French Revolution, or condemned the Communards as murderers, vandals, and cruel social levelers. In this the domestic commentators seemed to follow the lead of some Americans in Paris (like Pembroke Fetridge and Mrs. Willard) and of most of the French bourgeoisie, but the resemblance was more a matter of convergence than direct influence.

In 1871, the most compelling image of the French Revolution for most Americans was still the image presented by Charles Dickens, which led one magazine writer to note, "There is a 'Tale of Two Cities' worthy of the telling of a Dickens or [Thomas] Carlyle, in the Paris . . . of to-day."[6] The "Reds of Paris," added the *Nation,* have "indulged in the luxuries of an imitation Reign of Terror," and the *Atlanta Constitution* echoed that the Commune's red flag was "simply the emblem of Terror and Chaos." "In a word," concluded a tiny Western paper, the Commune "is but the mad restoration of those dark days when the guillotine was moistened in the blood of France's best men and women."[7]

As for crime, Linus P. Brockett wrote that "intemperance, debauchery, licentiousness, and murder ran riot in the city . . . Never had vice of all descriptions been so bold and unblushing as it was now." He continued, "We might easily fill the pages of a volume larger than this with narratives of the horrors of these two months, the murders, the blasphemies, the treasons, the avowals of doctrines and the commission of acts which fairly make the blood curdle; but we forbear."[8] The *New York Herald* simply concluded that "murderers let loose on society could not be worse than the Paris Commune."[9]

Perhaps the harshest language was reserved for attacking the supposed leveling tendencies of the Commune. The *Cleveland Leader* complained that the present revolution, like all previous French revolutions, was "a conspiracy of Socialists and Communists." With more than a hint of fear it then predicted that "property throughout France will be seized and distributed to the rabble should the Reds extend and maintain their power." The *New York Times* also fixed on the real Terror "which lie[s] back of the present revolution . . . the fear that it is a socialistic outbreak, a stroke at property itself." The *Philadelphia Ledger* simply noted that "'Property is robbery' with them."[10]

Even the *Youth's Companion,* a children's magazine published in Boston, felt compelled to attack the Commune (with an eye, perhaps, to the proper raising of a new generation of workers). "Some of the Reds," they warned their young readers, "are men so extreme in their ideas that they go for the equalization of property, and for similar absurdities . . . Perhaps they are best defined as men who are opposed to the present state of society, but who have not prepared a substitute for it . . . [They] are looked upon as enemies of order, and as seeking the destruction of life and property,—and as being opposed to everything that decent people like."[11] The decent people who wrote editorials for the Midwestern press seemed to agree. Thus, the *Cleveland Leader* yearned for a "benefactor . . . [to] curb the lawless vagabondism of the Commune," while the *Chicago Tribune* advocated "mowing down" the ruthless Parisians "without compunction or hesitation."[12]

This catalog of vitriol could be extended ad nauseam, but as Marxist historian Samuel Bernstein points out, "The denunciations of the Paris Revolution, often detailing the same alleged horrors, make monotonous reading."[13] This does not mean that American conservatism spoke with once voice, however. Consider the clergy. No group in the Gilded Age spoke so consistently for the status quo or was so quick to point out the dangers that threatened its continuation. Whether the danger was foreign or domestic, religious or secular—and in some ways the Commune was all four—an American clergyman was there to decry it.[14] Henry C. Bowen, the editor of the *Independent,* an influential religious weekly published in New York, was well aware of this fact. As the Commune ended he noted that the "terrible events . . . were the text of a few sermons last Sabbath, and every pulpit will have its say next Sunday. The applications to the state of things in this country are numerous and evident enough to give points enough to any thoughtful preacher."[15] Yet the pulpits presented a wider range of views than Bowen probably expected.

Most religious leaders reacted in horror to the Commune's irreligion, and some even feared it would spread to America via the International Workingmen's Association.[16] While a pious layman like George Templeton Strong was qualified to note that "*la belle France* is Satan's country seat and summer home," it took men of the cloth, with professional expertise in the ways of Evil, to fully realize the dangers of French atheism.[17] Before the Commune was half over, the prominent Boston Unitarian Edward Everett Hale observed that "the sans-culottes of to-day are persuaded, by their mad leaders, that in the overthrow of the churches they are striking out one of the vestiges of imperialism." In mid-April, the *Independent* denounced the "anti-religious animus of the Reds" and added for good measure that the "intellectual life of a nation cannot save it from the ruin that follows irreligion and immorality."[18] President Mark Hopkins of Williams College addressed the same theme in May when he spoke on "Modern Skepticism" at the International Convention of the Young Men's

Christian Association. Alluding to current events in Paris, he suggested that "corruption" and the "ridicule" of religion "have made France what she is to-day."[19] The Reverend Octavius B. Frothingham, a well-known Boston reformer, strongly agreed, noting that France had given itself over to "luxuriance, and became a nation without a religion . . . [T]he punishment of Providence [now] comes upon them for their skepticism."[20]

A few Sundays later, Frothingham's colleague, the Reverend Charles Brandon Boynton, preached a similar sermon at the Assembly Presbyterian Church in Washington, D.C., on "The French Commune as a Popular Medium of Evil." Boynton used this prominent pulpit to denounce Charles Darwin and the International as the two "great forces which are leading our modern world away from God." He reserved his greatest animus, however, for the godless IWA, "that almost world wide association in sympathy with the French Communist[,] which proposes the destruction of all government, all social order and all religion . . . [But] any attempt to construct a society without the recognition of God will fail as it has twice over failed in France, and on a smaller scale in many other places."[21]

Such sentiments were common among the Protestant clergy, though American Catholics probably had a better case against the Paris revolutionaries. After all, the Commune had expropriated Catholic churches and executed Catholic priests (plus an archbishop). Armed with these facts, the *Catholic World*, semiofficial organ of the Church in America, duly arraigned the Commune as "the enemies of God" and as "miscreants . . . in violation of law, religion, morality, and every principle of justice."[22] The strongest appeal to Divine justice did not come from the Catholic hierarchy, however. It came instead from the Presbyterian Reformed Synod, meeting in Philadelphia while Bloody Week raged in Paris.

The Reformed Synod was an outgrowth of the main body of American Presbyterianism, representing the denomination's most conservative members, both theologically and politically. On May 22, 1871, the Synod condemned the Commune in general terms and then adopted the following resolution:

That the present condition of France in general, as desolated by storm of war, and of the city of Paris in particular, as now drenched by the blood of her own citizens, is a righteous retribution for the martyrdoms of St. Bartholomew's Day [1572], and the tangible fulfillment of the Divine promise to the Church, "That no weapon that is formed against thee shall prosper."

Reaction to this "strange view of the French Civil War," as the *New York Evening Post* rightly called it, was swift but mixed. The next day, for example, political scientist Francis Lieber wrote to a colleague in Europe that "priestly arrogance like this is offensive to every one; still, the attention is aroused by such a declaration, and it is well that men should not wholly forget events like the butchery of the Protestants."[23] Others, like the *New York World*, were less restrained.

A lead editorial in the *World* berated the Synod as a "parcel of bigoted busybodies" in desperate need of "reforming itself in the three trifling particulars of Christian charity, common sense, and ordinary historical knowledge." The *World*, of course, was a Democratic newspaper with many loyal Catholic readers, and its attack on the Presbyterians was conditioned by long-standing ethnocultural hostilities. The editors knew they could score points with their readers by attacking the pretensions of WASP clergymen. Knowing this, they focused their sarcasm on the Protestants' newfound sympathy for the Catholic Church when the latter suffered at the Commune's hands:

> From the point of view of the Synod the weapon formed by the Commune was the very sword of the Lord and of Gideon; and if it were possible for such people to be logical they ought to pass a resolution of censure upon Providence for failing to make this weapon prosper, even to the hanging [i.e., shooting] of Archbishop Darboy . . . [It] must be admitted to be a hard measure for the Commune that the earnest desire of its leaders to murder an archbishop should not exonerate them in the eyes of the "Presbyterian Reformed Synod."

The *World* concluded that "from a purely human and humane point of view," the "horrors" of 1572 and the "abominations" of 1871 had yielded "blood enough . . . to satisfy the most exacting of misanthropic accountants with a God of retaliations." As for the Presbyterians, "when such a convocation deviates into secular questions in search of notoriety, and assumes to drag Divine Providence into the service of sectarian spite and stupidity, its practices dispense us from even pretending to respect its professions."[24]

Protestant clergymen were no kinder to their colleagues in the Reformed Synod. Henry Ward Beecher's newspaper, the *Christian Union*, reprinted the *World*'s attack verbatim under the blunt headline "Bigotry Well Rebuked." At the upscale Broadway Tabernacle, the Reverend Dr.

Joseph P. Thompson confessed to "feelings of deep mortification for Christianity" upon reading the Synod's resolution, "the tone and manner of which are monstrous." He added, "It seems to me that the spirit that penned such a resolution is a spirit that would burn Paris, assuming to be the executioners of divine justice. I protest against it in the name of Christianity, civilization, and humanity." To his eyes the Paris Commune was a tragedy rather than a manifestation of evil. Its origin was the religious intolerance of France, which prevented the Parisians from attaining a proper moral education or proper notions of self-government. Its actors deserved compassion rather than censure. Finally, Thompson drew a specific lesson for the well-to-do New Yorkers who sat in his congregation: show some compassion for the poorer classes in your *own* city, or "the rich would hear from them."[25]

A few days after Thomson's sermon, Henry Bowen used the pages of the *Independent* to advance yet another theological view of the Commune. It was almost as reactionary as the one offered by the Presbyterian Reform Synod. Bowen began with a text from the Apocalypse, and then went on:

> The Babylon of the Apocalyptic vision has generally been assumed to be Rome, as the seat of the Papacy, by Protestant divines and commentators. Morally and theologically, perhaps, the description of the Scarlet Woman and her Cup of Abomination may apply [to Rome]; . . . but literally and physically the prophecy would seem to be satisfied by the fate of Paris. The 18th chapter of the Revelation conveys almost as accurate a description of the city of Paris a year ago and now as any that could be written by a contemporary and an eyewitness.

From there Bowen proceeded to gloss the entire chapter, showing how Paris had displayed the vices and suffered the fate of the Scarlet Woman, first at the hands of burly Prussians and then at the hands of barbaric Communists.

His dubious exegesis done, Bowen then took an overt step from theological to political conservatism. (To their credit, the Presbyterian Reformed Synod had resisted this extra step.) Drawing on religious imagery, Bowen gloated, "The Commune has gone down in blood, and we may hope will never have a hideous resurrection." Switching to politics, he added that the Commune's "very excesses and enormities will perhaps be found to work for good . . . by inspiring a general horror of the political and moral heresies from which they sprang." These heresies, as Bowen went on to define them, included any attempt to form a government from men "with no stake of property or character in society"—such as working-men and *déclassé* reformers.[26]

Many Protestant clergymen shared Bowen's harsh view of the Paris Commune.[27] But Joseph Thompson also had his followers in advocating a compassionate view of the events in France. For example, when members of the American Board of Foreign Missions met at Salem, Massachusetts, in October 1871, they managed to discuss the Commune without calling down the wrath of God. Their guest speaker was the Reverend Athanase Coquerel, a well-known French Protestant, who explained the sad fact that French workers "had come to believe that all religion was a species of despotism, and this has destroyed their faith in God. They firmly believed that if they embraced any religion they must give up every civil and political right." Not surprisingly, he blamed the Roman Church for this state of affairs, as he "analyzed the irreligious elements in the late insurrection." Then he encouraged the board members to focus their efforts on teaching rather than preaching in their attempt to evangelize Europe—a suggestion they took to heart as they resolved to fight the ignorance, rather than the evil, in France.

After a fair-handed summary of the meeting, *Woodhull & Claflin's Weekly* described Coquerel (and by extension the American missionaries) as "well-meaning . . . seemingly as much of a philanthropist as a sectarian." But the *Weekly* nonetheless argued that French churches, of whatever denomination, were "part of the machinery of oppression" against which the Communards had struggled. In fact, the *Weekly* concluded that "Jesus Christ, if he had lived in Paris, would have been behind the barricades with *La Commune,* just as he is said to have driven the bankers and brokers out of the temple; and because he promised always to be where truth is found . . . the Commune would consider him a sanguinary Red, and worship him more intelligently than Coquerel or [the archbishop of Paris]."[28] Significantly, even this extreme view found one or two adherents among the American clergy.[29]

In 1871, the Reverend Henry Ward Beecher was "one of the most popular and respected clergymen in the nation," and without doubt the most famous. He was the handsome scion of a particularly distinguished American family: his sisters were Harriet Beecher Stowe, the novelist, and Catherine Beecher, the feminist reformer; his father and several brothers were noted churchmen.[30] But his popularity sprang even more from an ability to articulate middle-class hopes and fears while epitomizing the middle-class "respectability" of his age (a respectability, I suspect, that broadly corresponds to the "conservatism" evoked by the historians cited above). His optimistic theology, usually referred to as "evangelical liberalism" or "the Gospel of Love," replaced the harsh neo-Calvinism that reigned in the time of his father, Lyman Beecher, with a new creed that stressed salvation through loving-kindness. Like his theology, the junior Beecher's support for social reform (abolition, women's suffrage) *and* social stability was aimed at "nurturing, supporting, and reassuring the anxieties of the Victorian public."[31] In this context, his preaching on the Paris Commune is proof that moderation was a viable American response to events in France, even from those who spoke for the status quo.

As biographer Clifford E. Clark argues, Beecher was the "spokesman for middle-class America," both reflecting and affecting a large body of public opinion. He edited the *Christian Union* (circulation 102,000), wrote popular fiction and essays, and earned top dollar on the lecture circuit. His weekly sermons were widely reprinted and discussed. As a result, when he rose to the pulpit at Brooklyn's Plymouth Church, he spoke not only to his congregation but to the nation at large. On Sunday, May 28, 1871, he rose to speak on "The Lesson from Paris."[32]

Like Henry Bowen, the Reverend Beecher drew his text from the eighteenth chapter of Revelation, concentrating on the verse "she shall be burned with fire; for strong is the Lord God who judgeth her" (Rev. 18:8). He began by denouncing the actions of the Paris workers. The scenes of the Commune, he claimed, "which have transpired in Paris during the last month, increasing in horror every week and every day, have filled the world with amazement, and shocked every sensibility." Beecher then claimed that the Commune rehearsed the terrors of the French Revolution; argued that the Commune was not just a political upheaval, but one aimed at society itself; and hinted that the Commune was simply part of a global revolution being hatched by the International.[33]

Conservatives like Bowen would have stopped right there, but Beecher continued. Although he condemned the acts of the Commune, he willingly ascribed both honesty and heroic commitment to a few of the Communards. "The wantonness of the deeds," said the Brooklyn preacher, "admit of no extenuation, and no apology. They may, however, admit of some explanation." Despite the negative press aimed at the Commune, Beecher refused to believe that Communards were "monsters," "beasts," or even insane. Instead, they were on a misguided "crusade in favor of certain distinct, moral, political and social ideas." Ultimately, "they acted in a bad cause as good men would fain act in a good cause."[34]

One explanation that Beecher offered for the terrible events in Paris was that French workers lacked religion, and thus were inclined towards "materialism." Yet he recognized that French people had legitimate complaints about the ruling institutions of their country, which could be genuinely stifling; for unlike lucky Americans, whose society had arisen from the wilderness, Europeans were subjected to the worst evils of church and state. He also believed, like Thompson and the American Board of Foreign Missions, that evangelical Protestantism was the last, best hope for preventing future outbreaks of "communism" in France. Finally, Beecher joined Thompson in chastising the well-to-do people of his own country for not giving sufficient notice to the real cares of the working class.[35]

To his credit, Beecher refused to join in the auto-da-fé against the people of Paris. Instead, in a short prayer before his sermon, Beecher evoked the travails of the American Civil War and the long train of suffering throughout human history to plead for compassion:

> While we look abroad upon nations that are drinking blood and passing away, we pray that we may not forget our own suffering, or the dark days and trying hours which we have known, and that we may not arrogate to ourselves such superiority over others, because for this hour we are secure and they are tempest-tossed and not comforted.
>
> We pray for all nations of the earth. Pity and spare those which thou art chastising, and bind up where thou hast bruised, and establish again the goings of those who have been cast down.[36]

Beecher's compassion and moderation were not unique among clergymen, but the need for such a plea suggests that most of his colleagues were less forgiving towards the Commune. In 1871, therefore, the Commune was neither uniformly condemned by conservatives, nor uniformly described as an exercise in class warfare.

To use the American clergy to describe all of American conservatism is to take a dangerous path. Yet no other group historically regarded as conservative offered a monolithic reaction to the Paris Commune either. Consider the Brahmin intelligentsia of New England, which proudly styled itself as "a conservative intellectual class based on learning and culture."[37]

Many Brahmins devoted themselves to humanitarian causes in the antebellum years, and during the Civil War they helped to forge a new concept of nationalism, often at the cost of their (or their sons') lives. But by 1871 they were spending more time defending the Northern industrial order than trying to improve humanity. James Russell Lowell was a paragon of this intellectual community: an eighth-generation New Englander, a Harvard-bred poet and scholar, a public figure, a former diplomat, and the editor of the most prestigious establishment organ, the *Atlantic Monthly*. When it came to the Commune, indeed he spoke for the Massachusetts industrialists—but reluctantly, and with a healthy sense of irony. In a letter to Leslie Stephen, the English belletrist, Lowell wrote sarcastically that "I have been selling my birthright for a mess of pottage, and find it so savory that I side with Esau more than ever." He explained, "I have just . . . been selling all that I held in my own right . . . I have gone over to the enemy and become a capitalist. I denounce the Commune with the best of them, and find it extremely natural that I should be *natus consumere fruges*— which means that I shall now grow consumedly frugal . . . Property, sir, is the Ponce-de-Leon fountain of youth. I am already regenerate."[38] Similar comments, though generally less self-aware, could be found in the writings of many other New England intellectuals.[39]

Not every member of Lowell's caste was so quick to denounce the Commune as a blow against capital. From the relative safety of Harvard Yard, William James noted that "the gallant Gauls are shooting at each other again!"—and decided, like Athanase Coquerel and others, that the Catholic Church was mostly to blame. As he admitted to a Brahmin companion, Henry T. Bowditch, "I wish we knew what it all meant. From the apparent generality of the movement in Paris, it seems as if it must be something more dignified than it at first appeared. But can anything great be expected now from a nation between the two factions of which there is such hopeless enmity and mistrust as between the religious and revolutionary parties in France?" Charles Eliot Norton, a former Harvard professor and the editor of the *North American Review*, even applauded the Commune as an attempt to redress grievous wrongs in Paris; although he generally believed in moderate reform, he thought that "occasional violent revolutionary action to remove deepseated evils" was sometimes in order.[40]

Louis Agassiz, the Harvard zoologist and a Brahmin by adoption if not by birth, never went quite as far as his friend Norton. Nonetheless, he also thought that the Commune deserved Americans' sympathy as a failed attempt at reform. On the occasion of the French Fair, organized by Boston's female elite to relieve the civilian suffering of the Franco-Prussian War, he confessed that "Parisians . . . are now guilty of acts which shock and alienate their best friends." But he begged his readers to "remember that there are good men even among the dreaded 'reds'; men who have been cheated of their hoped-for republic again and again . . . It is true that the idea of a republic has danced before the eyes of France like a *'feu follet'* rather than a steady light; it has led her through bog and morass . . . But on the other side of the marsh is stable ground and the dawn of day. Let us help her to reach it."[41]

New England intellectuals south of Cambridge also displayed a laudable open-mindedness about the Commune. At commencement time in New Haven, for example, a youthful Eli named Orville Bliss delivered a Class Day oration on "The Educated Man in American Society." According to a report in the *New York Evening Post,* the young scholar "commenced by analyzing society, showing its penalties and rewards, and spoke on the triumph of labor in England," and then went on to support "the Communist troubles in France as a step in the reform of society."[42]

In 1871, the American Protestant clergy spoke with many voices about the Paris Commune, even if most of those voices could be described as conservative. By the end of the decade, however, one voice would dominate all the others: a voice that cried out against the workingman. In particular, the Commune would be used to explain and condemn the acute wave of labor unrest that swept across the United States in the summer of 1877. American interpretations of the Commune changed (and narrowed) with the changing social conditions of the 1870s, and the clergy is a useful place to start examining that transformation. In the rest of this book I focus on the rise and fall of the "American Commune," a term that some critics used to decry domestic labor activism in the 1870s. What follows, by way of a brief introduction, is a "before and after" snapshot of American political culture.

Though he spoke to the better angels of their nature in 1871, Henry Ward Beecher also spoke to the fears of the American middle class, particularly its fear of social upheaval. In his sermon on the Commune he wondered out loud if the tragic events in Paris might some day reproduce themselves on the near side of the Atlantic. After all, "there is a certain general likeness in human nature." Anticipating Charles Loring Brace's description of *The Dangerous Classes of New York,* Beecher even noted that if we "take the account that is given of New York (and perhaps it is not much exaggerated); . . . [we] will be apt to suppose that we are in imminent danger, and that we, too, may have a Paris." The source of this anxiety, which Beecher tried to ease, was the fear that social conditions in Europe and America were rapidly converging.[43]

He admitted that the New World, like the Old, was fast becoming the locus of gaping class divisions; more and more, an "upper class full of riches" seemed to hold sway over the national economy, while the working people suffered. Even Beecher recognized that "if this country stratifies itself [like Europe], . . . we shall come into very imminent perils, and very deadly ones." But American society had a long way to go before it became Europeanized. There was no aristocracy in the United States, and far more religious sentiment than the poor French could ever hope to muster. For the time being, we were further protected from the social woes of Europe by our sparse population and comparative lack of urbanization, our cheap western lands ("that will not fail for generations to come"), a system of education that fostered equality, and the American free press.[44] Yet Beecher's optimism was perilously undercut by the apprehensive concession, early in his sermon, that the United States "may not always be so secure."[45] In this, too, he spoke for middle-class America.

When economic times were good (as they were in 1871), it was easy to sustain an air of optimism, to believe that the United States would never go the way of Europe. When economic times turned bad (as they did after 1873), it was easy to become anxious. Economic times were at their worst when Beecher rose to the Plymouth Church pulpit on July 22, 1877, and his sermon on "The Railroad Riots" reflected some unsettling changes in American social conditions.[46]

"In a time of profound peace," began Beecher, "suddenly there has broken out along the great [railway] routes of . . . our country a riot of unusual magnitude and persistency—a riot of industrious men who have taken the law into their own hands." Yet he quickly consoled his Brooklyn parishioners with the observation that the riot was "only a paroxysm. A few days, or a few weeks at farthest, and the tumult will have subsided." In the meantime, the riots provided an excellent opportunity for all of them to think about the "principles of political economy which are based upon morality."

For his own part, Beecher seemed to let morality get in the way of his political economy, which otherwise was sound. He knew that the railroad strike was a result of the lingering economic depression, which in turn was a result of postwar overexpansion, speculation, and financial instability. He explained this to his congregation clearly and frankly. Yet he also suggested that the railroad strikes had a more important, more ominous, cause: "an organized conspiracy [of the workers] which has in it every element both of opprobrium and peril." With some appearance of liberality, Beecher noted that "every generous mind . . . [has] a disposition to take sides with the weak as against the strong, [and] with the poor as against the rich . . . [Y]et poor men may be in the wrong, and rich men may be in the right," and such was the case right now.

According to Beecher, the "general sobriety" of individual American workers was "unquestionable," and for this reason he sympathized with the hardships they suffered. But their labor organizations were another matter entirely, for "a foreign element . . . has come into these 'unions' in America." This was a "poisonous element," spreading ideas about collective action that "surpasse[d] the most bitter tyranny of Europe" in that they denied "personal independence and popular liberty." This foreign element was also immoral, playing upon the workers' ignorance to lead them into "a very great crime": the railroad strike, which "strikes at the [very] foundation of organized society, and at universal industry." "The philosophy on which [the railroad strikers] . . . are acting is a false one," concluded Beecher. "It may do for the Communes of Paris and the slums of Europe, but it should be scorned by the intelligent workingmen of America."

Wasn't America supposed to be immune from such elements and ideas in the first place? So Beecher had claimed in 1871, and so he tried to preach again in July 1877. He stated with confidence, "It is just as sure that . . . [the strikers and their philosophy] will be overthrown, as that natural laws in the long run will prevail against any momentary infraction or overslaughing of them." But his words sounded tremulous and shrill, and a week later, on July 29, Beecher returned to the pulpit to reconsider "The Strike and Its Lessons."[47]

Beecher's first lesson was that "the working men of the world [are] oppressed . . . Yes, undoubtedly [so], by governments, by rich men, and by the educated classes." They are oppressed, he continued, because whenever men are "ignorant and weak and poor they cannot help being oppressed." The primary example of this was the "working population of Europe[, which] is largely ignorant—that is the trouble." To the extent that they were simply ignorant, Beecher still "sympathize[d] with European laborers in their efforts to right themselves," just as he had done in 1871. He sympathized with "their demand for education"; he even sympathized with "their demand for participation in the management of public affairs." Yet he "abhor[red] the modes and theories that thus far have been devised for the accomplishment of such . . . purposes"—especially because they were being imported into the United States.

Forgetting his former sympathy for the European workers, Beecher announced that they were "not fit to be teachers of Americans." Here was the next important lesson that he drew from the American strikes: "The importation into America of European emissaries and European theories and European methods for the relief of labor . . . [are] an importation of abominations. The theory of these emissaries is un-American . . . [I]t is Tzarism, it is Caesarism, it is absolute monarchy, . . . [and it is] none the less despotic because it takes on a democratic form, as it exists in the communes." Any sort of "combinations in trades-unions, communes, etc.," he continued, "destroy the liberty of the individual." And so Beecher protested "against the political economy of the French communes, in the name of labor and of laboring men. Communism is a deadly poison . . . We will give citizenship to foreigners, but we will give no citizenship to foreign theories of this kind."

Unfortunately, the theories were already here, and Beecher was unsure why—or perhaps he was just unwilling to admit to himself the reasons. He asserted that "the American idea recognizes no classes . . . [I]n the intense sense in which the term 'class' is now coming to be used in the controversies of the day it is un-American, it is unphilosophic, it is undemocratic, it is false." But he was unable to deny the existence of classes in America by wishing them away, or to solve the problem of class with a stiff lecture on Social Darwinism. It was not just that European socialists had come to America, but that the social differences between Europe and America had been dissolved, as he feared might happen in 1871. Because of that, "the nonsensical schemes of European theorists . . . [now] disturb men's minds and fill them with lies."

For Beecher, the ultimate lesson of the strike was that America's working people needed more education, more self-control, more diligence, and more "manhood after the pattern of Christ Jesus." This was the same lesson that he had drawn for the Parisian workers after the Commune, while vigorously denying that Americans needed such an active regimen themselves. But now his lesson contained a veiled threat to the domestic working class: "Because we are their brothers, we should rebuke them."[48]

Beecher's sermons on the railroad strikes produced an immediate reaction from the striking workers—not only because he was the most famous preacher attacking them, but also because he was the most insulting. In his July 22 sermon Beecher declared, "It is said that a dollar a day is not enough for a [workingman with a] wife and five or six children. No, not if the man smokes and drinks beer . . . but is not a dollar a day enough to buy bread with? Water costs nothing; and a man who cannot live on bread is not fit to live." It was a callous statement, and much more callous out of context, the way it appeared in scores of newspapers across the nation.[49] In a sarcastic response, labor advocate John Swinton congratulated a group of New York workers for not "look[ing] like a mob of rioters; . . . on the contrary, it seems to me that you are quite as good-looking, in my opinion, as Henry Ward Beecher's church." Swinton then attacked Beecher's utter audacity for telling strikers to be satisfied with a dollar a day when the Brooklyn cleric was earning $30,000 a year. A trade-union journal likewise called him a "sanctimonious hypocrite," while crowds of workers chanted "God damn Beecher!"[50] Fortunately, a flood of these negative comments—and not just from angry strikers—made Beecher realize that his statement was somewhat lacking in Christian charity, and he grudgingly apologized both before and during the next week's sermon.[51]

Henry Ward Beecher was not the only man of the cloth to condemn the strikes and the strikers, or to compare the domestic unrest with the distant Commune; far from it. When it came to criticizing the strikers, Beecher actually displayed more restraint than most of his colleagues. What had been a relatively minor note back in 1871—the notion that the Paris Commune was really a virulent form of labor unrest—now emerged from the background noise of Commune descriptions to become a dominant theme in clerical pronouncements. Henry Bowen's *Independent* called for "bullets and bayonets, canister and grape" to be used against the strikers, just as Adolphe Thiers had used them against the Communards.[52] The popular *Congregationalist* magazine called for similar measures, noting that "hundreds of these reckless desperadoes to whom the most fiendish excesses of the days of the Commune in Paris were due, may now be here, fervid apostles of the same red-handed and blazing license."[53] In Scranton, Pennsylvania, the local Presbyterian minister proclaimed, "The spirit abroad is that of the Commune; generated in the shades of moral death, and manifested in a lawless violence which can only be sin."[54] In the city of Chicago, the specter of the Paris Commune was waved about like a bloody shirt, and "along with other citizens, [the clergy] attacked workingmen in general as socialists and communists who should be hunted down like 'mad dogs.'"[55] And Chicago was not an isolated case, for nowhere in 1877 were American churchmen removed from the general run of antilabor opinion.[56]

The wave of clerical comparisons between the Paris Commune and the American strikes did not really crest until a year or so after the summer of 1877, once the clergy had had a chance to ponder what it all meant. By then their conclusions had become quite uniform (surprisingly so, given the diversity of clerical opinion in 1871): the Great Strike was essentially a repetition of the Commune, social distinctions between America and Europe were rapidly disappearing, and the nation was no longer immune to European Communism. In 1878, for example, Roswell D. Hitchcock, the president of Union Theological Seminary, wrote, "To-day there is not in our language, nor in any language, a more hateful word than Communism. In Paris seven years ago, [as] in Pittsburgh last year, . . . it meant, and still it means, wages without work, arson, assassination, anarchy. In this shape of it, the instant duty of society, without a second breath, is to smite it with the swiftness and fury of lightning." In former days, he noted, the Western frontier kept America free from communism: "No French engineering could barricade a prairie." But there had been barricades in 1877, and they were the result of "the unparalleled industrial paralysis of the last five years."[57]

The Reverend Joseph Cook agreed. In a series of popular lectures at the Tremont Temple in Boston in 1880, he railed against the new social convergence between America and Europe. The result, he thought, would be socialism, and socialism was bad. A "socialistic state," he declared, "will lift power away from the people, and give the government a tendency to tyranny such as the Commune exercised so mercilessly. The roughs . . . of Paris had their own way for a time . . . [and one] would think that a single historical example . . . would be enough to convince the world of the impolicy of socialistic political arrangements." France had been convinced by the Commune, but not, unfortunately, America. Instead, the United States had the Great Strike of 1877, and might have similar strikes again.[58] "The time will yet come," he ominously declared, "when America will be roughly awakened from th[e] dream" that she is immune to the social unrest of Europe:

I do not say that Gatling guns will easily be turned against honest property, but they were used against it in Paris . . . [B]y and by we are to have a half-dozen cities as large as Paris . . . [It is] coming; and to-day is the time to discuss the question whether some Thiers or McMahon will be needed before every great city at our second centennial to keep order when demagogues fan the Gehenna-flames of socialist revolution.

Yet Cook concluded, with a hint of the early Beecheresque optimism, that "schools and churches, and not Gatling guns, are to be the delivery of America from the socialistic abuse of universal suffrage."[59] For him, the final lesson of 1877 was this: "There is a French Revolution republicanism . . . [and there] is an American republicanism . . . Whoever does not perceive this vital distinction does not understand American history. There is red republicanism. There is American republicanism. We must insist on this distinction, or we are ruined."[60] But how could we maintain this distinction in the face of domestic labor unrest? Cook really could not say.

This sort of clerical analysis of the Great Strike, with all its attendant fears of the Commune, lasted from 1877 until well into the 1880s.[61] It was most surprising, however, when it flowed from the pen of Joseph Thompson. The Reverend Thompson, who had shown such sympathy for Parisians while rebuking the Presbyterian Reformed Synod in 1871, changed his mind entirely after 1877. The man who once described Paris as struggling for self-government concluded in 1878 that the "Paris commune did not represent the true democracy of France" and that America had "utterly lost in Europe that influence for republican institutions which was so potent [formerly]."[62] Even more significant than the divergence in politics was the dreaded convergence in social conditions that Thompson saw between America and Europe. The man who once predicted that the rich "would hear" from the workers was now clearly stunned by the fact that they had. This can be seen in his tract *The Workman: His False Friends and His True Friends;* it was truly *un*friendly to the Commune, and little more friendly to the working class at home.[63]

The very first sentence of the tract was a frightened reminder of "May, 1871, [when] the world was startled by the report that Paris was in flames . . . set on fire by an organized band of her own citizens, chiefly workmen" (5). Such was the Paris Commune, a great conspiracy "to destroy every vestige, work, and monument of former governments, to efface all distinctions of property and of society," to rule the entire nation, to redistribute wealth, and to make "Labor . . . [the only] thought and care of civil government" (6). That was too bad for France, but just six years later "the world was again startled by the news that the great lines of railway in the United States had been seized by the workmen . . . and all traffic brought to a stand . . . [until] this gigantic conspiracy of Labor against property and law was put down by military power" (6–7). Worse yet, the two conspiracies were somehow linked, for "the attack on the railroads in the United States was prompted by the same motives which actuated the Commune in setting fire to Paris—to assert for workmen the right of control in society and in the state; and the methods by which the right was asserted were the same—destruction and terror" (7).

"*Something* must be wrong in a system or a theory which seeks its ends . . . by such methods," concluded Thompson, and he knew that the system or theory had a name: Communism (8). To the extent that the Commune had simply been fighting centralized government, this clergyman still thought that "the end was good, though the means were evil." Yet as soon as it turned to "economical and social [re]organization"—to Communism as such—"the Commune became a danger and a curse to France" (182). Indeed, it was not just a danger to France but also to America, where the trade unions spent the 1870s striking and preaching socialism.[64]

In a burst of nostalgia, Thompson wrote, "Let American workmen devoutly thank God that in this country the madness of the [socialist] delusion renders it for ever impossible" (158). But he knew that the Great Strike had turned such prayers into so much wishful thinking, so he added a blatant threat to his working-class readers: "American society has been tolerant of . . . all sorts of social experiments, but let the attempt be made to force upon the people community of families or of goods and it would be put down as sharply and decisively as was the Commune in Paris in 1871" (141)—or, he might have added, as sharply and decisively as the American strikes in 1877.

This is a process we have seen before, especially with Edward King: what began as a sympathetic view of the Commune in 1871 was altered by subsequent changes in American society. The Paris Commune was used to describe those changes, and then the domestic transformations were read back into the Commune itself. In King's case, the impetus for this distortion was political change in the South; for Thompson and others, it was economic change in the North. Thompson and the others were also caught in the same historical gap that separated Alexander Stephens from Albert Parsons—the gap between political rebellion and social revolution that made earlier views of the Commune untenable when it came to describing America after the Great Strike.

8

1877: The Rise of the American Commune?

> It is not the proper and lawful refusal of laborers to be oppressed by capitalists, that threatens the public peace; but . . . "the red fool-fury of the Seine," transplanted here, taking root in our disasters, and drawing its life only from our misfortunes.
>
> —JAMES A. GARFIELD (1878)

The single worst threat to the desperate ideal that America was somehow immune to Commune-like unrest was the unavoidable, undeniable presence of a home-grown working class. The United States in the 1870s was wracked by economic turmoil, especially after the Panic of 1873 dragged the nation into deep depression. One result of the downturn was widespread unemployment. Out-of-work Americans were more conspicuous than ever and, together with numerous strikes and the growing militance of labor unions, the unemployed throng made the working class seem like an ominous source of domestic disorder. By 1874 the *New York Times* was already worried that "insane imitations of the miserable class warfare and jealousy of Europe" were beginning to afflict America.[1] It was unprecedented, but not nearly as remarkable as the great strike wave of 1877, which burst upon the land "like a thunderbolt out of a clear sky."[2]

Americans were suddenly confronted with a whole new quality of unrest, which had a distinctly foreign appearance. They went looking for explanations, and what they found was the Commune. For just as the Civil War could be used to make sense of the foreign upheaval in 1871, the Paris Commune—made so familiar by six long years of domestic circulation—could now be used to make sense of the labor unrest at home. In the process, however, the awkward balance between familiar and foreign was permanently upset, and the Paris Commune was transformed from a multivalent political image to a simple mask for the fears of the American bourgeoisie.

If the domestic working class was a threat to complacent views of the Commune, then so were two other groups: middle-class Americans who

161

still defended the Paris uprising, and French political exiles. Both groups were undeniably present in the United States—like little pieces of the Commune at home—but neither was present in any great number. As a result they could usually be disavowed, laughed off, or ignored by the dominant culture.

Consider the Communard refugees, fleeing from the wrath of the Thiers government. The United States was never the mecca for fleeing French revolutionaries that London or Geneva became. Despite the widespread anxiety that undesirable immigrants from France were about to flood the Great West, a mere trickle of French men and women ever reached these shores. In 1871, only 5,780 French immigrants entered the United States legally (as opposed to 107,201 Germans and 61,463 Irish), and for the rest of the decade the yearly average was only slightly higher.[3] Despite the dire warning in *Harper's Weekly* that a "great number of the working-men of Paris, of Communist principles, contemplate emigration to America," at best a few hundred émigrés could really be called Communards, and most of them settled in New York City.[4]

Decades later, Samuel Gompers, longtime president of the American Federation of Labor, remembered that New York in the 1870s was "vividly cosmopolitan with depths in its life that few understood." He also recalled that in "those days New York was the haven for . . . refugee leaders and soldiers from [all] the successive revolutionary movements" in Europe, including the Commune. Gompers even imagined that Manhattan in the early 1870s "looked like Paris during the Commune."[5] Despite Gompers's keen imagination, few participants in the Commune ever found a place in the American labor movement, and even fewer prominent ones. The most notorious was probably Edmond Mégy, who once commanded a legion of National Guardsmen under Cluseret in Paris and then became an active member of the International, an editor, and a loud exponent of revolutionary anarchism in America; one French newspaper even described him as "the head of the New York communards."[6] The most famous was probably Eugène Pottier, author of the "Internationale," who lived for a time in Paterson, New Jersey and became a propagandist for the fledgling Socialist Labor Party in the late 1870s.[7] However, both returned to France after the general amnesty of 1880.

Most of the Communards in America were soldiers rather than leaders in the Paris revolutionary movement. Nonetheless, their presence in the major cities certainly helped to feed the cosmopolitan radicalism of the 1870s and 1880s that Gompers later described. Leonora O'Reilly, who helped found the New York Women's Trade Union League in 1903, specifically recalled that she was motivated to a life of labor activism by her youthful friendship with Commune survivors; according to a co-worker, O'Reilly was profoundly inspired by their "self-sacrifice, . . . [their] renunciation of all those personal ties held dear by most of us, all their splendid, heroic deeds."[8] The survivors in New York formed their own Société des Réfugiés de la Commune, which became a section of the moribund First International in 1873.[9] In several cities they formed their own Masonic lodges.[10] Everywhere they kept to themselves.

Indeed, only on rare occasions did the Communards make their presence known to mainstream America. When they held public meetings, addressed workers' rallies, or gave interviews to the press, the larger community did take notice, but not very much.[11] When a small delegation of French trade unionists came to the Centennial Exposition in 1876, the press briefly turned its attention to the general problem of French workers in America: "Are our authorities cultivating an American Commune?" they asked, and then turned back to the fairground festivities.[12] In one of his more lurid moments, James Dabney McCabe wrote about the "chattering Frenchman with an irresistible smack of the Commune about him" who routinely terrified respectable visitors to the Bowery.[13] But in general, Communard refugees in America were most apparent at the annual commemorations of the civil war that had sent them hither.

As one middle-class observer reported at the end of the 1870s, "There still exists in New York a 'Société des Réfugiés de la Commune,' of whose presence the reader of the newspapers is reminded at yearly intervals." He may not have realized that the society had been celebrating the Commune's anniversary every March since 1873.[14] As individuals, the refugees also participated in the anniversary celebrations arranged by others, and continued to do so through the 1890s.[15] Outside observers regarded these celebrations with derision and wonder. The *New York Times* was amused that one of the meetings included "all the appurtenances of a more aristocratic ball, . . . including a coat-room . . . [with] a dandified colored gentleman." After a more modest gathering in Cleveland, a local journalist thankfully reported that the "long-haired, loud-talking refugees from France . . . who have come here to make wild speeches in attics and cellars to [American] workingmen about their rights and grievances, find that they have mistaken their field." Henry Ammon James, a sensible lawyer with a Yale education, summed up the ruling sentiment about Communard refugees: "They are accustomed to indulge in language of the most extravagent kind known to irresponsible impotence. They may occasionally cause a shock in the breast of some quiet citizen at his comfortable breakfast-table, or lend a hand in riotous demonstrations, but they are otherwise of little importance, as they have no particular influence outside of their own little circle." The refugees were far from desirable, but they were also far from dangerous; their numbers were small, and they were not about to transplant the "red fool-fury" of the Commune to American soil.[16]

The same could be said about native-born, middle-class supporters of the Paris Commune—and often it was. To be sure, the Commune never had more than a few uncritical defenders in the United States, but they did their best to get their views across. Sympathetic American reformers spent the entire summer of 1871 defending the Commune at public meetings and other forums, all of which was duly noted by a skeptical press.[17] At the end of the year, when a prominent group of native-born radicals in New York joined with local organizers of the European-based International to stage a parade in memory of the Parisian martyrs, their efforts drew even more notice.

After a week of delays during which the police tried to halt the demonstration, a parade was finally held on Sunday, December 17. The centerpiece of the demonstration was a somber horse-drawn catafalque, draped in red, decked with flowers, painted with the words "Honor to the Martyrs of the Universal Republic," and escorted by several refugees fresh from Paris. This was a tribute to Louis Rossel, a military hero of the Commune who had just been executed by the French government. The Communards marched to the muffled beat of an African-American honor guard, and they were followed by a procession that reflected the cosmopolitan milieu of New York City: the Skidmore Light Guard (a black militia unit); political refugees from Cuba and France; veteran soldiers of the Garibaldi Guard; French, German, Swiss, and Bohemian sections of the International; reformers such as Victoria Woodhull and Theodore Tilton; Irish nationalists; and many ordinary members of the working class. In all, the procession contained several thousand marchers, most of them wearing red rosettes in their lapels or black armbands on their sleeves. Many red flags and liberty caps were also in evidence, and a banner proclaimed "The Spirit of the Commune Expands As the Axe Falls On the Necks of the Martyrs."[18] One newspaper account mentioned "an unusually large crowd of spectators."[19] What it did not mention was a crowd of nervous bourgeois observers.

Much of the blame for the New York demonstration was pinned on the fiercesome IWA. After all, many people believed the International had started the Commune, and others believed it had started the recent Chicago Fire; thus, it was easy to believe that the International was up to its same terrible tricks in New York. Even before the big parade, the *Evening Telegram* predicted that, given half a chance, New York's Internationalists would prove to be the "same repulsive monsters" as their counterparts in France. Afterward, an association of Gotham's leading philanthropists warned that the International was secretly planning "to annihilate law and re-enact on American soil the atrocities of the Paris Communists."[20] Yet by the end of 1871 the IWA was a moribund organization: it was badly split by factional fights in Europe and badly stigmatized by the Commune. It never had more than 5,000 members in the United States anyway, and most of them were European immigrants. When Karl Marx, the Association's founder, contrived to have its headquarters moved to New York in 1872, he expected it to die a quiet death.[21] The IWA could not have created an American Commune if it tried. On its own, it could not even organize a major American rally in support of the *Paris* Commune; despite what the newspapers thought, native-born radicals and dissident American members of the International had as much to do with the New York solidarity parade as Friedrich Sorge and his European-born Marxists.[22]

Whoever organized it, most middle-class observers were soon convinced that neither the parade nor the International was a real threat to American society. In fact, most agreed with the glib assessment published in the *Cleveland Leader* just days before the march: "The worst that can be said of the New York Communists is that their society . . . is based upon ideas foreign to American citizens."[23] Observers were glad to be able to deny that native reformers had any real influence on the working class. Undeterred, American reformers continued to defend the Commune well into the 1870s.[24] No one paid much attention.

Wendell Phillips was always the exception. Because he was still a famous orator and abolitionist, people listened when he spoke about the Commune. But Phillips was also an infamous agitator, and in the end, complained a Philadelphia journal, "There is no logic in Mr. Phillips . . . [H]e is a rhetorician, a declaimer, a scolder, not a reasoner."[25] Other infamous supporters of the Commune could be similarly discounted: Ben Butler was politically unstable, George Francis Train was mentally unstable, Victoria Woodhull was a woman, and so on. As a result no one seemed to take them, or any other defender, very seriously. On the right, the *Cleveland Leader* awarded such Americans "the palm of lunacy," while the *New York Herald* scorned them as "Cackling Communists."[26] On the other side of the political spectrum, Sorge of the International could barely hide his contempt for the "motley gathering of bourgeois reformers, evangelists of free love, atheists and deists" who joined him in supporting the Paris uprising.[27] Like the scattered French refugees, these American radicals were easy to ridicule, easy to ignore.

It was much more difficult to ignore the presence of a domestic working class in the United States. From the start, the events of the Commune led some American observers to wonder about the future of labor relations in this country (though not, we have seen, to the exclusive degree described by later historians).[28] In Congress, Republican George Frisbie Hoar of Massachusetts was sufficiently inspired by the Commune to propose "the appointment of a commission on the subject of the wages and hours of labor and the division of profits between labor and capital in the United States."[29] According to one of the bill's supporters, it was France's inattention to the labor question that had "lighted the fires of the Commune in Paris," and now "we are following in the footsteps of the old nations." But opponents on both sides of the aisle scoffed that "there are great differences between the conditions of the working classes of Europe and here" and that "we can gather very little information from Europe which shall be of importance to us." John W. Killinger, a Pennsylvania Republican, added that American workers were striving for something "widely different from what I understand the Commune of Paris . . . to be striving for."[30] Others must have agreed: though grudgingly approved by the House in the last days of 1871, Hoar's bill perished in the Senate a few months later, a quiet sacrifice to party politics and American exceptionalism.

Outside Washington, antilabor voices also tried to compare domestic labor unrest to the Paris Commune. As early as April 1871 a strike in the Pennsylvania coal fields became "The Commune in Pennsylvania," and similar descriptions were repeated around the country.[31] The response to these comments was usually the same as the response that greeted Hoar's proposed labor commission in Congress: the "circumstances . . . which helped the leaders of the Paris Commune in their mad work" just did not obtain in the United States. As the *New York World* put it, "The social conditions in America tend incessantly to mitigate and to dissipate as the social conditions of Europe tend to embitter and concentrate, what may be called the 'class-life' of the laboring multitude."[32]

This confidence in the peculiar stability of American social conditions was badly tested by the Crash of 1873 and the long depression that followed. In September 1873 a financial panic swept through Wall Street, demolishing Jay Cooke's giant investment house along with dozens of smaller firms. Banks by the hundreds called their loans, market values tumbled, and the New York Stock Exchange was forced to suspend trading for the first time since it had opened its doors in 1792. What followed was the "longest period of uninterrupted economic contraction in American history," lasting fully sixty-five months.[33] Before it was over, thousands of businesses had failed, defaulting on more than a billion dollars in debt. All told, economic activity in the United States declined by a third between 1873 and 1878.

American workers bore the main brunt of this economic contraction. In some places consumer prices declined by as much as a fifth during the depression, but wages fell even more. In New York City, for example, a union carpenter might have earned $2.50 to $3.00 a day in 1872, and only $1.50 to $2.00 three years later (with a longer workday as well). The average decline in wages was 50 percent in Pennsylvania, with similar drops in other industrialized states. That was for workers who were lucky enough to have a job. According to one New York relief agency, there were 93,750 unemployed workers in that city during just the first winter of the depression, or about one-quarter of the available workforce. Nationwide, a million workers were out of work by 1874. The jobless walked the streets, tramps roamed the countryside, and famine darkened the homes of the poor. Finally, as Pennsylvania's Secretary of Internal Affairs pointed out in 1876, "the antagonism between rich and poor, learned and illiterate, . . . [was] making itself fearfully manifest."[34]

Suddenly, the United States resembled the tottering, class-riven nations of Europe. The collapse of American exceptionalism that Melville, Phillips, Child, Beecher, Brace, and dozens of others foresaw in the wake of the Paris Commune now looked as if it had come to pass. The proof was in the ragged American proletariat and the increasing amount of labor unrest. Labor historians are still unsure just how many strikes took place between 1873 and 1877, but they do know that the number of strikes was rapidly increasing.[35] The strikes also seemed to be growing more violent, especially in the coal-mining districts of Pennsylvania and the Midwest. And it was increasingly likely that strikes would be compared to the Paris Commune.[36]

Looking back on "the agitation in labor circles" that occurred during the long depression, noted detective Allan Pinkerton described it as having been "under [the] leadership of agents of the Commune," cleverly disguised as Molly Maguires and the Knights of Labor. Of course this was just a fantasy, but it was neither a post hoc fantasy nor Pinkerton's alone. Newspapers in the mid-1870s routinely reported strikes as being "perpetrated at the insistence of . . . Communist leaders." In 1875 one railroad manager even warned the Pennsylvania legislature that the Molly Maguires in the state's coal fields were "a class of agitators . . . brought here for no other purpose than to create confusion, to undermine confidence, and to stir up dissension between the employer and the employed . . . [They are] advocates of the Commune and emissaries of the International."[37] Not just strikes, but other forms of labor protest also received the Commune label. For example, from 1873 to 1875 Chicago witnessed a series of demonstrations by unemployed workers who demanded jobs and relief from the city government; the *Chicago Tribune* routinely described these demonstrations as the work of "the Commune in Chicago."[38] On January 13, 1874, more than 7,000 New Yorkers, most of them unemployed, gathered at Tompkins Square in lower Manhattan to make the same demands; they were met by the police and a riot ensued. A socialist speaker named Justus Schwab was arrested for carrying a red flag, among other offenses, and he supposedly told the magistrate, "It must come to the Commune at last. We intend to make the streets of New York run redder with blood than those of Paris did."[39] Across the country, newspapers were quick to describe this entire sordid episode as "The Commune in New York" or even the "American Commune." They were also quick to blame it on communists, the rump International, even the scattered Parisian refugees—anything except the hurting economy.[40]

Through all this mounting unrest and despite their own repeated allusions to the Paris Commune, spokesmen for the dominant culture somehow managed to maintain their faith in American exceptionalism. Just days after the Tompkins Square riot, George Templeton Strong confided to his diary that the tumult was caused by "German and French Communists or 'free-thinkers' (calling themselves unemployed workmen)," not by real Americans. Perhaps he had read in the *Times* that "Communism is not a weed of native growth"; certainly he agreed with the next issue of *Harper's*

Weekly that the "follies and ferocities of the Commune are alien to American thought and American methods."[41] As usual, the editors of the *Chicago Tribune* were less hopeful than their New York counterparts. But for all their references to local communism, they still conceded that any "attempt to organize the Commune presupposes a peculiar mental or moral state" that Americans did not display—at least not yet. All the American workingman needed was basic "comfort, [both] mental and physical," said the *Tribune* in 1874; give him that and "a larger share in the product of his labor, . . . and you make the Commune impossible."[42] Unfortunately, even this weak form of optimism was dashed by events in 1877.

By July 1877 workers on the Baltimore & Ohio railroad had had enough. Since 1873 they had watched their wages dwindle and their standard of living deteriorate. Early that month, managers at the B&O and other railroads announced a 10 percent pay reduction, the second such general cutback since the start of the depression. It went into effect on July 15. On July 16, forty firemen at Camden Junction near Baltimore refused to run their locomotives. At Martinsburg, West Virginia, a critical freight-handling center, 1,200 more B&O employees stopped the trains.[43]

These were spontaneous protests against hard times and exploitation. But the rest of the American working class was just as distressed by the dreadful economic conditions of the long depression, and just as angry about the callous indifference of railway managers and other bosses. The strikes in West Virginia and Maryland were contagious. In the next two weeks, almost a million workers across the land either walked off the job or engaged in some other form of protest. Nothing like it had ever been seen in the United States before. Of course there had been numerous strikes in the nation's history, but nothing of this magnitude. From the start it was called the Great Strike.

Actually, it was a series of strikes, simultaneous but never fully connected; mutual inspiration, not coordination, carried the day. From Martinsburg and Camden Junction the strike wave spread to Baltimore and Pittsburgh; Grafton and Wheeling, West Virginia; Chicago and St. Louis; Scranton and Reading, Pennsylvania; Buffalo and Cincinnati; Hornellsville, New York, and Newark, Ohio; Terre Haute and Peoria; to the capital cities of Columbus, Albany, and Trenton; and to dozens of other cities, large and small, across the Northeast and Midwest. The South alone remained largely unperturbed. From the B&O Railroad the wave spread to the Erie, the New York Central, the Pittsburgh and Fort Wayne, the Pennsylvania, the Atlantic and Great Western, and the Lakeshore Railroads, along with many smaller lines.[44] The strike expanded from railroad workers to longshoremen and freight handlers, then to coal miners and ironworkers, and quickly to dozens of other trades. In St. Louis, unrest at the railyards even induced a citywide "general strike," and for a week a committee of the Marxist Workingmen's Party "assume[d] the appearance of a rival city government"—the first time this social phenomenon had ever been seen on American soil.[45]

New York had noisy sympathy rallies. San Francisco had bloody race riots. In Pittsburgh, the state militia arrived from Philadelphia on July 21 and promptly gunned down twenty strikers and onlookers, wounding even more; in return, the strikers torched the Union Depot and reduced two miles of downtown Pittsburgh to a smoldering heap of ashes. Strikers also clashed with the militia and the police in other cities, and the result was more death and fire. For only the second time in American history (the first since 1834), federal troops were used to quell a labor disturbance. As quickly as it began, the Great Strike was over; by August 5 the Army was able to assure President Hayes that *pax semper ubique:* peace prevailed everywhere.[46]

This is merely a sketch of what happened in the Great Strike of 1877. The details have been told, and told well, many times before. Here I want to focus on just two points: the contemporary sense that the strikes were unprecedented and the overwhelming flood of comparisons between the American strikes and the Paris Commune. Why, in the midst of the worst domestic crisis "since the days of the Civil War," was this foreign event so ubiquitous?[47] What did the Paris Commune mean to Americans six years after it was crushed?

Americans should hardly have been surprised by the outbreak of strikes in 1877, but they were. Despite the growing intensity of labor protest in the 1870s, the middle class still clung to the belief that America was immune to social unrest. This complacency made the Great Strike all the more shocking. Immediately after the strikes, the editor of the conservative *Princeton Review* observed, "No event since the bombardment of Sumter has struck the country with such startling and ominous dismay, or been accepted as so loud a summons to rally to the defence of our altars and firesides as the mobocratic reign of terror in the latter part of July under the lead of railroad strikers."[48] "Sudden as a thunder-burst from a clear sky, the crisis came upon the country," wrote the first historian of the strikes in 1877, and his colleague, James Ford Rhodes, employed the same turn of phrase some forty years later: "[the strikes] came like a thunderbolt out of a clear sky, startling us rudely. For we had hugged to the delusion that such social uprisings belonged to Europe." Rhodes knew what he was talking about, having watched the 1877 strikes from behind an office desk in Cleveland.[49]

Perhaps they were wrong to be shocked by the fact, but contemporaries like Thomas A. Scott, president of the Pennsylvania Railroad, correctly observed that the latest strikes were "unexampled in American history."[50] They actually witnessed what modern scholars can only describe: "for the first time, a single strike action developed into a wave on a national scale."[51] And they were frightened by what they saw. At the very least, as E. L. Godkin warned them, the country was being menaced by "a rising of the worst elements," which he and other spokesmen for the dominant culture variously described as disaffected elements, roughs, mobs, hoodlums, the rabble, rioters, tramps, suspicious-looking individuals, bad characters, thieves, law-breakers, labor-reform agitators, bummers, bands of worthless fellows, malcontents, incendiaries, and riffraff.[52] That was bad enough. But where Godkin saw only "simple ruffianism," others sensed anarchy and revolution. "The danger was terrible and real," says James D. McCabe, "and for a moment the American people stood appalled, not knowing how far the revolt might extend, or what character it might assume."[53]

In the midst of this confusion, the Commune helped explain what was going on. Disorder and rebellion were the watchwords of the day, and even before 1877 the Commune had become a multivalent image of disorder and rebellion. In 1878, Henry Ammon James recalled an "alarming glimpse of the possibilities of disorder in this country . . . [that] bore an unpleasant resemblance to some of the methods of past revolutions in France." He could have been reading year-old newspapers, like the issue of *Frank Leslie's Illustrated* that explained how the strike "arose with the suddenness of the Parisian mob . . . and culminated, from extraneous sources, in the terrors of the Commune, in which fire and pillage and murders were, as usual, the instruments of short-lived popular frenzy." Or the issue of the *Pittsburgh Commercial Gazette* that complained, "It was as though the French Commune had suddenly been vomited over us, and all the scenes characteristic of the Commune were re-enacted in the city of Pittsburgh."[54]

References, allusions, and comparisons to the Commune were everywhere that summer. The word "Commune" probably appeared in more American headlines and editorials during the last week of July 1877 than during any week in 1871. The *Pittsburgh Commercial Gazette* fretted that "the elements of the Commune are not confined to Paris. We have them in our midst," and the *Baltimore American* identified "the gaunt spectre of Communism stalk[ing] through the land."[55] The *St. Louis Globe-Democrat* asserted, "Every trade-union and labor organization is infected with members of the American Commune"; for the *Philadelphia Inquirer* it was clear that labor had "declared war against society . . . They have practically raised the standard of the Commune in free America."[56] A headline blared in Cincinnati: "THE RED FLAG: IT CASTS ITS UGLY SHADOW OVER OUR QUEENLY CITY." In Manhattan, a volunteer soldier noted how the "red flag of the Commune had been raised in New-York."[57] According to papers in distant cities, there was "Something Like Communism at Cumberland [Maryland]," while the Baltimore "mob . . . [was] seeking to emulate the terrible deeds of the Commune."[58] Headlines in New York declared: "THE COMMUNE AT PITTSBURGH . . . BLOOD, FIRE, FLAME, PILLAGE AND PLUNDER . . . A CITY SURRENDERED TO ANARCHY." In Pittsburgh itself, the newspapers thought they heard "the howl of the Commune" and thought they saw a mob "as bloody, revengeful, and lawless as ever disgraced Paris."[59] Even at a safe distance from the violence, in Louisville, Kentucky, editors concluded that events in Pittsburgh and elsewhere were worse than the "wildest orgie[s] of the Paris Commune."[60]

Of course, newspapers were not alone in asserting a parallel between the Commune and the strikes. As we have seen, it flowed from the pulpits as well, where the "reverend clergy . . . assumed to interpret the Providence of the strike" by comparing it to the evil uprising in France.[61] The same sort of language also appeared in two "instant histories" of the Great Strike produced for the subscription-book trade by the end of 1877. In one, James D. McCabe waxed eloquent about "the horrors of the Parisian Commune" that had befallen poor America. In the other, Joseph Dacus evoked "the fiendish spirit of the Commune," which "inaugurate[d] a reign of terror more dreadful than that which appalled the civilized world in France."[62] These examples, from every medium, could be repeated ad nauseam, if not ad infinitum.[63] The point is that the Commune was widely used to describe the American strikes and was often used to evade the real issues involved in the labor unrest.

James Ford Rhodes was hardly the only person to notice that most comparisons between the strikes and the Commune were misguided, if not pernicious. His opinion is worth quoting: "Writers . . . who have based their accounts on newspaper sources, have pushed historical parallels too far when they have compared the riots of 1877 with the terrible days of the first French Revolution and of the Paris Commune of 1871. In truth a thorough study will show much more conspicuous diversities than resemblances between the American and the French uprisings."[64]

The spontaneous strike wave in America had little in common with the French civil war, except for the fact that both uprisings involved angry workers and ended in violence; only in St. Louis and a few other places did American strikers or their leaders act with the same political consciousness that the Commune displayed in its best moments. Rhodes was right about that. What he failed to mention was the important *cultural* function that the Commune served for many middle-class Americans in 1877, as a handy template for interpreting the events around them. Throughout the 1870s, the demands of commercial culture and domestic ideology had steadily rendered the foreign Commune familiar, at least in some Americanized version; economic change had suddenly caused domestic strikes that seemed foreign; and both processes came together in the last, hot days of July.

Individuals were probably comparing the strikes to the Paris Commune even before they read what the newspapers and other public sources had to say about the subject. In many cases, I suspect, newspaper headlines and editorials simply confirmed a latent comparison that was already forming in their readers' minds. Americans had spent six years reading and hearing about the Commune, and now those assorted descriptions of unrest came in handy to describe what they were seeing out their windows. Charles Loring Brace, who had spent long years worrying about the problem of the *prolétaire* in America, now wrote to a young female friend that he was "not afraid of the mob or commune-spirit in this country," but his brave words rang hollow. A more spontaneous reaction was recorded by Andrew Hickenlooper, the superintendent of the Cincinnati gas works, who confided to his private journal that the "rabble . . . forcibly brought to mind the days of the French Commune." A self-described "Tax-Payer" in Pittsburgh wrote to his local editor that "the furious beasts" of the city reminded him of the "Parisian mob that reeked [*sic*] its vengeance upon the monumental column of the Place Vendome." In a personal letter to a colleague, a militia officer agreed that events in Pittsburgh were "outrages which Paris in its days of butchery would have blushed at." Even Elihu Washburne, who should have known better, was unduly influenced by common images of the Paris uprising when he compared the recent strikes to the Commune as works of the "organized mob . . . [of] force and terror."[65]

As an image of disorder, the Commune was a useful way to describe the Great Strike, which to many Americans seemed otherwise inexplicable. But the history of the civil war in France also recommended a good solution to the present unrest: armed intervention by national troops.[66] Americans still remembered the effective use of military force in their own Civil War, and industrialists needed little prodding to call on President Hayes to deploy strikebreakers. Yet the Commune provided a certain historical justification: while the American army had not been used against strikers since Andrew Jackson's time, the French army had been used against the Commune just six years before.

The call for French-style repression came from many quarters. Philadelphia was the calmest big city in the East during the strike wave. Even so, notes one historian, the "Paris Commune was fresh in the memory of many Philadelphians and most newspaper editors, at least, felt that any means were legitimate if they tended to prevent such an outbreak in Philadelphia." The *Philadelphia Inquirer* panicked and wrote that the strikers have "practically raised the standard of the Commune in free America"; the *Philadelphia Record* agreed, and went on to argue that Americans should adopt the same "grape and canister" policy as Versailles in 1871.[67] In Pittsburgh, the *Evening Chronicle* likewise called for "grape and canister," while the *Commercial Gazette* insisted that the "spirit of the Commune is growing, and this cannot be tolerated . . . Law and order first, and justice afterwards."[68] One New York editor thought that the "Communistic element" needed to learn "the convincing arguments of the bullet and the bayonet"; the *Albany Journal* added that, "if need be," they would have to be taught "at the mouth of the cannon and the point of the bayonet, that this is a free country."[69]

In a surprising show of charity, the *New York Times* announced on July 30 that it was "not at all necessary to show the [same] vindictiveness" in the prosecution of stikers as "characterized the trials of the French Communists." By then the Great Strike was already winding down.[70] In the aftermath, the issue of punishment became less important than the question of why the strikes had started in the first place. As J. A. Dacus noted, "such spontaneous demonstrations by large masses of the people, as have been witnessed in the United States in 1877, do not take place without a sufficient cause."[71]

Fortunately, while the Commune provided bourgeois observers with useful descriptions and fierce solutions to the Great Strike, it also provided them with a simple explanation for the domestic upheaval: foreign agitators. Lydia Maria Child blithely assured a friend at the conclusion of the strikes that "most of these reckless rioters have had their training under European governments," as if that explained everything. When it appeared a few months later, *Appletons' Annual Cyclopaedia* agreed that the instigators of the strike were "nearly all foreigners," albeit with "active minds, thoroughly imbued with the doctrines of the French commune and the German social democracy." Along the same lines, a horrified army officer wrote in 1884 that "Russia has her Nihilists, England her Fenians, France her Communists, Spain her Carlists, and Italy her banditti, [but] we are liable to have *all* of these classes among us"—and *any one* of those refugee groups was likely to foment an insurrection.[72] But it was refugees from the Paris Commune who remained the primary focus for this sort of horror in 1877.

In the last days of the Great Strike, the *Philadelphia Ledger* speculated that the International had to be "the secret inspiration" behind the unrest. After all, the IWA had started the Paris Commune, and it was a "well-known fact that when the war there was over many of the leaders were obliged to seek refuge in the United States . . . [T]he pillaging and rioting now in progress in the West especially are really their handiwork." A New York journal agreed that this was probably the case. It recalled, with imperfect clarity, that "Communist refugees in New York" once organized a frightening parade in honor of the Paris Commune, and that the Communards "made an unseemly exhibition of themselves in Tompkins square" in 1874; given their record of disturbing the peace, it certainly made sense that French exiles were behind the current upheaval.[73] Others shared in the confidence born of this dubious logic: the strikes were like the Paris Commune, so Communards must be involved.[74]

Even a year later, Congressman James A. Garfield tried to argue that Parisian agitators were the underlying cause of the strikes. In a Fourth of July oration at Painesville, Ohio, he assured his home-state audience that the "so-called war between capital and labor" was never spawned in their beloved Midwest. It was not even "born on the Hudson" in New York City. Instead "it was born on the Seine, and [it] has no part in our life":

Eighty [*sic*] years ago, when the bloody Commune of France, after its march of cruelty and terror, was finally subjugated, the remnant fled across the ocean and took refuge in New-York, in Philadelphia, in Cincinnati, in Chicago, and in all our great cities. And this element has been working ever since and is working to-day to corrupt our people with the purpose of making a French hell in the heart of the United States . . . I tell you this element is foreign to us.[75]

At about the same time, novelist Lee O. Harris used the influx of treacherous Frenchmen as a major theme of his lurid post-strike opus *The Man Who Tramps*. After 1871, he wrote, America had become home to the worst representatives of "the dangerous communism of France." These were "vicious agitators, who had tasted the intoxication of anarchy and bloodshed, [and] when driven from France found a refuge here." Together with a few native-born "deadbeats" and "bummers," these aliens generated the "scenes of riot and bloodshed that made the nation grow pale" in 1877. Fortunately, he added, most American workers tried to avoid these villains, for they "did not care to invoke the demon of anarchy."[76]

As historian Lewis Barnett points out, using the Commune to describe the American strikes was just an "ingenuous . . . attempt to deny the flaws in American society." By the same token, blaming the strikes on a few scattered Communards would have to count as a *disingenuous* attempt.[77] The *Pittsburgh Daily Post*, which sympathized with the strikers, suggested as much in July 1877. Saying that refugees from France had caused the American strikes was all part of the "Commune nonsense," claimed the journal's editor (and historian Rhodes would have agreed). It was a "very absurd way of alarming timid people, by insinuating that the American working classes are influenced by the teachings of the Paris commune, whose foundation idea is that all 'property is crime.' The strike originated in well ascertained [domestic] grievances."[78] He was right. Despite the lingering assertions of Garfield and Harris, any serious analysis of the Great Strike would have to start somewhere else than among the miserable ranks of the Parisian refugees.

Adolf Douai, a German-born socialist and a refugee of European rebellion himself, was a much better analyst when he wrote that "our country is no longer a *new* country, but resembles the old countries of Europe in every respect." Reluctantly, the *New York Times* agreed: "The days are over in which this country could rejoice in its freedom from the elements of social strife which have abounded in old countries." Professor John B. Clark of Carleton College wrote that, once upon a time, "Communism could . . . have taken no root in America," because the national economy was both agricultural and decentralized. Sadly, all that changed with the spread of industry, and the strikes were proof that "conditions most favorable to order and harmony have thus yielded to conditions favorable to social agitation and class antagonism." The *New York World* used different words, but their meaning was the same: "The American laborer must make up his mind henceforth not to be so much better off than the European laborer."[79]

In the end, using the Commune to describe the strikes in America distorted American perceptions of both events, sometimes beyond recognition. Consider the image of labor unrest that appeared on the pages of the illustrated weeklies. Always quick to exploit a sensational story, *Harper's Weekly* and its rivals published dozens of "pictures" of the Great Strike, most of them dominated by scenes of mob violence.[80] In many cases, the stark images resembled six-year-old illustrations of the Paris Commune—images of fierce-eyed men, frenzied women, and wanton destruction that were already painfully distorted in 1871. After examining the more recent illustrations, the *Pittsburgh Leader* complained that "with the single exception of John Donaghy . . . [of] *Frank Leslie's Illustrated Newspaper*, not one of the artists were near enough to 'the mob' they assume to depict to know what it really looks like." As a result,

> they represent it [the mob] as a wild and heterogeneous collection of rough men and virago women, in every variety of costume . . . and all with coarse, brutish faces, exhibiting every phase of ignorance and malignity. Now this is a French mob, the traditional mob of the first French Revolution, as sketched by English artists, which again budded and bloomed and was plucked in the commune of June, 1870 [*sic*]. The artist who puts this mob in front of the American policemen and soldiers simply draws on his imagination and his memory of old [wood]cuts . . . [for the] American mob is a different sort of body altogether.[81]

Fear and fantasy obscured the reality of American crowds, not just here but in many evocations of the Paris Commune from 1877, while amnesia and ignorance obscured the reality of Parisian ones.[82]

The same thing had happened when Thomas Nast created his cartoons of the Vendôme Column in 1871–1872: accurate renditions became less important than familiar ideologies and were tossed aside. In 1877, accurate depictions of American strikers were less familiar (and therefore less comprehensible) than descriptions of Commune-like mobs. These descriptions had little to do with the actual events in Pittsburgh, or with the actual events in Paris six years earlier; instead, they were fearful projections of what American social unrest *might* look like. Bourgeois observers of the Great Strike were trying hard to make sense of America, and six years of using America to describe the Commune had made it progressively easier to reverse the analogy—even when the focus was being narrowed, and the Commune was being compared with labor unrest alone. After the long depression (and the social changes it wrought), and because of the unprecedented scale of events in 1877, descriptive and predictive Americanization had fully merged. Friedrich Sorge's premature lament of 1871 had finally come true: "The ruling classes [of America] had the 'Commune' on the brain."[83]

A closer look at contemporary accounts of the Great Strike reveals that despite all the talk about the Paris Commune, the strikers themselves hardly ever mentioned it. Although they waved the Commune's red flag in cities across the country, they also marched to the tune of the "Marseillaise" and carried placards demanding "Liberty, Equality, and Fraternity"—references to the French Revolution more than to the Commune itself.[84] The strikes' leaders and supporters were just as reticent about mentioning the Commune. In New York, for example, one of the strikers' warmest friends was the German saloon-keeper Justus Schwab, whose infamous bar was "adorned by pictures of the burning of the hotel de Ville, the destruction of the Column Vendome, and other scenes from the French commune; and flaring-red mottoes from Proudhon and other radical socialists."[85] But Schwab did not urge the Parisian example on American workers in 1877, at least not openly. The closest he came was on July 23, when he shared the stage at New York's Germania Hall with a former Communard and the labor organizer David Conroy, as the latter threatened to "Hang [Tom] Scott to a lamp post" and thereby launch a French-style revolution in America.[86]

Conroy and Schwab shared a stage again at a solidarity meeting in Tompkins Square on July 25. This time Conroy was even more vociferous, declaiming that the "railroad taskmasters . . . should not be allowed to revolutionize 40,000,000 of freemen. (Cheers.) They should be arrested forthwith, and sent to the Dry Tortugas Islands. They are the Commune, not us." (At this point Conroy became so vociferous that the chairman of the meeting declared him drunk and out of order.)[87] In St. Louis, another labor organizer also flirted with the example of the Commune, but after making vague reference to the time when Paris "became desperate with hunger and feasted on blood," he stopped without summoning the Commune by name, as either a curse or a model.[88]

The best historian of the St. Louis general strike notes that one enthusiastic politician from across the river in East St. Louis "struck a far more bloodthirsty note" than any striker ever did. On July 22, a warm Sunday night, Judge William G. Kase told a gathering of workers that he had been to church that very morning to *"render thanks . . . for property destroyed at the hands of the people."* The people cheered, and they cheered again when Kase reminded them about "that little affair in France between capital and labor in 1871," which might be repeating itself right then in the Midwest. On that ominous note, however, the meeting's organizers hurried the judge from the stage.[89]

In later months, the St. Louis press took a strange kind of pride in the fact that their city had weathered the only *"genuine Commune"* in the nation.[90] Yet all they could offer as testimonial proof of the strikers' desire to emulate the Paris Commune were the statements of the labor organizer and Judge Kase, given above. The same was true in New York. When the sympathy meeting in Tompkins Square was first announced, the *Commercial Advertiser* fully expected to hear "Communist refugees . . . obtrud[ing] their dangerous and revolutionary plans" as they plotted to make "Pittsburg in 1877 the parallel of New York in 1863 and Paris in 1871." The *New York Tribune* likewise expected to hear speeches "filled with demagoguery and Communism," both at Tompkins Square and the next day during a trade-union demonstration at the Cooper Union. But despite long columns of verbatim transcriptions, the *Tribune* did not produce a single direct reference to the Paris Commune.[91]

All told, there were precious few reports of American workers appealing to the memory of the Paris uprising in 1877—which is strange, given the eagerness of the contemporary press to compare the strikes to the Commune.[92] They would have been happy to print the slightest mention of the Commune by strikers as proof of malevolent foreign influence. Moreover, thanks to the telegraph, a Commune-spotting in any one newspaper would quickly have reappeared in dozens of others. But where were they? Perhaps all the journalists missed them; perhaps all the workers were remarkably circumspect; perhaps a profound discussion of the Commune as tactical and ideological model was taking place in the workers' secret councils, from which reporters were typically barred. Perhaps, but I doubt it. A simpler explanation is that very few workers were talking—or thinking—about the Paris Commune, and even fewer of the native-born workers who made up the bulk of the strikers in 1877.

Despite the best efforts of the International and the Workingmen's Party of the United States, two organizations dominated by foreign-born workers and intellectuals, American labor had always been reluctant to embrace the Paris Commune. Though native-born American workers, both black and white, had marched in the big parade honoring the Commune in December 1871, Sorge of the International was never really convinced of their commitment to the cause. In September 1871, he proudly reported to Marx and the General Council in London, "After the sublime struggle of the Commune in Paris the more intelligent workingmen have turned their eyes more eagerly towards the IWA." Yet Sorge also had to admit that the National Labor Union, the largest organization of native-born workers, was "very careful[ly] & anxiously trying not to mention the word 'Commune' in their proceedings." He saw the "labor movement gaining strength . . . since the downfall of the 'Commune,'" but he also noticed that the "American Workingman's mind is greatly biased against the Commune and its defenders."[93] In another letter two months later, Sorge wrote with some bitterness that Pennsylvania coal miners were "disclaiming all connection with the IWA & the 'Commune,'" which they blamed for the failure of a recent strike.[94] Although he did not mention it, by that point the leading American labor journal, the Chicago *Workingman's Advocate,* had also become distinctly cool in its attitude towards the Commune.[95]

A similar coolness spread throughout the native-born working class. When "Internationalists and Communists as individuals . . . renewed the European watch words of violence" in 1872, they were "universally condemned" by Eight-Hour demonstrators in New York. According to the Boston *American Workman,* the demonstrators rejected all "violence . . . and incendiary language" as the "acts of the minority with no approval from the leaders or the majority."[96] When a group of prominent trade-union leaders called for a labor convention in Cleveland in 1873 they began by explaining, "We desire it distinctly understood that we have no agrarian ideas; we neither believe [n]or preach the doctrine that capital is robbery. We are not followers of the 'Commune,' believing such an organization as the 'Commune' would be antagonistic to the best interests of labor in this country."[97] Two years later, another group of pure-and-simple unionists complained along the same lines: "Many persons hostile to the cause of labor have sought to bring . . . [the] labor movement into disrepute by persistently asserting that the movement is French, German, or Russian, but nothing can be further from the truth."[98]

Those who promoted the Commune as a model for American labor between 1871 and 1877 tended to be foreigners or middle-class reformers, not native-born workers. When members of the last group did invoke the Commune as a positive example it was almost always in response to extraordinary goading by their bosses or the dominant culture. In 1871, for example, a Philadelphia workman named Hammond stood up for the Paris Commune largely because "an unsympathetic world had denounced [them as] men who were barbarous and devoid of character."[99] In the middle of the long depression, the president of the Coopers' International Union explained to an Indiana audience that he was sick and tired of hearing about "the presumptuous absurdity of asking the government to interpose its protecting arm in behalf of the people in [these] emergencies and crises": "We are told that it *might* do for French Communists to demand governmental assistance in times of extreme want and privation, but that . . . [the] free American workmen should demand aid from the best of governments, is an outrageously preposterous absurdity." In response, he called for some of the same public works that the Communards had attempted in Paris.[100]

The *Workingman's Advocate* used a similar tone of disgust to respond to the "self-satisfied comments of the daily press" regarding America's immunity to "red republicanism." It noted, "We are afraid that . . . [they] have studied the Labor Movement to little advantage . . . [I]nstead of taking a warning from the past, instead of acknowledging the fact that the same causes will produce the same results, and determining to avoid the causes which have created communism in Europe, we hug the mantle of self-complacency, and shut our eyes to the precipice to which we are hurrying."[101] In 1877 the United States seemed to reach that precipice. Yet, despite an occasional threatening word, American workers continued to treat the Commune in the same way they always had. Left to themselves, they rarely mentioned it; but with enough Commune-baiting from non-workers, they could respond in kind.

William M. Grosvenor provided an extreme form of provocation on the pages of the *International Review* in September 1877.[102] Grosvenor was a

Missouri Republican, a former associate of Carl Schurz in the Liberal Republican movement, an expert on the tariff and national finance, and the "economic editor" of the *New York Tribune*. Like the *International Review* itself, he was resolutely pro-business and a firm believer in hard money and free trade. Just after the strikes ended, Grosvenor sat down "by the light of the flames at Pittsburg" to contemplate the future of America, and he concluded that "a terrible trial for free institutions in this country" was approaching: "The Communist is here." Already in other countries, the Communist had "forced property to prefer despotism to spoliation, and intelligent labor to prefer despotism to anarchy." Now the strikes were a sign that the "gaunt Communist has placed his foot on American soil . . . If this is but the beginning, what will be the end?" (585).

According to Grosvenor, the American Commune was a nasty blend of ignorance and envy, the misplaced "desire of the many who are poor to plunder the few who are rich, which has appeared in the insurrection of the Trades Unions" (586). To his mind, anyone who wanted to use the law to curb the power of the railway corporations (for example, the Grangers) was a communist; anyone who wanted to use the strike to improve the worker's situation (for example, the trade unions) was a communist and a criminal. They were to blame for the crash in 1873 and the strikes in 1877, not the railroads.[103] Indeed, as far as Mr. Grosvenor was concerned, the railroads were the real victims of the depression, because their profits were down by half. Yet selfless employers like Tom Scott had still tried their best to help the workers by sharing economic hardships. And what did they get in return for this benevolence? "As soon as hard times came, . . . [workers on the Pennsylvania Railroad] began to organize, threaten, and coerce, like other Communists" (590).

The result was the Great Strike, a wave of "banded lawlessness" (594) led by demagogues who thought that "we have . . . [a] right to rob the rich, or make war upon society, because we can not get all our accustomed comforts in times of general distress" (596). It was just like the French Commune, and Grosvenor was afraid that, just like France, the United States was about to slip into either despotism or anarchy. He only managed to soothe his fears with a shopworn anodyne: "another alternative than this may be found, and one not pregnant with [the] destruction of free institutions . . . [This] must be the hope of patriotic citizens" (599).

A "Red-Hot Striker" from Scranton, Pennsylvania, was quick to respond to Grosvenor's "slander of [the] working-people." His response appeared in the *Radical Review,* a magazine published by Benjamin Tucker and other American-born radicals (including a few who had defended the Commune in 1871).[104] It was withering in its sarcasm. "I blush through all the cinders and sweat my face ever carried," began the striker, "to think that an American citizen could produce an article like that, and that it should get a place in a respectable American publication" (524). But Grosvenor couldn't help himself: he was just a hired lackey of Scott and the other "railway kings." Plus, his view of the strikes was distorted by the light of the burning flames in Pittsburgh. You "must make allowance for that," said the striker. "Once I went to a theatre to see a play where they had a red light turned on, and every thing looked different. I suppose it did to Tom Scott [and Grosvenor, too]" (525).

The real cause of the recent strikes was the "few who are rich," and the Red-Hot Striker quipped that the "rich few ain't so cussedly bad at heart, when you can get at their hearts. The slave-holders wa'n't [either]." But like the slaveholders, the railway capitalists ought to be chastised by the government—and preferably by Ben Butler's committee in Congress![105] As for the "gaunt Communist" who stalked through Grosvenor's article, he was gaunt because "the railway manager isn't." Because of the managers, even honest workmen were poor, "and when scrimping-time comes, have got to scrimp down to hard-pan, and nothing in it to fry! They're the *'gaunt'* fellows that make up the Commune, and that's giving you that are *fat* just now such a scare" (526).

As for the Commune, the Red-Hot Striker was willing to accept it as a model of popular action against plutocracy. He reminded Grosvenor that "it isn't my word, but your's [*sic*]. I let you name it, and take the name because it's as good as any other." Then, in defiance of the capitalists' definition, he declared that "the 'Commune' *represents the cause of the poor in this: that its object is to give every human born into this world a chance to live; live long, and die well*" (527, original italics). It made no difference to the labor movement if the capitalists cry "Commune" in self-defense:

> If you can only scare the people with your cry of "Commune," you imagine they'll give up every thing—liberty and all. They won't . . . Caesar cried "Commune," or something like it; Napoleon cried it; MacMahon [the President of France] is crying it; and now Tom Scott is going it. Well, sir, Caesar is dead; Nap—both Naps are dead; MacMahon is dying; and Thomas Scott never'll be crowned! The game's been played once too much, even in France. (529)

This is not what Grosvenor wanted to hear—but in the end, he and the rest of the middle class only had themselves to blame for conjuring with the image of the Commune in the first place.

Conclusion:
That Once Dreaded Institution

> The Paris Commune . . . that once dreaded institution.
> —*NEW YORK TRIBUNE*, MARCH 20, 1904

In 1877 the "Red-Hot Striker" in the *Radical Review* observed that "every paper I take up most has a lot to say about the French Commune, and its getting started here in America," but he confessed that he did not really know what had happened in Paris back in 1871. He added, however, that "since my attention's been turned to it, I've been reading up some." Indeed, his reading had led him to a conclusion that must have chilled William Grosvenor right down to his capitalist bones: "Things got done in their frenzy that wa'n't right, but that's nothing against the principles they stand by . . . [W]hat I look at, and what I know, is, they've got a good cause, and sooner or later they'll hit the mark and do the right thing."[1]

Three years later, on the ninth anniversary of the Paris uprising, a labor organizer named Philip Van Patten went to Detroit to urge a working-class audience there to remember "the dying heroes of the Commune." He exhorted them, "Let us prove . . . that the lesson [of the Commune] has not been in vain . . . And let us hope that when the workmen of America have their Eighteenth of March, there will be sufficient intelligence, honor and courage in our people, to make this Republic what it was intended to be." Van Patten had been a prominent figure in the Chicago strikes of 1877, and now he was National Secretary of the tiny Socialist Labor Party (SLP). Although he was born in the United States himself, the party's membership was overwhelmingly foreign born; as the next party secretary was forced to admit, the SLP "is only a German colony, an adjunct of the German-speaking Social Democracy."[2] In any event, Van Patten's was a voice crying in the wilderness, for American workers were even less willing to follow the revolutionary model of the Paris Commune in the 1880s than they had been a decade before.

The Red-Hot Striker was unusual in his embrace of the Commune after the Great Strike, and even then he was mostly trying to *épater le bourgeois*. In most cases, explains one historian of the Greenback Labor movement,

184

skilled, native-born workers "rejected the radicalism of the socialists who loomed in the commercial press as a vast subversive conspiracy bent on establishing an American replica of the Paris Commune of 1871," and many of them "likewise downplayed the [1877] railroad strike."³ Even among socialists and anarchists the Commune seemed to be giving way to the Great Strike as a model for working-class revolution in America. As far as one observer in the mid-1880s could tell, the "red-letter era to the Anarchist-Socialist" was now July 1877: "He claims that the first 1877 took him unawares, but that he 'will be armed to the teeth and ready for the second, which ushers in the dawn of a new civilization.'"⁴

One reason for this move away from the Commune was that middle-class and elite Americans had used the events of 1877 to give the Paris Commune a worse name than ever before. American workers had never really supported the Commune anyway (in part because the dominant culture was also their own), and they were happy to keep distancing them-selves from the events in France. Adopting the voice of a workingman, in 1878 a prolabor poet emphatically declared "Not of the commune, we!": "Not of the Jacobins . . . not of the anarchists . . . not of the levelers . . . not of agrarians . . . not of infidels."⁵ That same year, the Greenback Labor Party of Indiana officially condemned the "red flag Communism imported from Europe which asks for an equal division of property," together with "the Communism of the National Banks, of the Bond Syndicates, and of the consolidated railroad corporations."⁶ In 1886, when Albert Parsons and his fellow anarchists rallied in Haymarket Square, the working people of Cincinnati were quick to reject the trappings of the Commune that the Chicagoans held so dear. The Bricklayers' Union began by declaring, "The carrying of a red flag at the head of a procession that pretends to represent the laboring class is acting a lie, for a red flag does not mean honest labor, but money or blood, and should not be tolerated in America." The car-penters, machinists, and typographers all rapidly joined them in denounc-ing the "red flag of the Commune," while the local Assembly of the Knights of Labor called "the red flag . . . un-American, and in itself an open proclamation against the Government and its institutions." How-ever, this never meant that they disapproved of the Chicago anarchists' proposal for an eight-hour day, which the Haymarket rally was all about.⁷

To give one more example, in 1891 striking coal miners in Tennessee went out of their way to disavow the slightest comparison between them-selves and the Paris Commune. At a meeting with the governor in Knoxville, a committee of the miners reminded him, "It is unnecessary on our part to point out the seriousness of the situation. We are neither nihilists nor adherents of the Commune." Yet they were no less class-conscious because of that disavowal: "We fight for the right to earn our bread through honest work, and we are fundamental foes of that system of labor which is used to humiliate us . . . and our families." Most of these workers were native-born.[8]

Indeed, the only workers in the United States who still celebrated the Paris uprising after 1877, or even consistently remembered it, were foreign-born workers—and not even all of them. More than anyone else, the Chicago anarchists became the guardians of the Commune's memory in America. It was part of their ideology and part of their movement culture.[9] They bestowed on the Paris Commune an almost holy aura, and Communards like General Dombrowski and Louise Michel became revolutionary saints. Every March, from 1872 to 1909, the Chicago anarchists came together to honor the memory of the Commune.[10]

But as one labor statistician noted as early as 1881, "the American artisan . . . [had] vanished from the scene," replaced by Germans, Bohemians, Poles, Scandinavians, and other foreign-born workers. Anarchism was a foreign movement, not just in Chicago but elsewhere, and except for rare cases like Albert Parsons it failed to attract many native-born followers.[11] In the 1880s ethnic differences reinforced the political split between workers who celebrated the Commune and those who did not. One Knight of Labor drew attention to this split when he explained to the union's national leader, Terence V. Powderly, that "I can not, either as a Catholic or as a true friend of my class, lend myself to or become the advocate of the teachings of a Carnot, a Danton, a Robespierre, a Most or a Louisa [*sic*] Michel."[12] In 1897, a Catholic University sociologist wrote that the only group in America still holding "sacred the memory of the Chicago anarchists and the Paris Communards" was the SLP, which was still tiny and still dominated by immigrants.[13] The Social Democratic Party, the remaining Chicago anarchists, and even a few Wobblies continued to celebrate the anniversary of the Commune after the turn of the century.[14] But for most American workers the Paris Commune had become a non-event.

What about the workers' class opponents in the bourgeoisie? Was the Paris Commune still a feature of their mental landscape after 1877? For all their talk about the Commune and all their thundering about "grape and canister," American businessmen, editors, and politicians never had the mettle to follow the 1877 strikes with wholesale repression à la Thiers in France. Blacklisting was the American way, not deportation or mass execution.[15] Nonetheless, a lurid image of the Commune continued to haunt their vision of domestic social unrest. Yet even this image dimmed shortly after the Great Strike, as the imaginary Commune ceased to be an active force in American culture.

It dimmed, for the most part, because the Paris Commune was no longer needed to describe what was happening in America. The Great Strike finally showed that the United States was not immune to "European" disorders, and it finally unbalanced the shaky twin identity of the Commune as something familiar but foreign. The memory of American strikes and the presence of a native proletariat could now become the focus of social unease in the dominant culture,[16] especially since the negative attributes of the Commune, fabricated piecemeal over six disorderly years, had been transferred as whole cloth to the Great Strike.

The consistency of Americans' response to both the Commune and the strikes is remarkable, even if the former had taken years to develop while the latter came out in a rush. Was the Paris Commune a repetition of the French Revolution? Contemporaries also thought that the 1877 strikes "bore an unpleasant resemblance to some of the methods of past revolutions in France," and "the reign of terror" was a common headline during the worst days of July and August.[17] Was the Commune a terrible result of republican incapacity? According to a summary of recent French politics published by *Harper's Weekly* in the midst of the Great Strike, France was still displaying a "total incapacity to comprehend free institutions," while here in America, complained Senator Vest of Missouri, "universal suffrage is a standing menace to all stable and good governments; its twin sister is the Commune with its labor unions, workingmen's leagues, red republicanism and universal anarchy."[18] Was the Commune a result of French ignorance? The *Christian Union* saw the strikes as proof that America itself had "a larger turbulent and uncontrolled population than we have supposed": "Our untamed savages have been suffered to grow up in savageness, much as they were in France before the revolution, and in the long run it is the cultured and the well-to-do who suffer from savage growths. Half the money wasted in this rebellion expended in processes of education would have made the strike impossible."[19]

Was the Commune a conspiracy of arsonists? If so, then St. Louis was also infested by the kind of "incendiary communists" who "burned the city hotel [*sic*], the Tuileries, and many other of the finest edifices in the city [of Paris]"; in Pittsburgh as well, Commune-like "scoundrels, the human vultures, [and] the wretched Pariahs" conspired to make the city "blaze with fire."[20] Was Paris overflowing with frenzied women in 1871? According to the *Pittsburgh Commercial Gazette,* the female strikers in America also "seemed to be more furious than the men, and indulged in combats and profanity shocking to observe and hear . . . A large amount of the pillaging was . . . [done by] middle aged dames of Amazoniac proportions."[21] Were the men of the Paris Commune deranged? The president of the New York Central described the strikes along his railroad as a "crazy émeute," while Tom Scott tapped "the insanity of passion" as the cause of strikes on his Pensylvania Railroad.[22] Did Communards of both sexes resemble American Indians? Well, so did American strikers. As historian Richard Slotkin notes, one "ideological task of the antilabor journalists [in 1877] was to enforce the association between strikers and Indian savages." The conflation of "redskin" and "Red" returned, and at least one observer called unemployed tramps the "Arabs of the cities and Apaches of the country."[23] Indeed, just like the Communards before them, the strikers of 1877 were likened to a whole array of savage "others." For E. L. Godkin the strikes even cast a shadow of doubt on "our superiority to the Ashantees or the Kurds," while the *Pittsburgh Daily Post* expressed its dismay at "how fearfully rapid is the descent to scenes of the most brutalizing and inhuman nature."[24]

So it went with every negative word that the Commune had attracted in six long years. Together, the descriptions provided a vocabulary of social unrest that was easily transferred to the Great Strike. As the Civil War had once been a convenient way to describe the Paris Commune, the homemade description of the Commune now became a convenient way to describe the unprecedented strikes. Once the translation was accomplished, the original version became less useful. Indeed, the Commune could now be discarded—but only with difficulty, because it had worked its way so fully into every corner of American culture.

Use of the Paris Commune to describe American unrest reached its peak in the two years after the Great Strike, at the time of the clerical pronouncements discussed at the end of Chapter 7. As early as 1878, however, newspapers had begun to chide the "Commune Bugbear," as the *New York Tribune* called it. According to the *New York Herald,* "Communism [was] one of the bugaboos that shallow people flaunt in the faces of a timid public," while another journal added that "few subjects have given rise to such a magnificent display of ignorance on the part of both speakers and writers" as communism and the Paris Commune.[25] In the early 1880s,

Unitarian minister R. Heber Newton, a leading evangelist of the new Social Gospel, wryly noted that "Communism is . . . the stock bogy of our dry nurses of the pulpit, the press, and the platform, wherewith they scare children of a larger growth from peeping into the dark places of our social system . . . In the popular mind it is the alias of the Parisian petroleuse and the railroad rioter, and stands for a social craze which is diseasing labor." He continued, "The extravagence of these misconceptions is not to be wondered at after the wild words and works of those who vaunt the name of Communist."[26]

Newton's idea was to examine the "social problem" in a rather more sober fashion, to define the "wild words" whose indiscriminate use made reform so difficult, and to return the notion of communism to its historical context. Some of America's leading scholars had the same idea, and they also began by defining what communism really meant. "Many who use the word commune glibly have a very imperfect understanding of its significance," explained a young Johns Hopkins economist named Richard T. Ely: it simply denoted a township. The "insurrection in Paris" was merely an effort to achieve "extreme local self-government," and had nothing to do with the "communism" that worried some Americans. President Woolsey of Yale added that "communism" was very different from "socialism," and he agreed with Ely that neither concept was strictly connected to the Paris Commune. They and many other scholars began to see the Commune as a purely historical event; interesting, no doubt, but not part of the American social problem. For the next twenty years serious thinkers continually strove to remove the Paris Commune from discussions of American social reform, even when they feared that workers' unrest was a threat to domestic tranquility.[27]

At the same time, there were others, perhaps less thoughtful, who continued to scream "Commune" whenever domestic unrest reared its head. This was especially true in 1886, when the chief of Chicago's police department blamed the Haymarket riot directly on "the propagation of communistic doctrines, not as they are understood by the teachers of social science, but as they were understood by the rabble who sought the communism of Paris only." The national press agreed: the "bloodthirsty wretches" in Chicago had "no likeness in modern history except in the Paris Commune."[28] Even Elihu Washburne, who *still* should have known better, told a reporter that "he had not known during the carnage enacted by the Commune of Paris so utterly and atrocious a murder as that [of policemen in Haymarket Square]."[29]

Chicago anarchists, who revered the Parisian experience, were not the only ones to be branded with the sign of the Commune. In the 1880s the Knights of Labor were routinely associated with the Paris Commune.[30] In the 1890s, a Republican senator from Kansas even claimed that, deep down, the mild-mannered Populists were just "as incendiary as . . . the communists in Paris in 1871."[31] A young fellow Republican named Theodore Roosevelt also seemed to like waving the bloody flag of the Paris uprising. Writing about the 1894 Pullman strike in *Forum* magazine, he declared that only federal troops had saved Chicago from a "repetition of what occurred during the Paris Commune." During the 1896 presidential campaign, he warned an audience of Illinois Republicans that, if elected, Democratic candidate William Jennings Bryan and Democratic governor John Peter Altgeld "would substitute for the government of Washington and Lincoln . . . a red welter of lawlessness and dishonesty as fantastic and as vicious as the Paris Commune itself." Indeed, as late as 1911 Roosevelt was still complaining to a supporter in California that "Debs and his people . . . [are] on a par with the creatures of the Paris Commune."[32] Yet despite the best efforts of Senator Ingalls and President Roosevelt, it was impossible to argue with the judgment of the *New York Tribune* in 1904: the Commune had become "that once dreaded institution," faded from the minds of most Americans.[33]

The Paris Commune did most of its fading from American culture in the two decades after the Great Strike, and for a time the epithet "communist" seemed to be fading with it. Throughout the 1870s, notes a leading student of American anarchism, "the press used both 'communist' and 'socialist' interchangeably." Eventually "socialist" gained the upper hand, only to be replaced in the 1880s by "anarchist" as the most feared and caustic label for undesirable social change.[34] Labor leaders noticed the change. In 1882, Terence Powderly of the Knights of Labor complained to a friend that "They . . . call me Molly McGuire, Communist, Socialist, Nihilist, and every epithet that the tongue of slander and malice can invent." But a decade later Eugene V. Debs calmly noted that even "the epithet 'anarchist' is being largely overworked" because the "subsidized press" liked to apply it to any "workingmen who resist[ed] oppression to the extent of striking for their rights." (Debs was sitting in Woodstock prison at the time.)[35] Yet some things remained constant in the transition from communist to socialist to anarchist (and later to Bolshevik and communist again), and not just the sense that alien forces were threatening to disrupt American society. When Debs noted that his men in the American Railway Union were called "anarchists," he included a list of the traits that always went with the label: "enemies of capital, blatant agitators, breeders of riots and sedition, conspirators, criminals," and so on. It was the same list, more or less, that had been used to describe the Commune and Communards in the 1870s.[36]

What was gone from these subsequent red-baiting labels was a powerful suspicion that still attached to the Paris Commune: a sense that the French civil war remained part of the Franco-American co-tradition of democratic revolution and republican governance. It was a sense that Alexander Stephens, for one, had never lost, and that still led an editor to write in 1879 that the "French nation is the Republican progress of Europe. Her history, through kingship, feudal right, third estate, and commune, fills the mind with wonder as she ends in an established Republic." As Edward King continued to remind his readers in 1895, the Commune was started "in the name of liberty and local self-government," even if later it was "perverted to a Socialistic revolution"; at least in its origins, it shared something with our own Civil War.[37]

This is the final reason that the Paris Commune disappeared from American culture in the 1880s and 1890s: it was too firmly linked to what can be called the age of democratic civil wars. In the early 1860s, it was a positive thing for Americans to imagine that the United States was on a convergent path with the rest of the world. Indeed, this idea was valorized at the highest levels, for as President Lincoln told them, America was the "last, best hope of earth." Many Northerners believed (or came to believe, or were led to believe by the force of Lincoln's rhetoric) that a world-historical struggle was unfolding around them, a struggle to test whether *any* polity, "conceived in Liberty" and dedicated to human Equality, could "long endure."[38] In their own way, many Southerners also believed what Lincoln said, and their belief helped sustain both sides through a long and bloody war.

It also persuaded Americans to give their approbation to similar struggles in foreign lands. Not two weeks after the Gettysburg Address, the *New York Commercial Advertiser* published an editorial on the Polish revolution that had taken place that very summer. The editor claimed, "the cause of Poland is indeed the cause of oppressed humanity throughout the world": like the United States, Poland was fighting for liberty. According to a stunned British diplomat three years later, "Ireland [was] looked upon as a second Poland" for much the same reason, and Americans displayed a similar attitude toward other European reform movements in the 1860s and 1870s.[39] If the world would only emulate the United States—whose mere existence, claimed Gustave Cluseret, "republicanises Europe by . . . example"—a better age would follow.[40]

When the Civil War ended, however, many Americans were dismayed to discover that the United States and Europe were indeed converging, but in the wrong direction. Instead of exporting self-government, free labor, and liberty, the United States seemed to be importing ignorance, class warfare, and tyranny. Returning from their bloody affirmation of America's ideals, they found that the path of American exceptionalism was suddenly clogged with two-way traffic, and they began to question the basic ideals that the war had been fought to preserve.[41]

The Paris Commune burst upon this two-way traffic in 1871, a moment when American society was particularly unsettled; and, thanks to endogenous developments in American mass culture, the Commune rapidly became ubiquitous. As the raw material for ad hoc descriptions and wayward allegories, it became a convenient way to make sense of postwar unrest, whether social, sectional, or economic. (Unfortunately, as we have seen, the allegorical process often distorted the reality of events in both America and France.)[42] At the same time, the Commune became a focal point in America's changing view of popular uprisings abroad, which shifted "from the romantic traditions of rebellion towards the new traditions of social revolution and terrorism"; this shift was inspired by fears of domestic unrest.[43]

The year 1877 was a crucial moment in this passage from the optimism of the early 1860s. Most historians consider 1877 the end of Reconstruction, as marked by the Great Strike, the contested election of President Hayes, and the withdrawal of American troops from the South. The hopeful attempt to democratize Southern society was over; henceforth, said *Appletons' Annual Cyclopaedia,* "the Southern States . . . [would be] entirely abandoned by the Federal Government to the care and reconstruction of their own citizens." In Europe, meanwhile, Turkey and Russia had concluded a major war and France had weathered a major political crisis. In all, said the *Cyclopaedia,* "1877 witnessed the culmination of many important events."[44]

One of these events was the age of democratic civil wars, at least for Americans. Its passing was little noted; but when this age ended, the Americanization of the Paris Commune ended with it.

In the summer of 1917 a Southern-born president of the United States assured his nation that the painful issues of the Civil War were finally behind them. Woodrow Wilson explained to a gathering of Confederate veterans, "There are some things that we have thankfully buried, and among them are the great passions of division which once threatened to rend this nation in twain . . . [W]e are forgetting the things that once held us asunder."[45] Five months later, Americans witnessed a foreign revolution that, like the Paris Commune a half-century earlier, seemed to hold tremendous implications for American culture and society. The result was a widespread fear of the Russian Bolsheviks, a fear of social unrest at home, and a fear that somehow the two were connected. "RED PERIL HERE," cried the newspaper headlines.[46] In 1919, a committee of the New York state legislature set out to investigate the forces of upheaval that threatened to rend the nation asunder again, forces that seemed both foreign and just around the corner. The result was four fat volumes, *Revolutionary Radicalism: Its History, Purpose and Tactics,* a compendium of middle-class apprehensions that was also "the most complete and detailed published repository of radical literature and information available" (according to the best historian of the 1919 Red Scare).[47] In more than four thousand pages of text, however, the Paris Commune was mentioned just once, and then in a purely historical reference.[48] What had once been a potent description of domestic unrest—what had once been used to make sense of the Civil War, the Great Strike, and a dozen other disruptions—what had once been Americanized—was now forgotten. It was no longer needed.

Appendix A:
Chronology of the
Paris Commune

For a more complete chronology, see Stewart Edwards, *The Paris Commune, 1871* (London, 1971), 369–376.

August 9, 1792   Declaration of a revolutionary Commune (municipal government) in Paris to replace the monarchic Communal Council.

1870

July 4   Gala celebration of American Independence at the Paris home of Dr. Thomas Evans.

July 19   France declares war on Prussia.

September 2   Surrender of Napoleon III and most of his army at Sedan.

September 4   French Republic declared.

September 18   German siege of Paris begins.

September 28   Failed insurrection in Lyons.

November 1   Failed insurrection in Marseilles.

1871

January 5   Germans begin to bombard Paris.

January 28   Armistice signed. Siege of Paris ends.

March 18   French government attempts to seize the National Guard cannon at Montmartre. Generals Thomas and Lecomte are killed by the crowd. The Thiers government flees to Versailles.

March 19   Central Committee of the National Guard announces elections for a Commune in Paris.

March 22   The "Friends of Order" demonstrate against the Commune in the Place Vendôme.

March 22–26   Failed Commune uprising in Lyons.

March 22–April 4   Failed Commune uprising in Marseilles.

March 26	Elections in Paris.
March 28	Paris Commune formally proclaimed at the Hôtel de Ville.
March 30	Fighting breaks out between the Commune and the Versailles government.
April 2	Versailles begins to bombard Paris. Commune declares separation of church and state.
April 3–4	Failed Commune offensive.
April 4	Gustave Cluseret named Minister of War.
April 6	Commune begins to seize hostages.
April 12	Versailles begins a major offensive to the south and west of Paris.
April 16	Paris by-elections. Cluseret elected a member of the Commune.
May 1	Cluseret arrested and removed as War Minister. Committee of Public Safety created. New bombardment of Paris.
May 9	Fort d'Issy, south of Paris, falls to the French army.
May 16	Destruction of the Vendôme Column.
May 18	French government ratifies the treaty of Frankfurt, officially ending the Franco-Prussian War.
May 21	Last regular meeting of the Commune Council. Gala in support of the Commune at the Tuileries gardens. Troops from Versailles enter Paris. Cluseret released in the midst of his trial.
May 21–28	The *semaine sanglante* (Bloody Week), with violent suppression of the Commune by the French government.
May 24–25	Commune executes 63 hostages, including Archbishop Darboy.
May 28	The last barricade of the Commune falls at 2:00 P.M.
May 30	Karl Marx gives his address, *The Civil War in France*, to the International.
November 28	Execution of Louis Rossel and other leading Communards.
December 17	Large parade in New York City honoring Rossel and the other martyrs of the Commune.
1871–1874	More executions and deportations of Communards.
July 11, 1880	Complete amnesty for Communards.

Appendix B:
Two American Poems about the Paris Commune

The Hero of the Commune: An Incident of the Paris Siege

MARGARET JUNKIN PRESTON
(originally published in *Scribner's Monthly* 3, April 1872, 660–661)

I
     "Garçon!—You—*you,*
Snared along with this cursed crew?
(Only a child, and yet so bold,
—Scarcely as much as ten years old)
     —Do you hear? Do you know
Why the *gendarmes* put you there, in the row,—
You,—with those Commune wretches tall,
     With face to the wall?"

II
"'Know?'—To be sure I know! Why not?
     We're here to be shot;
And there by the pillar's the very spot,
Fighting for France, my father fell,
     —Ah, well!
That's just the way I would choose to fall,
     With my *back* to the wall!"

III
"(*Sacré!*—Fair, open fight, I say,
Is right magnificent in its ways,
And fine for warming the blood; but who

197

Wants wolfish work like this to do?
Bah! 'Tis a butcher's business).—*How?*
(The boy is beckoning to me now:
I knew his poor child's heart would fail;
   —Yet his cheek's not pale).
—Quick! Say your say: for don't you see,
When the church-clock yonder tolls out *Three,*
   You're all to be shot?
   —*What?*
'Excuse you one moment?' O ho, ho!
D'ye think to fool a *National* so?"

IV

"But, sir, here's a watch that a friend, one day,
—My father's friend, just over the way,—
Lent me; and if you'll let me free
(It still lacks seven minutes of *Three*),
I'll come back, on the word of a soldier's son,
Straight back into line, when the errand's done."

V

"Ha, ha! No doubt of it! Off! Begone!
—(Now, good Saint Martin! speed him on!
The work will be easier since *he's* saved;
For I hardly think I could have braved
The ardor of that innocent eye,
   As he stood and heard
   Me give the word,
Dooming him like a dog to die.)"

VI

"*In time!*—Well, thanks that my desire
Was granted; and now I'm ready. Fire!
   One word; that's all:
You'll let me turn my *back* to the wall?"

VII

"*Parbleu!*—Come out of the line, I say!
Come out!—(Who said that his name was *Ney?*
Ha! France will hear of him yet one day!)"

A Triumph of Order

JOHN HAY

(originally published in *Atlantic Monthly* 30, August 1872, 219)

> A squad of regular infantry,
>   In the Commune's closing days,
> Had captured a crowd of rebels
>   By the wall of Père-la-Chaise.
>
> There were desperate men, wild women,
>   And dark-eyed Amazon girls,
> And one little boy, with a peach-down cheek
>   And yellow clustering curls.
>
> The captain seized the little waif,
>   And said, "What dost thou here?"
> "*Sapristi*, Citizen captain!
>   I'm a Communist, my dear!"
>
> "Very well! Then you die with the others!"
>   "Very well! That's my affair!
> But first let me take to my mother,
>   Who lives by the wine-shop there,
>
> "My father's watch. You see it,
>   A gay old thing, is it not?
> It would please the old lady to have it,
>   Then I'll come back here, and be shot."
>
> "That is the last that we'll see of him,"
>   The grizzled captain grinned,
> As the little man skimmed down the hill,
>   Like a swallow down the wind.
>
> For the joy of killing had lost its zest
>   In the glut of those awful days,
> And Death writhed gorged like a greedy snake
>   From the Arch to Père-la-Chaise.
>
> But before the last platoon had fired,
>   The child's shrill voice was heard!

"*Houp-là!* the old girl made such a row
    I feared I would break my word."

Against the bullet-pitted wall
    He took his place with the rest,
A button was lost from his ragged blouse,
    Which showed his soft, white breast.

"Now blaze away, my children!
    With your little one—two—three!"
The Chassepots tore the stout young heart,
    And saved Society!

Appendix C: Novels and Plays about the Paris Commune

Novels about the Paris Commune, 1872–1904

The following is a chronological list of novels published in the United States set wholly or partly in the Paris Commune. Authors in capital letters are British.

LINTON, MRS. ELIZABETH [LYNN]. *The True History of Joshua Davidson, Communist.* Philadelphia: Lippincott, 1872. Originally published in London, 1871, as *The True History of Joshua Davidson.* Another edition was published by Tauschnitz at Leipzig in 1873, under the original title.

ORR, MRS. A[LEXANDER] S[TEWART]. *The Twins of Saint-Marcel: a Tale of Paris Incendié.* Boston: Shepard & Gill, 1874. Originally published in Edinburgh by William P. Nimmo, 1872; a second American edition was published in Boston by A. W. Lovering, 1875.

Trammell, William DuGas. *Ça Ira.* New York: United States Book Co., 1874.

COBB, JAMES F. *Workman and Soldier.* New York: E. P. Dutton and Co., 1880. First published in London, 1880; another English edition appeared in 1896, under the title *In Time of War: a Tale of Paris Life during the Siege and Rule of the Commune.*

Chambers, Robert W. *The Red Republic: a Romance of the Commune.* New York: Putnam, 1895.

Gribble, Francis H. *The Red Spell.* New York and London: Frederick A. Stokes, 1895.

202 | Appendix C

HENTY, GEORGE A. *A Girl of the Commune*. New York: R. F. Fenno, 1895. Originally published in London as *A Woman of the Commune* (F. V. White & Co., 1895), and variously republished in England as *Cuthbert Harrington* and *Two Sieges of Paris*.

King, Edward S. *Under the Red Flag; or, The Adventures of Two American Boys in the Days of the Commune*. Philadelphia: Henry T. Coates & Co., 1895.

Savidge, Eugene C. *The American in Paris, a Biographical Novel of the Franco-Prussian War; The Siege and Commune of Paris from an American Stand-Point*. Philadelphia and London: Lippincott, 1896.

OXENHAM, JOHN. *Under the Iron Flail*. London and New York: Cassell, 1902.

BARRY, DR. WILLIAM. *The Dayspring*. New York: Dodd, Mead, 1904. Preceded by an English edition.

Isham, Frederick S. *Black Friday*. Indianapolis: Bobbs-Merrill, 1904.

American Plays about the Paris Commune, 1871–1911

The following chronological list is derived from a United States Copyright Office publication, *Dramatic Compositions Copyrighted in the United States, 1870–1916*, 2 vols. (Washington, D.C., 1918), which contains an alphabetical listing, by title, of plays submitted to the Library of Congress for copyright purposes. The short descriptions that immediately follow some titles are copied verbatim from this source. Although this list was checked against subject catalogues at the Library of Congress, the Harvard Theatre Collection, the New York Public Library's Theatre and Drama Collection, and the Princeton University Library's Theatre Collection, there remains a strong possibility that some plays were missed. Plays that were never submitted for copyright, or that were pirated from abroad (a common practice before the Anglo-American copyright arrangement of 1891), would be difficult to locate without sorting through thousands of playbills, newspaper advertisements, and other sources. For example, in a letter to her daughter dated April 18, 1897, Julia Ward Howe mentions that she had recently "see[n] Laura Cushing's wonderful acting in a French play of the Commune. She possesses great tragic power and reminds one of [Eleanora] Duse and of Sarah Bernhardt."[1] I have not been able to identify this play.

Dramatic pieces designed for working-class audiences have also proved elusive. These were never formally copyrighted, and they were often impromptu works put together to celebrate the anniversary of the Commune. In 1892, for example, a lively group of Francophone anarchists from Spring Valley, Illinois, calling themselves "La Revanche des Mineurs" (The Miners' Revenge), commemorated the Commune with a play that toured the tiny mining towns of western Pennsylvania; a year later they returned for repeat performances.[2] The German-American socialists of Chicago were also fond of marking the Commune's passing with dramatics, whether *tableaux vivants* representing the fall of the Commune (at anniversary celebrations in 1878, 1893, 1896, and 1897), or political plays like *Die Nihilisten* (*The Nihilists,* 1882), *Die Tochter des Proletariers* (*The Proletarian's Daughter,* 1883), *The Poor of New York* (1885), or *Im Frühroth* (*Dawn,* 1907), only the last of which was actually set in the Commune.[3]

William Humphreys. *La Commune.* Copyright: New York, July 1871.

T[homas] C. De Leon. *Paris, or Days of the Commune,* a drama in prologue and three acts. Copyright: New York, August 1871. Opened at New York's Grand Opera House on November 27, 1871, for a short run. Reviewers were unanimous in their scorn for this play, which "failed lamentably."[4] According to the *New York Times,* the play had been announced as "an entirely new, pictorial, romantic and realistic drama . . . [which] appears to be a delusion of the author, unless, indeed, a new, pictorial, romantic and realistic drama can be constructed without either characters, dialogue or plot. The commendable ambition of our native playwrights has doubtless achieved worse plays than this, but it has not been our fortune to see them. It is but simple justice to say that from beginning to end, 'Paris' is unmitigated trash of the dreariest and most common-place sort." The only thing this reviewer could find to praise was the scenery.[5]

The *Times*'s reviewer refused even to describe the plot. According to another review, the melodramatic story began with a duel between an American diplomat and a bigamous Frenchman just after the coup d'état of 1852, and ended with a love story between their children (a French camp follower and an American cavalry officer) eighteen years later. "Love, jealousy, affection, hatred, treachery, and fidelity, with other qualities, work through the different characters till the good are happy and the bad punished." This reviewer also praised the vivid recreations of the fall of Paris.[6]

A third reviewer, clearly sympathetic to the Commune, noted with keen disappointment that De Leon had wasted "a subject so full of possibilities." At the hands of the right playwright, the "public might have been cheated into taking a small dose of wisdom and truth [about the Commune] without knowing it, under the delicate disguise of an entertaining play . . . With such a vast subject as the fall of an Empire, and with such motives as the mighty passions that were let loose, and in their Titanic convulsions seemed an upheaval of all the moral and political forces, giving play to the most prodigious influences, a dramatist might surely evoke spirits that would touch the sympathies of his audience. The dramatist of the Commune is yet in the unknown future."[7]

St. John Molyneux and William Rose. *The Revolt of the Commune; or, Paris in 1871,* a drama in three acts. Copyright: New York, December 1871. Opened at Brooklyn's Park Theatre, December 11, 1871, with actress Kate Ranoe in a leading role.[8]

Edward Greey. *Vendome,* a drama. Copyright: Manchester, Mass., 1875. Opened at the Boston Museum on November 27, 1876. According to a reviewer, "The piece is of the scenic order, as well as the military, and is rather bloodthirsty in its tendencies. It is a story of French life during the reign of the Commune of '71, and the opportunity thus afforded of introducing striking situations and tableaux is not wholly lost. The plot is like most plots in plays of this kind, and is therefore scarcely worth detailing."[9]

According to the playbill, the action included "GRAND SCENIC EFFECTS," "BRILLIANT COSTUMES," and "STIRRING MUSICAL COMPOSITIONS," together with tableaux of the destruction of the Vendôme Column and the burning of the Hôtel de Ville. There was also a scene depicting a Communist trial. Yet despite "the richness of the materials at hand," wrote the reviewer for the *Boston Evening Transcript,* "the scenes are so poverty-stricken in incident that the house sits in silent wonder and amaze[ment] at the miraculous stupidity of the piece." One theatergoer agreed, calling it a "very poor piece, what little strength there is, being in the situations . . . [A]ll the skill of good acting cannot save the dialogue and conventional characters from being wearisome."[10]

Greey also wrote a short story about an American artist who remained in Paris during the Franco-Prussian War and Commune, "Models; an Episode of the Franco-German War," *Frank Leslie's Illustrated Newspaper,* November 16, 1872.

Hyp[polyte?] A. Magendie. *Parent by Proxy*, a comedy-drama in four acts, founded on the Commune. Copyright: San Francisco, September 1881.

Lou Leubrie. *Fall of Paris and Reign of the Commune*, a drama without words. Copyright: Memphis, August 1888.

Charles Harvey Palmer. *1871* (based on Alphonse Daudet's *Le Siège de Berlin*). Copyright: Milwaukee, 1896. Performed at the Falmouth, Mass., Town Hall in 1896. Also performed at Boston's Hollis Street Theatre, October 19–22, 1896, in a double bill with the three-act comedy, *A Superfluous Husband*.[11]

Evelyn Greenleaf Sutherland. *At the Barricade*. Copyright: 1898. Published in her *Po' White Trash and Other One-Act Dramas* (Chicago, 1900), 187–211. Produced as a benefit performance at the Hollis Street Theatre, Boston, April 28, 1898, and presented as a "Pupils' Matinee" at the American Academy of Dramatic Arts, Boston, December 14, 1899.[12] A short melodrama, it was apparently geared toward a younger audience. It opens with three *pétroleuses*, captured on the barricades, as prisoners of the advancing Versailles troops. The three are waiting to be shot. As a contrast, the playwright then introduces a refined noblewoman and her maid, who are trying to flee the revolution. The Comtesse and the French lieutenant in charge are lovers, and she confesses to him amidst the rubble that "my love leaped its barricade" (200). The *pétroleuses* are softened by the sight of this love. A shady French Marquis then enters, and we discover that the lieutenant is, unknowingly, his illegitimate son. Suddenly, the Comtesse's maid is hauled on stage, wrongly accused of being a *pétroleuse;* she is saved by the voluntary surrender of Yvonne de Guimperle, the "Queen of the *Pétroleuses*," who demonstrates a nobility befitting her aristocratic birth. Amazingly, Yvonne turns out to be the French lieutenant's mother! And because she is his mother, the lieutenant offers to free her; but she refuses, knowing that this will lead to his disgrace as an officer and gentleman. When he insists, she commits suicide rather than let him traduce his honor. Finally, Communards overrun the barricade—but the *pétroleuses* make sure that the lieutenant and his lover remain unharmed.

The theme that runs throughout this play seems to be that a woman's place is *not* at the barricade. As one of the French regulars tells his lover, "man's work is here; but a woman?" (196); another points out to an innocent bystander that "no woman who values her life or honor is found in Paris streets to-day!" (197). Finally, it is implied that Yvonne began the long descent into the life of a *pétroleuse* with her youthful indiscretion in the Marquis's bed (207–208).

Maurice Mikol, *The Communard's Daughter,* a play in four acts. Copyright: New York, December 1911. This play exists only as a copyright typescript on deposit at the Library of Congress (deposited December 29, 1911, number D28231); mercifully, there is no sign that it was ever performed. It might be debated whether Mikol, a Frenchman, was least proficient as a typist, a dramatist, or a master of the English language. Here is a typical line of dialogue, spoken by a disillusioned priest as he rips off his clerical collar: "This sign of reverence is supposititious!" (18). Set in lower Manhattan in 1893, the play is the story of an old Frenchman (who fought in both the American Civil War and the Paris Commune), his beautiful adopted daughter, her long-lost mother (a Communard's widow who later became a wealthy prostitute in the Montana copper-mining country), and the radical ex-priest (who eventually marries the Communard's daughter). The play is equal parts melodrama and propaganda, though obviously written by someone familiar with the Paris Commune and New York's radical Franco-American community.

Notes

Introduction

1. Edmond Lepelletier, *Histoire de la Commune de 1871,* 3 vols. (Paris, 1911–1913), 3:405. As a young man Lepelletier played a minor role in the Paris Commune and later became a Radical Republican. The title for my introduction was suggested by one writer's observation that "since the early years of the century there has been no epoch more fruitful of stirring events than that comprised between the years 1861 and 1871"; see *North American Review* 125 (1877), 171.

2. James A. Rawley, "The American Civil War and the Atlantic Community," *Georgia Review* 21 (1967), 185; for a complementary Marxist view, see George Novack, "The Civil War—Its Place in History," in Novack, ed., *America's Revolutionary Heritage* (New York, 1976), 256–257.

3. The recent literature is summarized in Ian Tyrrell, "American Exceptionalism in an Age of International History," *American Historical Review* 96 (October 1991), 1031–1055, and Carl J. Guarneri, "Out of Its Shell: Internationalizing the Teaching of United States History," *Perspectives* 35 (February 1997), 1, 5–8.

4. Rudd quoted in Edward T. Gargan, "The American Conservative Response," in Jacques Rougerie, ed., *1871: Jalons pour une histoire de la Commune de Paris* (Assen, the Netherlands, 1972), 249. Gargan draws a different conclusion from the Rudd episode than I do.

5. Henri Lefebvre, *La Proclamation de la Commune* (Paris, 1965), 137–140. Among the legion of works that have been written about the Commune, I have found the following to be most useful: Stewart Edwards, *The Paris Commune: 1871* (London, 1971)—still the best general study in English; George Haupt, "The Commune as Symbol and Example," *Aspects of International Socialism, 1871–1914,* trans. Peter Fawcett (Cambridge, Eng., and Paris, 1986), 23–47; Roger Magraw, *France, 1815–1914: The Bourgeois Century* (Oxford, 1983), 197–205; Karl Marx, *The Civil War in France* (1871), in Marx and Frederick Engels, *Collected Works,* 46+ vols. (London, 1975–), 22:307–359; and R. D. Price, "Ideology and Motivation in the Paris Commune of 1871," *Historical Journal* 15 (1972), 75–86.

6. Haupt, "Commune as Symbol," 34 (quote); Price, "Ideology and Motivation," 80–86.

7. Hans Mommsen, "Paris Commune," in C. D. Kernig, ed., *Marxism, Communism, and Western Society*, 8 vols. (New York, 1972–1973), 6:177 (quote); Jean T. Joughin, *The Paris Commune in French Politics, 1871–1880* (Baltimore, 1955); Haupt, "Commune as Symbol," 23–25, 40–47.

8. Haupt, "Commune as Symbol," 25. The studies in question are: Rose Bernstein and Samuel Bernstein, "Répercussions de la Commune de Paris aux Etats-Unis," *Cahiers Internationaux* no. 24 (1951), 11–32; Samuel Bernstein, "American Labor and the Paris Commune," *Science & Society* 15 (1951), 144–162 (an English version of the previous item); idem, "The American Press Views the Commune," *Essays in Political and Intellectual History* (New York, 1955), 169–183; idem, "The Impact of the Paris Commune in the United States," *The Massachusetts Review* 12 (1971), 435–446; A. Landy, "La Commune et la class ouvrière aux Etats-Unis," *La Pensée* no. 37 (1951), 99–106; idem, "La Commune et les intellectuels américains," *Europe* no. 70 (1951), 111–126; idem, "Témoins américains oculaires de la Commune de Paris," *Cahiers Internationaux* no. 34 (1952), 65–74; and Jean-Jacques Recht, "La Commune de Paris et les Etats-Unis," *La Pensée* no. 164 (1972), 99–120.

9. Gargan, "The American Conservative Response"; George L. Cherry, "American Metropolitan Press Reaction to the Paris Commune of 1871," *Mid-America* 32 (1950), 3–12; and Eugene N. Curtis, "American Opinion of the French Nineteenth-Century Revolutions," *American Historical Review* 29 (1924), 249–270. The most recent discussions can be found in Nell Irvin Painter, *Standing at Armageddon: The United States, 1877–1919* (New York, 1987), 17–24; M. J. Heale, *American Anticommunism: Combating the Enemy Within, 1830–1970* (Baltimore, 1990), 21–30; and David A. Shafer, "Les répercussions de la Commune aux États-Unis, le cas de la presse: la Commune de Paris et la grève générale de 1877," *Cahiers d'histoire de l'Institut de Recherches Marxistes* 44 (1991), 7–23. Painter and Heale provide brief but perceptive discussions, while Shafer's article is a throwback to the works cited in note 7.

10. As Max Weber pointed out, the purpose of an ideal type is to be illuminating rather than strictly "typical" or modal; this should be kept in mind during the following discussion, which focuses on one very *atypical* individual. See Weber, *Economy and Society*, 2 vols. (Berkeley and Los Angeles, 1978), 1:20–21.

1. The Two Civil Wars of General Cluseret

1. This portrait of Cluseret, one of two that Courbet eventually painted, is reproduced in the *Bulletin des Amis de Gustave Courbet* 39 (1968), 5; the actual canvas seems to have disappeared some time prior to World War II.

The two Gustaves were not just fellow travelers in politics but also fellow artists; see Hélène Toussaint, *Gustave Courbet, 1819–1877* (London, 1978), 131, and "Cluseret peintre," *L'Intermédiaire des Chercheurs et Curieux* 64 (1911), 229–231.

2. At the time, Cluseret boasted of capturing eleven barricades and three flags; years later this boast came back to haunt him, and he was forced to apologize for his role in 1848, which he blamed on youth and inexperience. See Arthur Lehning, ed., *Michel Bakounine sur la Guerre Franco-Allemande et la Révolution Sociale en France, 1870–71* (Leiden, 1977), lxxxv–lxxxvi. In general, see Jean Maitron, ed., *Dictionnaire biographique du mouvement ouvrier français,* 43 vols. (Paris, 1964–93), 5:134–136, and "Général" Bourelly, *Le Ministère de la Guerre sous la Commune* (Paris, [1901]). Unless otherwise noted, information on Cluseret's life is derived from these two sources.

3. Gustave P. Cluseret, *Mémoires,* 3 vols. (Paris, 1887–1888), 2:194.

4. Ella Lonn, *Foreigners in the Union Army and Navy* (Baton Rouge, 1951), 273–275; Cluseret to Charles Sumner, April 1862. See also Lowell L. Blaisdell, "A French Civil War Adventurer: Fact and Fancy," *Civil War History* 12 (1966), 246–247. Both here and elsewhere, the Cluseret-Sumner correspondence is cited from the microfilm edition of the Sumner Papers, published by Chadwick-Healey, Inc. (Alexandria, Va., 1988). Cluseret's letters were written in French.

5. A. Landy, "A French Adventurer and American Expansionism after the Civil War," *Science & Society* 15 (1951), 318; George B. McClellan, *McClellan's Own Story* (New York, 1887), 143; Elihu B. Washburne, *Recollections of a Minister to France,* 2 vols. (New York, 1887), 2:107; Lowell L. Blaisdell, "Cluseret and the Frémont Campaign of 1864," *Mid-America* 46 (1964), 253–268.

6. Cluseret, "My Connection with Fenianism," *Fraser's Magazine,* n.s., 2 (1872), 31–46; Washburne, *Recollections,* 2:212; Landy, "French Adventurer," 325–328; Samuel Bernstein, *The First International in America* (New York, 1962), 26–27, 41–43; *New York World,* April 28, 1871.

7. Lehning, *Michel Bakounine,* lx–xci, 385–386.

8. Theodore Stanton to editor, *New York Times,* April 5, 1920. Stanton's account of the work that Cluseret did for the U.S. government is not quite accurate, and should be compared with *H. Repts.,* 50th Cong., 1st sess. (1888), Rpt. 784.

9. Marx to Frederick Engels, September 10, 1870, in Marx and Engels, *Collected Works,* 46+ vols. (London, 1975–), 44:70; *New York Times,* January 30, 1880. For typical remarks by historians, see Bernstein, *First International,* 42, and Louis M. Greenberg, *Sisters of Liberty: Marseille, Lyon, Paris, and the Reaction to a Centralized State, 1868–1871* (Cambridge, Mass., 1971), 98.

10. Unsigned article by Cluseret in the *Army and Navy Journal,* May 6, 1865, 579.

11. Edmond Lepelletier, *Histoire de la Commune de 1871*, 3 vols. (Paris, 1911–1913), 3:194. Cluseret's obituarist in the *New York Herald* strongly disagreed, writing that "The Frenchman's love of an idea animated him, and its pursuit led him [onward]" (August 24, 1900).

12. When Cluseret came to fight the American Civil War, he already counted among his acquaintances the leading figures of the French republican opposition (the strongest French supporters of the Union): Henri Martin, Eugène Pelletan, Emile Girardin, Alexandre Ledru-Rollin. In 1862, he considered himself a representative of the French republican party. Even so, his own sentiments seem to have been more anti-Bonapartist than pro-republican. See Cluseret to Sumner, mid-April, April 30, and August 19, 1862, and April 16, 1865; Landy, "French Adventurer," 318; Serge Gavronsky, *The French Liberal Opposition and the American Civil War* (New York, 1968).

13. Cluseret, *Idée d'un Corps Spécial pour l'Armée Italienne* (Turin, 1861). On Cluseret's course through the 1860s, see his *Mémoires,* 2:267, and "Connection with Fenianism," 46.

14. Cluseret to Sumner, September 22, 1864; see also Cluseret to Sumner, March 1, 1865.

15. A classic study of this is Leon Festinger et al., *When Prophecy Fails* (1956; paperback ed., New York, 1964).

16. Cluseret to Sumner, April 1861 (no date specified), August 19, 1862 (quote), and March 1, 1865; see also Cluseret, *Armée et Démocratie* (Paris, 1869), 7.

17. One can follow Cluseret's forlorn search for a general's star through his correspondence with Sumner from February through April 1862; see also Cluseret to William H. Seward, January 24, February 16, and March 10, 1862, and May 1, 1863, Seward Papers, University of Rochester.

18. McClellan, *McClellan's Own Story,* 143; *War of the Rebellion . . . Official Records of the Union and Confederate Armies,* 128 vols. (Washington, D.C., 1880–1901), ser. 1, vol. 12, pt. 1, 655–666 (cited hereafter as *Official Records*). Cluseret's account of the battle appears in a letter to Sumner, June 13, 1862, and in his *Mémoires,* 2:163–167; see also Blaisdell, "French Civil War Adventurer," 248–249.

19. Cluseret to General-in-Chief Henry W. Halleck, November 29, 1862, enclosed in a letter to William Seward, same date; Cluseret to Frederick W. Seward, December 29, 1862, Seward Papers, University of Rochester; Cluseret to Sumner, August 19, 1862.

20. Years later, the *New York Times* recalled him as an "irrepressible grumbler" (November 27, 1888). See Gen. Halleck to Gen. William S. Rosecrans, January 23, 1863, in *Official Records,* ser. 1, vol. 23, pt. 2, 11–12.

21. Cluseret to William Seward, April 19, 1863; Cluseret elaborated these charges in a letter to an unidentified Frenchman, copy enclosed in John Bigelow to William Seward, February 8, 1863, Seward Papers, University of Rochester; compare Cluseret to Sumner, January 1863.

22. Jacob D. Cox, *Military Reminiscences of the Civil War,* 2 vols. (New York, 1900), 1:426–427; *Official Records,* ser. 1, vol. 23, pt. 2, 11; Cluseret to Sumner, March 1, 1865; Blaisdell, "French Civil War Adventurer," 250–252.

23. Cluseret to Sumner, March 1, 1864; see also Cluseret to Sumner, April 19, April 28, and May 1, 1863. Cluseret also compared himself to Lafayette in a card addressed to the *Cincinnati Commercial* in early 1863 (reprinted in the *New York Times,* February 1, 1863) and in a personal letter to Abraham Lincoln, April 7, 1862, quoted in Blaisdell, "French Civil War Adventurer," 250.

24. Cluseret to Sumner, May 11, 1862; Cluseret, *Armée et Démocratie,* 20 (quote), 101–102, 110–111; compare his *Mémoires,* 2:165n.

25. Cluseret, *Armée et Démocratie,* 101–102 (italicized phrase in English in original); see also *Army and Navy Journal,* May 6, 1865, 579, and Cluseret to Sumner, April 27, 1865.

26. Blaisdell, "Cluseret and the Frémont Campaign," 254–255; Cluseret to Sumner, March 31, 1864; *New Nation,* September 24, 1864. The *New Nation* was based in New York and appeared weekly from March 5 through November 12, 1864; after a nine-month hiatus, it briefly resurfaced in the autumn of 1865.

27. Blaisdell, "Cluseret and the Frémont Campaign," 255; compare *New York Times,* September 12, 1872.

28. These themes were laid out in the first issue of the *New Nation,* March 5, 1864, and constantly reiterated; see also *New York Herald,* March 11, 1864.

29. *New Nation,* March 12, 1864. For more of his attacks on Lincoln, see *New Nation,* June 18, 1864, and Blaisdell, "Cluseret and the Frémont Campaign," 260–261.

30. Cluseret to Sumner, late February 1864. For the French context of these views, see Cluseret to Sumner, April 10, 1865; Gavronsky, *French Liberal Opposition,* passim; and Greenberg, *Sisters of Liberty,* 13–65.

31. The estimate of 400 supporters is provided by the *New Nation,* June 4, 1864. In a subsequent letter to Sumner, September 22, 1864, Cluseret estimated that the paper had only four thousand readers, but he revised his earlier estimate of attendance at the Cleveland convention to "not even 900 Frémont *men*" (English word in the original), "most of them men disgusted with the present parties . . . [and] looking for a new one."

32. Cluseret to Sumner, September 1 (quote), September 22, December 31, 1864; Blaisdell, "Cluseret and the Frémont Campaign," 258–265.

33. Cluseret to Sumner, September 22, November 25, December 31, 1864, and January 18, 1865 (inaccurately dated "January 10?" in the microfilm edition of the Sumner Papers). Cluseret never forgave Frémont, and cheered when the otherwise hated French government convicted his former commander of fraud in 1873; see Landy, "French Adventurer," 329, and Cluseret to Sumner, April 4, 1873.

34. Cluseret to Sumner, September 22, 1864.
35. "The New Nation to the Public," prospectus enclosed with Cluseret to Sumner, November 10, 1864; compare Cluseret, "Connection with Fenianism," 46.
36. Cluseret, *Mémoires,* 2:194; *New York Times,* February 1, 1863. Blaisdell, "French Civil War Adventurer," 254–256, is almost certainly right that Jefferson Davis never singled out Cluseret for condemnation, but it is also clear that he had genuine antislavery sentiments. This was one of the things that initially attracted Cluseret to Frémont, one of the first military commanders to try freeing slaves as part of the war effort.
37. Cluseret to Sumner, late February 1864. On the French liberals' reception of the Emancipation Proclamation see Gavronsky, *French Liberal Opposition,* 181–205.
38. *New Nation,* March 5, March 19, May 21, June 4, 1864; Cluseret to Sumner, late February 1864, and October 7, 1865 (incorrectly dated "February 7, 1865" in microfilm edition of Sumner Papers).
39. Cluseret to Sumner, April 27, 1865.
40. Cluseret to Sumner, April 16, 1865; see also his letter of November 10, 1864. Cluseret also made an explicit analogy with the *biens nationaux* of the French Revolution, lands seized from royalists and the Catholic Church in order to be sold to small proprietors. Most of the *biens nationaux* wound up in the hands of the original owners or the wealthy bourgeoisie—which made them, ironically, a better analogy than Cluseret perhaps intended.
41. Cluseret to Sumner, May 4, April 27, 1865.
42. Cluseret to Sumner, November 10, 1864, February 3, February 21, March 1, 1865.
43. Cluseret, "The Paris Commune of 1871: Its Origin, Legitimacy, Tendency, and Aim," *Fraser's Magazine,* n.s., 7 (1873), 364, 367–368; *Mémoires,* 2:194–195; Bourelly, *Le Ministère de la Guerre,* 8.
44. Greenberg, *Sisters of Liberty,* 228, 235–237; Lehning, *Michel Bakounine,* lxxxv–xci. According to Cluseret, he was "sent to Lyons by the [Parisian] Committee of the Twenty Arrondissements," a revolutionary group that later played a key role in initiating the Paris Commune (*Mémoires,* 2:137).
45. Cluseret, *Mémoires,* 2:138–139.
46. Greenberg, *Sisters of Liberty,* 176–183; Cluseret, *Mémoires,* 2:139.
47. See Train, *My Life in Many States and in Foreign Lands* (New York, 1902), a memoir that makes up in charm what it lacks in reliability; many of the worst exaggerations are corrected in the standard biography by Willis Thornton, *The Nine Lives of Citizen Train* (New York, 1948).
48. Train, *My Life,* 302–305. The text of Train's speech is printed in Maxime Aubray and Sylla Michelesi, *Histoire des Évènements de Marseille du 4 Septembre 1870 au 4 Avril 1871* (Marseilles, 1872), 126–128; on the impact of his oratory, see Cluseret, *Mémoires,* 2:182.
49. Train, *My Life,* 303–304; Aubray and Michelesi, *Évènements de Marseille,* 136–139.

50. Train, *My Life*, 306–309; Cluseret, *Mémoires*, 2:100–101; Thornton, *Citizen Train*, 204–205. Aubray and Michelesi, *Évènements de Marseille*, 97, incorrectly place Cluseret at Marseilles in late September.

51. Thornton, *Citizen Train*, 205; Greenberg, *Sisters of Liberty*, 181–183; Aubray and Michelesi, *Évènements de Marseille*, 141–153.

52. Proclamation of November 1, 1870, reprinted in Aubray and Michelesi, *Évènements de Marseille*, 143.

53. Train, *My Life*, 307–308.

54. Ibid., 309–313; Benjamin Moran to Elihu B. Washburne, December 16, 1870, Washburne Papers, Library of Congress (hereafter LC).

55. Cluseret, "Paris Commune," 380; *Mémoires*, 2:139.

56. Cluseret, "Paris Commune," 367–368, 379–381; *Mémoires*, 1:29–31; Bourelly, *Le Ministère de la Guerre*, 9–10; Stewart Edwards, *The Paris Commune: 1871* (London, 1971), 125–128.

57. Bourelly, *Le Ministère de la Guerre*, 11, 51–54; Edwards, *Paris Commune*, 198, 220, 225–226.

58. Bourelly, *Le Ministère de la Guerre*, 13–14. Cluseret was later accused of having conspired with the Germans and American general Philip Sheridan (an observer with the Prussian army) to bollix the April 3 sortie; see Ernest A. Vizetelly, *My Adventures in the Commune, Paris, 1871* (New York, 1914), 151.

59. Bourelly, *Le Ministère de la Guerre*, 16–18, 24–27; Cluseret, "Behind the Scenes at the Commune," *Fraser's Magazine*, n.s., 6 (1872), 782–787; Edwards, *Paris Commune*, 220–223.

60. Bourelly, *Le Ministère de la Guerre*, 84, 14–20, 24–27. The story of Cluseret's attempt to reorganize the Commune's armies is beyond the scope of this study, but see the account in his *Mémoires*, 1:56–136, and the assessment in Bourelly, *Le Ministère de la Guerre*, 81–86.

61. Bourelly, *Le Ministère de la Guerre*, 21, 35.

62. Proclamation of April 7, 1871, reprinted in Cluseret, *Mémoires*, 1:75; compare Bourelly, *Le Ministère de la Guerre*, 82–83; Edwards, *Paris Commune*, 209–210.

63. Cluseret, *Armée et Démocratie*, 20.

64. Bourelly, *Le Ministère de la Guerre*, 86; see also Vizetelly, *Adventures*, 99.

65. The first photograph is reproduced as an engraving in L. P. Brockett, *Paris Under the Commune; or, The Red Rebellion of 1871* (New York, 1871), opposite p. 56; the second is (poorly) reproduced in Gregor Dallas, "An Exercise in Terror? The Paris Commune, 1871," *History Today* 39 (February 1989), 40.

66. Cluseret, *Mémoires*, 2:165n. These words are part of a long self-description of his American career that appears as a footnote to Cluseret's account of his trial before the Commune in May 1871.

67. Cluseret, *Mémoires*, 2:86, 158; Cluseret, "Behind the Scenes," 784–785; Bourelly, *Le Ministère de la Guerre*, 13–14. See R. D. Price, "Ideology and Motivation in the Paris Commune of 1871," *Historical Journal* 15 (1972),

76–77, for a discussion of ideology and military necessity under the Commune.

68. Cluseret, "Behind the Scenes," 786.

69. Ibid., 782, 785; *Mémoires*, 2:161. More of Cluseret's strained relationship with the politicians can be glimpsed in Bourelly, *Le Ministère de la Guerre*, 9, 40–46, 53–54; Cluseret, "My Connection with Fenianism," 42–43; Cluseret, "The Interview at Aubervilliers," *Fraser's Magazine*, n.s., 5 (1872), 427–428.

70. Bourelly, *Le Ministère de la Guerre*, 66; Cluseret, "Behind the Scenes," 800–801. The charge of dictatorship was pervasive enough to get itself reprinted in American newspapers; see, e.g., *New York World*, April 26, 1871, and *The Spirit of the Times*, April 29, 1871.

71. Bourelly, *Le Ministère de la Guerre*, 35–37, 50–51, 54–55 (quote); Edwards, *Paris Commune*, 234–235; Washburne, *Recollections*, 2:105.

72. Edwards, *Paris Commune*, 226–227.

73. Bourelly, *Le Ministère de la Guerre*, 61–65; Cluseret, "Behind the Scenes," 792–800; "Interview at Aubervilliers," 425, 429; *Mémoires*, 2:85; "Paris Commune," 374.

74. Washburne, *Recollections*, 2:108.

75. W. Pembroke Fetridge, *The Rise and Fall of the Paris Commune in 1871* (New York, 1871), 199, 200 (quoting another American in Paris); Cluseret to Washburne, June 5, 1872, Washburne Papers, LC; Cluseret, "Interview at Aubervilliers," 425; Elihu B. Washburne, *Account of the Sufferings and Death of the Most Rev. George Darboy, Late Archbishop of Paris* (New York, 1873). See the next two chapters for a more detailed account of American activities during the Commune.

76. Quoted in Cluseret, *Mémoires*, 2:154–155.

77. Edwards, *Paris Commune*, 308–311 (Vallès quoted on 311); Bourelly, *Le Ministère de la Guerre*, 72; Washburne, *Recollections*, 2:108. Cluseret's own detailed account of the trial, containing long extracts from the *Journal Officiel* of the Commune, can be found in his *Mémoires*, 2:128–171.

78. Cluseret, *Mémoires*, 2:190–192; Bourelly, *Le Ministère de la Guerre*, 73–78. On Huntington, see Royal Cortissoz, *The Life of Whitelaw Reid*, 2 vols. (New York, 1921), 1:172–173. Cluseret's disappearance from the streets of Paris prompted the *New York Times* to print the first of two obituaries it would eventually run on him (May 31, 1871); the second appeared thirty years later (August 24, 1900). Fetridge, meanwhile, reported that "it is generally believed [Cluseret] made his escape from Paris disguised as a cabman, and has landed safely in the United States, and that he will probably remain there until Satan 'finds some work for idle hands'" (*Rise and Fall*, 508).

79. Edwards, *Paris Commune*, 313–343, 346; the quoted passage appears on 313.

80. Ibid., 313. When I went there on March 18, 1993, the anniversary of the

Commune's commencement, a bouquet of red roses was lying against the wall.

81. Bourelly, *Le Ministère de la Guerre,* 78; Cluseret, *Mémoires,* 2:192–193.
82. The same analysis, often in the same words, appears in his *Mémoires,* which were composed contemporaneously.
83. The Commune was clearly an uprising of the working class, but this does not mean that it was either a socialist revolution or a manifestation of the International; indeed, the International played a minor role in the Commune, compared to the large role it assumed in post facto interpretations. For a discussion of both roles, see Roger Magraw, *France, 1815–1914: The Bourgeois Century* (Oxford, 1983), 197–205; Edwards, *Paris Commune,* 67–68, 210–212; and Henri Lefebvre, *La Proclamation de la Commune* (Paris, 1965), esp. 166–167, 390–392.
84. Cluseret, "Aux Travailleurs Américains," *Le Marseillaise* (Paris), April 2, 1870.
85. Cluseret, "Interview at Aubervilliers," 425 (quote), 427; see also his article "Paris Commune," 384, and his *Mémoires,* 2:197.
86. Cluseret, "Interview at Aubervilliers," 423.
87. Cluseret, "Paris Commune," 360, 362; see also his "Interview at Aubervilliers," 426, and "Connection with Fenianism," 46. Cluseret's comment on the struggle to emancipate the slaves was a specific reference to Wendell Phillips, whose reaction to the Commune will be discussed below.
88. Cluseret, "Paris Commune," 360; minutes of the Commune Council, March 30, 1871, quoted in Edwards, *Paris Commune,* 204. Similarly, the Central Committee of the National Guard wanted to declare Paris an "independent Republic" (Lefebvre, *La Proclamation,* 202).
89. Cluseret, "Interview at Aubervilliers," 423–424. For many years, American historians have been able to discover "republicanism" wherever they sought it, without being able to agree on a definition. One element common to many definitions is "virtue," which Cluseret also placed at the center of republicanism. I have little desire to enter the historiographic tangle described by Daniel T. Rodgers in "Republicanism: The Career of a Concept," *Journal of American History* 79 (1992), 11–38. However, the fact that Americans were vitally concerned with "republicanism" and "the republic" in the Reconstruction era can be seen in the following (and the list could easily be extended): Charles O. Lerche, Jr., "Congressional Interpretations of the Guarantee of a Republican Form of Government during Reconstruction," *Journal of Southern History* 15 (1949), 192–211; C. C. P. Clark, *Nova Instauration Reipublicae (The Commonwealth Reconstructed)* (Oswego, N.Y., 1872); T[homas] M. Cooley, "The Guarantee of Order and Republican Government in the States," *International Review* 2 (January 1875), 57–87; and E[mily] H. Watson, *Is Our Republic a Failure?* (New York, 1877).
90. Cluseret, "Behind the Scenes," 788; see also his "Paris Commune," 368,

376. On his growing opposition to standing armies, an old republican bugbear, see *Army and Navy Journal,* May 6, 1865, 579, and Cluseret, *Armée et Démocratie,* esp. 20, 28, 64.

91. Cluseret, "Paris Commune," 383.

92. Proclamation of the Commune Council, April 19, 1871, quoted in Lefebvre, *La Proclamation,* 357. On the importance of decentralization, see ibid., 32–33, 136, 149–154, 312–313; Edwards, *Paris Commune,* 25–29, 153, 174–175, 217–219; and Greenberg, *Sisters of Liberty.* In French, the word *commune* can simply mean "municipality."

93. Albert D. Vandam, *An Englishman in Paris,* 2 vols. (London, 1892), 2:332.

94. Cluseret, *Mémoires,* 1:39 (quote), 139, 2:3, 220; "Interview at Aubervilliers," 423–424, 429; "Paris Commune," 374, 383.

95. Greenberg, *Sisters of Liberty,* 17; Jean T. Joughin, *The Paris Commune in French Politics, 1871–1880: The History of the Amensty of 1880* (Baltimore, 1955), 14.

96. Cooley, "Guarantee of Order," 57, 82.

97. Cluseret, "Paris Commune," 383.

98. Fetridge, *Rise and Fall,* 120; Washburne, *Recollections,* 2:108; Benjamin Moran to Elihu Washburne, April 5, 1871, Washburne Papers, LC. John Leighton, a Briton, wrote that Cluseret "is not a Frenchman; nor is he an American; for the honour of France I prefer his being an American"; see his *Paris Under the Commune; or, Seventy-Three Days of the Second Siege* (London and New York, 1871), 151.

99. *Appleton's Journal,* June 10, 1871, 868–869; *The Spirit of the Times,* April 29, 1871, 168; compare *New York World,* April 26, 1871.

100. Carl E. Schorske, "Politics in a New Key: An Austrian Trio," in his *Fin-de-Siècle Vienna: Politics and Culture* (New York, 1980), 120 (my thanks to Jane Dailey of Rice University for drawing my attention to this apt passage). Cluseret's obituary in *Le Temps* (August 27, 1900) also notes his microcosmic qualities.

101. The idea of an "age of democratic civil wars" is, of course, inspired by R. R. Palmer's classic study, *The Age of the Democratic Revolution,* 2 vols. (Princeton, 1959–1964).

102. James A. Rawley, "The American Civil War and the Atlantic Community," *Georgia Review* 21 (1967), 185. A similar perspective is suggested by A. R. Tyrner-Tyrnauer, *Lincoln and the Emperors* (New York, 1962), xiii–30; David M. Potter, "The Civil War," in C. Vann Woodward, ed., *The Comparative Approach to American History* (New York, 1968), 135–145; Cluseret, *Mémoires,* 2: 241. In addition to the Commune, the American Civil War, and the other civil wars mentioned in the text, a partial list of important events in the "age of democratic civil wars" might include Italian and German unification (both culminating in 1870); the end of Russian serfdom (1861); the Polish civil war (1863); the Fenian uprising, the partial inde-

pendence of Canada and Hungary, the British Reform Bill (all 1867); and the rise of the First International.

103. François Bourricaud, "Cotradition et traditions chez Tocqueville," *Tocqueville Review* 2 (Winter 1980), 25–39; Marvin Trachtenberg, *The Statue of Liberty* (1976; rev. ed., New York, 1986), 21–40 (quoted passage on 22); Gavronsky, *French Liberal Opposition,* 35–50. Many works have been written on the special relationship between France and the United States, and most concur with Albert Guérard that "France and America . . . are near enough to be intelligible to each other, far enough to be mutually interesting"—an assessment I find much too optimistic. Guérard, *Beyond Hatred: The Democratic Ideal in France and America* (New York, 1925), ix.

2. La Colonie Américaine

1. The epigraph is from John Sherman, *Recollections of Forty Years in the House, Senate, and Cabinet,* 2 vols. (Chicago, 1895), 1:406. Oliver Wendell Holmes, *The Autocrat of the Breakfast-Table* (1858), in *The Writings of Oliver Wendell Holmes,* Riverside Edition, 14 vols. (Boston, 1899), 1:124–125.

2. The population estimate of 13,000 is derived from John Meredith Read, diary entry of December 5, 1870, Read Diary, New York Public Library (NYPL). Read was the American consul-general in Paris, well positioned to judge the size of the American colony. Wickham Hoffman, a secretary at the American Legation, suggested a more conservative figure of 6,000 Americans in *all* of France at the start of the war; see his *Camp, Court, and Siege: A Narrative of Personal Adventures and Observations during Two Wars* (New York, 1877), 149. The official French census, meanwhile, counted some 7,223 "American" inhabitants of Paris in 1866 and 6,859 in 1872; however, these figures do not distinguish between North and South Americans and drastically undercount temporary residents; see Bureau de la statistique générale [de la France], *Dénombrements des étrangers en France: résultats statistiques du dénombrement de 1891* (Paris, 1893), xvi. At the other extreme, a contemporary traveler put the number of Americans in France at 30,000; see Charles Carroll Fulton, *Europe Viewed through American Spectacles* (Philadelphia, 1874), 175.

3. "The American Colony in France," *Nation,* April 18, 1878, 258 (cited hereafter as "American Colony"); François Boucher and Frances W. Huard, *American Footprints in Paris* (New York, 1921), 24–26; Gerald Carson, *The Dentist and the Empress: The Adventures of Dr. Tom Evans in Gas-Lit Paris* (Boston, 1983), 76; John Russell Young, *Around the World with General Grant,* 2 vols. (New York, 1879), 1:136–140.

4. Joseph Wilson Cochran, *Friendly Adventurers: A Chronicle of the American Church of Paris (1857–1931)* (Paris, 1931); Frederic Hudson, *Journalism in the United States, from 1690 to 1872* (New York, 1873), 314.

5. Young, *Around the World,* 1:136–137 (including the remarks about beverages and bazaars); André Léo (pseud. of Léodile de Champceix), *The American Colony in Paris in 1867; From the French of André Léo* (Boston, 1868); "Nebulae," *Galaxy Magazine* 12 (1871), 294; Lucy H. Hooper, "The American Colony in Paris," *Appleton's Journal* 11 (1874), 779–781; Edward Gould Buffum, *Sights and Sensations in France, Germany, and Switzerland* (New York, 1869), 200–203.

6. "American Colony," 258; Young, *Around the World,* 1:142.

7. Léo, *American Colony in 1867,* 5.

8. "American Colony," 258.

9. John A. Dix, American minister to France in 1869, quoted in Thomas W. Evans, *The Memoirs of Dr. Thomas W. Evans: Recollections of the Second Empire,* ed. Edward A. Crane, 2 vols. (London, 1905), 1:135; "American Colony," 258; Léo, *American Colony in 1867,* 4.

10. Catty observers loved to point out that any daughter of the nouveaux riches, "no matter what her parentage or antecedents," could catch a minor nobleman by dangling the right bait from "the commercial whirlpool of New York, or the oil regions, or the [Western] mines." Lucy H. Hooper, *Under the Tricolor; or, The American Colony in Paris* (Philadelphia, 1880), 77.

11. "American Colony," 258. See also Carson, *Dentist and Empress,* 78; Young, *Around the World,* 1:142, 161–164.

12. Léo, *American Colony in 1867,* 5; Carson, *Dentist and Empress,* 77–78; Elihu B. Washburne, *Recollections of a Minister to France, 1869 to 1877,* 2 vols. (New York, 1887), 1:36–38; Hoffman, *Camp, Court, and Siege,* 122.

13. Evans, *Memoirs,* 1:128–129. For more on Evans's unique career, see the Carson biography cited above; also Alan Albright, "T. W. Evans, a Philadelphian 'Yankee' at the Court of Napoleon III," *1853–1947: Les Américains et la Légion d'Honneur* (Paris, 1993), 129–131.

14. "American Colony," 258; Young, *Around the World,* 1:147–149.

15. H. Barbara Weinberg, "Nineteenth-Century American Painters at the École des Beaux-Arts," *American Art Journal* 13 (1981), 66–84; "Americans in Paris: Catalogue of an Exhibition," *Princeton University Library Chronicle* 17 (1956), 227–228; Albert Boime, "Olin Levi Warner's Defense of the Paris Commune," *Archives of American Art Journal* 29 (1989), 2–22.

16. *The Revolution,* September 14, 1871; "Paris in 1870: Letters of Mary Corinna Putnam," *American Historical Review* 22 (1917), 836.

17. Young, *Around the World,* 1:136, 142.

18. Evans, *Memoirs,* 1:137–138; A[mbrose] Dudley Mann to Jefferson Davis, April 2, 1871, in Dunbar Rowland, ed., *Jefferson Davis, Constitutionalist,* 10 vols. (Jackson, Miss., 1923), 7:290–293.

19. Young, *Around the World,* 1:137–138; Hooper, *Under the Tricolor,* 28. The festivities of July 4, 1870, are described in Carson, *Dentist and Empress,* 101–102, and a special issue of the *American Register,* July 9, 1870.

20. Carson, *Dentist and Empress,* 102.

21. *American Register,* July 1, 1871.

22. Roger Magraw, *France, 1815–1914: The Bourgeois Century* (Oxford, 1983), 187–197.

23. Dale Clifford, "Elihu Benjamin Washburne: An American Diplomat in Paris, 1870–71," *Prologue* 2 (1970), 163; Washburne, *Recollections,* 1:34–35; Robert Lowry Sibbet, *The Siege of Paris, by an American Eye-Witness* (Harrisburg, Pa., 1892), 289; Ruth Putnam, ed., *Life and Letters of Mary Putnam Jacobi* (New York, 1925), 118, 252–253.

24. *American Register,* October 22, 1870.

25. *American Register,* July 16, August 27, October 22, November 26, December 24, 1870; January 14, March 18, 1871. There were also a number of naturalized American citizens, born in France, who fought for their native country; see Nathan Sheppard, *Shut Up in Paris* (London, 1871), 118, and Washburne, *Recollections,* 2:46–48.

26. Marie Caroline [de Trobriand] Post, *Life and Mémoirs of Régis de Trobriand* (New York, 1910), frontispiece, 50–52, 171, 227n, 432–434.

27. New York *World,* June 9, 1871.

28. *Every Saturday,* April 8, 1871, 335. On Porter, see *American Register,* April 1, 1871, and *Frank Leslie's Illustrated Newspaper,* April 8, 1871.

29. Sibbet, *Siege of Paris,* 51 (from a letter he wrote in August 1870); compare Clara Barton to Elihu B. Washburne, August 3, 1870, Washburne Papers, Library of Congress (LC).

30. Sibbet, *Siege of Paris,* 1, 47; Washburne, *Recollections,* 1:92–95, 196–201; *The Americans in Paris* (Paris, 1887; rpt. San Francisco, 1987), 43–44.

31. Hoffman, *Camp, Court, and Siege,* 149.

32. See John Meredith Read to President Grant, n.d., copy in Read Diary, December 5, 1870, NYPL; Washburne to Hamilton Fish, December 3, 1870, in "Franco-German War and Insurrection of the Commune. Correspondence of E. B. Washburne," *Sen. Ex. Doc.* 24, 45th Cong., 2d sess. (1878), 104. Their estimate was almost certainly low, as "during the siege Americans came to light of whose existence the legation was not aware" (Young, *Around the World,* 1:148).

33. Augustus L. Chetlain [American consul in Brussels], *Recollections of Seventy Years* (Galena, Ill., 1899), 148–149; Nicholas Fish to E. B. Washburne, February 1, 1871, Washburne Papers, LC; *American Register,* January 28, 1871.

34. On the general hardships of the siege, see Washburne, *Recollections,* 1:133–134. Food is a common topic in American memoirs of the Prussian siege. The most interesting account is Wickham Hoffman's, which lists "elephant, yak, camel, reindeer, porcupine, etc." among the exotica consumed during the Prussian siege (*Camp, Court, and Siege,* 212; see also 209–214); see also Louis Judson Swinburne, *Paris Sketches* (Albany, N.Y., 1875), 139–152, and *The Revolution,* September 14, 1871.

35. Washburne to Hamilton Fish, February 2, 1871, "Franco-German War Cor-

respondence," 141. One victim of the Prussian bombardment was a young medical student who died with these words on his lips: "O to suffer and die for France! I am an American." "Un étudiant américain, victime du Siège," *L'Intermédiaire des Chercheurs et Curieux* 54 (1906), 275.

36. Colonel R. Lloyd Lindsay to *London Times,* quoted in *American Register,* November 11, 1870. See also Carson, *Dentist and Empress,* 108–110; Ralph Keeler, "With the American Ambulance Corps at Paris," *Lippincott's Magazine* 12 (1873), 84–93; Swinburne, *Paris Sketches,* 19–31, 47–48; *American Register,* July 23, July 30, August 6, October 8, November 19, 1870, and April 8, 1871.

37. Sibbet, *Siege of Paris,* 86–87; Swinburne, *Paris Sketches,* 11.

38. Henry Vizetelly, *Paris in Peril,* 2 vols. (London, 1882), 2:11–23; Sheppard, *Shut Up in Paris,* 208–209; Washburne, *Recollections,* 1:168–170.

39. Hoffman, *Camp, Court, and Siege,* 166–169; Vizetelly, *Paris in Peril,* 2:19–20; Henry Blumenthal, *A Reappraisal of Franco-American Relations, 1830–1871* (1959; rpt. Westport, Conn., 1980), 197–198.

40. Washburne, *Recollections,* esp. 1:39–43, 69–71, 96, 226–231, and 2:239–40; "Franco-German War Correspondence," 12, 16, 27–28; Stephen Hess, "An American in Paris," *American Heritage* 18 (February 1967), 26–27, 71.

41. Washburne, *Recollections,* 1:43 (quote), 1:308–309; "An American Lady" [Mrs. F. J. Willard], *Pictures from Paris in War and in Siege* (London, 1871), 237; Sheppard, *Shut Up in Paris,* 290–291.

42. Washburne to Benjamin Moran, January 1, 1871, quoted in *Recollections,* 1:308; in the same letter, Washburne requests that no more outside newspapers be sent to him. The controversy over the American diplomatic mail-bag is discussed on 1:165–166, 306–313.

43. John C. Davis to E. B. Washburne, telegraphic dispatch, September 7, 1870, Washburne Papers, LC; see also Chapter 5 below.

44. Sibbet, *Siege of Paris,* 134; Read Diary, September 9, 1870, NYPL. Some sense of the French republicans' resentment of American neutrality can be found in Willard, *Pictures from Paris,* 262–263; Joseph Aron, *Les Deux Républiques Soeurs, France et États-Unis* (Paris and New York, 1885); Theodore Stanton, "General Grant and the French," *Cornell Magazine* 2 (1889), 9–26.

45. Henry Blumenthal, *France and the United States: Their Diplomatic Relations, 1789–1914* (New York, 1972), 57–58.

46. E. B. Washburne to Hamilton Fish, September 5, 1870, in "Franco-German War Correspondence," 63; Erskine quoted in Washburne, *Recollections,* 1:118–119. See Edward King, *Europe in Storm and Calm* (Springfield, Mass., 1887), 226–240, for another firsthand account of the declaration of the Republic, which King reported for the *Boston Journal.*

47. Journal entry of September 4, 1870 (as copied in personal letterbook), and E. B. Washburne to Mary Washburn, September 8, 1870, Washburne Papers, LC; Clifford, "Elihu Benjamin Washburne," 163–164.

48. "The Fourth of September in Paris. Familiar Letter from a Young American," *Putnam's Magazine*, n.s., 6 (1870), 553, 559 (also reprinted in Putnam, *Life and Letters*); *American Register*, September 10, 1870. In general, see *American Register*, January 14, February 11, 1871.

49. Hoffman, *Camp, Court, and Siege*, 164–165; Blumenthal, *Reappraisal*, 12–15.

50. Letters between Washburne and Favre reprinted in Washburne, *Recollections*, 1:120–122.

51. Washburne, *Recollections*, 1:123–125; *American Register*, September 10, 1870.

52. Quoted in Sheppard, *Shut Up in Paris*, 32–33. On Hugo's speech, see Melville D. Landon, *The Franco-Prussian War in a Nutshell* (New York, 1871), 265.

53. Sibbet, *Siege of Paris*, 127–128.

54. *American Register*, October 8, October 29, 1870.

55. *American Register*, October 22, October 31, November 19, 1870.

56. *American Register*, October 8, October 15 (quote), November 12, 1870.

57. *American Register*, December 17, 1870; see also the issues of October 29 and November 12, 1870.

58. E. B. Washburne to Mary Washburn, September 8, 1870, Washburne Papers, LC; Willard, *Pictures from Paris*, 32–33.

59. Evans, *Memoirs*, 2:346–351; the story of his flight with the empress is most conveniently found in Carson, *Dentist and Empress*, 112–131.

60. Read Diary, September 4–5, 1870, NYPL; compare King, *Europe in Storm and Calm*, 226, and Willard, *Pictures from Paris*, 102–103. On contemporary usage of the term, see "Agrarianism," *Atlantic Monthly* 3 (1859), 393–394.

61. Willard, *Pictures from Paris*, 102–104, 109. A handwritten note on the title page of the copy of her book at the Library of Congress identifies Willard as the "authoress of Louisiana."

62. Ibid., 148, 153, 43.

63. Ibid., 43–45.

64. On the vicissitudes of the American colony in the short weeks before the Commune, see Emma Bullet, *The Autobiography of Emma Bullet, Twenty-Five Years Paris Correspondent of "The Brooklyn Daily Eagle"* (Brooklyn, 1906), 29; also the March 16 dispatch from "Lux" in the *New York Evening Post*, April 5, 1871. According to the *American Register*, more than 126 Americans had returned to Paris and registered with Bowles Brothers bank as of March 4, 1871.

65. Dale L. Walker, *Januarius MacGahan: The Life and Campaigns of an American War Correspondent* (Athens, Ohio, 1988), 35–36, 40 (quote).

66. Lillie Moulton to her mother, March 19, 1871, in L[illie Moulton] de Hegermann-Lindencrone, *In the Courts of Memory, 1858–1875, from Contemporary Letters* (New York, 1912), 271 (at the time of the Commune the

author was married to American banker Charles Moulton); E. B. Washburne to Benjamin Moran, March 19, 1871, Washburne Papers, LC.

67. On the flight of the colonists, see Chetlain, *Recollections,* 160–161, and *American Register,* March 25, 1871. On those who remained in Paris, see Washburne, *Recollections,* 2:77; *American Register,* April 10, 1871; and E. B. Washburne to Marshal MacMahon, May 25, 1871, Washburne Papers, LC.

68. *American Register,* April 29, 1871; Clifford, "Elihu Benjamin Washburne," 169.

69. Cluseret and Witton are the only Americans to appear on the list of 49 foreign participants in the Commune first published by *Le Figaro* on May 31, 1871 (and often reproduced since), though Washburne had his doubts about the nationality of the latter (see his *Recollections,* 2:236). On the Franco-American battalion, see Clifford, "Elihu Benjamin Washburne," 169. On Block, see Georges-Ferdinand Gautier, *Les Francs-Tireurs de la Commune* (Paris, 1971), 34, 37–38. On Trammell, see George B. Benham, *The Proletarian Revolt* (San Francisco, 1898), 220.

70. *Harper's Weekly,* February 1, 1873, 91.

71. Hegermann-Lindencrone, *In the Courts of Memory,* 289–295, 310–311; Washburne, *Recollections,* 2:77.

72. Jean Maitron, ed., *Dictionnaire Biographique du Mouvement Ouvrier Français,* 43 vols. (Paris, 1964–1993), 4:236. This source gives the name as either Beer, Ber, or Berr; it might even be the Nathaniel Berry mentioned earlier.

73. Walker, *Januarius MacGahan,* 36–37; *New York Herald,* May 23, 1871.

74. Frank M. Pixley quoted in Benham, *Proletarian Revolt,* 213.

75. Clifford, "Elihu Benjamin Washburne," 169; John R. Young, *Men and Memories,* ed. May D. Russell Young, 2 vols. (New York, 1901), 1:184; Hoffman, *Camp, Court, and Siege,* 267–270; Washburne, *Recollections,* 2:85, 89, 120–21. See also C.W.T., "What an American Girl Saw of the Commune," *Century Magazine* 45 (1892), 61–63.

76. Washburne, *Recollections,* 2:157.

77. Benham, *Proletarian Revolt,* 213; King, *Europe in Storm and Calm,* 476–477.

78. *Christian Union,* August 9, 1871, 89; [W. F. Chermside], "Two Nights in a French Prison during the Civil War," *MacMillan's Magazine* 24 (1871), 215; E. B. Washburne to Jules Favre, June 15 and June 21, 1871, Washburne Papers, LC.

79. Washburne, *Recollections,* 2:160–161; King, *Europe in Storm and Calm,* 488–490, 514.

80. At the time there was some confusion about the man's real name. As Washburne explained to Secretary Fish, the passport read "George S. Hanna," but the personal papers gave "George H. Teniel" (dispatch of March 23, 1871, in "Franco-German War Correspondence," 163); meanwhile, American

newspapers rendered it as George Tinnel, George Hannah Tinnel, and George S. Hanna (see *New York Evening Post*, March 24, April 6, 1871).

81. Frank Moore to E. B. Washburne, March 22, 1871, in "Franco-German War Correspondence," 165–166; Chetlain, *Recollections*, 158–159; Edward Forbes, "The Massacre in the Place Vendôme," *Appleton's Journal*, May 13, 1871, 560.

82. Sheridan quoted in Colonel Henry C. Lockwood, "General Philip Henry Sheridan," *Frank Leslie's Popular Monthly* 26 (1888), 527. See also *American Register*, March 25, 1871; Washburne, *Recollections*, 2:18, 43–44, 53–54; W. Pembroke Fetridge, *The Rise and Fall of the Paris Commune in 1871* (New York, 1871), 66–67.

83. *Every Saturday*, May 6, 1871, 415; Ernest A. Vizetelly, *My Adventures in the Commune, Paris, 1871* (London, 1914), 283; Clifford, "Elihu Benjamin Washburne," 169. In general, see Fetridge, *Rise and Fall*, 134–135, 262–265.

84. Young, *Men and Memories*, 1:201; Vizetelly, *My Adventures*, 281.

3. First Impressions

1. A. Landy, "Témoins américains oculaires de la Commune de Paris," *Cahiers Internationaux* 34 (1952), 65–74.

2. W. Pembroke Fetridge, *The Rise and Fall of the Paris Commune in 1871* (New York, 1871), 15, iv. For the French bourgeoisie's view of the Commune, see Martin R. Waldman, "The Revolutionary as Criminal in 19th Century France: A Study of the Communards and *Déportés*," *Science & Society* 37 (1973), 31–55, and Paul Lidsky, *Les écrivains contre la Commune* (Paris, 1970). According to Michel Fabre, *From Harlem to Paris: Black American Writers in France, 1840–1980* (Urbana, Ill., 1991), 16, their view was also shared by Victor Séjour, an African-American playwright who had been living in Paris for many years.

3. See also Fetridge, *Rise and Fall*, 22, 60–61, 86, 414.

4. Emmeline Raymond, "The Second Siege of Paris, Described by an Eye-Witness," *Harper's Weekly*, July 15, 1871, 646–647; compare A. Dudley Mann to Jefferson Davis, April 2, 1871, in Dunbar Rowland, ed., *Jefferson Davis, Constitutionalist*, 10 vols. (Jackson, Miss., 1923), 7:293.

5. Mann to Davis, April 2, 1871, in Rowland, *Jefferson Davis*, 7:291. Mary Surratt was hanged in 1865.

6. Mann to Davis, December 5, 1871, in ibid., 7:300.

7. "An American Lady" [Mrs. F. J. Willard], *Pictures from Paris in War and in Siege* (London, 1871), 312–313.

8. John Meredith Read to his father, May 17, June 16, 1871, copy in Read Diary, New York Public Library (NYPL).

9. Washburne to Secretary Fish, March 19, 1871, in "Franco-German War and

Insurrection of the Commune: Correspondence of E. B. Washburne," *Sen. Ex. Doc.* 24, 45th Cong., 2d sess. (1878), 159; compare his letter to Bismarck, March 22, 1871, in ibid., 162.

10. Elihu B. Washburne, *Recollections of a Minister to France, 1869 to 1877,* 2 vols. (New York, 1887), 2:67. Compare Washburne's diary entry for March 31, 1871, reprinted in ibid., 58; also Washburne to Secretary Fish, March 25, 1871, in "Franco-German War Correspondence," 166–168.

11. Dale Clifford, "Elihu Benjamin Washburne: An American Diplomat in Paris, 1870–71," *Prologue* 2 (1970), 170–171. Washburne did not present his official credentials to the Thiers government until May 8, 1871.

12. Washburne to Secretary Fish, April 6, 1871, in "Franco-German War Correspondence," 178; see also Washburne, *Recollections,* 2:32–33, 77; Wickham Hoffman, *Camp, Court, and Siege: A Narrative of Personal Adventures and Observations during Two Wars* (New York, 1877), 256–258.

13. Clifford, "Elihu Benjamin Washburne," 173; Hoffman, *Camp, Court, and Siege,* 247–248; *New York World,* June 20, 1871; *American Register,* July 8, 1871; International Workingmen's Association, *Mr. Washburne, The American Ambassador in Paris* (London, 1871).

14. Washburne, *Recollections,* 2:126, 88.

15. Washburne to Secretary Fish, May 25, 1871, in "Franco-German War Correspondence," 207; see also Clifford, "Elihu Benjamin Washburne," 167–174.

16. The story of Darboy's imprisonment and assassination is related in Washburne, *Recollections,* 2:163–189; Hoffman, *Camp, Court, and Siege,* 262–265; Elihu B. Washburne, *Account of the Sufferings and Death of the Most Rev. George Darboy, Late Archbishop of Paris* (New York, 1873).

17. Washburne, *Recollections,* 2:192, 42; see also Clifford, "Elihu Benjamin Washburne," 171–174.

18. Washburne to Fish, quoted in Henry Blumenthal, *France and the United States: Their Diplomatic Relations, 1789–1914* (New York, 1972), 127n31; compare Washburne to Fish, May 31, June 2, 1871, in "Franco-German War Correspondence," 209–212.

19. *American Register,* November 11, 1870; see also Nathan Sheppard, *Shut Up in Paris* (London, 1871), 85–89.

20. *American Register,* March 25, 1871.

21. *American Register,* April 1, 1871. On April 22, the *Register* ran an article on municipal corruption in the United States, which is also pertinent; after citing Wendell Phillips on "the value of municipal institutions," the article concluded that some corruption in a free city would still be an improvement on imperial despotism.

22. *American Register,* May 13, 1871. Of special interest is Girardin's short-lived newspaper *Le Bonhomme Franklin,* published in Paris during the Commune, which derived both its name and its ideas from the American political tradition. Note that Girardin was also one of Cluseret's French republican "patrons" in 1862.

23. Washburne, *Recollections,* 2:191–192; Fetridge, *Rise and Fall,* 23–24, 93–94 (quote). For an alternative view, see John Russell Young, *Men and Memories,* ed. May D. Russell Young, 2 vols. (New York, 1901), 1:193–195.

24. *American Register,* April 29, May 13, June 3, June 17, and July 15, 1871.

25. *American Register,* May 27, 1871.

26. *American Register,* June 6, May 27, and April 1, 1871.

27. See especially the *American Register*'s editorial on republicanism versus socialism in France, June 10, 1871.

28. Gerald Carson, *The Dentist and the Empress* (Boston, 1983), 78–80; Washburne, *Recollections,* 1:233.

29. Letter dated March 24, 1871, in L[illie Moulton] de Hegermann-Lindencrone, *In the Courts of Memory, 1858–1875, from Contemporary Letters* (New York, 1912), 285.

30. Washburne, *Recollections,* 2:192; Lillie Moulton to her mother, March 31, 1871, in Hegermann-Lindencrone, *Courts of Memory,* 298–300.

31. Lillie Moulton to her mother, May 7, May 15, May 18, and May 23, 1871, in Hegermann-Lindencrone, *Courts of Memory,* 317–318, 328, 330, 333.

32. *Life and Letters of Mary Putnam Jacobi,* ed. Ruth Putnam (New York, 1925), 171–172, 218–220, 238–239, 280–281; Paul Reclus, *Les Frères Élie et Élisée Reclus* (Paris, 1964), 71, 74.

33. Putnam, *Life and Letters,* 281.

34. Mary Putnam to George Haven Putnam, May 7, 1871, in Putnam, *Life and Letters,* 278.

35. Simon Newcomb, *The Reminiscences of an Astronomer* (Boston, 1903), 322–323 (quotes), 321–327; see also Landy, "Témoins américains oculaires," 68–69.

36. The *American Register* described Pixley as "one of the representative men of the Pacific coast" (July 1, 1871).

37. Daniel Lévy, *Les Français en Californie* (San Francisco, 1884), 253; see also Jerome A. Hart, *In Our Second Century: From an Editor's Note-Book* (San Francisco, 1931), esp. 120–123, 128–130.

38. Pixley quoted in George B. Benham, *The Proletarian Revolt* (San Francisco, 1898), 211–212 (emphasis in original); see also Landy, "Témoins américains oculaires," 69–70. Pixley's memoirs of the Commune first appeared in the San Francisco *Argonaut* in 1878–1879. John Russell Young provides a similar description of orderliness under the Commune (*Men and Memories,* 1:199–202).

39. Pixley in Benham, *Proletarian Revolt,* 212.

40. Young, *Men and Memories,* 1:195–196. This and the quotations that follow come from Young's long dispatch to the *New York Tribune* dated May 28, 1871.

41. Young, *Men and Memories,* 1:192–193, 196.

42. Ibid., 1:205, 207.

43. Benham, *Proletarian Revolt,* 220.

44. In 1863, popular historian James Parton claimed that Wilkes was one of the three great writers produced by the Civil War, along with Abraham Lincoln and Benjamin Butler; see his *General Butler in New Orleans* (New York, 1863), 9.

45. *Nation*, July 2, 1874, 10. Note that, like many Southern books, *Ça Ira* was published in New York.

46. Trammell, "Review of an *Address delivered before the Alumni Society of the University of Georgia*," *Southern Magazine*, n.s., 3 (1872), 756, 761; compare *Ça Ira*, 28, 183, 211.

47. *Ça Ira*, 239–240. These words are spoken by the autobiographical hero of the novel.

48. Ibid., 19–21, 56–57. This conspiracy, involving secret college societies, the Klan, and expatriate Southrons, was almost certainly the most fictional aspect of Trammell's book.

49. Benham, *Proletarian Revolt*, 220.

50. *Ça Ira*, 5, 270–271; see also 138, 150–151, and esp. 264–271.

51. *Ça Ira*, 197, 185, 191; see also 205–207.

52. The most important letters to the *Herald* were reprinted in *The Spirit of the Times*, from which they will be cited. The two pamphlets are *A Defence of the Commune* (London, 1871) and *The Internationale: Its Principles and Purposes* (New York, 1871).

53. Wilkes letter of May 16, 1871, in *The Spirit of the Times*, June 24, 1871, 289–291.

54. Ibid., September 23, 1871, 88–89, and October 7, 1871, 120–121.

55. Ibid., October 7, 1871, 120, 121; compare Wilkes, *The Internationale*, 4, 6.

56. Wilkes, *The Internationale*, 14–20; see also the *New York Sun*, November 27, 1871, quoted in *The Spirit of the Times*, December 2, 1871, 249; *American Register*, September 23, 1871.

57. Wilkes, *The Internationale*, 19.

58. Wilkes letter of June 17, 1871, in *The Spirit of the Times*, July 1, 1871, 310; see also ibid., June 24, 1871, 291. For compelling literary treatments of "denationalized Americans," see Lucy Hooper's *Under the Tricolor* (Philadelphia, 1880), or almost any of the early works by Henry James.

59. Young, *Men and Memories*, 1:203–205.

60. Fetridge, *Rise and Fall*, 512–515; Fetridge to Washburne, May 5, 1871; Washburne to Fetridge, May 10, 1871; Washburne to Charles de Rémusat, November 20, 1871, Washburne Papers, Library of Congress.

61. Letter of May 8, 1871, in Hegermann-Lindencrone, *Courts of Memory*, 319.

62. Washburne, *Recollections*, 2:241.

4. Ripples across the Atlantic

1. The epigraphs in this chapter are from M. Hildegarde Yeager, *The Life of James Roosevelt Bayley, First Bishop of Newark and Eighth Archbishop of Balti-*

more, 1814–1877 (Washington, D.C., 1947), 317, and Samuel Bernstein, "The American Press Views the Commune," *Essays in Political and Intellectual History* (New York, 1955), 182. Benton (1898) quoted in Robert J. Greef, "Public Lectures in New York, 1851–1878: A Cultural Index of the Times" (Ph.D. diss., University of Chicago, 1941), 28–29; see also David A. Wasson, "The Modern Type of Oppression," *North American Review* 119 (1874), 262–264.

2. George P. Rowell & Co., *American Newspaper Directory* (New York, 1873), 29–31. The growth of the American press far outstripped population growth. Between 1850 and 1870, the U.S. population expanded by 72 percent (from 23.2 million to 39.8 million) while the number of periodicals grew by 133 percent, and their aggregate circulation by an impressive 254 percent, as calculated from the statistics in Rowell and those in U.S. Bureau of the Census, *Historical Statistics of the United States, 1789–1945* (Washington, 1949), 25. See also Frank L. Mott, *American Journalism, A History: 1690–1960* (1941; 3rd ed., New York, 1962), 404.

3. *British Quarterly Review* (1871) quoted in Mott, *Journalism*, 405. The comparative publishing statistics are from Rowell, *Newspaper Directory*, 31, and Mott, *Journalism*, 404–405.

4. S. N. D. North, *History and Present Condition of the Newspaper and Periodical Press* (Washington, 1884), 105. On technical innovation and the press, especially during the Civil War years, see Edwin Emery and Michael Emery, *The Press and America: An Interpretive History of the Mass Media* (5th ed.; Englewood Cliffs, N.J., 1984), 205–206, and Mott, *Journalism*, 400–402.

5. North, *History of the Newspaper*, 105.

6. In 1868, for example, the average price for a press dispatch of about thirty words was approximately $1.05—not cheap, but cheaper than it would have been before the war. See Donald L. Shaw, "News Bias and the Telegraph: A Study of Historical Change," *Journalism Quarterly* 44 (Spring 1967), 6–7.

7. Michael Schudson, *Discovering the News: A Social History of American Newspapers* (New York, 1978), 66–67. The discussion of Civil War journalism that follows is derived from Mott, *Journalism*, 329–338; Emery and Emery, *The Press and America*, 205–206; and John Hohenberg, *Foreign Correspondence: The Great Reporters and Their Times* (New York, 1964), 62–72.

8. Mott, *Journalism*, 329.

9. Ibid., 380.

10. Hohenberg, *Foreign Correspondence*, 69; see also Mott, *Journalism*, 330, and *New York World*, May 26, 1871. Another unintended consequence of the reporting style was that the brief dispatches *appeared* to lack any editorial content, at a time when a newspaper's editorial stance was often its strongest selling point.

11. Havilah Babcock, "The Press and the Civil War," *Journalism Quarterly* 6 (March 1929), 2–3.

12. Charles Seymour (1872), quoted in Shaw, "News Bias," 10.

13. "Culture and Progress," *Scribner's Monthly* 8 (1874), 117. Donald Shaw argues that Wisconsin editors in the early 1870s were well aware of their readers' appetite for telegraphic news of dubious veracity or importance (Shaw, "News Bias," 10).

14. Shaw, "News Bias," 6–8.

15. Strictly speaking, this was the second transatlantic cable; Field's first cable was completed in 1858 but quickly failed, and could not be replaced until after the war.

16. Edward King, *Europe in Storm and Calm* (Springfield, Mass., 1887), v–vi.

17. Hohenberg, *Foreign Correspondence*, 77; *Scribner's Monthly* 8 (1874), 117; John G. Gazley, *American Opinion of German Unification, 1848–1871* (New York, 1926), 87.

18. Gazley, *American Opinion*, 320.

19. Reid to Smalley, July 20, 1870, in Royal Cortissoz, *The Life of Whitelaw Reid*, 2 vols. (New York, 1921), 1:170.

20. On the *Tribune*'s coverage of the Franco-Prussian War, see Henry W. Baehr, Jr., *The New York Tribune since the Civil War* (New York, 1936), 76–79; Cortissoz, *Life of Reid*, 1:168–179; Hohenberg, *Foreign Correspondence*, 74–80.

21. Gazley, *American Opinion*, 530–533; Frederic Hudson, *Journalism in the United States, from 1690 to 1872* (New York, 1873), 606. Hudson, the managing editor of the *New York Herald* during the Civil War, added, "No record of previous wars can surpass those of the years between 1861 and '71. Anterior to these events we spoke of Napier, Thiers, Gibbon, Bancroft. They were compilers from old documents. Now we speak of the *Tribune, Times, World, Herald*. They have been eye-witnesses" (Hudson, 719).

22. Hohenberg, *Foreign Correspondence*, 77; Dale L. Walker, *Januarius MacGahan: The Life and Campaigns of an American War Correspondent* (Athens, Ohio, 1988), 16, 33.

23. Baehr, *The New York Tribune*, 79; Cortissoz, *Life of Reid*, 1:170–172; Mott, *Journalism*, 380–381.

24. Melville D. Landon, for example, relied heavily on clippings from Conway and Halstead when he wrote *The Franco-Prussian War in a Nutshell* (New York, 1871). See also Hohenberg, *Foreign Correspondence*, 77–78; Donald Walter Curl, "An American Reporter [Murat Halstead] and the Franco-Prussian War," *Journalism Quarterly* 49 (1972), 480–488; and Edward King's novel *Kentucky's Love; or, Roughing It around Paris* (Boston, 1873), a semi-autobiographical account of American journalists during the Prussian siege.

25. North, *History of the Newspaper*, 106–108; Shaw, "News Bias," 7.

26. Hudson, *Journalism in the United States*, 606.

27. *The Independent*, March 23, 1871.

28. Notably the *New York Herald*'s trio of MacGahan, Dr. George Hosmer, and Alvan Southworth, whom Washburne later claimed "had a more intelligent knowledge of all that was taking place at that time than any [other men] . . .

in Paris" (quoted in Walker, *Januarius MacGahan*, 33). See ibid., 33–38; Southworth, "The Commune of Paris," *Frank Leslie's Popular Monthly* 4 (1877), 416–432.

29. Samuel Bernstein, "The American Press Views the Commune," *Essays in Political and Intellectual History* (New York, 1955), 171.

30. *New York World*, May 26, 1871.

31. *Daily Corinne Reporter*, April 8, 1871.

32. Diary entries of February 15, April 8, 10, 17, May 23, 24, 26, 1871, *Diary of George Templeton Strong*, ed. Allan Nevins and Milton H. Thomas, 4 vols. (New York, 1952), 4:346, 350–351, 358–359 (cited hereafter as *Strong Diary*).

33. Diary entries of May 27 and 29, 1871, *Strong Diary*, 4:360–361.

34. Bartholdi to his mother, July 28, 1871, in Bartholdi Papers, New York Public Library; Fetridge, *The Rise and Fall of the Paris Commune in 1871* (New York, 1871), iii; Brockett, *Paris Under the Commune* (New York, 1871), 3; see also *Woodhull & Claflin's Weekly*, May 20, 1871, and *New York World*, May 26, 1871. New York merchant Elliot C. Cowdin, an eyewitness to the Commune, was one of very few observers to feel that "you at home were better informed of events than we who were detained in Europe": *France in 1870–71: An Address, Delivered before the Cooper Union . . . , New-York, February 10, 1872* (New York, 1872), 5–6.

35. A. Landy, "La Commune et les intellectuels américains," *Europe* no. 70 (1951), 112, 118, and passim.

36. Clifford Geertz, "Thick Description: Toward an Interpretive Theory of Culture," *The Interpretation of Cultures* (New York, 1973), 5. My own thinking about culture and ideology has been particularly influenced by Geertz and Max Weber, as well as François Bourricaud, *Le Bricolage Idéologique* (Paris, 1980).

37. Arthur L. Stinchcombe, *Theoretical Methods in Social History* (New York, 1978), 117.

38. Caroline Barrett White diary, March 20, 1871, microfilm of original at the American Antiquarian Society, Worcester, Massachusetts; Walter van Tilburg Clark, ed., *The Journals of Alfred Doten, 1849–1903*, 3 vols. (Reno, 1973), 2:1129.

39. Frans H. Widstrand to Charles Sumner, April 15, 1871, Sumner Papers (microfilm edition). Étienne Cabet was a French Utopian socialist with many followers in the United States.

40. *New Orleans Daily Picayune*, March 26, 1871.

41. The last of these conditions was probably the least restrictive, since a newspaper cost only 2 cents in 1871, and a ticket in the family circle at New York's Grand Opera House cost only 30 cents.

42. *Every Saturday*, April 22, 1871, 380–381; July 1, 1871, 20–21; July 8, 1871, 25; September 16, 1871, 265. Every one of these illustrations also appeared in *Harper's Weekly*, with slightly different captions.

43. See, e.g., *Every Saturday,* June 17, 1871, 572; July 8, 1871, 32–33.

44. Frank L. Mott, *A History of American Magazines, 1865–1885* (Cambridge, Mass., 1938), 359.

45. Contra Landy, "La Commune et les intellectuels américains" (esp. 116), articles about the Commune were a minor staple for two generations of serious American magazines, from the stodgy *North American Review* in the 1870s to the middle-brow *Munsey's* in the 1890s. For example, see A. S. Hill, "Causes of the Commune," *North American Review* 116 (1873), 90–109, and Molly Elliot Seawell, "The Commune of Paris," *Munsey's Magazine* 17 (1897), 705–719, 810–824, and 18 (1897), 113–132.

46. Fetridge bears a striking resemblance to Charles Schermerhorn Schuyler, the fictional author of *Paris Under the Commune* in Gore Vidal's novel *1876* (New York, 1976), 9. Nonetheless, though Vidal understood that the Commune was "emblematic . . . for the Americans of 1876," he did not base Schuyler on any specific historical figure (Vidal to author, September 26, 1996).

47. On the subscription book trade, see Michael Hackenburg, "Hawking Subscription Books in 1870: A Salesman's Prospectus from Western Pennsylvania," *Papers of the Bibliographic Society of America* 78 (1984), 137–153; John Tebbel, *A History of Book Publishing in the United States,* 5 vols. (New York, 1972–1981), 2:511–520; and the entire contents of the James Dabney McCabe Papers, Johns Hopkins University (JHU).

48. *Appleton's Cyclopaedia of American Biography,* 7 vols. (New York, 1888–1901), 4:74.

49. McCabe to National Publishing Co., August 8, 1870 (quote), February 8 and 11, 1871, McCabe Papers, JHU. Brockett and Fetridge also reproduced numerous engravings from the illustrated weeklies in their books.

50. McCabe to National Publishing Co., March 9, 1871, McCabe Papers, JHU.

51. McCabe to National Publishing Co., April 10, May 30, 1871, McCabe Papers, JHU; see also the review of Brockett in the *New York Herald,* September 25, 1871, noting the interest of the "general reader" in the Commune.

52. McCabe to National Publishing Co., June 2, 1871; McCabe to E. Hannaford (a book distributor in Cincinnati), July 7, 1871, McCabe Papers, JHU.

53. See Appendix C for a list of "American" novels set in the Paris Commune, with complete bibliographic information. About half of these were British imports, or simply pirated from British editions before the Anglo-American copyright agreement in 1891.

54. Eugene C. Savidge, *The American in Paris* (Philadelphia, 1896), [3]. His statement appears in the Preface.

55. For example: [Grenville Murray], "Consule Julio: An Episode under the Commune de Paris," *Littell's Living Age* 110 (1871), 718–737 (reprinted from *Cornhill Magazine* in London); idem, "The Pétroleuse: A Souvenir of Versailles," *Every Saturday,* November 25, 1871, 514–515, and December 2, 1871, 550–551 (also reprinted from *Cornhill*); Edward Greey, "Models:

An Episode of the Franco-German War," *Frank Leslie's Illustrated Newspaper*, November 16, 1872, 150 (part of the action is set in the Commune); Alfred Esmery, "Muguette: or, The Last Day of the Column (Episode of the Paris Commune)," *Frank Leslie's Illustrated Newspaper*, March 7, 1874, 422–423; and "The Stranger's Money," *Frank Leslie's Popular Monthly* 1 (1876), 614–622.

56. I have been able to locate only one dime novel set in the Paris Commune: Anthony P. Morris, Jr., *The French Spy; or, The Bride of Paris. A Thrilling Story of the Commune* (New York, 1878; reprinted 1880). But Edward T. LeBlanc, a leading collector of dime novels and the editor of *Dime Novel Round-Up* magazine, suggests there were probably others (LeBlanc to author, September 17, 1990).

57. "Cacique: A Story of the Commune," *Frank Leslie's Popular Monthly* 3 (1877), 217–222.

58. Mott, *Magazines*, 511. The 100,000 is a circulation figure, and thus a very conservative estimate of actual readership.

59. "O Star of France," *Galaxy* 11 (June 1871), 817. Whitman wrote the poem in mid-April 1871; see *Correspondence of Walt Whitman*, ed. Edwin H. Miller, 5 vols. (New York, 1961–1977), 2:121. A slightly different version appears in *Leaves of Grass: Comprehensive Reader's Edition*, ed. Harold W. Blodgett and Sculley Bradley (New York, 1965), 396–397.

60. "Paris and the Lessons of Adversity," reprinted in *Every Saturday*, February 10, 1872, 162.

61. Landy, "La Commune et les intellectuels américains," 115–116; Larry J. Reynolds, *European Revolutions and the American Literary Renaissance* (New Haven, 1988), 135–142, 152.

62. John P. McWilliams, Jr., *Hawthorne, Melville, and the American Character: A Looking-Glass Business* (Cambridge, Eng., 1984), 211–217.

63. Reynolds, *European Revolutions*, 13–14, 100–108.

64. *Clarel: A Poem and Pilgrimage in the Holy Land*, ed. Walter E. Bezanson (New York, 1960), 587–588.

65. Robert H. Walker, *The Poet and the Gilded Age: Social Themes in Late Nineteenth-Century American Verse* (Philadelphia, 1963), 12–13, and passim.

66. Landy, "La Commune et les intellectuels américains," 124.

67. *Scribner's Monthly* 2 (1871), 500. Perhaps because of its female protagonist, King's poem was quickly reprinted in *The Woman's Journal*, September 2, 1871, and *Woodhull & Claflin's Weekly*, September 9, 1871.

68. "A Triumph of Order," *Atlantic Monthly* 30 (1872), 219; the text is reprinted in Appendix B. Hay was Lincoln's former secretary and Theodore Roosevelt's future Secretary of State, but in 1871–1872 he was merely an assistant editor at the *New York Tribune*.

69. *Galaxy* 12 (September 1871), 326–327.

70. "Paris-Berlin (Summer, 1871)," *Harper's Weekly*, July 8, 1871, 626; see also her poem "France, 1871," *Harper's Weekly*, April 15, 1871, 350.

71. Margaret J. Preston, "Rossel" (circa 1872), in *Cartoons* (Boston, 1875), 161–162. Preston's poem "The Hero of the Commune," which originally appeared in *Scribner's Monthly* 3 (1872), 660–661, was reprinted in the same collection (151–153); the text is also included in Appendix B.

72. John Boyle O'Reilly, "From the Earth, a Cry," in *The Statues in the Block, and Other Poems* (Boston, 1881), 37–44; [William J. Linton], "Delescluze on the Barricade," in *Voices of the Dead* (New Haven, 1879), 11–14; see also Linton's essay "The Paris Commune," *The Radical* 9 (1871), 81–104.

73. Carl Sahm, "The Song of the Commune," *Die Fackel*, March 18, 1883, reprinted in Hartmut Keil and John B. Jentz, eds., *German Workers in Chicago: A Documentary History of Working-Class Culture from 1850 to World War I* (Urbana, Ill., 1988), 334–335; Charles E. Markham, "The Song of the Workers: Remembering the Martyrs of Paris in 1871," *Denver Labor Enquirer*, February 12, 1887, reprinted in Philip S. Foner, ed., *American Labor Songs of the Nineteenth Century* (Urbana, Ill., 1975), 303–304; John Leslie, "Seventy-One" (circa late 1880s), reprinted in Marcus Graham, ed., *An Anthology of Revolutionary Poetry* (New York, 1929), 91–92.

74. Helen H. Bessey, ed., *Granger's Index to Poetry and Recitations* (3rd ed.; Chicago, 1940).

75. Versions of the anecdote can be found in Stewart Edwards, *The Paris Commune: 1871* (London, 1971), 296; *New York Herald*, July 13, 1871; *Harper's Weekly*, July 15, 1871; *Appleton's Journal*, August 19, 1871; Fetridge, *Rise and Fall*, 419–420; Trammell, *Ça Ira* (New York, 1874), 179–180; Gribble, *The Red Spell* (New York, 1895), 127–128; see also George B. Benham, *The Proletarian Revolt* (San Francisco, 1898), 149–150. A few details in Hay's ironic version of the story are distinctive: for example, the watch once belonged to the boy's father, and the young lad is actually executed by the French troops when he returns from the errand.

76. Redpath to Washburne, July 7, 1871, Washburne Papers, Library of Congress.

77. Coquerel spoke in New York on October 18, 1871 (Greef, "Public Lectures in New York," 91). Earlier that month he gave two lectures at Boston's fashionable Music Hall, where he was introduced to the audience by Senator Charles Sumner; see Sumner, *Complete Works*, 20 vols. (Statesman ed., Boston, 1900), 19:159–160. He also lectured on the Commune at the October meeting of the American Board of Foreign Missions in Salem, Massachusetts (see Chapter 7 below).

78. Greef, "Public Lectures in New York," 91; Cowdin, *France in 1870–71*; idem, *Capital and Labor: An Address Delivered before the American Institute of the City of New York . . . October 11, 1877* (New York, 1877). Despite the provocative title, Cowdin's second lecture focused on the Commune and barely mentioned the recent wave of domestic strikes (the Great Strike discussed in Chapter 8 below).

79. Greef, "Public Lectures in New York," 91; *New York Tribune*, November 10, 1876.

80. *New York Times*, November 16, 1877. In 1878, Washburne gave a similar talk to students at the University of Michigan (*Forney's Progress*, November 16, 1878).

81. Phillips quoted in "The International Association," *Catholic World* 14 (1872), 705; compare *New York Times*, December 7, 1871, which contains a less accurate transcription of Phillips's remarks. For a general discussion of Phillips's postbellum radicalism, see Richard Hofstadter, "Wendell Phillips: The Patrician as Agitator," *The American Political Tradition* (New York, 1948), 137–163; Samuel Bernstein, "The Impact of the Paris Commune in the United States," *Massachusetts Review* 12 (1971), 443–444.

82. *New National Era*, May 18, 1871; see also the *Christian Union*, May 17, 1871, 310; *Nation*, June 8, 1871, 394; Hofstadter, "Wendell Phillips," 162.

83. See Chapter 8 for a discussion of what middle-class reformers later had to say about the Commune, and the reaction of their conservative peers.

84. F. O. Mattheissen, ed., *The American Novels and Stories of Henry James* (New York, 1947), 732–740; see also Matthiessen's "Introduction," xix–xx. Like others at the time, especially in the genteel classes, James rhetorically connected the Commune and American feminism (see Chapter 6 below).

85. George C. D. Odell, *Annals of the New York Stage*, 15 vols. (New York, 1927–1949), 9:70; *New York Herald*, July 30, August 4, 1871.

86. See Appendix C for the details of these and other American plays set in the Commune.

87. *New York Times*, November 28, 1871.

88. *Woodhull & Claflin's Weekly*, December 9, 1871.

89. See Appendix C.

90. Robert Wernick, "Getting a Glimpse of History from a Grandstand Seat," *Smithsonian* 16 (August 1985), 68–69, 78.

91. *The Great Siege of Paris, 1870–71: From Authentic Historical Data* (New York and Philadelphia, 1875–1876). The description of Desbrosses's picture is taken from an unpaginated insert in the New York Public Library's copy of the pamphlet, which also describes the painting as "Just Added."

92. James D. McCabe, *The Illustrated History of the Centennial Exhibition* (Philadelphia, 1877), 311; *The Great Siege of Paris: 1870–71; Also, The Assassination of the Archbishop of Paris, at the Hands of the Commune of 1871* [Philadelphia, 1876], 21–23; see also Philip S. Foner, "The French Trade Union Delegation to the Philadelphia Centennial Exposition, 1876," *Science & Society* 40 (1976), 277n63.

5. Civil Wars by Analogy

1. *Harper's Weekly*, August 24, 1872, 655.

2. Edward T. Gargan, "The American Conservative Response," in Jacques Rougerie, ed., *1871: Jalons pour une histoire de la Commune de Paris* (Assen, the Netherlands, 1972), 245.

3. This is a good example of what some philosophers have called "metaphorical

tension," in which the "creative interaction between diverse perspectives" extends the range of possible meanings for *both* sides of the comparison, even when the intention is merely to explain *one* side. See Douglas Berggren, "The Use and Abuse of Metaphor," *Review of Metaphysics* 16 (1962–1963), esp. 244, and Martin Landau, "On the Use of Metaphor in Political Analysis," *Social Research* 28 (1961), 334–335.

4. For a sampling of military comparisons between the Franco-Prussian War and the Civil War, see the newspaper extracts in Melville D. Landon, *The Franco-Prussian War in a Nutshell* (New York, 1871), 90, 304, 337–338, 434. For other comparisons between Paris and Richmond under siege, see General Adam Badeau, "Two Great Wars: An Historical Parallel," *Fraser's Magazine,* n.s., 2 (1870), 804; *Every Saturday,* September 10, 1870, 578, and February 25, 1871, 187.

5. Badeau, "Two Great Wars," 793. The two wars are extensively compared in Stig Förster and Jörg Nagler, eds., *On the Road to Total War: The American Civil War and the German Wars of Unification, 1861–1871* (Washington, D.C., 1997); see also J. P. T. Bury's trenchant discussion in *Gambetta and the National Defence: A Republican Dictatorship in France* (1936; rpt. Westport, Conn., 1971), 303–307.

6. Diary entry of July 16, 1870, *Diary of George Templeton Strong,* ed. Allan Nevins and Milton H. Thomas, 4 vols. (New York, 1952), 4:296 (cited hereafter as *Strong Diary*).

7. Eugene N. Curtis, "American Opinion of the French Nineteenth-Century Revolutions," *American Historical Review* 29 (1924), 270; Elizabeth Brett White, *American Opinion of France from Lafayette to Poincaré* (New York, 1927), 179–180.

8. Grant to Elihu B. Washburne, August 22, 1870, in *General Grant's Letters to a Friend, 1861–1880* (1897; rpt. New York, 1973), 68; Grant interview, *New York Sun,* August 6, 1870, quoted in Landon, *Franco-Prussian War,* 43; Theodore Stanton, "General Grant and the French," *Cornell Magazine* 2 (1889), 9–26; Curtis, "American Opinion," 264–265; White, *American Opinion of France,* 174–175.

9. The discussion that follows is drawn from Gazley, 313–380, and from other sources as noted.

10. Grant to Elihu B. Washburne, August 22, 1870, in *General Grant's Letters,* 68; *Richmond Whig,* August 6, 1870, quoted in White, *American Opinion of France,* 181; Henry Blumenthal, *A Reappraisal of Franco-American Relations, 1830–1871* (1959; rpt. Westport, Conn., 1980), 192.

11. Jean-Baptiste Ravold, *Français et Allemands aux États-Unis pendant l'Année Terrible (1870)* (Nancy [France], 1883), 22–24. At a similar rally in St. Louis, one Fenian speaker argued that "the French had redeemed America, and Americans would be cowards and dastards if they were to forget what the French had done for them" (*New York Tribune,* September 23, 1870, quoted in Gazley, *American Opinion of German Unification,* 362).

12. Ravold, *Français et Allemands,* 22, 33–34; Gazley, *American Opinion of German Unification,* 367–370.

13. Carl Schurz, editorial, St. Louis *Anzeiger des Westens,* quoted in Curtis, "American Opinion," 265n57; *Harper's Weekly,* September 24, 1870, 610–11; Gazley, *American Opinion of German Unification,* 359–361, 379; White, *American Opinion of France,* 181–183.

14. [Parke Godwin], "Editorial Notes: American Sympathy in the War," *Putnam's Magazine,* n.s., 6 (1870), 456; clearly, Godwin wrote this before the declaration of the new French republic. Landon, *Franco-Prussion War,* 68–69, and Gazley, *American Opinion of German Unification,* 322–324, offer further examples of the overwhelming Northern and Republican support for Prussia at the start of the war.

15. Godwin, "Editorial Notes," 456–457.

16. General John Cochrane, quoted in Ravold, *Français et Allemands,* 19; see also White, *American Opinion of France,* 173–179.

17. *New York Times,* September 4, 1866, quoted in Gazley, *American Opinion of German Unification,* 208–209; George Bancroft to Secretary of State Fish, November 29, 1870, quoted in Joseph Aron, *Les Deux Républiques Soeurs, France et États-Unis* (Paris and New York, 1885), 58; see also *Harper's Weekly,* January 14, 1871, 36; Badeau, "Two Great Wars," 793; Gazley, *American Opinion of German Unification,* 356–358. For negative views of German unity, see Landon, *Franco-Prussian War,* 463; Gazley, *American Opinion of German Unification,* 413–416.

18. White, *American Opinion of France,* 183.

19. James A. Rawley, "The American Civil War and the Atlantic Community," *Georgia Review* 21 (1967), 192–194; Karl Heinzen, *What Is Real Democracy? Answered by an Exposition of the Constitution of the United States* (Indianapolis, 1871), 10–27, 58–60.

20. "The United States of Europe," *Old and New* 3 (1871), 260–267.

21. Eric Foner, *Reconstruction: America's Unfinished Revolution, 1863–1877* (New York, 1988), 232–233; Charles O. Lerche, Jr., "Congressional Interpretations of the Guarantee of a Republican Form of Government during Reconstruction," *Journal of Southern History* 15 (1949), 192–211; T[homas] M. Cooley, "The Guarantee of Order and Republican Government in the States," *International Review* 2 (1875), 60–61; E[mily] H. Watson, *Is Our Republic a Failure?* (New York, 1877), 163–164.

22. Landon, *Franco-Prussian War,* 69n (quote), 258–259, 280; Ravold, *Français et Allemands,* 27–31, 47–49.

23. Curtis, "American Opinion," 269–270; David Brion Davis, *Revolutions: Reflections on American Equality and Foreign Liberations* (Cambridge, Mass., 1990), 80–81.

24. Charles Sumner, "The Duel between France and Germany," *Complete Works,* 20 vols. (Statesman ed., Boston, 1900), 18:204. This speech, delivered in Boston on October 26, 1870, was widely reprinted.

25. Grant, annual message to Congress, December 5, 1870, quoted in Curtis, "American Opinion," 268; Cadwallader C. Washburn to Elihu B. Washburne, December 25, 1870, Washburne Papers, Library of Congress (LC).

26. *Harper's Weekly*, January 21, 1871, 50; Gazley, *American Opinion of German Unification*, 388. The various older studies disagree about how large or permanent a shift in American sympathies was occasioned by the new French Republic. Curtis claims that "public opinion made a complete [and lasting] *volte-face*" when the Republic was declared ("American Opinion," 265), while Gazley argues that there was merely a temporary change of opinion, which largely evaporated by January 1871 (*American Opinion of German Unification*, 381, 392). Elizabeth Brett White, though writing a few years before Gazley, charged that "a careful study of the facts" would not sustain the argument that the change of opinion "was only temporary, and that the balance swung back toward Germany as the war progressed" (*American Opinion of France*, 197). I think that Americans simply got confused as they tried to reconcile their faith in republicanism with their distrust of both European combatants.

27. J. Lothrop to Washburne, September 26, 1870, Washburne Papers, LC.

28. Ravold, *Français et Allemands*, 31–34; see also Gazley, *American Opinion of German Unification*, 382–383; *Harper's Weekly*, September 24, 1870, 610–611.

29. Jonathan Baxter Harrison, "Limited Sovereignty in the United States," *Atlantic Monthly* 43 (1879), 186. See also Michael E. McGerr, *The Decline of Popular Politics: The American North, 1865–1928* (New York, 1986), 45–52.

30. Harrison, "Limited Sovereignty," 186.

31. Michael E. McGerr, "The Meaning of Liberal Republicanism: The Case of Ohio," *Civil War History* 28 (1982), 307; Russell B. Nye, *Midwestern Progressive Politics: A Historical Study of Its Origins and Development, 1870–1958* (Michigan, 1959), 30–31; James G. Sproat, *"The Best Men": Liberal Reformers in the Gilded Age* (New York, 1968).

32. Child to Anna Loring Dresel, January 1, 1871, *The Collected Correspondence of Lydia Maria Child, 1817–1880*, ed. Patricia G. Holland and Milton Meltzer (Milwaukee, 1979), microfiche edition.

33. *Nation*, December 1, 1870, 360; see also February 2, 1871, 69.

34. *Harper's Weekly*, January 28, 1871, 74; see also October 1, 1870, 626, and March 3, 1871, 186; Ravold, *Français et Allemands*, 34–35; White, *American Opinion of France*, 194–196.

35. Lerche, "Congressional Interpretations," 198–208.

36. Harold M. Hyman argues this briefly in *A More Perfect Union: The Impact of the Civil War and Reconstruction on the Constitution* (New York, 1973), 532–533; see also M. J. Heale, *American Anticommunism* (Baltimore, 1990), 24.

37. *Frank Leslie's Illustrated Newspaper*, July 12, 1873.

38. Gazley, *American Opinion of German Unification*, 285, 347–348; "Table-Talk," *Putnam's Magazine*, n.s., 5 (1870), 120–121.

39. *Scribner's Monthly* 1 (1870), 106; *Harper's Weekly*, October 1, 1870, 626, and January 1, 1871, 2. Similar indictments of the French capacity for republican government can be found in *Every Saturday*, October 8, 1870, 642–643; *Scribner's Monthly* 2 (1871), 206–207; *Nation*, February 2, 1871, 69–70; and Rev. John Crowell, *Republics* (Philadelphia, 1871), 40–41, 163, 210–211, 226.

40. Interview in *New York Herald*, July 30, 1871. Butler first defended the Commune in a widely reported campaign speech at Gloucester, Massachusetts, on June 29 (*New National Era*, July 6, 1871; *Independent*, June 29, July 13, 1871).

41. *Woodhull & Claflin's Weekly*, November 25, 1871; Samuel Bernstein, "The American Press Views the Commune," *Essays in Political and Intellectual History* (New York, 1955), 179.

42. A. Cridge to editors, *Woodhull & Claflin's Weekly*, September 15, 1871 (emphasis added).

43. *San Francisco Morning Bulletin*, quoted in Bernstein, "American Press," 171. Frank Pixley's dispatches from Paris to the San Francisco press were making the opposite claim, more proof that American interpretations of the Commune were largely unrestrained by events in Paris, even when those could be accurately ascertained.

44. *New Orleans Daily Picayune*, April 4, 1871; *New York Times*, May 31, 1871.

45. *New York Evening Post*, April 4, 1871.

46. *Frank Leslie's Illustrated Newspaper*, May 6, 1871, 121.

47. Crowell, *Republics*, 226.

48. *Independent*, June 8, 1871.

49. *Civil Rights: The Hibernian Riot and the "Insurrection of the Capitalists," A History of Important Events in New York in the Midsummer of 1871* (New York, 1871), 20. For specific comparisons between the Commune and the political activity of immigrants in American cities, see the *New York Herald*, July 11, July 13, 1871; George Templeton Strong's diary entries for July 10 and 13, 1871, *Strong Diary*, 4:368, 371; Joel T. Headley, *The Great Riots of New York, 1712 to 1873* (New York, 1873), 18–19; and the *Nation*, April 9, 1874, 230–31. For general attitudes about immigrants and their limited capacity for self-government, see John Higham, *Strangers in the Land: Patterns of American Nativism, 1860–1925* (1955; 2nd ed., New York, 1973), esp. Chapter 2.

50. *Every Saturday*, June 3, 1871, 523. For the debate over women's capacity for self-government, see Ellen Carol DuBois, *Feminism and Suffrage: The Emergence of an Independent Women's Movement in America, 1848–1869* (Ithaca, 1978). For contemporary comparisons between women's suffrage and the Commune, see the *Nation*, June 22, 1871, 426–427; G. Thomas Edwards, *Sowing Good Seeds: The Northwest Suffrage Campaigns of Susan B. Anthony*

(Portland, Ore., 1990), 75–76, 101. I will return to this theme in the next chapter.

51. Frelinghuysen quoted in William E. Nelson, *The Fourteenth Amendment: From Political Principle to Judicial Doctrine* (Cambridge, Mass., 1988), 88; William Gillette, *The Right to Vote: Politics and the Passage of the Fifteenth Amendment* (Baltimore, 1965), 21–50.

52. *Oswego (N.Y.) Daily Palladium*, June 3, 1867; Rep. Michael C. Kerr (D–Indiana), both quoted in Nelson, 97. Many similar statements are quoted by Nelson, *Fourteenth Amendment*, 96–104.

53. Guion Griffis Johnson, "The Ideology of White Supremacy, 1876–1910," in Fletcher M. Green, ed., *Essays in Southern History* (Chapel Hill, 1949), 128; Vincent P. De Santis, *Republicans Face the Southern Question: The New Departure Years, 1877–1897* (Baltimore, 1959), 44, 49–52.

54. "Ought the Negro to Be Disfranchised? Ought He to Have Been Enfranchised?," *North American Review* 128 (1879), 266.

55. *Nation*, April 16, 1874, 247–248. The comparison to the Commune is implicit but clear.

56. Karl Marx and Frederick Engels, *Collected Works*, 46+ vols. (London, 1975–), 20:20.

57. Ibid., 22:458; compare 22:464.

58. "S.K.B." to editor, *Cleveland Leader*, May 2, 1871; *New Orleans Daily Picayune*, May 5, 1871; *New York Herald*, July 4, 1871.

59. *New York Evening Post*, June 29, 1871.

60. Ibid., September 16, 1871; compare "Parisiana," *Fraser's Magazine*, n.s., 5 (1872), 481–482.

61. *New York Times*, April 28, 1871; compare *Harper's Weekly*, July 1, 1871, 594.

62. "General Butler and the Commune," *Independent*, July 13, 1871. Note how this is almost exactly an opposite version of the Civil War analogy that Marx employed.

63. *Independent*, March 23, 1871; see also "Reconstruction in France," *Independent*, August 24, 1871.

64. Laura E. Richards and Maud Howe Elliott, *Julia Ward Howe, 1819–1910*, 2 vols. (Boston, 1916), 2:308–309. Compare Howe's view of the Commune as the "military enforcement of political opinions" with Philip Sheridan's eyewitness version of the Commune in Chapter 2 above; unlike Howe, the general seemed willing to sanction military enforcement almost without regard for the political opinions involved.

65. Alcorn quoted in J. S. McNeilly, "The Enforcement Act of 1871 and the Ku Klux Klan in Mississippi," *Publications of the Mississippi Historical Society* 9 (1906), 135.

66. *The Republic* 6 (1876), 126–127. Four years earlier, a similar view was presented in a campaign pamphlet entitled *The Republican Party, the Standard-Bearer of Civilization and National Progress* (n.p., 1872), 6. In 1875, the

staunchly Republican *Chicago Tribune* also compared the endemic political violence in New Orleans to the earlier Commune, noting that "the barricade, the *coup d'état,* the revolution, are the means to an end with these people"; finally, it called for the same armed suppression that Thiers had used in 1871 (*Chicago Tribune,* February 12, 1875).

67. Sister Mary Cortona Phelan, *Manton Marble of the New York "World"* (Washington, D.C., 1957), v, 23–26, 43–46, 54–58. In general, see George J. McJimsey, *Genteel Partisan: Manton Marble, 1834–1917* (Ames, Ia., 1971).

68. Phelan, *Manton Marble,* 50–53, 84–86, 95.

69. On the *World*'s editorial coverage of the Franco-Prussian War, see McJimsey, *Genteel Partisan,* 142–145. For Marble's relatively sympathetic treatment of the Commune, see Bernstein, "American Press," 178–179; "The Red Revolution," *New York World,* April 5, 1871; and the *World*'s interview with Karl Marx, July 18, 1871 (reprinted in Marx and Engels, *Collected Works,* 22:600–606).

70. *New York World,* March 26, 1871.

71. Ibid., May 18, 1871. One specific "ultra-loyalist" that Marble had in mind was the hated Ben Butler, whose wartime reputation for vandalism was still current among Southerners and their supporters; ironically Butler, like Marble, was sympathetic toward the Commune in its quest for local autonomy.

72. Jean T. Joughin, *The Paris Commune in French Politics, 1871–1880* (Baltimore, 1955), 14.

73. Phelan, *Manton Marble,* 45–46; compare Edward L. Burlingame, "Commune de Paris," *The American Cyclopaedia,* 16 vols. (New York, 1873–1876), 5:160–161.

74. McJimsey, *Genteel Partisan,* 154–155.

75. *New Orleans Daily Picayune,* June 8, 1871.

76. Ibid., April 26, 1871. Compare this to the *Daily Picayune*'s hostile anti-Commune editorial of April 4, 1871.

77. Samuel S. Cox (D–N.Y.), speech against the last Enforcement Act, April 4, 1871, *Congressional Globe,* 42d Cong., 1st sess., 453. "Sunshine" Cox was primarily the congressman from Tammany Hall, but here he was mouthing the views of his Southern allies. Positive but qualified comparisons of the Klan and the Commune also appeared in the *New York World,* May 14, 1871, and in a dispatch from "Bourrieff" (a Paris correspondent) to the *Atlanta Constitution,* April 27, 1871.

78. *Woodhull & Claflin's Weekly,* January 27, 1872 (quote); A. Landy, "La Commune et la classe ouvrière aux États-Unis," *La Pensée* no. 37 (1957), 104–105. Green's introduction was quickly reissued as a separate pamphlet, with a title that evoked the sectional crisis of the 1850s: *The Irrepressible Conflict Between Labor and Capital* (Philadelphia, 1872).

79. *Atlanta Constitution,* May 25, 1871 (quote); *Charleston Republican* quoted in *Woodhull & Claflin's Weekly,* July 15, 1871.

80. "An Interesting Interview," reprinted in [Lucy E. Parsons, ed.], *The Life of*

Albert R. Parsons, with a Brief History of the Labor Movement in America (1889; 2nd ed., Chicago, 1903), 65–67; the interview originally appeared in the *Chicago Daily Telegraph,* January 20, 1880.

81. Paul Avrich, *The Haymarket Tragedy* (Princeton, 1984), 18–19. This brief account of Parsons's life is also drawn from the "Autobiography of Albert R. Parsons" in Philip S. Foner, ed., *The Autobiographies of the Haymarket Martyrs* (1969; rpt. New York, 1977), 27–58, and Hugh D. Duncan, *Culture and Democracy: The Struggle for Form in Society and Architecture in Chicago and the Middle West during the Life and Times of Louis H. Sullivan* (Totowa, N.J., 1965), 171–175.

82. Duncan, *Culture and Democracy,* 172.

83. Parsons (1886), quoted in Avrich, *Haymarket Tragedy,* 140.

84. Charles W. Hubner, *Modern Communism* (Atlanta, 1880), 89–92.

85. James Ford Rhodes, *History of the United States from the Compromise of 1850,* 7 vols. (New York, 1893–1906), 3:120–123. On the popularity of the "Marseillaise" in the Confederacy, see Richard Harwell, *Confederate Music* (Chapel Hill, 1950), 62.

86. Stephens to J. Henley Smith, July 10, 1860, quoted in James L. Roark, *Masters without Slaves: Southern Planters in the Civil War and Reconstruction* (New York, 1977), 4–5.

87. Stephens to J. Henley Smith, September 16, 1860, quoted in Roark, *Masters without Slaves,* 19. Roark, 1–32, perceptively dissects the ambiguities inherent in the idea of a "Planters' Revolution"; see also Emory M. Thomas, *The Confederacy as a Revolutionary Experience* (1971; rpt. Columbia, S.C., 1991), 23–42.

88. Unidentified Southern paper, reprinted in *New York Evening Post,* June 15, 1871.

89. [Mrs. F. J. Willard], *Pictures from Paris in War and in Siege* (London, 1871), 281.

90. Worth to Charles A. Eldridge, June 15, 1868, in J. G. de Roulhac Hamilton, ed., *Correspondence of Jonathan Worth,* 2 vols. (Raleigh, N.C., 1909), 2:1221–1222; Robert L. Dabney, *Discussions,* ed. C. R. Vaughan, 4 vols. (Richmond [and elsewhere], 1890–1897), 4:56–8, 105; see also George C. Rable, *But There Was No Peace: The Role of Violence in the Politics of Reconstruction* (Athens, Ga., 1984), 7, 62–63.

91. *Charlottesville (Va.) Weekly Chronicle,* April 7, 1871; *Nashville Republican Banner,* October 29, 1871, quoted in Philip S. Foner, *American Socialism and Black Americans: From the Age of Jackson to World War II* (Westport, Conn., 1977), 38; see also Heale, *American Anticommunism,* 17.

92. *Galveston Daily News,* June 7, 1871, quoted in Foner, *American Socialism and Black Americans,* 38. In much the same spirit, and on the very same day, the *New York World* printed an article about a strike among black public employees in the nation's capital under the headline "A Negro Commune in Washington."

93. *Edgefield (S.C.) Advertiser,* August 17, 1876 (recalling a parade of the 9th

Regiment, South Carolina militia, two years earlier), quoted in Vernon Burton, "Race and Reconstruction in Edgefield County, South Carolina," *Journal of Social History* 12 (1978), 40–41.

94. *New York Tribune,* June 21, 1871; also quoted in Kenneth M. Stampp, *The Era of Reconstruction, 1865–1877* (New York, 1965), 205.

95. Interview reprinted in *Atlanta Constitution,* June 14, 1871.

96. Dabney, "The State Free School System" (1876), *Discussions,* 4:204–205; Thompson (circa 1880?), quoted in Mary L. Crosby, "Hugh Smith Thompson and the Establishment of the Public School System in South Carolina" (master's thesis, University of South Carolina, 1950). My thanks to Steve Kantrowitz for this citation.

97. However, at least one African-American spokesman also took the Commune as a sign that his people required more education and experience before they became fully competent as citizens of the republic; see J[ohn] F. Quarles, "The Social Problem of the South," *Proceedings of the Southern States' Convention of Colored Men . . .* (Columbia, S.C., 1871), 100–101.

98. Lamar quoted in McNeilly, "The Enforcement Act of 1871," 371; Hampton quoted in George M. Fredrickson, *The Black Image in the White Mind: The Debate on Afro-American Character and Destiny, 1817–1914* (New York, 1971), 265.

99. *New York World,* January 8, 1873.

100. Pike to Chase, August 8, 1865, quoted in Robert F. Durden, *James Shepherd Pike: Republicanism and the American Negro, 1850–1882* (Durham, N.C., 1957), 164.

101. Page citations are from Pike, *The Prostrate State: South Carolina under Negro Government,* ed. Henry S. Commager (New York, 1935). For the background of this book, see Durden, *James Shepherd Pike,* 201–219.

102. Paul H. Buck, quoted in W. Magruder Drake and Robert R. Jones, "Editors' Introduction" to Edward King, *The Great South* (Baton Rouge, 1972), xxiii. Page references to *The Great South* are from this edition.

103. See Drake and Jones, "Editors' Introduction," xxvi–xxxvi, for the background on King's book.

104. Ibid., xlii–xliii, lii–liii.

105. Ibid., lvi–lix.

106. See note 3 above.

107. Edward King, "Clubs and Club Life in Paris," *Cosmopolitan* 4 (1887), 377.

6. The View from the 1870s

1. The epigraph is from Charles Eliot Norton to Frederick Harrison, December 24, 1872, in Sara Norton and M. A. De Wolfe Howe, eds., *Letters of Charles Eliot Norton,* 2 vols. (Boston and New York, 1913), 1:446. J. Chal Vinson, *Thomas Nast, Political Cartoonist* (Athens, Ga., 1967), 9; see also Morton Keller, *The Art and Politics of Thomas Nast* (New York, 1968).

2. Vinson, *Thomas Nast,* 11.

3. Tweed quoted in ibid., 19.

4. Ibid., 15–22; Seymour J. Mandelbaum, *Boss Tweed's New York* (New York, 1965).

5. Samuel Bernstein, *The First International in America* (New York, 1962), 73.

6. Norton to E. L. Godkin, November 3, 1871, quoted in Ari Hoogenboom, "Civil Service Reform and Public Morality," in H. Wayne Morgan, ed., *The Gilded Age* (rev. ed.; Syracuse, 1970), 80–81.

7. *Scribner's Monthly* 2 (1871), 206; see also *New York Times,* May 30, 1871.

8. *Nation,* September 28, 1871, 205–206.

9. *Harper's Weekly,* October 14, 1871, 970; *New York Herald,* June 2, 1871, quoted in Matthew P. Breen, *Thirty Years of New York Politics* (New York, 1899), 342; *New York Times,* May 8, 1871.

10. *Nation,* June 1, 1871, 309; June 29, 1871, 442; September 28, 1871, 205–206. *Report of the New York City Council of Political Reform, for the Years 1872, '73, and '74* (New York, 1875) contains a wealth of similar antidemocratic statements by New York's elite.

11. Jonathan Baxter Harrison, "Limited Sovereignty in the United States," *Atlantic Monthly* 43 (1879), 186. See Chapter 5 above.

12. *New York World,* n.d., quoted in *Christian Union,* April 19, 1871, 246. John F. Dillon, a noted legal scholar, took a comparable but less enthusiastic view than the *World:* "The *commune* movement was but the natural result of a popular uprising against centralized power . . . But a scheme which made cities, and not the nation, practically the sovereign, is radically defective": Dillon, *The Law of Municipal Corporations,* 2 vols. (2nd ed.; New York, 1873), 1:84. At the other extreme, the *New York Herald* bluntly suggested that the Committee of Seventy (a nonpartisan group of leading Gothamites determined to oust the Tammany regime), not the Tweed Ring, was the real parallel to the Commune: "What we contend is that the principles of the Commune . . . and the irresponsible Committee of Seventy are the same. They are revolutionary. They do violence to our free institutions" by arrogantly opposing the municipal government elected by the people (*New York Herald,* September 19, 1871).

13. *New York Times,* May 4, 1871. Fernando Wood, a Tammany Democrat, was mayor of New York in 1861, at which time he urged the city to secede along with the South.

14. "Hash—or, A Tale of Two Cities," *Harper's Weekly,* July 1, 1871, 609.

15. *Harper's Weekly,* July 27, 1872, 585; also reprinted in Keller, *Nast,* ill. 39.

16. As early as April 26, 1871, the *New York World* archly compared Horace Greeley to General Cluseret for the amount of political mischief that each was capable of fomenting. In the midst of the 1872 presidential campaign, at least one satirist again equated Greeley with the Commune, although in more general terms; see *The Sorehead War: A Campaign Satire for 1872* (New York, [1872]), 7–8.

17. This is strange, since Nast drew the Vendôme Column quite accurately the

year before. He could also have found an accurate engraving of the column in the *Harper's Weekly* of June 10, 1871.

18. Nell Irvin Painter, *Standing at Armageddon: The United States, 1877–1919* (New York, 1987); see also Carl Smith, *Urban Disorder and the Shape of Belief: The Great Chicago Fire, the Haymarket Bomb, and the Model Town of Pullman* (Chicago, 1995).

19. J. L. Gillin, "The Development of Sociology in the United States," *Publications of the American Sociological Society* 21 (1926), 3; see also Morton Keller, *Affairs of State: Public Life in Late Nineteenth Century America* (Cambridge, Mass., 1977), 127, 489–491.

20. *New York Times*, April 28, 1871.

21. John J. Pauley, "The Great Chicago Fire as a National Event," *American Quarterly* 36 (1984), 682; see also Fred Fedler, "Mrs. O'Leary's Cow and Other Newspaper Tales About the Chicago Fire," *American Journalism* 3 (1986), 24–38; Smith, *Urban Disorder*, 28–29.

22. Rev. E. J. Goodspeed, *History of the Great Fires in Chicago and the West* (New York, 1871), 207; "Paris and Chicago," reprinted in James W. Sheahan and George P. Upton, *The Great Conflagration: Chicago, Its Past, Present and Future* (Chicago, 1871), 367; *Appleton's Journal,* January 6, 1872, 23. See also John B. Carson to E. B. Washburne, November 11, 1871, Washburne Papers, Library of Congress (LC); Smith, *Urban Disorder*, 48–49.

23. See Ross Miller, *American Apocalypse: The Great Fire and Myth of Chicago* (Chicago, 1990), 2, 251n1, 252n14; Smith, *Urban Disorder*, 301n36; Pauley, "The Great Chicago Fire," 670.

24. Fedler, "Mrs. O'Leary's Cow," 30–32; H. A. Musham, "The Great Chicago Fire, October 8–10, 1871," *Papers in Illinois History* (Springfield, Ill., 1941), 148; Smith, *Urban Disorder*, 64, 77–81.

25. Pauley, "The Great Chicago Fire," 33.

26. Frank Luzerne reprinted the "confession" and gave it serious consideration in *Through the Flames and Beyond, or Chicago as It Was and as It Is* (New York, 1872), 185–196 (from which it is quoted here); see also Smith, *Urban Disorder*, 49–50. The confession was denounced as a fabrication by Elias Colbert and Everett Chamberlin, *Chicago and the Great Conflagration* (Cincinnati and New York, 1872), 372. A similar story emerged after the giant Boston fire of November 1872, when the *New York Herald* published the tale of a self-proclaimed chemist and Communard who supposedly bragged at a labor-reform meeting that he had started the Boston fire with a petroleum bomb; see Diane Tarmy Rudnick, "Boston and the Fire of 1872: The Stillborn Phoenix" (Ph.D. diss., Boston University, 1971), 179–180.

27. *Chicago Times*, October 23, 1871, quoted in Pauley, "The Great Chicago Fire," 33; *Chicago Tribune*, n.d., quoted in Goodspeed, *History of the Great Fires*, 215; *Chicago Tribune*, January 20, 1872; see also *Every Saturday*,

December 9, 1871, 571, and Goodspeed, *History of the Great Fires,* 125–127. See Chapter 8 below for a fuller discussion of the IWA in America.

28. Train, *My Life in Many States and in Foreign Lands* (New York, 1902), 321–322. A more trustworthy account can be found in Willis Thornton, *The Nine Lives of Citizen Train* (New York, 1948), 221–232.

29. *Woodhull & Claflin's Weekly,* May 13, 1871; *Frank Leslie's Illustrated Newspaper,* April 12, 1873, 70.

30. *American Register,* November 18, 1871; see also Thornton, *Citizen Train,* 218, and [John Wesley Nichols], *The Man of Destiny* (New York, 1872), 48.

31. "The International Association," *Catholic World* 14 (1872), 704–705. Carl Smith makes a similar point in *Urban Disorder:* "Observers of the Chicago fire . . . saw in the smoke and flames a fulfillment of their deepest fears about urban life . . . [and] the precariousness of the social order. The tales of arson . . . and crime [not to mention the International] spoke mainly on a symbolic level, revealing a desire for greater control of 'dangerous' elements. The anxiety behind this desire was that social chaos, not fire, was the most severe threat to the future of the city" (55).

32. Stewart Edwards, *The Paris Commune, 1871* (London, 1971), 346–348; *American Register,* August 19, 1871; *New York Herald,* August 29, 1871.

33. Alexander Saxton, *The Rise and Fall of the White Republic: Class Politics and Mass Culture in Nineteenth-Century America* (London and New York, 1990), 215–216; *American Register,* July 29, 1871.

34. The glowing prospectus that Wilkes submitted to the French government is reprinted in *The Spirit of the Times,* August 12, 1871. The actual state of the Lower California Company is described in Ruth Elizabeth Kearney, "The Magdalena Bubble," *Pacific Historical Review* 4 (1935), 25–29, and Pablo L. Martinez, *A History of Lower California,* trans. Ethel Duffy Turner (Mexico City, 1960), 389–392.

35. Kearney, "Magdalena Bubble," 28–38; Martinez, *History of Lower California,* 392–393; Saxton, *White Republic,* 216–218; "The Explosion of a Great Bubble," *New York Evening Post,* July 24, 1871.

36. *New York Herald,* July 11, 1871; *American Register,* July 29, 1871; *The Spirit of the Times,* August 12, 1871, 409.

37. Kearney, "Magdalena Bubble," 37; *American Register,* August 12, 1871; *New York Herald,* August 13, 1871.

38. *American Register,* September 23, 1871; *Le Temps* (Paris), December 22, 1871. In the absence of any colony, in September 1871 the Mexican government revoked the Lower California Company's charter (Kearney, "Magdalena Bubble," 38).

39. There may also have been a third scheme, to send Communards to Texas; see Wickham Hoffmann to N. A. Cowdray, August 28, 1871, and the index entry under "Cowdray" in the General Correspondence letterbooks, vol. 127, Washburne Papers, LC.

40. Saxton, *White Republic,* 218; *New York Herald,* July 29 (quote), August 13,

1871; *Christian Union*, August 2, 1871, 77; *American Register*, August 19, 26, 1871; *(Tucson) Arizona Citizen*, August 26, 1871, clipping in the Poston Collection, Arizona Historical Society.

41. *New York Herald*, August 13, 1871.

42. *American Register*, August 12, 1871.

43. *Le Figaro*, July 2, 1871, quoting *Le Soir*.

44. *La Patrie*, quoted in *Le Temps*, August 11, 1871.

45. *La Verité*, quoted in *American Register*, August 19, 1871.

46. Kearney, "Magdalena Bubble," 37.

47. "Immigration," *Colorado Monthly*, September 1871, quoted in Levette Jay Davidson, "The Colorado Monthly," *Colorado Magazine* 16 (1939), 139.

48. *(Tucson) Arizona Citizen*, August 26, 1871, clipping in the Poston Collection, Arizona Historical Society.

49. *Every Saturday*, September 16, 1871, 283, and September 2, 1871, 219.

50. Wickham Hoffmann to N. A. Cowdray, August 28, 1871, Washburne Papers, LC.

51. *New York Herald*, July 11, 1871.

52. *American Register*, August 26, 1871.

53. Ibid., August 19, 1871.

54. *Christian Union*, August 2, 1871, 77; *New York Herald*, August 9, 1871. Such optimism about the redemptive power of the West stands in stark counterpoint to the common antebellum belief that "bring[ing] the polished man in contact with savage nature [on the American frontier], . . . the one must succumb to the other, or both will undergo a change. As man civilizes the wilderness, the wilderness more or less brutalizes him": Alexander Mackay (1849), quoted in Ray A. Billington, *Land of Savagery/Land of Promise: The European Image of the American Frontier in the Nineteenth Century* (New York, 1981), 180.

55. *Every Saturday*, September 16, 1871, 283; see also the *San Francisco Chronicle*, August 18, 1871, quoted in Kearney, "Magdalena Bubble," 38.

56. *Santa Fe Daily New Mexican*, May 30, 1871; *Colorado Monthly*, September 1871, quoted in Davidson, "The Colorado Monthly," 139; see also *Arizona Citizen*, August 26, 1871, clipping in the Poston Collection, Arizona Historical Society; "A Communist Colony for Arizona," *New York Herald*, July 29, 1871.

57. Nathan Sheppard, *Shut Up in Paris* (London, 1871), 140. This statement may have owed as much to his own class fears as to those of Adolphe Thiers.

58. *Harper's Weekly*, August 5, 1871, 735; the remarks in single quotes are Mazzini's, reprinted from the *Roma del Popolo*.

59. *Harper's Weekly*, May 27, 1871, 485; *Nation*, June 22, 1871, 426; *Chicago Tribune*, March 22, 1871; see also *New York Herald*, July 13, 1871.

60. One dime novel of particular note was Frederick Whittaker's *The Mustang-hunters; or, The Beautiful Amazon of the Hidden Valley* (New York, 1871), published by Beadle just weeks after the Paris Commune. (Henry Nash

Smith, in *Virgin Land: The American West as Symbol and Myth* [Cambridge, Mass., 1950], 113 and note 4, questions the date of publication; but the edition I consulted at the New York Public Library was published in 1871.) Set in Texas, an "enormous state, as large in its area as . . . France" (9), the characters include a reclusive French radical, his beautiful daughter, and a dashing American hero. The Frenchman is a self-described "red republican . . . the friend of Louis Blanc, Mazzini, and Kossuth," who did his part "in '48 toward lighting the flame of Revolution" (59); but when the Second Empire began he fled into self-imposed exile. After fifteen years of banishment to the frontier (56), however, he is allowed to redeem himself by helping the American trap and massacre a band of Comanches (76–77); afterward the American and the daughter marry, and all three return from the wilderness to civilization. In contemporary thinking the revolutions of 1848 and 1871 were often linked, and this Frenchman's career in the West strongly parallels the most optimistic predictions for Communard emigrants.

61. "The Jesuit Martyrs of the Commune," *Catholic World* 19 (1874), 512; G. M. Lambertson, "Indian Citizenship," *American Law Review* 20 (1886), 188–189; compare Richard Slotkin, *The Fatal Environment: The Myth of the Frontier in the Age of Industrialization, 1800–1890* (New York, 1985), 338–339.

62. Slotkin, *Fatal Environment,* 311, makes the same argument.

63. *New York World,* June 16, 1871.

64. Ibid., May 2, May 21, July 2, 1871.

65. Francis Paul Prucha, *American Indian Policy in Crisis: Christian Reformers and the Indian, 1865–1900* (Norman, Okla., 1976), vi; Robert W. Mardock, *The Reformers and the American Indian* (Columbia, Mo., 1971), 86–87 (quoting a Nebraska editor and a Montana congressional delegate, both in the late 1860s).

66. Dan L. Thrapp, *The Conquest of Apacheria* (Norman, Okla., 1967), 70.

67. Ibid., 79–94.

68. Slotkin, *Fatal Environment,* 301, 309.

69. Ibid., 311. I will return to this argument in Chapter 8 and the Conclusion.

70. Brace was not a practicing clergyman, but he was clearly part of the clerical establishment discussed in Chapter 7. On Brace's life and career see Paul Boyer, *Urban Masses and Moral Order in America, 1820–1920* (Cambridge, Mass., 1978), 94, 96–107.

71. Charles Loring Brace, *The Dangerous Classes of New York and Twenty Years' Work Among Them* (1872; 3rd ed., 1880), 97, 29–30. Here I am largely following Slotkin, *Fatal Environment,* 310–311, who cites some of the same passages.

72. Brace, *Dangerous Classes,* 25–26, 29–30 (quote), 130–31; *Nation,* October 10, 1872, 237–238; *Cleveland Leader,* November 15, 1871; Slotkin, *Fatal Environment,* 310. Significantly, Brace's worried reflections on the Commune came in a chapter called "The Proletaires of New York," which was

one of the first times that an American used the French term *prolétaire* to describe the domestic working class.

73. Prucha, *American Indian Policy*, 342–347. Ironically, the treaty system came to an end on March 3, 1871, just before Paris began to redefine itself as a semisovereign city-state; although no one made the explicit connection, the public debate surrounding this policy change might have predisposed some observers to think about the Commune in relation to both federalism and the Indians.

74. Russell Errett (R–Pa.), quoted in Wilcomb E. Washburn, *The Assault on Indian Tribalism: The General Allotment Law (Dawes Act) of 1887* (Philadelphia, 1975), 38; Robert F. Berkhofer, Jr., *The White Man's Indian: Images of the American Indian from Columbus to the Present* (New York, 1978), 153–156, 169–171; Prucha, *American Indian Policy*, 238–239.

75. *New York Herald*, August 8, 23, 1871; *Every Saturday*, June 17, 1871, 571; *New York Times*, May 25, 1871; *Nation*, May 25, 1871, 351; "Editor's Easy Chair," *Harper's New Monthly Magazine* 42 (1871), 136; *New York Times*, June 7, 1871.

76. *New York Evening Post*, May 25, 1871; *Atlanta Constitution*, May 28, 1871; see also [Mrs. F. J. Willard], *Pictures from Paris in War and in Siege* (London, 1871), 126–127. Similar bestial imagery was used by French opponents of the Commune; see Paul Lidsky, *Les écrivains contre la Commune* (Paris, 1970), 154–156.

77. *Independent*, March 23, 1871; *Christian World* 22 (1871), 267; "The Stranger's Money," *Frank Leslie's Popular Monthly* 1 (1876), 621; L. P. Brockett, *Paris Under the Commune* (New York, 1871), 129. See also James D. McCabe, Jr., *History of the War between Germany and France . . .* (Philadelphia and elsewhere, 1871), 762. Another evolutionary argument was mooted by E. L. Godkin, who saw the Commune as a retrogression from "contract" to "status," the polarities of which had recently been described by Sir Henry Maine (*Nation*, June 1, 1871, 375).

78. Keller, *Art and Politics of Thomas Nast*, esp. 109, 244–245.

79. *Harper's Weekly*, February 7, 1874; cartoon reprinted in Keller, *Art and Politics of Thomas Nast*, ill. 74, and Denis Tilden Lynch, *The Wild Seventies* (New York, 1941), 443. Other skeleton cartoons appeared in *Harper's Weekly* as late as the 1880s.

80. For the toadstool cartoon, see *Harper's Weekly*, March 7, 1874; for the frog cartoons, see *Harper's Weekly*, February 18, 1871, May 25 and June 1, 1878.

81. Norman Dain, *Concepts of Insanity in the United States, 1789–1865* (New Brunswick, N.J., 1964), esp. 88–91, 191–193.

82. Edward T. Gargan, "The American Conservative Response," in Jacques Rougerie, ed., *1871: Jalons pour une histoire de la Commune de Paris* (Assen, the Netherlands, 1972), 242.

83. Henry Ward Beecher, "The Lesson from Paris," *The Sermons of Henry Ward Beecher, in Plymouth Church, Brooklyn*, Sixth Series (New York, 1872), 237.

84. *Nation,* May 25, 1871, 360; *New York Herald,* July 4, 1871; Brockett, *Paris Under the Commune,* 28; Charlotte M. Yonge, *Young People's History of France* (New York, 1874), 170; *New York Evening Post,* May 10, 1871; *Nation,* March 30, 1871, 211.

85. Andrew Jackson Davis, *Mental Disorders; or, Diseases of the Brain . . . Developing the Origin and Philosophy of Mania, Insanity, and Crime . . .* (New York and elsewhere, 1871), 67. The French doctor's diagnosis also appeared in the *Nation,* June 15, 1871, 411; *Daily Corinne (Utah) Reporter,* June 20, 1871; *Harper's Weekly,* July 8, 1871, 31; *Every Saturday,* July 8, 1871; and *Boston Journal of Chemistry* 6 (August 1871), 24.

86. Lydia Maria Child to Anna Loring Dresel, January 7, 1872, *The Collected Correspondence of Lydia Maria Child, 1817–1880,* ed. Patricia G. Holland and Milton Meltzer (Milwaukee, 1979), microfiche edition.

87. *New York Times,* June 2, 1872; *New York Tribune,* June 6, 1871.

88. *Every Saturday,* May 20, 1871, 459; *New York Evening Telegram,* April 14, 1871, quoted in *Public Opinion* (London), April 29, 1871, 515.

89. "Editor's Easy Chair," *Harper's New Monthly Magazine* 42 (1871), 137.

90. Eugene Benson, "The Fire-Fiend," *Galaxy* 8 (1869), 655, 648; *Appleton's Journal,* January 6, 1872, 23; George B. Benham, *The Proletarian Revolt* (San Francisco, 1898), 57.

91. The reality behind the *pétroleuse* myth is thoroughly discussed in Edith Thomas, *The Women Incendiaries* (New York, 1966), and Gay L. Gullickson, *Unruly Women of Paris: Images of the Commune* (Ithaca, 1996). Gullickson notes that "while women may have participated in the burning of the Tuileries Palace, the vast majority of the fires [at the end of the Commune] were set by men" (170).

92. *New York Evening Post,* June 15, 1871; see also Henry B. Blackwell, "Women in Paris," *The Woman's Journal,* June 24, 1871, 200; *Nation,* December 28, 1871, 416; Elizabeth W. Latimer, *France in the Nineteenth Century, 1830–1890* (Chicago, 1892), 346.

93. Willard, *Pictures from Paris,* 43–45.

94. *Harper's Weekly,* July 8, 1871, 620; Howard Glyndon [Laura C. Searing], "Paris-Berlin (Summer, 1871)," *Harper's Weekly,* July 8, 1871, 626. Similar adjectival screeds appear in *Every Saturday,* July 8, 1871, 29, and the anonymous "Cacique: A Story of the Commune," *Frank Leslie's Popular Monthly* 3 (1877), 217–222. The Communarde was also a popular subject in the illustrated weeklies, where she appeared as a hussy or harridan.

95. *Harper's Weekly,* July 22, 1871, 686; *Every Saturday,* July 8, 1871, 47; Gullickson, *Unruly Women of Paris,* 176–180.

96. *New York Herald,* July 10, 1871 (emphasis added). *The Revolution,* June 29, 1871, discussed a similar sermon preached in New York.

97. *New York Evening Telegram,* April 14, 1871, quoted in *Public Opinion* (London), April 29, 1871, 515; see also *Woodhull & Claflin's Weekly,* June 10, 1871; *Cleveland Leader,* June 26, 1871; "The New Order of Amazons," *Frank Leslie's Illustrated Newspaper,* March 16, 1872.

98. Ellen Carol DuBois, *Feminism and Suffrage: The Emergence of an Independent Women's Movement in America, 1848–1869* (Ithaca, 1978), 93–101.

99. *Albany (Oregon) Democrat,* October 13, 1871, quoted in G. Thomas Edwards, *Sowing Good Seeds: The Northwest Suffrage Campaigns of Susan B. Anthony* (Portland, Ore., 1990), 75–76.

100. Meredith Tax, *The Rising of the Women: Feminist Solidarity and Class Conflict, 1880–1917* (New York, 1980), 42–43; F. O. Matthiessen, ed., *The American Novels and Stories of Henry James* (New York, 1947), 745.

101. *New York Times,* July 4, 1871; "Communism in New-York," ibid., December 12, 1873; see also "Communism in America," ibid., December 28, 1873; "Why the Commune is Possible in America," *Chicago Tribune,* May 24, 1874.

102. *New York Times,* July 25, 1877; see also H. Wayne Morgan, "Toward National Unity," in Morgan, ed., *The Gilded Age,* 8; Painter, *Standing at Armageddon,* 1–71.

7. Apocalypse Where? Apocalypse When?

1. The epigraph is from *The Diary of George Templeton Strong,* ed. Allan Nevins and Milton H. Thomas, 4 vols. (New York, 1952), 4:357 (cited hereafter as *Strong Diary*). Sorge to General Council, June 20, 1871, North American Federal Council (NAFC) letterbook, IWA Papers, State Historical Society of Wisconsin (SHSW). Karl Marx himself concluded, "The daily press and the telegraph, which in a moment spread inventions over the whole earth, fabricate more myths (which the bourgeois cattle believe and enlarge upon) in one day than could have formerly been done in a century." See Marx to Dr. Kugelmann, July 27, 1871, quoted in George Haupt, *Aspects of International Socialism, 1871–1914,* trans. Peter Fawcett (Cambridge, Eng., and Paris, 1986), 23.

2. *Woodhull & Claflin's Weekly,* July 22, September 2, 1871; see also July 8, October 7, 1871.

3. *Woodhull & Claflin's Weekly,* September 2, 1871; "The Press and the Commune," *New York Standard,* undated clipping (from late summer 1871) in Thomas Phillips Papers, SHSW. See also the *Workingman's Advocate,* August 5, 1871; *The Revolution of the Commune: Humanity First, Glory Afterward—The Paris Rebels Vindicated from the Aspersions of a Money-Shackled Press—The Truth at Last Told in Vigorous English* (New York, 1871).

4. Robert Justin Goldstein, *Political Repression in Modern America, from 1870 to the Present* (Boston, 1978), 25; see also Patricio Cayo Sexton, *The War on Labor and the Left: Understanding America's Unique Conservatism* (Boulder, 1991), 124–126; Denis Tilden Lynch, *The Wild Seventies* (New York, 1941), 1.

5. Gargan, "The American Conservative Response," in Jacques Rougerie, ed., *1871: Jalons pour une histoire de la Commune de Paris* (Assen, the Netherlands, 1972), 245; Albert Boime, "Olin Levi Warner's Defense of the Paris

Commune," *Archives of American Art Journal* 29 (1989), 3–4. Similar conflations of 1871 with 1877 can be seen in Samuel Bernstein, "The American Press Views the Commune," *Essays in Political and Intellectual History* (New York, 1955), 174; Peter H. Buckingham, *America Sees Red: Anti-Communism in America, 1870s to 1980s: A Guide to the Issues and References* (Claremont, Calif., 1988), 3–4; Joseph J. Holmes, "Red Baiting as Used against Striking Workingmen in the United States, 1871–1920," *Studies in History and Society* 5 (1974), 2, 6; Harvey Wish, ed., *Reconstruction in the South, 1865–1877* (New York, 1965), 142.

6. Philip Quilibet [pseud.], "Drift-Wood," *Galaxy* 11 (1871), 731; see also *Harper's Weekly*, May 20, 1871, 458. Like many other Americans, Mark Twain was compelled by the events of 1871 to read (or reread, in his case) Carlyle's *French Revolution;* see Twain to William Dean Howells, August 22, 1887, in Frederick Anderson et al., eds., *Selected Mark Twain–Howells Letters, 1872–1910* (Cambridge, Mass., 1967), 276; Wesley Britton, "Carlyle, Clemens, and Dickens: Mark Twain's Francophobia, the French Revolution, and Determinism," *Studies in American Fiction* 20 (1992), 197–204.

7. *Nation*, April 13, 1871, 251; *Atlanta Constitution*, May 28, 1871; *Daily Corinne (Utah) Reporter*, April 11, 1871.

8. Linus P. Brockett, *Paris Under the Commune* (New York and elsewhere, 1871), 71, 90.

9. *New York Herald*, August 11, 1871. Similar diatribes were published in the *Cleveland Leader* (see esp. April 8, May 19, and June 1, 1871) and many other newspapers. Gargan, "American Conservative Response," 242, and Martin R. Waldman, "The Revolutionary as Criminal in 19th Century France: A Study of the Communards and *Déportés*," *Science & Society* 37 (1973), 31–55, describe a similar discourse on criminality that was prevalent among the French bourgeoisie. These languages of class generally developed in parallel, not conjunction.

10. *Cleveland Leader*, March 22, April 1, 1871; *New York Times*, March 24, 1871; *Philadelphia Ledger*, April 12, 1871, quoted in George L. Cherry, "American Metropolitan Press Reaction to the Paris Commune of 1871," *Mid-America* 32 (1950), 6.

11. *Youth's Companion*, May 4, 1871, 141; see also June 15, 1871, 188–189.

12. *Cleveland Leader*, May 3, 1871; *Chicago Tribune*, March 22, 1871, quoted in Gargan, "American Conservative Response," 243–244.

13. Bernstein, "American Press," 180.

14. See Henry F. May, *Protestant Churches and Industrial America* (New York, 1949), 37–87; Sidney E. Mead, *The Lively Experiment: The Shaping of Christianity in America* (New York, 1963), 142, 156–157. "Conservative" is a slippery label, especially when applied to the American clergy in the third quarter of the nineteenth century. I am using it here, as George M. Fredrickson does, to describe "men with an allegiance to well-established organizations or coherent social groups [who] had a stake in the preservation of the

traditional forms of social control": see his *Inner Civil War: Northern Intellectuals and the Crisis of the Union* (New York, 1965), 23–24. Because their primary interest was preserving an idealized status quo, they could still be active reformers as long as reform was construed as a return to the ideal. This variety of conservatism described a much larger portion of the American middle class than the narrow conservatism condemned by the historians cited above.

15. *Independent,* June 1, 1871.
16. Sidney Warren, *American Freethought, 1860–1914* (New York, 1943), 216; May, *Protestant Churches,* 46, 58–59 (citing several negative reactions to the Commune in the contemporary religious press).
17. Entry of June 12, 1871, *Strong Diary,* 4:364; compare Brockett, *Paris Under the Commune,* 87–89.
18. *Boston Balloon Post,* April 17, 1871; *Independent,* April 13, 1871.
19. Hopkins, "Modern Skepticism," *Association Monthly* 2 (1871), 145–147.
20. *New York Times,* May 29, 1871.
21. *New York Herald,* July 10, 1871.
22. "The Recent Events in France," *Catholic World* 14 (1871), 303; "The International Association," *Catholic World* 14 (1872), 705–706. See also Orestes A. Brownson, "Essay in Refutation of Atheism" (1872), in Henry F. Brownson, ed., *The Works of Orestes A. Brownson,* 20 vols. (Detroit, 1882–1898), 2:3–4; Elihu B. Washburne, *Account of the Sufferings and Death of the Most Rev. George Darboy, Late Archbishop of Paris* (New York, 1873); "The Jesuit Martyrs of the Commune," *Catholic World* 19 (1874), 505–525.
23. *New York Evening Post,* May 22, 1871; Lieber to Prof. Bluntschli, May 23, 1871, in Thomas Sergeant Perry, ed., *Life and Letters of Francis Lieber* (Boston, 1882), 411. The powerful image of the St. Bartholomew's Day massacre was not the sole property of conservatives; in 1872, a radical newspaper referred to the suppression of the Commune as "the ghastly horrors of the modern St. Bartholomew's days of the Barricades" (*Woodhull & Claflin's Weekly,* June 8, 1872); see also "A Socialist," *Reply to Roswell D. Hitchcock, D.D., on Socialism* (New York, 1879), 16.
24. *New York World,* May 23, 1871.
25. *Christian Union,* May 24, 1871, 329. Parts of Thompson's sermon were reprinted in the *New York Times,* May 29, 1871 (quoted here), the *New York World,* May 29, 1871, and the *Independent,* June 1, 1871.
26. "The End of the Commune," *Independent,* June 1, 1871. Herman Melville made a similar claim for the identity of the Commune with the Scarlet Woman in *Clarel:* "The Red Republic slinging flame / In Europe—she's your Scarlet Dame"; see *Clarel: A Poem and Pilgrimage in the Holy Land,* ed. Walter E. Bezanson (1876; New York, 1960), II.xxv.110–111.
27. May, *Protestant Churches,* 58–59.
28. "Jesus Christ and La Commune," *Woodhull & Claflin's Weekly,* January 6, 1872; ironically, this article was published next to a large portrait of Karl

Marx, the subject of another article on the same page. Three decades later, American Protestants were still interested in mission work among French workers; see Louise S. Houghton, *The Silent Highway: A Story of the McAll Mission* (New York, 1900).

29. One prominent bourgeois supporter of the Commune was Theodore Tilton, the editor of a New York religious newspaper and a former colleague of Bowen's and Henry Beecher's, though not a minister himself (*Woodhull & Claflin's Weekly,* November 25, 1871, March 6, 1875; *Cleveland Leader,* August 26, 1871; Bernstein, "The American Press," 179). The *Independent,* which Tilton once edited, snidely pointed out that public supporters of American labor and the Commune tended to be "ex-clergymen" (May 18, 1871). See also the *New York World,* June 5, 1871 (an account of a meeting of the New York Positivists); and James Dombrowski, *The Early Years of Christian Socialism in America* (New York, 1936), 77–78.

30. Clifford E. Clark, Jr., *Henry Ward Beecher: Spokesman for a Middle-Class America* (Urbana, Ill., 1978), 197. Beecher's moral influence, though not his fame, declined somewhat after the scandalous Beecher-Tilton adultery trial of the mid-1870s; see Altina L. Waller, *Reverend Beecher and Mrs. Tilton: Sex and Class in Victorian America* (Amherst, 1982).

31. Clifford, *Henry Ward Beecher,* 190 (quote); Waller, *Reverend Beecher and Mrs. Tilton,* 12–14, 18–28, 30–31, 37.

32. The sermon was reported in many newspapers, but the text as quoted is from Henry Ward Beecher, *The Sermons of Henry Ward Beecher, in Plymouth Church, Brooklyn,* Sixth Series (New York, 1872), 235–248.

33. Ibid., 235–236, 238–239, 241.

34. Ibid., 236–239.

35. Ibid., 239–242.

36. Ibid., 239; he returned to this theme in the final words of his sermon.

37. Fredrickson, *Inner Civil War,* 49.

38. Lowell to Leslie Stephen, July 31, 1871, in Charles Eliot Norton, ed., *Letters of James Russell Lowell,* 2 vols. (New York, 1894), 2:72–73; see also A. Landy, "La Commune et les intellectuels américains," *Europe* no. 70 (1951), 117–118.

39. Landy, "La Commune," 113–121; Jean-Jacques Recht, "La Commune de Paris et les États-Unis," *La Pensée* no. 164 (1972), 109–116.

40. James to Bowditch, April 8, 1871, in Henry James, ed., *The Letters of William James,* 2 vols. (Boston, 1920), 1:161–162; Norton to E. L. Godkin, November 1871, quoted by Ari Hoogenboom, "Civil Service Reform and Public Morality," in H. Wayne Morgan, ed., *The Gilded Age* (revised ed.; Syracuse, 1970), 80–81. Hoogenboom adds that "Norton's radicalism . . . [was] a temporary romantic aberration" (81).

41. *Boston Balloon Post,* April 11, 1871. Agassiz added that Americans ought to offer France the sort of "help which cheers and encourages, not that depressing alms-giving which lacks the warmth and graciousness of sympathy." Ob-

viously he knew his audience; after all, this was the same upper-crust Boston society that produced Mrs. Josephine Shaw Lowell, who would soon be launching a crusade to systematize charity and strip it of human sympathy. Indeed, one Boston magazine responded to Agassiz's plea for charity with the "hope [that] no food will be sent to the mob infesting Paris, as the sooner they starve the better": *Folio* 4 (1871), 102.

42. *New York Evening Post,* July 13, 1871. According to Barbara Miller Solomon, the young men at Harvard were much more likely to rail against "Socialists, Communists, Nihilists, [and] Irish Leaguers" (to quote an 1883 oration) than to support them; see Solomon, *Ancestors and Immigrants: A Changing New England Tradition* (1956; Chicago, 1972), 98–99.

43. Beecher, *Sermons,* 236.

44. Ibid., 242–246. Not every clergyman was so sanguine about the influence of the press; the (Episcopal?) Bishop of Western New York, for example, wondered, "If journalism is so powerful, who shall save us from such journalism as made the Commune possible in Paris?" Quoted in Frederic Hudson, *Journalism in the United States, from 1690 to 1872* (New York, 1872), xix.

45. Beecher, *Sermons,* 236.

46. The sermon, which was reprinted many times, is quoted here from the *Christian Union,* August 1, 1877; see Robert V. Bruce, *1877: Year of Violence* (1959; rpt. Chicago, 1989), 312–314.

47. *Christian Union,* August 8, 1877.

48. One year later, Beecher returned to some of these themes in a speech to Northern veterans. He told them that "communism . . . is not of American origin" and that "labor-unions are the worst forms of despotism that ever were bred by the human mind," a statement that was greeted with applause. He then waved a stronger threat at strikers: in the future, "enraged mob[s]" would have to "submit to the regular army of the United States." Beecher, "Address: Society of the Army of the Potomac, . . . Springfield, Mass., June 5, 1878," in John R. Howard, ed., *Patriotic Addresses* (Boston, 1887), 819–821.

49. *Christian Union,* August 1, 1877.

50. *New York Sun,* July 26, 1877, quoted in Philip S. Foner, *The Great Labor Uprising of 1877* (New York, 1977), 120; Bruce, *1877,* 313.

51. *Christian Union,* August 1, August 8, 1877; *New York Tribune,* July 30, 1877.

52. *Independent,* August 2, 1877, quoted in May, *Protestant Churches,* 92; see also Bruce, *1877,* 313.

53. *Congregationalist,* July 25, 1877, quoted in May, *Protestant Churches,* 93.

54. Samuel C. Logan, *A City's Danger and Defense; or, Issues and Results of the Strikes of 1877* (Scranton, 1887), 122 (quoting one of his sermons from the time of the strikes).

55. Bessie L. Pierce, *A History of Chicago,* 3 vols. (New York, 1937–1957), 3:438, 251–252, 438–439.

56. On conservative opinion in 1877, see Chapter 8 below. There were a few notable exceptions to the clerical Commune-bashing in 1877, such as Congregationalist minister Jesse H. Jones, a leading figure in the Christian Labor Union, who wrote a series of pro-strike, pro-Commune editorials for his journal *The Labor-Balance*. On Jones, see Dombrowski, *Early Years of Christian Socialism*, 82–83, and Charles H. Hopkins, *The Rise of the Social Gospel in American Protestantism, 1865–1915* (New Haven, 1940), 46–47.

57. Roswell D. Hitchcock, *Socialism* (1878; revised ed., New York, 1879), 24, 42, 40–41; see also May, *Protestant Churches*, 166.

58. Joseph Cook, *Socialism, With Preludes on Current Events. Boston Monday Lectures* (Boston, 1880), 44–45; see also May, *Protestant Churches*, 164–166.

59. Cook, *Socialism*, 50–51.

60. Ibid., 189.

61. See the *New York Tribune*, July 30, 1877; Lyman H. Atwater, "The Great Railroad Strike," *Princeton Review*, n.s., 6 (1877), 719–744; May, *Protestant Churches*, 92–95; Charles W. Hubner, *Modern Communism* (Atlanta, 1880); M. B. Anderson, "The Lessons of Fifty Years," *Baptist Home Missions in North America* (New York, 1883), 263–270; Lawrence B. Davis, *Immigrants, Baptists, and the Protestant Mind in America* (Urbana, Ill., 1973), 55–56.

62. "The Drift of Europe, Christian and Social" (1878), reprinted in *American Comments on European Questions, International and Religious* (Boston, 1884), 19, 6.

63. *The Workman: His False Friends and His True Friends* (New York, 1879); see also May, *Protestant Churches*, 166.

64. Thompson, *The Workman*, 103–106. Like many other critics at the time, Thompson considered socialism to be no different from communism (144–160).

8. 1877: The Rise of the American Commune?

1. The epigraph is from Burke A. Hinsdale, ed., *The Works of James Abram Garfield*, 2 vols. (Boston, 1883), 2:549. *New York Times* quoted in Herbert Gutman, "The Workers' Search for Power: Labor in the Gilded Age," in *Power and Culture: Essays on the American Working Class*, ed. Ira Berlin (New York, 1987), 75.

2. James Ford Rhodes, *History of the United States from Hayes to McKinley, 1877–1896* (New York, 1919), 46.

3. Edward Young, *Special Report on Immigration* (Washington, D.C., 1872), 231; Henry Cabot Lodge, "The Restriction of Immigration," *North American Review* 152 (1891), 28. These statistics are based on calendar years.

4. *Harper's Weekly*, July 1, 1871, 595. There is no adequate study of the Com-

munard refugees in America, and I have not been able to find a reliable estimate of how many came to the United States. According to one fugitive, a gathering of New York–based Communards in 1876 attracted "almost all the refugees of the Commune" in that city, but he was able to list only twenty-two by name; see Jean Maitron et al., eds., *Dictionnaire biographique du Mouvement Ouvrier Français,* 43 vols. (Paris, 1964–1993), 6:58–59 (hereafter cited as *Dict. biographique*). For some idea of the French exile community in New York, see William H. Rideing, "The French Quarter of New York," *Scribner's Monthly* 19 (1879), 1–9; Michel Cordillot, "Les Blanquistes à New York (1871–1880)," *1848: révolutions et mutations au XIXe siècle* no. 6 (1990), 77–92; Ronald Creagh, *Nos cousins d'Amérique* (Paris, 1988), 342–350, 359–360, 366–367.

5. Samuel Gompers, *Seventy Years of Life and Labor,* 2 vols. (1925; rpt. New York, 1943), 1:50–51, 61; Charles A. Beard and Mary R. Beard, *The Rise of American Civilization,* 2 vols. (New York, 1927), 2:214–215.

6. *Le Temps* (Paris), May 12, 1878; *New York World,* March 29, 1878; *New York Times,* May 9, 1878; George B. Benham, *The Proletarian Revolt* (San Francisco, 1898), 219; *Dict. biographique,* 7:315–316.

7. Eugène Pottier, *Oeuvres complètes,* ed. Pierre Brochon (Paris, 1966), 17, 20–21, 110–126, 208–215.

8. Meredith Tax, *The Rising of the Women: Feminist Solidarity and Class Conflict, 1880–1917* (New York, 1980), 97.

9. *Woodhull & Claflin's Weekly,* January 20, 1872; F. A. Sorge to Société des Réfugiés de la Commune, June 13, 1873, General Council letterbook, IWA Papers, State Historical Society of Wisconsin (SHSW). According to Bernard A. Cook, "Section 15 of the IWA: The First International in New Orleans," *Louisiana History* 14 (1973), 302, refugees from the Commune were also active in the International in New Orleans.

10. Creagh, *Nos cousins,* 342; Pottier, *Oeuvres complètes,* 208–209.

11. See, for example, Samuel Bernstein, *The First International in America* (New York, 1962), 89, 230–234; *New York Times,* December 5, 1873, May 9, 1878; *Frank Leslie's Illustrated Newspaper,* June 13, June 20, 1874.

12. Philip S. Foner, "The French Trade Union Delegation to the Philadelphia Centennial Exposition, 1876," *Science & Society* 40 (1976), 264–265.

13. James D. McCabe, Jr., *Lights and Shadows of New York Life* (1872; rpt. New York, 1970), 192; compare *New York Times,* June 26, 1878.

14. Henry Ammon James, *Communism in America* (New York, 1879), 24; F. A. Sorge to Société des Réfugiés de la Commune, March 15, 1874, General Council letterbook, IWA Papers, SHSW; *New York Times,* March 15, 18, 19, 1874, and March 18, 1878; *American Socialist,* March 28, 1878.

15. See, for example, "Strike for the Universal Commune!" (broadside for an anniversary celebration at New York City's Germania Hall, 1881), New York State Library, Albany, N.Y.; *La Torpille,* commemorative issue of March

1886 (an anarchist paper published in Pennsylvania); *Libertas,* March 17, 1888 (a German anarchist paper published in Boston); and *Freedom,* April 1, 1892 (an anarchist paper published in Chicago).

16. *New York Times,* March 18, 1878; *Cleveland Leader,* April 30, 1874; James, *Communism in America,* 24.

17. In New York alone, the Paris Commune was defended at meetings of the New England Labor Reform League (*New York Times,* May 8, 9, 1871), the Positivists (*New York Times* and *New York World,* June 5, 1871), the Cosmopolitan Conference (*New York World,* June 19, 1871; *New York Herald,* July 3, 1871; *Workingman's Advocate,* July 29, 1871), and the Liberal Club (*New York Times* and *New York World,* July 15, 1871). Additional forums for a defense of the Commune included the lecture stage (see Chapter 4 above) and letters to *Woodhull & Claflin's Weekly* and other radical publications. Among the veteran reformers who defended the Commune that summer (including figures mentioned elsewhere in this book) were Stephen Pearl Andrews, Theodore Banks, Benjamin Butler, William B. Greene, Ezra H. Heywood, Robert W. Hume, Lewis Masquerier, Wendell Phillips, Theodore Tilton, George Francis Train, Benjamin Tucker, Cyrenus Osborne Ward, William West, George Wilkes, and Victoria C. Woodhull.

18. For descriptions of this parade, see the New York press accounts of December 18, 1871; also *Frank Leslie's Illustrated Newspaper,* December 30, 1871, 243, 247, and January 6, 1872, 263–265; Bernstein, *First International,* 89–90; Creagh, *Nos cousins,* 346; Theodore F. Watts, *The First Labor Day Parade* (Silver Spring, Md., 1983), 13–15.

19. *Frank Leslie's Illustrated Newspaper,* January 6, 1872, 263. This account offers a low estimate of 600 marchers; an inflated estimate of 10,000 marchers is offered by Philip S. Foner, *American Socialism and Black Americans: From the Age of Jackson to World War II* (Westport, Conn., 1977), 37. Neither gives a reliable figure for the size of the crowd.

20. *New York Evening Telegram,* June 27, 1871, quoted in Bernstein, *First International,* 85; New York Association for Improving the Condition of the Poor, *Twenty-Eighth Annual Report . . . for the Year 1871* (New York, 1871), 52–53 (quote), 76, 80–81.

21. Samuel Bernstein, "The Impact of the Paris Commune in the United States," *Massachusetts Review* 12 (1971), 438; Bernstein, *First International,* 155–156.

22. Mark A. Lause, "The American Radicals and Organized Marxism: The Initial Experience, 1869–1874," *Labor History* 33 (1992), 67–68. According to Lause, at first Sorge even opposed the demonstration.

23. *Cleveland Leader,* December 8, 1871; see also the *New York Times,* December 16, 1871; *Every Saturday,* December 30, 1871, 626; and the selection of editorial views in *Public Opinion* (Philadelphia), December 20, 1871, 182.

24. To cite one example: Edwin M. Chamberlin, who once ran for governor of Massachusetts on a Labor Reform ticket, explained to a Boston audience in

1875 that "the French Revolution, the Revolution of 1848, and the Commune, are the legitimate results of the ill-calculated attempts to forcibly confine within too narrow limits the natural expression of the popular heart for greater fraternity, sympathy and love"; see Chamberlin, *The Sovereigns of Industry* (1875; rpt. Westport, Conn., 1976), 97 (quote), 32–33, 51–52; compare *Workingmen's Advocate*, March 6, 1875. For other defenses of the Commune by American radicals after 1871, see *Woodhull & Claflin's Weekly*, March 30, 1872, March 6, 1875; William B. Greene, *Socialistic, Communistic, Mutualistic, and Financial Fragments* (Boston, 1875), 234–235, 255; Lewis Masquerier, *Sociology; or, The Reconstruction of Society, Government, and Property* (1877; rpt. Westport, Conn., 1970), 34, 62.

25. *Philadelphia Age*, quoted in *Public Opinion* (Philadelphia), December 20, 1871, 179.

26. *Cleveland Leader*, August 26, 1871; *New York Herald*, July 3, 1871. Similar comments appeared on the editorial pages of the *Independent*, May 18, 1871, and the *Christian Union*, June 26, 1872.

27. *Friedrich A. Sorge's "Labor Movement in the United States": A History of the American Working Class from Colonial Times to 1890*, ed. Philip S. Foner and Brewster Chamberlin (Westport, Conn., 1977), 17 (quote), 133–134, 158.

28. See the historiographic discussion at the start of Chapter 7.

29. Although he disagreed with many of their actions, Hoar applauded the Communards' heroism, adding, "I do not believe that a cause which inspired that heroism is a cause which is not entitled to the respect of Americans everywhere" (speech of December 13, 1871, *Congressional Globe*, 42d Cong., 2d sess., 102). See also Richard E. Welch, Jr., *George Frisbie Hoar and the Half-Breed Republicans* (Cambridge, Mass., 1971), 32–34.

30. *Congressional Globe*, 42d Cong., 2d sess., 104, 223, 225, 227.

31. *New York Evening Post*, April 24, 1871; see also *New York Tribune*, April 8, 1871; *Woodhull & Claflin's Weekly*, September 9, 1871, 9 (complaining that the press "calumniate[s] every workingmen's movement" by comparing it to the Commune); *Chicago Tribune*, January 16, 23, 1872; *New York World*, February 25, 1872; Joseph J. Holmes, "Red Baiting as Used against Striking Workingmen in the United States, 1871–1920," *Studies in History and Society* 5 (Spring 1974), 2; Robert V. Bruce, *1877: Year of Violence* (1959; rpt. Chicago, 1989), 226–227.

32. *New York World*, June 1, 1871. According to one overconfident editor, the doctrines of the Paris Commune, which appealed so much to the "pauper laborers of Europe," were "no lure to the intelligent, thoughtful and well paid workingmen of the United States, for, in nine cases out of ten he has considerable property of his own" (unidentified newspaper clipping, July 19, 1872, IWA Papers, SHSW, box 1, folder 9); see also *New York Times*, June 6, 7, 13, 18, 1871; *Frank Leslie's Illustrated Newspaper*, March 15, 1873, 2, and March 22, 1873, 18.

33. Bruce Levine et al., *Who Built America?*, 2 vols. (New York, 1989–1992),

1:546. My account of the long depression is based on ibid., 1:545–553; Bernstein, *First International,* 197–216; and Samuel Rezneck, "Distress, Relief, and Discontent in the United States during the Depression of 1873–78," *Journal of Political Economy* 58 (1950), 494–512.

34. Quoted in Bernstein, *First International,* 209.

35. See the discussion of strike statistics in Bruno Cartosio, "Strikes and Economics: Working-Class Insurgency and the Birth of Labor Historiography in the 1880s," in Dirk Hoerder, ed., *American Labor and Immigration History, 1877–1920s: Recent European Research* (Urbana, Ill., 1983), 19–20; compare David Montgomery, "Strikes in Nineteenth-Century America," *Social Science History* 4 (1980), 81–104.

36. Bernstein, *First International,* 208–211; M. J. Heale, *American Anticommunism* (Baltimore, 1990), 25–27; Gutman, "Workers' Search for Power," 70–71, 74–76, 85–88.

37. Allan Pinkerton, *Strikes, Communists, Tramps and Detectives* (1878; rpt. New York, 1969), 89; *New York Times,* January 13, 1874; Franklin B. Gowen (1875), quoted in J. Walter Coleman, *Labor Disturbances in Pennsylvania, 1850–1880* (Washington, D.C., 1936), 22n6.

38. Bessie L. Pierce, *A History of Chicago,* 3 vols. (New York, 1937–1957), 3:234–244; *Chicago Tribune,* December 23–27, 1873, and February 23–27, 1875; Carl Smith, *Urban Disorder and the Shape of Belief: The Great Chicago Fire, the Haymarket Bomb, and the Model Town of Pullman* (Chicago, 1995), 103–106.

39. *Freeman's Journal,* January 24, 1874, quoted in M. Hildegarde Yeager, *The Life of James Roosevelt Bayley* (Washington, D.C., 1947), 389–390.

40. *New York Times,* January 14, January 23, 1874; *Frank Leslie's Illustrated Newspaper,* January 24, 1874, 323, and January 31, 1874, 343; *Harper's Weekly,* January 31, 1874, 98; *Philadelphia Inquirer,* February 4, 1874, quoted in Herbert G. Gutman, "The Tompkins Square 'Riot' in New York City on January 13, 1874: A Re-Examination of Its Causes and Its Aftermath," *Labor History* 6 (1965), 56. Newspapers on both sides of the Atlantic drew special attention to the handful of Communards who were known to have participated in the Tompkins Square demonstration; compare the *New York Tribune,* January 14, 1874, and *Le Temps* (Paris), January 30, 1874.

41. Diary entry of January 24, 1874, *Diary of George Templeton Strong,* ed. Allan Nevins and Milton H. Thomas, 4 vols. (New York, 1952), 4:512; *New York Times,* January 13, 1874; *Harper's Weekly,* January 31, 1874, 98; see also "Communists in America," *Christian Union,* December 31, 1873, 536.

42. *Chicago Tribune,* May 24, 1874.

43. These episodes are vividly described by Robert Bruce in *1877: Year of Violence.* Bruce's work is easily the best history of the Great Strike, followed by Philip S. Foner, *The Great Labor Uprising of 1877* (New York, 1977). The best contemporary accounts are J[oseph] A. Dacus, *Annals of the Great Strikes* (1877; rpt. New York, 1969), and Edward Winslow Martin (a pseu-

donym for James Dabney McCabe, Jr.), *The History of the Great Riots* (Philadelphia, 1877), cited hereafter as Martin/McCabe. My account of the strikes is based on these books and other sources as noted.

44. See the extensive list of affected railroads in Foner, *Great Labor Uprising*, 10.

45. David T. Burbank, *City of Little Bread: The St. Louis General Strike of 1877* (St. Louis, 1957), 34; David R. Roediger, "America's First General Strike: The St. Louis 'Commune' of 1877," *Midwest Quarterly* 21 (1980), 196–206.

46. Bruce, *1877,* 291, quoting a dispatch from the Army Signal Corps, which served as the federal government's eyes and ears during the unrest. The literal translation of *pax semper ubique* is "peace, always, everywhere."

47. Martin/McCabe, 4; Thomas A. Scott, "The Recent Strikes," *North American Review* 125 (1877), 357.

48. Lyman H. Atwater, "The Great Railroad Strike," *Princeton Review,* n.s., 6 (1877), 720.

49. Dacus, *Annals,* iv (quote), 23, 28, 31; Rhodes, *History of the United States,* 46; see also Pinkerton, *Strikes,* 13.

50. Scott, "Recent Strikes," 352; see also Ainsworth R. Spofford, ed., *An American Almanac and Treasury of Facts . . . for the Year 1878* (New York and Washington, 1878), 105; H.C.C. [Lt. Henry C. Cochrane, USMC], "The Naval Brigade and the Marine Battalions in the Labor Strikes of 1877," *United Service* 1 (1879), 115–116.

51. Cartosio, "Strikes and Economics," 21.

52. *Nation,* July 26, 1877, 49. The list of epithets is derived from Samuel Yellen, *American Labor Struggles* (New York, 1936), 21–22, who compiled these and twenty-two more from a single issue of the *New York Times;* it represents an adequate cross-section of the negative labels that were applied to the strikers by the press.

53. *Nation,* July 26, 1877, 50; Martin/McCabe, 4.

54. James, *Communism in America,* 29; *Frank Leslie's Illustrated Newspaper,* August 11, 1877, 382; *Pittsburgh Commercial Gazette,* July 23, 1877.

55. *Pittsburgh Commercial Gazette,* July 26, 1877; *Baltimore American,* quoted in *Pittsburgh Daily Dispatch,* July 25, 1877.

56. *St. Louis Globe-Democrat,* July 28, 1877; *Philadelphia Inquirer,* July 23, 1877, quoted in Bruce, *1877,* 232.

57. *Cincinnati Enquirer,* July 23, 1877, quoted in Foner, *American Socialism and Black Americans,* 50; *"Who Was G.W.?" Being a Truthful Tale of the Seventh Regiment in the Armory during the Railroad Strikes in July, 1877* (New York, 1879), 10.

58. *Pittsburgh Evening Chronicle,* July 20, 1877; *New York Tribune,* July 23, 1877.

59. *New York Illustrated Times,* August 4, 1877; *Pittsburgh Telegraph,* July 24, 1877; *Pittsburgh Commercial Gazette,* July 23, 1877.

60. *Louisville Courier-Journal,* n.d., quoted in Lewis David Barnett, "Depictions

of Labor-Related Violence in American Periodicals, Newspapers, and Novels, 1877–1900: A Study in the Mythologizing of Deviance" (Ph.D. diss., Brown University, 1977), 149.

61. *Pittsburgh Commercial Gazette,* July 30, 1877; see also Chapter 7 above.

62. Martin/McCabe, 4; Dacus, *Annals,* 129, 55.

63. See Gerald N. Grob's excellent discussion of Commune bashing during the Great Strike in "The Railroad Strikes of 1877," *The Midwest Journal* 6 (Winter 1954–1955), 16–34.

64. Rhodes, *History of the United States,* 47.

65. Brace to Miss G. Schuyler, [July or August 1877], quoted in Emma Brace, *The Life of Charles Loring Brace* (New York, 1894), 355; Hickenlooper quoted in Steven J. Ross, *Workers on the Edge: Work, Leisure, and Politics in Industrializing Cincinnati, 1788–1890* (New York, 1985), 248; "Tax-Payer" to *Pittsburgh Telegraph,* July 28, 1877; Gen. Robert M. Brinton to Gen. A. L. Pearson, July 26, 1877, quoted in *Pittsburgh Daily Post,* July 31, 1877; Washburne quoted in *New York Times,* November 6, 1877.

66. Some contemporary discussion of the army's role in both the Commune and the Great Strike can be found in the *Pittsburgh Daily Post,* July 30, 1877; Thomas B. Nichols, "The Pittsburg Riots," *United Service* 1 (1879), 256–262; and Cochrane, "Naval Brigade," esp. 116, 618.

67. Philip English Mackey, "Law and Order, 1877: Philadelphia's Response to the Railroad Riots," *Pennsylvania Magazine of History and Biography* 96 (1972), 198; *Philadelphia Inquirer,* July 23, 1877; *Philadephia Record,* July 21, July 23, 1877, both quoted in Mackey, 198n33.

68. *Pittsburgh Evening Chronicle,* July 26, 1877; *Pittsburgh Commercial Gazette,* July 25, 1877.

69. *New York Commercial Advertiser,* July 23, 1877, and quoting the *Albany (N.Y.) Journal,* n.d.

70. *New York Times,* July 30, 1877; see also the *Nation,* August 2, 1877, 68; the *Independent,* August 2, 1877, 16; Foster Rhea Dulles, *Labor in America: A History* (New York, 1949), 121; Roediger, "America's First General Strike," 201.

71. Dacus, *Annals,* 16–17.

72. Child to Sarah Shaw, July 31, 1877, *The Collected Correspondence of Lydia Maria Child, 1817–1880,* ed. Patricia G. Holland and Milton Meltzer (Milwaukee, 1979), microfiche edition; *Appletons' Annual Cyclopaedia . . . for 1877* (New York, 1878), 751; Maj. William R. King, "The Military Necessities of the United States, and the Best Provisions for Meeting Them," *Journal of the Military Service Institution of the United States* 5 (1884), 390.

73. *Pittsburgh Daily Dispatch,* July 30, 1877; "An Impending Danger," *National Guardsman,* June 1, 1878, 177; Dacus, *Annals,* 229; Pinkerton, *Strikes,* 87–89; Denis Tilden Lynch, *The Wild Seventies* (New York, 1941), 444.

74. *Philadelphia Ledger,* n.d., quoted in *Pittsburgh Daily Post,* July 30, 1877; *New York Commercial Advertiser,* July 23, 1877.

75. *New York Times,* July 7, 1878; compare the version reported in the *Chicago Tribune,* July 10, 1878. See also Garfield's speech in Congress on May 21, 1878, *Works,* 2:549.

76. Lee O. Harris, *The Man Who Tramps: A Story of To-Day* (Indianapolis, 1878), 19–20, 272. One of the most dangerous conspirators in the book is "Toney Bazin," a tramp who is also a Communard refugee. Along the same lines, see "A Spectator," *The Commune in 1880: Downfall of the Republic!* (New York, 1877), esp. 8, 10–11.

77. Barnett, "Depictions of Labor-Related Violence," 50–51; Dulles, *Labor in America,* 115.

78. *Pittsburgh Daily Post,* July 30, 1877; compare *New York Daily Graphic,* July 28, 1877, 182.

79. Adolf Douai, *Better Times!* (1877; 2nd ed., New York, 1894), 6; *New York Times,* July 25, 1877; J. B. Clark, "How to Deal with Communism," *New Englander* 37 (1878), 533; *New York World,* n.d., quoted in Burbank, *City of Little Bread,* 185. See also *New York Times,* August 8, 1877; Scott, "Recent Strikes," 357, 361; James, *Communism in America,* 63, 70–71; George D. Wolff, "Socialistic Communism in the United States," *American Catholic Quarterly Review* 3 (1878), 534–535.

80. These could be found in all the illustrated newspapers from the start of August until nearly wintertime; similar "pictures," often reproduced from the same sources, also appear in the lurid accounts of the strikes produced by Dacus, Martin/McCabe, and Pinkerton.

81. *Pittsburgh Leader,* July 31, 1877, quoted in *Frank Leslie's Illustrated Newspaper,* August 18, 1877, 399.

82. Marianne Debouzy persuasively argues that crowds of American strikers in 1877 were orderly, self-controlled, and quite selective in their use of violence; see her "Grève et violence de classe aux États-Unis en 1877," *Le Mouvement Sociale* 102 (1978), 41–66. Just a few months after the Great Strike, Commune eyewitness Frank M. Pixley argued much the same thing about Communards on the pages of the San Francisco *Argonaut;* see Benham, *Proletarian Revolt,* 211, and Jerome A. Hart, *In Our Second Century: From an Editor's Note-Book* (San Francisco, 1931), 120, 123.

83. Sorge to General Council, August 6, 1871, NAFC letterbook, IWA Papers, SHSW. On the interactive distortion between images of the Great Strike and those of the Commune (yet another example of metaphorical tension), see Barnett, "Depictions of Labor-Related Violence," 150.

84. Burbank, *City of Little Bread,* 103, 107, 130; *New York Times,* July 25, 1877.

85. *Pittsburgh Daily Post,* August 4, 1877; Martin/McCabe, 299.

86. *New York Times,* July 24, 1877; *New York Tribune,* July 24, 1877; Dacus, *Annals,* 242–243 (who inaccurately places the meeting on July 24).

87. *New York Times,* July 26, 1877. For other descriptions of the meeting at Tompkins Square, see *New York Tribune,* July 26, 1877; *Frank Leslie's Illustrated Newspaper,* August 4, 1877, 7; Martin/McCabe, 292–326.

88. Joseph N. Glenn, speech of July 23, 1877, quoted in Burbank, *City of Little Bread,* 70.

89. Ibid., 48–49; italics in the original, which Burbank quotes from a contemporary newspaper.

90. Roediger, "America's First General Strike," 204–205; Burbank, *City of Little Bread,* 171–172.

91. *New York Commercial Advertiser,* July 23, 1877; *New York Tribune,* July 26, July 27, 1877; Martin/McCabe, 283–285.

92. Debouzy, "Grève et violence de classe," 59–60, 64–65; Barnett, "Depictions of Labor-Related Violence," 149.

93. Sorge to General Council, September 3, September 22, 1871, NAFC letterbook, IWA Papers, SHSW. According to a later Marxist, American workers at the time were at "a stage of development which hardly permitted them . . . to seize the full historical significance of the Commune": A. Landy, "La Commune et la classe ouvrière aux États-Unis," *La Pensée* no. 37 (1951), 106.

94. Sorge to General Council, November 5, 1871, NAFC letterbook, IWA Papers, SHSW.

95. Philip S. Foner, ed., *Wilhelm Liebknecht: Letters to the Chicago "Workingman's Advocate," November 26, 1870–December 2, 1871* (New York, 1982), 20.

96. *American Workman* (Boston), June 15, 1872.

97. *Workingman's Advocate,* July 5, 1873. Among the signers of this circular was Martin A. Foran, president of the Coopers' International Union and later a congressman from Ohio.

98. Hugh McGregor to Editor, *National Labor Tribune,* September 17, 1875, reprinted in Gompers, *Seventy Years,* 1:210–211. Gompers, McGregor, and others had just been involved in a failed attempt to launch a national labor federation.

99. Minutes of Philadelphia Section 26, vol. 1, 31, IWA Papers, SHSW.

100. Speech by Martin A. Foran, December 20, 1873, quoted in *Coopers' New Monthly* 1 (1874), 5 (emphasis in original).

101. *Workingman's Advocate,* February 14, 1874.

102. W. M. Grosvenor, "The Communist and the Railway," *International Review* 4 (1877), 585–599.

103. Ibid., 585–590, 597.

104. "A Red-Hot Striker," "So the Railway Kings Itch for an Empire, Do They?" *Radical Review* 1 (1877), 523–534. Grosvenor was also attacked by utopian reformer Ezra H. Heywood in this issue, in an article titled "The Great Strike: Its Relations to Labor, Property, and Government," 553–577. In 1871, Heywood was one of the Commune's leading American defenders. Here he writes that "the 'Communist,' when stripped of the blood-red

outfit, the daggers and revolvers with which imaginative capitalists clothe him, is a mild-eyed thinker, foolish enough to suppose people should be permitted to mind their own business. That king of terrors, the Paris Commune, simply proposed local self-government of cities and towns, like what we have in New England, instead of military centralization, which now, under the so-called 'Republic,' as formerly under the Empire, prevails in France" (571).

105. "Red-Hot Striker," "Railway Kings," 524–525, 528–529.

Conclusion

1. "A Red-Hot Striker," "So the Railway Kings Itch for an Empire, Do They?" *Radical Review* 1 (1877), 527.

2. Van Patten's address appears in *Labor Review* 1 (1880), 15–16 (an SLP organ published in Detroit); V. L. Rosenberg (1885), quoted in Nathan Fine, *Labor and Farm Parties in the United States, 1828–1928* (1928; rpt. New York, 1961), 115.

3. John D. French, "'Reaping the Whirlwind': The Origins of the Allegheny County Greenback Labor Party in 1877," *Western Pennsylvania Historical Magazine* 64 (1981), 119.

4. T. Edwin Brown, *Studies in Modern Socialism and Labor Problems* (New York, 1886), 61.

5. James A. Martling, "Song of the Workingmen" (1878), in his *Poems of Home and Country* (Boston, 1886), 526–528. The same sentiments reappear in Martling's 1878 poem "London Bridge; or, Capital and Labor," 408–433, which his wife "rededicated . . . to the Workingmen of America" (408). Martling was a Hoosier schoolmaster with a lifelong sympathy for the workingman; see Robert Harris Walker, *The Poet and the Gilded Age: Social Themes in Late Nineteenth Century American Verse* (Philadelphia, 1963), 74, 349.

6. Quoted in Fred E. Haynes, *Third Party Movements since the Civil War with Special Reference to Iowa* (Iowa City, 1916), 126; a similar statement by the Ohio Greenbackers is quoted on 127.

7. *Cincinnati Commercial Gazette,* May 4, 5, 7, 10, 11, 1886.

8. Quoted in Friedrich A. Sorge, *Friedrich A. Sorge's "Labor Movement in the United States": A History of the American Working Class from 1890 to 1896,* trans. Kai Schoenfels (Westport, Conn., 1987), 18.

9. Eric L. Hirsch, *Urban Revolt: Ethnic Politics in the Nineteenth-Century Chicago Labor Movement* (Berkeley and Los Angeles, 1990), 43–85; Bruce C. Nelson, "Anarchism: The Movement behind the Martyrs," *Chicago History* 15 (Summer 1986), 4–19.

10. Nelson, "Movement behind the Martyrs," 11, 17–19.

11. Ibid., 8–13; see also Chester McArthur Destler, "Shall Red and Black Unite? An American Revolutionary Document of 1883," *American Radicalism,*

1865–1901 (1946; rpt. Chicago, 1966), 78–104. In this document, the anarchists point to "1871 in France and 1877 in America" as proof that "the great mass of the people are *always* ready for revolt and revolution" (85–86).

12. Dan [no last name] to Powderly, December 8, 1884, quoted in Bruce C. Nelson, "'We Can't Get Them to Do Aggressive Work': Chicago's Anarchists and the Eight-Hour Movement," *International Labor and Working Class History* 29 (1986), 12. The first three names he mentions come from the French Revolution; Johann Most was an important ideologue of the anarchist movement; Michel was a famous Communarde.

13. W. J. Kerby, *Le Socialisme aux États-Unis* (Brussels, 1897), 14.

14. *Social Democratic Herald* (Milwaukee), March 10, 17, 24, 1900, and March 4, 1905; Bruce C. Nelson, "Dancing and Picknicking Anarchists? The Movement below the Martyred Leadership," in David Roediger and Franklin Rosemont, eds., *Haymarket Scrapbook* (Chicago, 1986), 76–79 (describing anarchist celebrations of the Commune as late as 1910); *Mother Earth* 7 (March 1912), 10–15 and inside back cover; William D. Haywood, *Bill Haywood's Book* (New York, 1929), 181.

15. David T. Burbank, *City of Little Bread: The St. Louis General Strike of 1877* (St. Louis, 1957), 183; *New York Times,* July 30, 1877.

16. Eugene M. Leach presents a similar argument in "Unchaining the Tiger: The Mob Stigma and the Working Class, 1863–1894," *Labor History* 35 (1994), 187–215.

17. Henry Ammon James, *Communism in America* (New York, 1879), 29; Lewis D. Barnett, "Depictions of Labor-Related Violence in American Periodicals, Newspapers, and Novels, 1877–1900: A Study in the Mythologizing of Deviance" (Ph.D. diss., Brown University, 1977), 150; *Harper's Weekly,* August 11, 1877, 626.

18. *Harper's Weekly,* August 11, 1877, 619; George G. Vest (1877), quoted in Philip S. Foner and Brewster Chamberlin, eds., *Friedrich A. Sorge's "Labor Movement in the United States": A History of the American Working Class from Colonial Times to 1890* (Westport, Conn., 1977), 205 (which misidentifies him as George *A. Best*); see also Robert V. Bruce, *1877: Year of Violence* (1959; rpt. Chicago, 1989), 316–317.

19. *Christian Union,* July 25, 1877, 62; *Nation,* August 2, 1877, 68; Barnett, "Depictions of Labor-Related Violence," 157–159. The president of the National Education Association was more sanguine, arguing that "the good sense of an immense majority of working people, created, fostered, and developed by education, . . . saved us from the terrors of the French Commune" in 1877; quoted in David B. Tyack, "Education and Social Unrest, 1873–1878," *Harvard Educational Review* 31 (1961), 194.

20. *St. Louis Republican,* July 27, 1877, quoted in Burbank, *City of Little Bread,* 139; *Frank Leslie's Illustrated Newspaper,* August 11, 1877, 382; see also *Pittsburgh Commercial Gazette,* July 23, 1877; *Pittsburgh Daily Post,* July 24,

1877; J[oseph] A. Dacus, *Annals of the Great Strikes* (1877; rpt. New York, 1969), 129–140.

21. *Pittsburgh Commercial Gazette,* July 23, 1877; Dacus, *Annals,* 94–95, 111, 122, 326.

22. William H. Vanderbilt (July 1877), quoted in Edward Winslow Martin [James D. McCabe, Jr.], *The History of the Great Riots* (Philadelphia, 1877), 262 (hereafter Martin/McCabe); Thomas A. Scott, "The Recent Strikes," *North American Review* 125 (1877), 352; *New York Tribune,* July 26, 1877; Barnett, "Depictions of Labor-Related Violence," 161–164.

23. Richard Slotkin, *The Fatal Environment: The Myth of the Frontier in the Age of Industrialization, 1800–1890* (New York, 1985), 480; William H. Brewer, "What Shall We Do with Our Tramps?" *New Englander* 37 (1878), 522; see also the *Nation,* August 9, 1877, 85.

24. *Nation,* August 2, 1877, 69; *Pittsburgh Daily Post,* July 23, 1877; Martin/McCabe, 387; Barnett, "Depictions of Labor-Related Violence," 154–157.

25. *New York Tribune,* June 15, 1878; *New York Herald,* April 29, 1878; *New York Graphic,* n.d., quoted in *American Socialist,* March 28, 1878.

26. R. Heber Newton, "Communism," *Unitarian Review* 16 (1881), 485–486.

27. Richard T. Ely, *French and German Socialism in Modern Times* (New York, 1883), quoted in George B. Benham, *The Proletarian Revolt* (San Francisco, 1898), 7; Theodore D. Woolsey, *Communism and Socialism* (New York, 1883), 2–3 and passim. Other scholarly discussions of the difference between communism (and/or socialism) and the Paris Commune can be found in William Alfred Hinds, *American Communities* (Oneida, N.Y., 1878), 158–160; W. G. H. Smart, "Three Mis-Used and Ab-Used Words," *American Socialist,* April 25, 1878, 130–131; John B. Clark, "The Nature and Progress of True Socialism," *New Englander* 38 (1879), 566; Brown, *Studies in Modern Socialism,* 21–22, 27–28; Philip Gilbert Hamerton, *French & English, a Comparison* (London and New York, 1889), xii–xiii; Charles Sotheran, *Horace Greeley and Other Pioneers of American Socialism* (1892; rpt. New York, 1915), 4–6; and William D. P. Bliss, ed., *The Encyclopedia of Social Reform* (New York, 1897), 310–314, 971.

28. John J. Flinn, *History of the Chicago Police* (1887; rpt. New York, 1973), 231; *Philadelphia Record,* May 6, 1886, quoted in *Public Opinion* (Washington, D.C.), May 15, 1886, 83. The extracts in this issue of *Public Opinion* include several more comments along the same lines.

29. *Cincinnati Commercial Gazette,* May 6, 1886.

30. Garrett Pendleton, "Spartan Communism," *Forney's Progress,* February 28, 1880, 344; Henry J. Browne, *The Catholic Church and the Knights of Labor* (Washington, D.C., 1949), 79–81, 88–90.

31. Sen. John J. Ingalls (1890), quoted in James C. Malin, *Confounded Rot about Napoleon* (Lawrence, Kan., 1961), 102.

32. Theodore Roosevelt, "True American Ideals," *Forum* 18 (1895), 747; Roosevelt, "The Menace of the Demagogue" (October 15, 1896), *The Works of Theodore Roosevelt*, 20 vols. (New York, 1926), 14:273; Roosevelt to Marshall Stimson, October 27, 1911, *The Letters of Theodore Roosevelt*, ed. Elting Morison et al., 8 vols. (Cambridge, Mass., 1951–1954), 7:422–423.

33. *New York Tribune*, March 20, 1904.

34. Nelson, "Movement behind the Martyrs," 11.

35. Powderly to William Hickey, May 17, 1882, quoted in Browne, *Catholic Church and Knights of Labor*, 79; Debs, "The Cry of 'Anarchist,'" *Public Opinion* (Washington, D.C.), April 11, 1895, 377–378.

36. Debs, "Cry of 'Anarchist,'" 377. On this continuity of antilabor language, see Barnett, "Depictions of Labor-Related Violence," 78; M. J. Heale, *American Anticommunism* (Baltimore, 1990), esp. xiii–xiv, 21–41; Joseph J. Holmes, "Red Baiting as Used against Striking Workingmen in the United States, 1871–1920," *Studies in History and Society* 5 (1974), 1–19.

37. *Forney's Progress*, August 16, 1879, 785; Edward King, *Under the Red Flag* (Philadelphia, 1895), 357–358.

38. See Garry Wills, *Lincoln at Gettysburg: The Words That Remade America* (New York, 1992).

39. *New York Commercial Advertiser*, December 1, 1863, quoted in Arthur P. Coleman and Marion M. Coleman, *The Polish Insurrection of 1863 in the Light of New York Editorial Opinion* (Williamsport, Pa., 1934), 104; Ambassador Sir Frederick Bruce (1866), quoted in M. J. Sewell, "Rebels or Revolutionaries? Irish-American Nationalism and American Diplomacy, 1865–1885," *Historical Journal* 29 (1986), 729. In general, see James A. Rawley, "The American Civil War and the Atlantic Community," *Georgia Review* 21 (1967), 185–194.

40. Cluseret, "The Audience at Aubervilliers," *Fraser's Magazine*, n.s., 5 (1872), 24.

41. The irony of this was captured by Dixon Wecter in a study of postwar demobilizations: "Is it possible," he asks, "that an upsurge of conservatism is as symptomatic of a victorious nation as radicalism appears to be in a defeated one?" *When Johnny Comes Marching Home* (Cambridge, Mass., 1944), 17–18.

42. François Bourricaud's general description of ideology formation is apposite here: the Commune became the basis of "a series of ad hoc constructions, tied together by a very tenuous line of analogies, and with a very indirect relationship to general principles": *Le Bricolage Idéologique* (Paris, 1980), 67.

43. Sewell, "Rebels or Revolutionaries," 723.

44. *Appletons' Annual Cyclopaedia . . . for 1877* (New York, 1878), iii.

45. Woodrow Wilson, "Remarks to Confederate Veterans in Washington" (June 5, 1917), *The Papers of Woodrow Wilson*, ed. Arthur S. Link, 69 vols. (Princeton, 1966–1993), 42:451–452.

46. Quoted in Robert K. Murray, *Red Scare: A Study in National Hysteria, 1919–1920* (1955; rpt. New York, 1964), 98.
47. Ibid., 284. On the so-called Lusk Committee, see 98–102.
48. Lusk Committee, *Revolutionary Radicalism: Its History, Purpose and Tactics,* 4 vols. (Albany, N.Y., 1920), 1:42.

Appendix C

1. Julia Ward Howe to her daughter Maud, April 18, 1897, in Laura E. Richards and Maud Howe Elliott, *Julia Ward Howe, 1819–1910,* 2 vols. (Boston, 1916), 2:227. Presumably the play was performed in Boston.
2. Ronald Creagh, "Socialism in America: The French-Speaking Coal Miners in the late Nineteenth Century," in Marianne Debouzy, ed., *In the Shadow of the Statue of Liberty: Immigrants, Workers and Citizens in the American Republic, 1880–1920* (Saint-Denis, 1988), 162.
3. Hartmut Keil and Heinz Ickstadt, "Elements of German Working-Class Culture in Chicago, 1880 to 1890," in Hartmut Keil, ed., *German Workers' Culture in the United States, 1850 to 1920* (Washington, D.C., and London, 1988), 94–97; Christine Heiss, "Popular and Working-Class German Theater in Chicago, 1870 to 1910," in Keil, *German Workers' Culture,* 193–195, 200; Carol J. Poore, *German-American Socialist Literature, 1865–1900* (Berne, 1982), 103–106.
4. George C. D. Odell, *Annals of the New York Stage,* 15 vols. (New York, 1927–1949), 9:163.
5. *New York Times,* November 28, 1871.
6. *The Spirit of the Times,* December 2, 1871, 256.
7. *Woodhull & Claflin's Weekly,* December 9, 1871.
8. Odell, *Annals,* 9:217.
9. Unidentified newspaper clipping, Harvard Theatre Collection.
10. *Boston Evening Transcript,* November 28, 1876; Boston Museum playbill, December 1, 1876 (with handwritten comments on the play), Harvard Theatre Collection.
11. Playbills, Theatre and Drama Collection, New York Public Library; advertisement in the *Boston Evening Transcript,* October 17, 1896.
12. Sutherland, *Po' White Trash,* 231.

Index